# PRINCIPLES OF NEGOTIATION, MEDIATION, AND OTHER PROCESSES OF DISPUTE RESOLUTION

**Stephen J. Ware**
*Frank Edwards Tyler Distinguished Professor of Law*
*University of Kansas*

CONCISE HORNBOOK SERIES™

WEST ACADEMIC

860 Blue Gentian Road, Suite 350
Eagan, MN 55121
1-877-888-1330

Published in the United States of America

ISBN: 979-8-88786-516-4

*for Sarah*

# Preface

Lawyers negotiate frequently. Of all the skills that contribute to a successful legal career, few if any contribute more than negotiation skills. Negotiation is also the foundation for mediation, which has become a routine part of many law practices. Lawyers represent clients in mediation, and some lawyers become mediators.

This book surveys the theory, practice, and law of negotiation and mediation. It summarizes negotiation theory and mediation theory; it offers practical tactics to help negotiators and mediators reach their goals; and it summarizes relevant law.

Negotiation theory helps people decide when to negotiate and with whom. Negotiation theory also helps people combine their goals and what they know about a situation to negotiate in ways likely to move toward their goals. The specifics are negotiation tactics—different tactics for different situations, different goals, and different people. Negotiating the sale of a small family business to a friend of the family probably calls for different tactics than negotiating the settlement of mass tort litigation involving thousands of parties, dozens of law firms, and enormous amounts of animosity. And each of these negotiations probably calls for different tactics than negotiating the plea bargain of a low-level felony charge.

Nevertheless, all three sorts of negotiations and many others are governed by rich bodies of law, replete with statutes, rules (including lawyers' rules of professional responsibility), and cases that vary somewhat from state to state, and even more across nations. The global stage of international treaties and multinational corporations finds lawyers negotiating every bit as much as the local courthouse full of divorces, misdemeanors, and evictions. Lawyers' careers vary tremendously, but negotiation is one of the strongest through lines connecting them all.

This book was written with the support of the University of Kansas School of Law, for which I am grateful. Thanks also to Gilat Bachar, Robin Craig, and Sharon Brett for helpful suggestions and comments. Finally, thanks to the student research assistants who contributed to this book: Thea Hack Schneider, Tara Phipps, Val French, Josh Hukill, Preston Knight, Zarah DeMeire, David Quirk, Paulina Rivera-Soto, Blake Millman, Maria Almirudis, Michael Calavera, Natalie Franklin, Braedon Bush, and Kevin Duperon.

As I expect to write future editions of this book, I welcome comments and suggestions by email.

STEPHEN J. WARE
Frank Edwards Tyler Distinguished Professor of Law
University of Kansas
ware@ku.edu
(785) 864-9209

2026 March 3

# Note to Teachers

This Hornbook is designed to be the primary or secondary text in a law school course. In the United States, casebooks, rather than Hornbooks or other treatises, are the primary texts in many law school courses, and casebooks work well in courses that emphasize Socratic dialog and "thinking like a lawyer." In contrast, many negotiation and mediation teachers design their courses to develop a wider array of practice skills, generally through the use of role-playing exercises. This Hornbook is especially well-suited to be the primary text for such courses. Because this book is clear and concise, students reading it can quickly gain a solid understanding of the concepts and legal doctrines central to negotiation and mediation. This efficient use of time enables the teacher to devote many class sessions to role-playing exercises, and discussion of them.

Excellent role-playing exercises are available from several sources, including:

- Suffolk University ADR Teaching Center https://sites.suffolk.edu/adrvideo/
- Laboratory for Advancing Dispute Resolution Skills Teaching https://mitchellhamline.edu/dri-skills-lab/resources/
- Collection of Negotiation, Mediation, Arbitration, and Client Counseling Simulations https://mitchellhamline.edu/dri-skills-lab/collections/marjorie-aaron/
- Harvard Program on Negotiation http://www.pon.harvard.edu/store/
- Negotiation & Team Resources https://www.negotiationandteamresources.com/
- University of Missouri Center for the Study of Dispute Resolution https://law.missouri.edu/academics/csdr/drle/dispute-resolution-teaching-materials/
- American Bar Association's Dispute Resolution Resource Database, (scroll to Legal Education) https://www.americanbar.org/groups/dispute_resolution/resources/ which links to several resources, including https://www.adrvideo.org/

Of course, individual instructors can also create their own role-playing exercises.

In addition to serving as the primary text for courses that emphasize role-playing exercises, this Hornbook can also serve as the primary text for seminars. In a seminar, students generally read scholarly articles and write their own substantial papers. Before venturing into a field of scholarship, students generally need a solid foundation in the field's central concepts and legal doctrines. This book provides that foundation with only a limited amount of reading, thus enabling students to devote substantial time to the seminar's more-advanced work of reading scholarly articles and writing original papers.

# Summary of Contents

# Table of Contents

1. THE ADVERSARIAL/COMPETITIVE APPROACH



2. THE COOPERATIVE APPROACH AND THE PRISONER'S DILEMMA



3. THE PROBLEM-SOLVING APPROACH AND THE NEGOTIATOR'S DILEMMA

## D. MEDIATION CONTEXTS

# PRINCIPLES OF NEGOTIATION, MEDIATION, AND OTHER PROCESSES OF DISPUTE RESOLUTION

# Chapter 1

# NEGOTIATION

*Table of Sections*

---

## A. NEGOTIATION CONTEXTS

### § 1.1 Negotiation and Lawyers

To negotiate is to "communicate or confer with another to arrive at the settlement of some matter."[1] So defined, negotiation is a pervasive form of human interaction, common among families and friends, cohabitants and coworkers. "Whenever any person, couple, community, company, organization, or country needs someone else to accomplish something, they must negotiate—*seeking agreement with*

---

[1] Negotiate, Webster's Third New International Dictionary 1514 (Merriam-Webster 1971). See also Marriam-Webster, *Negotiate*, https://www.merriam-webster.com/dictionary/negotiate (last visited 7 Oct. 2024) (definition of negotiate is "to confer with another so as to arrive at the settlement of some matter").

*one or more people to do that which one cannot do alone.*"[2] And sometimes one *could* do it alone, but it will be so much easier or cheaper or more fun to involve others, so we choose to engage in interactions that may require us to negotiate.

Lawyers, in addition to negotiating for themselves, often negotiate on behalf of their clients. Lawyers are especially likely to negotiate on behalf of a client with respect to a case the lawyer is litigating for the client or a big transaction—such as the sale of a business—in which the lawyer is helping the client assess risks and opportunities, draft documents, and ensure regulatory compliance. Parties to litigation and big transactions hire lawyers to negotiate on the client's behalf for a lot of reasons, such as:

- the lawyer's knowledge about the case or transaction,
- the lawyer's knowledge of relevant law and practices,
- the lawyer's skill at negotiating,
- to signal of how seriously the client takes the matter,[3] and
- to have a dispassionate ally who enables the client-lawyer team to use negotiation tactics that require two or more people on the same side.[4]

While hiring a lawyer to negotiate can have many benefits for the client, it also has costs, the most obvious of which is the lawyer's fee (discussed below in § 1.36(b)). In addition, a lawyer and client may have diverging opinions, interests, preferences, and personalities.[5] So the lawyer-client relationship can complicate all aspects of negotiation from preparing for negotiation (§§ 1.29–1.33), and conducting it (§§ 1.12–1.28), to the big question of whether to accept a particular deal (§§ 1.4–1.11, 1.34–1.39) and then possibly navigating law governing the deal (§§ 1.40–1.44).

The lawyer-client relationship is a principal-agent relationship, so discussions of principal-agent problems provide useful lenses through which to view lawyers negotiating on behalf of their clients.[6]

---

[2] Carrie Menkel-Meadow, Negotiation: A Very Short Introduction 1 (2022).

[3] As two non-lawyers writing for businesspeople put it, "[i]ntroducing lawyers into the process of negotiation puts the parties on notice that any breach could be costly and that promises made initially must be kept, even if these prove inconvenient." Fons Trompenaars & Charles Hampden-Turner, Riding the Waves of Culture: Understanding Diversity in Global Business 50 (2021).

[4] See Russell Korobkin, Negotiation Theory and Strategy ch. 11.A. (4th ed. 2024).

[5] Id. ch. 11.B.

[6] See, e.g., Richard A. Rosen et al., Settlement Agreements in Commercial Disputes § 7.01 (2022) ("As is the case in most types of legal disputes, the negotiation

Agency law (§ 1.41) provides another such lens, especially when supplemented by the law of lawyers' professional responsibilities, which often imposes on lawyers duties not imposed on other agents. So, the Model Rules of Professional Responsibility are noted throughout this book.

Because much of the work lawyers do is either litigation or transactional, lawyers negotiating for their clients are often engaged in *dispute negotiation* or *transactional negotiation*.[7] Negotiation is the most frequently used process of dispute resolution, including disputes that are already the subject of arbitration, litigation (civil or criminal), or adjudication before a government agency. Negotiation is also the foundation for other important processes of dispute resolution, such as mediation, which is the focus of this book's Chapter 2.

In addition, negotiation unrelated to any dispute looms large in the work of many lawyers. Such transactional negotiation often precedes a wide variety of agreements—from the previously mentioned sale of a business to the earlier agreement among its founders to create the business, its loan from a bank, hiring of a high-level employee, lease of a manufacturing facility, purchase of sophisticated equipment, license of intellectual property, and so forth. Non-business transactional negotiation is also central to many lawyers' practices, especially if they work in the government or non-profit sectors.

## § 1.2 Settlement Negotiation and the Shadow of the Law

### *(a) Settlement Negotiation and Plea Bargaining Defined*

Most dispute negotiation occurs without the involvement of lawyers. Think, for example, about disputes among family members or roommates about who will do various household chores. Parties to such disputes almost never hire lawyers to help them win, or negotiate a resolution of, the dispute. In contrast, when *do* parties to a dispute tend to hire lawyers? When the dispute is in, or likely to go,

---

and settlement of complex commercial litigation is often the work of servants (attorneys) rather than masters (clients). Indeed, the more sophisticated and multifaceted the controversy, the more a client must rely on its counsel to protect its interests and preserve its business strategy"); Ronald J. Gilson & Robert H. Mnookin, Disputing Through Agents: Cooperation and Conflict Between Lawyers in Litigation, 94 Colum. L. Rev. 509 (1994).

7 "Sometimes negotiations are designed to create something new—a relationship, a treaty, a new entity, partnership, contract (called a transactional or *deal negotiation*). Other times negotiations are used to resolved conflicts, resolving past disputes or providing for future relations, including ending relationships—think Brexit or divorce (called *dispute negotiation*)." Carrie Menkel-Meadow, Negotiation: A Very Short Introduction 2 (2022).

to litigation or another form of legally binding adjudication, such as arbitration.

*Adjudication* is the process by which somebody (the adjudicator) decides the result of a dispute, in contrast to the disputing parties agreeing on the result of the dispute, as occurs in negotiation and mediation. *Litigation* can be defined as adjudication in a court or other *government* forum, such as the Social Security Administration or a state department of labor, while *arbitration* is adjudication in a private sector forum, basically a private "court."[8]

Adjudication centers on the disputing parties, often through their lawyers, presenting evidence and argument to the adjudicator who then decides the result of the dispute based on that evidence and argument.[9] Parties often hire lawyers to represent them in adjudication because lawyers are trained in presenting evidence and argument (so they're typically good at it!) and a license to practice law is generally required to represent a party in litigation. So, it makes sense that the disputes parties bring to lawyers are especially likely to go to litigation or, to a lesser extent, arbitration. While adjudication can be non-binding, litigation is legally binding and so, typically, is arbitration.

Negotiation of these disputes is commonly called *settlement negotiation* (§§ 1.34–1.43). In other words, settlement negotiation is the negotiation of disputes that are already in binding adjudication (litigation or arbitration) or are likely to go there if negotiation does not result in agreement. *Plea bargaining* (§ 1.44) is the settlement negotiation of criminal cases.

### *(b) Selling Claims in the Shadow of the Law*

The previous paragraph defined *settlement negotiation* as the negotiation of disputes that are already in binding adjudication (litigation or arbitration) or are likely to go there if negotiation does not result in agreement. A *settlement* is generally defined as an agreement resolving a dispute and thus preventing or ending litigation or arbitration. Some settlements address multiple claims each party has against the other, or many parties' claims. But leaving

---

[8] Stephen J. Ware & Ariana R. Levinson, Principles of Arbitration Law § 1 n.1 (2d ed. 2023).

[9] Lon Fuller, The Forms and Limits of Adjudication, 92 Harv. L. Rev. 353, 364 (1978) ("[T]he distinguishing characteristic of adjudication lies in the fact that it confers on the affected [disputing] party a peculiar form of participation in decision, that of presenting proofs and reasoned arguments for a decision in his favor."); id. at 365 (from this participation by the parties, "the office of judge or arbitrator and the requirement of impartiality follow as necessary implications.") Lon Fuller is well described as "the leading jurisprudential thinker about ADR." Carrie Menkel-Meadow, Mothers and Fathers of Invention: The Intellectual Founders of ADR, 16 Ohio St. J. on Disp. Resol. 1, 16 (2000).

those more complex settlements aside, let's first consider the settlement of just one claim a plaintiff or potential plaintiff (P) has against the defendant or potential defendant (D). In that context, a settlement is the sale of a claim by P to D,[10] and the sales price is whatever D pays or promises to pay P, which is typically but not necessarily money. Perhaps more controversially, we might think similarly of a plea bargain as the prosecuting government's "sale" of a charge with the "price" to be paid by the defendant often expressed in months of incarceration rather than in dollars.[11]

While settlement negotiation is negotiation about the sale of a claim (or perhaps a criminal charge) to the defendant, claims differ from other sell-able things in the legal consequences that follow when the negotiators do not agree on a sale price. If a car, for example, is not sold because the negotiators do not agree on a price, the potential buyer will keep his money, and the potential seller will keep her car. Nobody will force a sale. In contrast, if a claim is not sold because the negotiators do not agree on a price, the plaintiff (or prosecution) can force a sale through litigation. The court's judgment will transfer (or "sell") the claim from Plaintiff to Defendant and will set the price Defendant is obligated to pay.[12]

This impending "forced sale" looms over settlement negotiation. This impending forced sale casts what is widely known as the "shadow of the law."[13] Settlement negotiation is conducted in the *shadow of the law* because the negotiators' expectations about the

---

[10] Keith N. Hylton, Selling Out: An Instrumentalist Theory of Legal Ethics, 34 Geo. J. Legal Ethics 19, 54 (2021) ("A settlement occurs when the defendant, the violator of the plaintiff's right, purchases the claim from the plaintiff."); id. ("As is well known in the literature on settlement, the plaintiff and the defendant are likely to arrange a transaction where the plaintiff sells the claim to the defendant when the expected net reward to the plaintiff is less than the expected payout by the defendant, or equivalently, when the expected judgment differential is less than the joint litigation cost"); D. Theodore Rave, Tort Claims As Property Rights, 69 DePaul L. Rev. 587, 591 (2020) ("there are several ways in which tort claims are alienable. Most fundamentally, the plaintiff can sell the claim to the defendant in a settlement").

[11] Frank H. Easterbrook, Criminal Procedure as a Market System, 12 J. Legal Stud. 289, 308 (1983) ("Plea bargaining establishes the price for most crimes.")

[12] Robert J. Rhee, A Price Theory of Legal Bargaining: An Inquiry into the Selection of Settlement and Litigation Under Uncertainty, 56 Emory L.J. 619, 670 (2006) ("A plaintiff asserts a legal claim, which may be 'bought' by a defendant either voluntarily or by forced purchase"); id. at 675 ("It is often said that a defendant is a buyer of the plaintiff's claim.")

[13] Robert H. Mnookin & Lewis Kornhauser, Bargaining in the Shadow of the Law: The Case of Divorce, 88 Yale L.J. 950 (1979); In re OHT Hawk AS, No. 21-60796, 2022 WL 1486778, at *2 (5th Cir. May 11, 2022) ("To borrow a phrase, settlements are negotiated 'in the shadow of the law' "); United States v. Khattak, 273 F.3d 557, 562 n.6 (3d Cir. 2001) ("criminal sentences in most cases are, at least in part, bargained for; that is, they are negotiated between the defendant and the government. In this sense, the sentencing regime has come to resemble the negotiation of civil settlements, also conducted in the shadow of the law.")

results of litigation, that is, the forced sale, shape the negotiators' attitudes toward various possible settlement terms.[14] Negotiators' expectations about the "price" of a forced sale, should it come to that, influence the price at which they will agree to settle.[15]

While settlement negotiation is conducted in the shadow of the law, other dispute negotiation is not. Ordinary day-to-day disputes among family members, roommates, and the like will never be the subject of litigation or binding arbitration, so negotiation of these disputes largely occurs beyond the shadow of the law. That is, dispute negotiation that is not settlement negotiation is dispute negotiation not influenced by the possibility of a court's or arbitrator's ruling on the dispute. So other factors influence its outcome.

## § 1.3 Settlement Negotiation Contrasted with Transactional Negotiation

Settlement negotiation tends to be more *adversarial* (§§ 1.13–1.18) than transactional negotiation. This is partly because parties whose disputes have made it to litigation or arbitration tend to be displeased with each other, while parties coming together to discuss their possible transaction tend to be more positive toward each other. Relatedly, settlement negotiation is less likely than transactional negotiation to involve parties who want or expect their relationship to continue after the negotiation.[16] The parties' expectation that their relationship will continue after the negotiation tends to make the negotiation more *cooperative* (§ 1.20) and *problem-solving* (§§ 1.22–1.26) than adversarial because the parties don't want to jeopardize the good vibes they hope will continue for their further interactions.

Also contributing to settlement negotiation's tendency to be adversarial is the fact that parties opposing each other in litigation or arbitration are usually stuck with each other in a way that is not true of most parties engaged in transactional negotiation. The buyer in a transactional negotiation is not typically stuck with any particular seller but can instead "shop around" for the seller from whom the buyer most wants to buy. Conversely, a negotiating seller is not typically stuck with only one potential buyer but can instead

---

14 See Robert H. Mnookin & Lewis Kornhauser, Bargaining in the Shadow of the Law: The Case of Divorce, 88 Yale L.J. 950, 968 (1979) ("the outcome that the law will impose if no agreement is reached gives each [party] certain bargaining chips—an endowment of sorts.")

15 As noted above, the "price" of a claim (or criminal charge), whether agreed to in settlement or imposed by litigation, is not necessarily an amount of money. The price includes whatever the plaintiff (or prosecuting government) receives in exchange for the claim (or charge).

16 Donald G. Gifford & Robert J. Rhee, Legal Negotiation: Theory and Practice 43–46 (3d ed. 2017).

tell any potential buyer, "You will have to raise your offer, or I will sell it to somebody else."

In contrast, cases in litigation or arbitration are between particular disputing parties, so those parties are typically stuck with each other. That is, they are stuck with each other for as long as it takes to adjudicate, or negotiate a settlement of, the case. To put it another way, negotiation to settle a lawsuit (sell a claim) generally occurs in a market with only one buyer (Defendant) and only one seller (Plaintiff). Defendant cannot "shop around" to find some other plaintiff who is charging a lower price, because only Plaintiff can sell what Defendant seeks to buy, which is an end to Plaintiff's case against Defendant. Similarly, Plaintiff cannot shop around to find some other defendant willing to pay more for Plaintiff's claim against Defendant because that claim threatens only Defendant with liability imposed by a court or arbitrator.[17] So in their negotiation, Plaintiff and Defendant are stuck with each other in a *bilateral monopoly*—a phrase suggesting that the negotiating parties can only get what they seek by dealing with each other. This bilateral monopoly characteristic affects most settlement negotiation[18] and contributes to its adversarial feel compared to transactional negotiation.

In addition, settlement negotiation is more likely than transactional negotiation to be *zero-sum*, (§ 1.9), that is, negotiation in which the better a deal is for one party, the worse it is for the other party.[19] Zero-sum negotiations tend to be more adversarial than *positive-sum* (§ 1.10) negotiations. So, settlement negotiation tends to be more adversarial for all four reasons just discussed:

1. personal animosity toward the opposing party,
2. lack of interest in a continuing relationship with that opponent,
3. being stuck with them in a bilateral monopoly, and
4. a zero-sum situation.

---

[17] If the plaintiff is suing many defendants, this analysis applies to each defendant, although multi-party issues raise additional issues, some of which are discussed in Section 1.42. See generally Russell Korobkin, Negotiation Theory and Strategy, ch. 12 (4th ed. 2024).

[18] Richard A. Posner, Economic Analysis of Law 779 (9th ed. 2014) ("Settlement negotiations are a classic example of bilateral monopoly. The plaintiff can settle only with the defendant and the defendant only with the plaintiff.")

[19] Robert H. Mnookin, Scott R. Peppet & Andrew S. Tulumello, Beyond Winning: Negotiating to Create Value in Deals and Disputes 224 (2000) (dispute "negotiations are often very distributive—a dollar more for one side is a dollar less for the other. As a result, litigators typically focus on dividing the pie, not enlarging it."); Donald G. Gifford & Robert J. Rhee, Legal Negotiation: Theory and Practice 43–46 (3d ed. 2017) ("Often transactional negotiations also present more opportunities for value creation").

In contrast, transactional negotiation tends to be more cooperative and problem-solving because transactional parties:

1. are at least okay with each other,
2. hope for a continuing relationship, but
3. have alternatives to each other, and
4. see positive-sum opportunities to "grow the pie."[20]

## B. NEGOTIATION THEORY

### § 1.4 Agreements

Agreements occur because, at the time parties make them, each party thinks making the agreement is better than that party's alternatives. In that sense, agreements create value; they improve each party's position in that party's estimation.[21] People make mistakes of course, so a party may look back on an agreement and regret making it. But at the time they made it, they must have thought (after thorough analysis or the impulsivity with which many of us click "Agree" on our phones) that making the agreement was better than whatever alternatives the party had. So, a lot can turn on those alternatives. They are discussed next.

### § 1.5 Best Alternative to a Negotiated Agreement (BATNA)

The better your alternatives to making any particular agreement, the less pressure you feel to make that agreement. If you can do without the agreement Party A is proposing because it is not as good for you as some alternative Party B is offering, then you can confidently encourage A to offer you better terms. But if A's offer is by far your best option, and A knows that, then A may tell you that its offer is nonnegotiable ("take it or leave it,") or even rescind that offer and replace it with an offer of terms more favorable to A and less favorable to you.

Sometimes your best alternative to an agreement with one party is a roughly comparable agreement with another party. For instance, if you're buying a new car and one car dealer's price for the model you seek seems a bit high, you may be able to get a lower price on the same model of car from another dealer not too far away. Or if you're selling your house, and one potential buyer's offer seems a bit low,

20 Robert H. Mnookin, Scott R. Peppet & Andrew S. Tulumello, Beyond Winning: Negotiating to Create Value in Deals and Disputes 224 (2000).

21 Id. at 12 ("whenever there's a negotiated agreement, both parties must believe that the negotiated outcome leaves them at least as well off as they would have been if there were no agreement. In this narrow sense, any negotiated outcome, if better than your best alternative away from the table, could be said to create value.")

you may be able to hold out for a higher offer from the other potential buyer who is touring your house next week.

By contrast, in other situations your best alternative to an agreement with one party may be no agreement at all. For example, instead of selling your house, you might just keep living there. So being happy remaining in your house helps you fetch a high price for leaving it because you can turn down any not-quite-high-enough offers with a sincere smile of contentment.

In a third category of situations, your best alternative to an agreement with one party is neither of the two extremes already discussed: a comparable agreement with a different party or no agreement at all. In this third, intermediate category, your best alternative to an agreement with one party is an agreement with a different party, but a very different sort of agreement. For example, your best alternative to buying a car from A might not be buying a car from B, but instead taking the bus or Uber, which may involve you making frequent smaller agreements to pay bus or Uber fare. Or you might keep your old car, which may involve you making frequent agreements with an auto repair shop to keep your old car moving. Brainstorming various possible alternatives to the negotiation under consideration can be wise, because attractive alternatives are not always "just sitting there waiting for you," so you may "have to develop them."[22]

The previous few paragraphs illustrate what negotiation theorists call *BATNA* (the Best Alternative to a Negotiated Agreement), which is your best alternative to reaching an agreement in the negotiation under consideration.[23] As suggested by the examples above, "the set of a negotiator's alternatives is made up of all those actions that the negotiator can take away from the [negotiating] table if no agreement is reached. The BATNA is the best alternative in that set."[24] (We still talk about the "negotiation table" even though most negotiations no longer occur, if they ever did, at a table.)

## § 1.6 Bottom Line

The previous section explains an important concept in negotiation theory—the Best Alternative to a Negotiated Agreement

---

[22] Roger Fisher, William Ury, & Bruce Patton, Getting to Yes 105–06 (3d ed. 2011).

[23] "BATNA" is a term "invented" by the influential negotiation book, *Getting to Yes*. Alan Scott Rau, Edward F. Sherman & Scott R. Peppet, Processes of Dispute Resolution 89 n.3 (4th ed. 2002) (citing Roger Fisher, William Ury, & Bruce Patton, Getting to Yes 100 (2d ed. 1991)).

[24] Alan Scott Rau, Edward F. Sherman & Scott R. Peppet, Processes of Dispute Resolution 89 n.3 (4th ed. 2002).

(BATNA). Determining your BATNA helps you negotiate because your *bottom line* in negotiation, which is the worst deal you will accept,[25] "should be tied to" your BATNA.[26] The value you place on your best alternative to a negotiation (your BATNA) should determine your bottom line in that negotiation because agreeing in a negotiation to something worse than your best alternative to it would be "the most basic negotiating mistake—agreeing to a deal when [you] would have been better off walking away from the table with no agreement."[27]

For example, if you decide your Best Alternative to a Negotiated Agreement with Auto Dealer A to buy A's new car is buying an identical new car from Auto Dealer B, and you can think of nothing else that makes buying from either A or B more appealing than buying from the other of them, then paying B's price is your BATNA, and thus your bottom line, in negotiating with A.[28] Your BATNA (paying B's price) would give you the same result (an identical car) as your negotiation under consideration (with A) in all respects except price, so the price of your BATNA should be your bottom line price in negotiating with A. Put simply, you shouldn't pay A more than you'd pay B for an identical car.

A bit more complex is where the negotiator's BATNA would produce a slightly different result than the negotiation under consideration. For example, suppose Auto Dealer B will charge you $20,000 for a lower mileage, but otherwise similar, used car to the used car about which you and Auto Dealer A are negotiating. Before negotiating price with A, you should decide how much you value the

---

25 "[T]he bottom line is a fundamental bargaining concept on which much of modern negotiation theory is built. It is the minimum acceptable level you require to say 'yes' in a negotiation." G. Richard Shell, Bargaining for Advantage: Negotiation Strategies for Reasonable People 27 (1999). See also Robert H. Mnookin, Scott R. Peppet & Andrew S. Tulumello, Beyond Winning: Negotiating to Create Value in Deals and Disputes 34 (2000); Jay E. Grenig, 1 Alt. Disp. Resol. § 3:7 (4th ed. Sept. 2021) ("The reservation value represents the minimum or maximum a negotiator would accept given the alternatives to a negotiated settlement."); Peter Reilly, Was Machiavelli Right? Lying in Negotiation and the Art of Defensive Self-Help, 24 Ohio St. J. on Disp. Resol. 481, 492 n. 39 (2009) ("In a negotiation, the reservation point is one's 'bottom line,' or the maximum amount that a buyer will pay for a good, service, or other legal entitlement.").

26 Alan Scott Rau, Edward F. Sherman & Scott R. Peppet, Processes of Dispute Resolution 89 n.3 (4th ed. 2002).

27 Russell Korobkin, A Positive Theory of Legal Negotiation, 88 Geo. L.J. 1789, 1797 (2000). See also Roger Fisher, William Ury, & Bruce Patton, Getting to Yes 100 (3d ed. 2011) ("Establishing a BATNA is crucial as it is the standard against which a negotiator should compare any proposed agreement: if the BATNA would result in a better outcome than the negotiated agreement, the agreement should not be concluded").

28 Korobkin, 88 Geo. L.J. at 1795 ("If the negotiator's BATNA and the subject of the negotiation are perfectly interchangeable, determining the reservation price is quite simple: the reservation price is merely the value of the BATNA.")

lower mileage of B's car. If, for example, you value the lower mileage at $3000, then your bottom line in negotiating with A should be $17,000 because paying more than that would be worse for you than your best alternative, which is buying B's car for $20,000.

This example of a mileage difference is only slightly more complex than the original example of identical cars from A and B because it added only one variable, mileage. More realistic examples of used car purchases would include more variables, and thus more valuations needed to determine the buyer's bottom line.

These valuations are subjective. For example, one buyer might highly value a used car that looks good, without dents or scratches, while another buyer barely cares about the car's looks at all. One buyer might love that a car is pink while another buyer considers pink a big negative. So, what counts as a positive or a negative, and the degree to which it counts, is subjective. But the rational person must, at least implicitly, place a numerical value on each difference between the BATNA and the subject of the negotiation under consideration, and then combine those valuations to produce a bottom line in that negotiation. For example, "I value this car's lack of dents and scratches at $4000 but value the pink color at negative $3000, so I would pay $1000 more for this car than for the otherwise-similar non-pink car with dents and scratches." A negotiator failing to do this "cannot be sure to avoid the most basic negotiating mistake—agreeing to a deal when he would have been better off walking away from the table with no agreement."[29]

## § 1.7 Expected Value

The previous section explains how the value you place on your BATNA—your best alternative to an agreement in the negotiation under consideration—helps you determine your *bottom line* in that negotiation. It also explains how that valuation can become increasingly complex as more factors distinguish your BATNA from the outcome of the negotiation under consideration. But the previous section nevertheless achieves some simplicity by assuming the negotiator knows the positives and negatives of each option and merely has to value them, as in "I value this car's lack of dents and scratches at $4000 but value the pink color at negative $3000, so I would pay $1000 more for this car than for the otherwise-similar non-pink car with dents and scratches."

In contrast, further complexity arises if some positives or negatives are uncertain, so the negotiator must predict their probability to value them. For example, in comparing your old car to

[29] Id. at 1797.

a newer—but still used—car you might buy, you may try to predict the likelihood of various mechanical problems each vehicle will experience in the coming years so you can try to estimate each vehicle's expected maintenance costs.

Or suppose you receive job offers from two employers. Employer A offers you a salary of $6000 per month. Employer B offers you a salary of $5000 per month, but B has been known to raise salary offers when pressed, so you're going to call B to try to negotiate a higher salary. The two jobs seem identical to you except you believe—but are not certain—you'd have nicer coworkers at B. To determine your bottom line in your negotiation with B, you need to value in dollars the likelihood B would give you nicer coworkers. Suppose that if you were certain that B had nicer coworkers you would value that at $400 per month. Then your bottom line in negotiating with B would be a salary of $5600 per month because if you cannot get at least that much money from B then you believe you'd be better off with the extra money from A, even at the expense of its less-nice coworkers.

But suppose you are only 75% confident that B has nicer coworkers, leaving a 25% chance you will like A's coworkers as much as you like B's. Under these circumstances, the *expected value* of B's nicer coworkers is $300 because:

$$\$400 \times .75 = \$300$$

This *expected value* calculation discounts the value you place on B's nicer coworkers ($400) by its probability (.75).[30] With the expected value of B's nicer coworkers at only $300, your bottom line in your negotiating with B would be a salary of $5700 per month. If you cannot get at least that much money from B then you believe you'd be better off with the extra money from A, even at the expense of its (75% likely) less-nice coworkers.

In sum, the *expected value* of an outcome is the value of that outcome multiplied by the probability that it will occur.

## § 1.8 Zone of Possible Agreement

As discussed in Sections 1.5 and 1.6, determining your Best Alternative to a Negotiated Agreement (BATNA) in the negotiation under consideration helps you in that negotiation because valuing your BATNA helps you determine your *bottom line* in negotiation. For example, suppose you decide your best alternative to negotiating with A to buy A's used car is paying B $23,000 for a dented pink car

[30] For more on expected utility theory and its application to negotiation, see Chris Guthrie, Better Settle Than Sorry: The Regret Aversion Theory of Litigation Behavior, 1999 U. Ill. L. Rev. 43, 47–54.

that is otherwise-similar to A's car. If you negatively value B's car's dents and pink at $7000, then $30,000 is your bottom line in negotiating with A.

If A's bottom line is $28,000, then you and A should reach a deal at a price between $28,000 and $30,000. You believe such a deal with A is better for you than your best alternative, and A believes such a deal with you is better for A than A's best alternative. This is depicted in Diagram 1-1 which uses a thick line to show prices better for Seller A than its bottom line and a thin line to show prices better for you (Buyer) than your bottom line.

**Diagram 1-1**

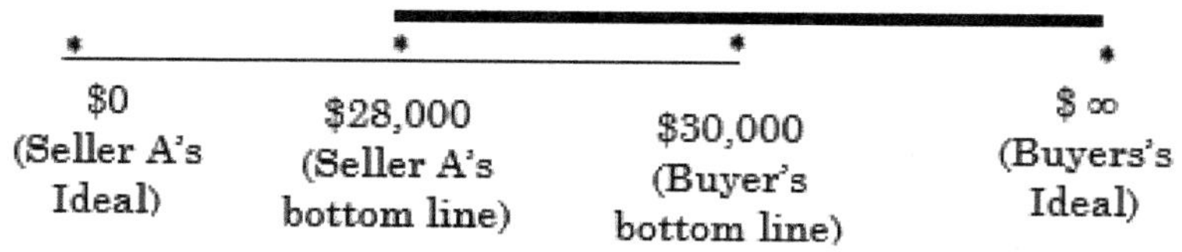


In this example, the Zone of Possible Agreement (ZOPA) is from $28,000 to $30,000. Agreement cannot occur outside this ZOPA (or "bargaining zone"[31]) because any agreement must be at least as good for each party as its bottom line. This follows from the fact that a party's bottom line is the worst deal that party will accept.

If a party announces its bottom line and then accepts a deal worse than that, either the party has changed its bottom line since the announcement (§ 1.32(b)) or the party's announcement misstated that party's actual bottom line (§ 1.15(a)).

## § 1.9 Zero-Sum (Distributive) Negotiation

Section 1.8 gives an example of *zero-sum* negotiation—your negotiation to buy a car from Auto Dealer A. It is zero-sum because any change in the proposed agreement results in increased value for one party and decreased value for the other party.

From your perspective as Buyer, $28,000 is better than $29,000, which is better than $30,000. Seller's (Auto Dealer A's) perspective is exactly the opposite: $28,000 is worse than $29,000 which is worse than $30,000. This complete opposition of interests applies to all possible agreements and is the essence of zero-sum negotiation. Any change in the proposed agreement, say from $28,500 to $29,000,

[31] See, e.g., Russell Korobkin, Negotiation Theory and Strategy, 25–31 (4th ed. 2024) ("The bargaining zone is defined as the space below a buyer's reservation price but above the seller's reservation price.")

results in increased value for one party and decreased value for the other party. The more Seller A gets, the less Buyer gets, and vice versa.

This is emphasized by the double arrow (pointing in opposite directions) in Diagram 1-2.

**Diagram 1-2**

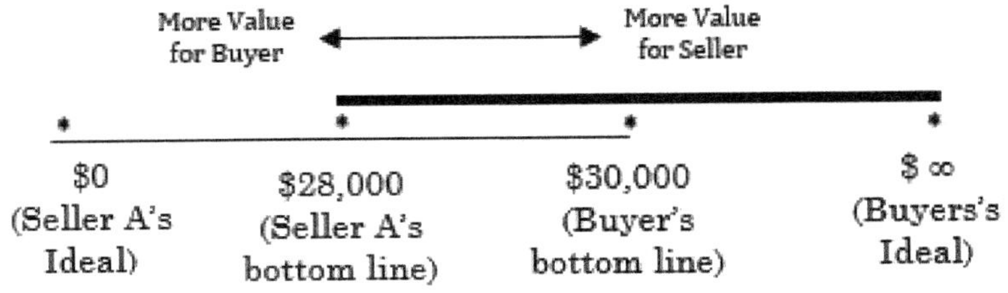


As the double arrow emphasizes, in zero-sum negotiation, the interests of the parties (you, the Buyer, and A, the Seller,) are diametrically opposed with respect to the choice among all possible agreements. So, any change in the proposed agreement results in increased value for one party and decreased value for the other party.

However, the choice among possible agreements is different from the choice between agreeing and not agreeing. You, the Buyer, and A, the Seller, will never agree on which of two possible agreements, say $28,500 or $29,000, is more attractive. But you and A agree that selling the car to you for, say, $28,500 is more attractive than you two not reaching an agreement with each other. To put it another way, $28,500 is better for each party than its *bottom line*, and thus within the Zone of Possible Agreement (ZOPA) (§§ 1.6–1.8). More broadly, an agreement reached in zero-sum negotiation makes each party, in its estimation at the time, better off than it would have been in the absence of a deal (§ 1.4).

## § 1.10 Positive-Sum (Integrative) Negotiation

### *(a) Distinguishing Positive-Sum from Zero-Sum Negotiation*

A classic metaphor for distinguishing *zero-sum* (§ 1.9) from *positive-sum* negotiation is the contrast between dividing a pie and expanding it. In zero-sum negotiations, negotiators discuss only how to divide a pie, while in positive-sum negotiations, negotiators find ways to expand the size of the pie. This metaphor is fine unless it leads people to forget that even purely zero-sum division of a pie is better for each party than spending time and money litigating until a court awards the by-then-spoiled pie to one of the parties. Any agreement—even if purely zero-sum—creates value in the sense that it gives each side something it values more than whatever alternatives it had (§§ 1.4–1.5). So, we might think of zero-sum negotiation as dividing a pie neither side gets any of if they fail to agree on how to divide it.

What makes an agreement positive sum is that it's not only better for each party than no agreement; it's better for each party than other possible agreements between them. That is, positive-sum negotiation finds possible agreements that appeal to *both parties* more than other possible agreements between them.[32] While zero-sum deals appeal to each party more than no deal, positive-sum deals appeal to each party more than both no deal and other possible deals.

Whether or not they use the pie metaphor, negotiation theorists distinguish creating value from dividing it.[33] Many negotiation analysts call zero-sum negotiation *distributive* bargaining because it distributes (divides) among the parties value that existed prior to the negotiation. These theorists call positive-sum negotiation *integrative* bargaining because it integrates or combines different topics to add new value created by negotiating. This terminology, like the pie metaphor, is fine unless it leads people to forget that any agreement, even if purely distributive, creates value in the sense that it gives each side something it values more than whatever alternatives it had, such as further litigation (§§ 1.4–1.5).

Some negotiations are purely zero-sum (§ 1.10(e)), and many negotiations have both a positive-sum part and a zero-sum part. Few if any negotiations are purely positive-sum because "No matter how much creative problem solving enlarges the pie, it must still be divided; value that has been created must be claimed."[34]

### *(b) An Example of Positive-Sum Negotiation*

An example of positive-sum negotiation is the sale of a business in Diagram 1-3.

---

[32] Robert H. Mnookin, Scott R. Peppet & Andrew S. Tulumello, Beyond Winning: Negotiating to Create Value in Deals and Disputes 12 (2000) ("The Goal: Creating Value Through Problem-Solving Negotiation."); id. ("When we talk about creating value, we typically mean reaching a deal that, when compared to other possible *negotiated* outcomes, either makes both parties better off or makes one party better off without making the other party worse off." (emphasis in original)).

[33] David A. Lax & James K. Sebenius, The Manager as Negotiator: Bargaining for Cooperation and Competitive Gain 33 (1986).

[34] Id. Accord Gerald B. Wetlaufer, The Limits of Integrative Bargaining, 85 Geo. L.J. 369, 373 (1996).

Diagram 1-3

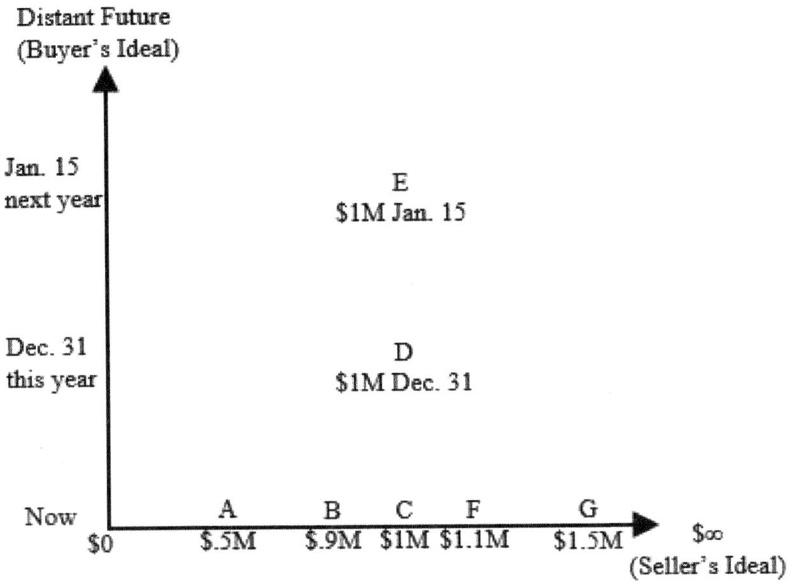


The horizontal line at the bottom of the diagram represents the price Buyer will pay Seller for the business. The vertical line on the left represents the time of that payment, with the bottom of the vertical line representing an immediate payment and the top of the vertical line representing payment in the distant future. Any time in between is a point on the line.

Several possible deals for immediate payment are noted along the line at the bottom of the diagram. Deal A is an immediate (now) payment of $.5M for the business. Deal B is a $.9M payment now, Deal C is a $1M payment now, and so forth.

Deal D, like Deal C, is a $1M payment for the business, but Deal D delays that payment until December 31 of this year. Deal E is also a $1M payment for the business but Deal E delays that payment until January 15 of next year.

In general, those receiving payment of a fixed amount of money prefer the payment as soon as possible, while those making payment prefer to delay payment as long as possible.[35] This is due to the *time value of money*, "a basic financial concept that holds that money in the present is worth more than the same sum of money to be received in the future . . . because money that you have right now can be invested and earn a return, thus creating a larger amount of money

[35] Tax laws create exceptions to this generalization. See § 1.10(d).

in the future."[36] Accordingly, the diagram shows that Seller prefers to receive payment as soon as possible (lower on the diagram), and Seller's ideal would be in the lower right corner of the diagram (large payment now). In contrast, Buyer prefers to delay paying as long as possible (higher on the diagram), and Buyer's ideal would be in the upper left corner (low payment in the distant future).

Compare the possible deals involving $1M. From Buyer's perspective, Deal E is better than Deal D which is better than Deal C. Seller's perspective is exactly the opposite: Deal E is worse than Deal D which is worse than Deal C. This complete opposition of interests applies to all possible agreements involving just a one-time payment of $1M for the business. In other words, the negotiation about the time of payment is zero-sum. Any change in the proposed time of payment results in increased value for one party and decreased value for the other.

Considered in isolation, both the amount of payment and the time of payment are topics for zero-sum negotiation. But considering them together may create a positive-sum negotiation. For example, compare Deal B ($.9M now) and Deal E ($1M on Jan. 15 of next year). The choice between these two possible terms involves a tradeoff between time and amount. The parties may assess this tradeoff differently so, for example, each prefers Deal E to Deal B. That is, Seller may prefer receiving $1M on Jan. 15 of next year to receiving $.9M now, and Buyer may prefer paying $1M on Jan. 15 of next year to paying $.9M now. This might occur because Buyer—perhaps a large corporation—can invest $.9M now with confidence that its investment will be worth more than $1M on Jan. 15 of next year, while Seller—perhaps a risk-averse individual who has reached retirement age—lacks tolerably safe investment opportunities as likely to turn $.9M into $1M by Jan. 15 of next year.

One might loosely say the issue of *time*-of-payment is more important to Buyer than to Seller, while the issue of *amount*-of-payment is more important to Seller than to Buyer.[37] These differing

---

[36] Corporate Finance Institute Time Value of Money, https://corporatefinanceinstitute.com/resources/valuation/time-value-of-money/ (last visited Nov. 30, 2024). See also Jeffrey J. Haas, Corporate Finance ch. 4 (2021) ("The 'time value of money' is directly related to two concepts in corporate finance known as 'present value' and 'future value.' . . . [T]hese concepts are basically two sides of the same valuation coin. Future value (FV) is simply the value of a current sum of money on some future date, assuming it was invested and earns a specified rate of interest between now and that future date.").

[37] More precisely, Seller's discount rate is lower than Buyer's. A discount rate is a rate of return used to convert a monetary sum, payable or receivable in the future, into a present value. See, e.g., Robert W. Hamilton & Richard A. Booth, Business Basics for Law Students Ch. 2 (4th ed. 2006). The general formula for the present value of a future amount X years in the future is:

priorities about time versus amount enable this negotiation to be positive sum. Because of these differing priorities, both parties prefer Deal E ($1M on Jan. 15 of next year) to Deal B ($.9M now). That *both parties* prefer some possible settlement terms to other possible settlement terms is the essence of positive-sum negotiation.

Another way to visualize this example is in Diagram 1-4.

Diagram 1-4

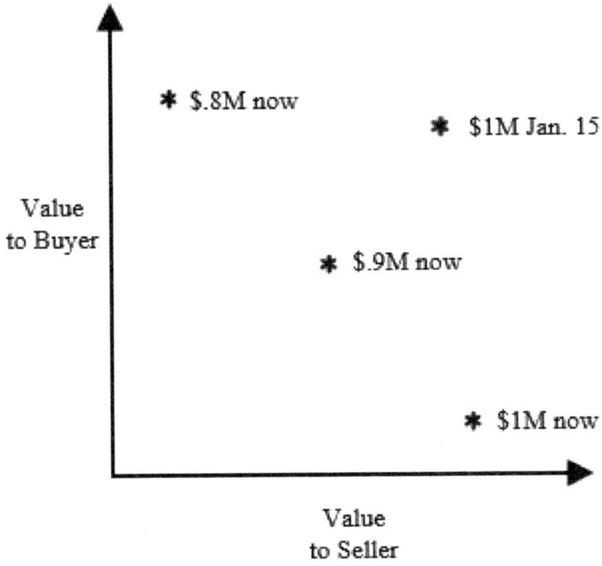


Diagram 1-4 shows three possible payment amounts now ($.8M, $.9M and $1M), which fall along an invisible diagonal line reflecting the fact that as the amount-of-payment rises, the value of deal to Seller rises, while the value of the deal to Buyer falls by a corresponding amount. Diagram 1-4 also shows that delaying payment until Jan. 15 of next year adds value because, for example, both parties prefer $1M on Jan. 15 to $.9M now.[38] That Buyer prefers $1M on Jan. 15 to $.9M

Present Value = (Future Value) / (1 + Discount Rate)$^{X}$

Different parties may have different discount rates because, as in the previous footnote, they face different investment and borrowing options. Even parties with the same investment and borrowing options may have different discount rates because they have different preferences about the tradeoff between present and future consumption. See, e.g., Russell B. Korobkin & Thomas S. Ulen, Law and Behavioral Science: Removing the Rationality Assumption from Law and Economics, 88 Cal. L. Rev. 1051, 1119 (2000).

38 The value created by the idea of delaying payment is analogous to the economics concept of expanding, or pushing outward, the production possibility curve.

now is shown by the fact that $1M on Jan. 15 is higher on the graph (more value to Buyer) than $.9M now. The Seller prefers $1M on Jan. 15 to $.9M now is shown by the fact that $1M on Jan. 15 is farther right on the graph (more value to Seller) than $.9M now.

### *(c) The Importance of Multiple Issues: Logrolling*

If the hypothetical parties discussed in the previous subsection had considered only the *amount* of the price for the business, and assumed immediate payment, they might have agreed on an immediate payment of $.9M. This would have squandered an opportunity to add value. By choosing "$1M on Jan. 15 of next year" over "$.9M now," the negotiators made each party better off (in its estimation at the time) than it would have been had the issue of time not been considered. The key to creating this additional value was considering an additional issue. Positive-sum negotiation almost never occurs if only one issue is considered, especially if that issue is the amount of money Buyer will pay Seller (or Defendant will pay Plaintiff).

In contrast, considering multiple issues can enable negotiation to create value (be positive sum) in two ways. Suppose Seller cares a lot about Issue A, but not much about Issue B, while Buyer cares a lot about Issue B, but not much about Issue A. The parties can create value if Buyer concedes on Issue A in exchange for Seller's concession on Issue B. Each party gives up something it cares about a little in exchange for getting what it cares about a lot. This is what happened in the previous subsection's example of choosing "$1M on Jan. 15 of next year" over "$.9M now." Seller conceded on the issue of time, while Buyer conceded on the issue of amount. This sort of trade, often called *logrolling*,[39] is the basis of most positive-sum negotiation. It works to create value, even where the parties disagree on every issue, if they prioritize the issues differently.

The example of positive-sum negotiation just discussed, choosing "$1M on Jan. 15 of next year" over "$.9M now," is exceptionally simple. In adding the issue of time, the negotiators still assumed that there would be just one payment by Buyer to Seller. Expanding the options to include a series of smaller payments might create still more value than the value created by delaying a single payment. And considering topics beyond payment amount and timing

---

Production Possibilities Curve, ReviewEcon.com (Mar. 21, 2024), https://www.reviewecon.com/production-possibilities-curve.

[39] The name logrolling apparently comes "from a former American custom of neighbors assisting one another in rolling logs into a pile for burning," so "logrolling" became more widely used to mean "the exchanging of assistance or favors." Logrolling, Merriam-Webster, https://www.merriam-webster.com/dictionary/logrolling (last visited Apr. 2, 2026).

opens countless other possibilities for creating additional value through negotiation. The sale of a business might involve a long contract with hundreds of clauses, each of which is a topic the negotiators can trade off against other topics, so each party keeps getting more and more of its higher priorities while giving up only its lower priorities. The more topics considered, the more likely the negotiators are to find more opportunities for positive-sum negotiation. Creativity often adds value.

### *(d) Coinciding Interests (with a Tax Law Example)*

Most positive-sum negotiation occurs through the *logrolling* process just discussed, in which each party gives up its lower priority to gain its higher priority. But occasionally negotiators find an issue on which the parties' interests coincide, so neither party has to give up anything to get something.

For an example of an issue on which the parties' interests coincide, consider settlement of a negligence claim for compensatory damages arising from a physical injury Defendant caused while engaged in its ordinary business activities. Both Plaintiff and Defendant may prefer that a settlement payment be made in late December, rather than early in the next month, January. Ordinarily, the *time-value of money* (§ 1.10(b)) causes plaintiffs to want settlement payments they receive to occur sooner and defendants to want the settlement payments they make to occur later. Tax law, however, probably permits Defendant to deduct this payment from its income because tax law generally permits deductions of settlement payments arising out of Defendant's business activities.[40] The time value of money leads taxpayers (here Defendant) to take deductions in the current tax year, rather than waiting until next year.[41] In other words, Defendant's tax benefit of paying money in

---

[40] Generally, payments pursuant to a settlement or judgment (along with attendant legal fees) are deductible if the payments arose out of defendant's business activities, as opposed to personal or family activities. See Deductibility of legal expenses, generally, 5 Mertens Law of Fed. Income Tax'n § 24A:18 (2022) ("If the origin of the claim arises out of the taxpayer's business, the taxpayer may deduct legal expenses paid or incurred in connection with such claim under Section 162. Similarly, if the origin of the claim arises out of an income-producing or investment activity, the taxpayer may deduct legal expenses paid or incurred in connection with such claim under Section 212. If the origin of the claim is for a personal matter unconnected with a business or the production of income, litigation expenses are not deductible.") However, no deduction is generally allowed for fines paid to government, 26 U.S.C. § 162(f), or for settlement payments and legal fees paid in connection with cases of sexual harassment or sexual abuse if such payment is subject to a nondisclosure agreement. 26 U.S.C. § 162(q).

[41] See, e.g., Mark J. Cowan & Joshua Cutler, Cross-Fertilizing the Tax Classroom, 19 Pitt. Tax Rev. 329, 358 (2022) ("Tax planning is often presented as a time value of money exercise: all else being equal, defer income and accelerate deductions where possible"); Karie Davis-Nozemack & Sarah Webber, Paying the IRS Whistleblower: A Critical Analysis of Collected Proceeds, 32 Va. Tax Rev. 77, 122–23

late December of this year may exceed the interest it could earn on that money by waiting until early January of next year to pay. If so, Defendant would likely prefer making its payment in late December, rather than early January. Plaintiff also prefers the payment to occur in late December rather than early January because no tax law or other factor offsets Plaintiff's desire to start earning interest on the money sooner rather than later.[42] In sum, both parties prefer the payment to occur in late December, rather than early January. A settlement providing for payment in early January would make both parties worse off than a settlement providing for payment in late December. Agreeing on payment in late December is a clear example of positive-sum negotiating because the parties' interests coincide on the question of when the payment occurs.

Issues on which parties' interests coincide are rare. They tend not to become issues precisely because the parties' interests coincide, and the negotiators realize that, so they agree to the terms that both parties prefer. On the other hand, tax issues are examples of issues that litigators and their clients may forget or misunderstand.[43]

### *(e) Positive-Sum (Integrative) Negotiation Is Not Always Worthwhile, or Even Possible*

Negotiators trying to find a positive-sum opportunity may fail because no such opportunity exists. The parties' interests may be so diametrically opposed that they have no coinciding interests. And the parties may prioritize issues so similarly that it is not possible to trade concessions on low priority issues for gains on higher priority issues (logrolling). In short, the situation may be zero-sum, thus precluding positive-sum negotiation. Negotiation theorists disagree about the frequency of zero-sum situations.[44]

---

(2012) ("Taxpayers have an incentive to defer income recognition into subsequent years to delay paying tax, and taxpayers have an incentive to accelerate deductions to minimize current taxable income").

[42] Carina Bryant, Proceeds of lawsuits, 1 Mertens Law of Fed. Income Tax'n § 5:17 (2022) ("Amounts received in settlement of a claim for damages on account of a personal physical injury or physical sickness are excluded from income"). By contrast, recoveries for many other sorts of losses generally are taxable income. Id.

[43] See, e.g., French v. Domnarski, No. CV94 0048532S, 1995 WL 573787, at *1 (Conn. Super. Sept. 15, 1995) (describing a client who settled a claim, relying on an attorney's mistaken advice that alimony and certain mortgage payments would be tax deductible); Jalali v. Root, 1 Cal. Rptr. 3d 689 (Ct. App. 2003) (plaintiff "Jalali claimed that, before she accepted the $2.75 million settlement, [her lawyer] Root told her that her taxes on the settlement would be 'forty percent of your share,' that is, Jalali's share after deducting Root's contingency fee. However, Jalali ended up paying taxes on the whole $2.75 million received, not just her portion after deducting her attorney's fee.").

[44] Compare, e.g., Carrie Menkel-Meadow, Toward Another View of Legal Negotiation: The Structure of Problem Solving, 31 UCLA L. Rev. 754, 784 (1984) ("true zero sum games are empirically quite rare"), with James J. White, The Pros and Cons of "Getting to Yes", 34 J. Legal Educ. 115, 115–117 (1984) (influential book "is

While negotiators can only have zero-sum negotiations in zero-sum situations, they can have either positive-sum or zero-sum negotiations in positive-sum situations. A zero-sum negotiation in a positive-sum situation is not necessarily a failure because the value created by exploiting a positive-sum opportunity may be lower than the value of the time and effort required to find it.

### *(f) The Zone of Possible Agreement in Positive-Sum Negotiation*

Section 1.8 provides a simple example of negotiators' bottom lines and thus their Zone of Possible Agreement (ZOPA): a car buyer who is willing to pay up to $30,000 while the seller is willing to sell for as low as $28,000. In this example, reproduced in Diagram 1-5, the Zone of Possible Agreement (ZOPA) is from $28,000 to $30,000. A thick line shows prices better for Seller A than its bottom line and a thin line shows prices better for Buyer than its bottom line.

Diagram 1-5

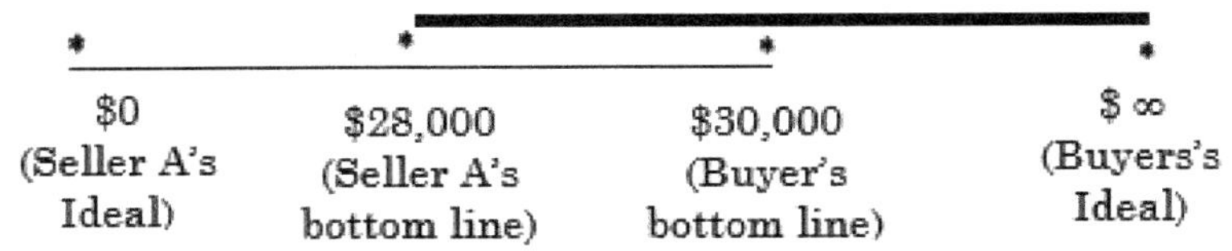


This ZOPA example is simple because it is zero sum. When the only issue parties consider up for negotiation is the amount of money, each party can determine its bottom line through the process discussed in Sections 1.5 and 1.6.

In contrast, as Section 1.10(c) explains, positive-sum negotiation nearly always requires negotiators to consider multiple issues. However, considering multiple issues complicates a party's determination of its bottom line.

Suppose, for example, that if all the seller of a business (Seller) was receiving from Buyer was money, the Seller's bottom line price for the business would be $5 million. But Seller genuinely wants from Buyer not only

(1) money, but also

---

frequently naive" for under-emphasizing prominence of zero-sum/distributive negotiation).

(2) a promise that Buyer will keep the business's headquarters in Seller's hometown for at least five more years, and

(3) a promise that Buyer will not disclose certain information Buyer learned about Seller while investigating the business.

In negotiating for these promises, Seller must at least implicitly quantify the values she places on them. For example, if she values them at $2 million, then Seller's bottom line price for the business can be expressed as "$3 million plus the promises about the headquarters and nondisclosure" or "$5 million without those promises."

Conversely, suppose Buyer's bottom line price for a purchase requiring only money from Buyer is $4 million. And suppose further that Buyer plans to keep the headquarters in Seller's hometown for the foreseeable future and Buyer does not mind keeping confidential what Buyer has learned about Seller. So, Buyer's willingness to pay for the business if it makes those two promises drops only from $4 million to $3.5 million.

This is depicted in Diagram 1-6 in which Part A shows Seller receiving only money from Buyer, while Part B shows Seller also receiving Buyer's promises regarding the headquarters (HQ) and nondisclosure. In both Parts A and B, the thick lines represent possible agreements better for Seller than her bottom line, while thin lines represent possible agreements better for Buyer than its bottom line.

Diagram 1-6

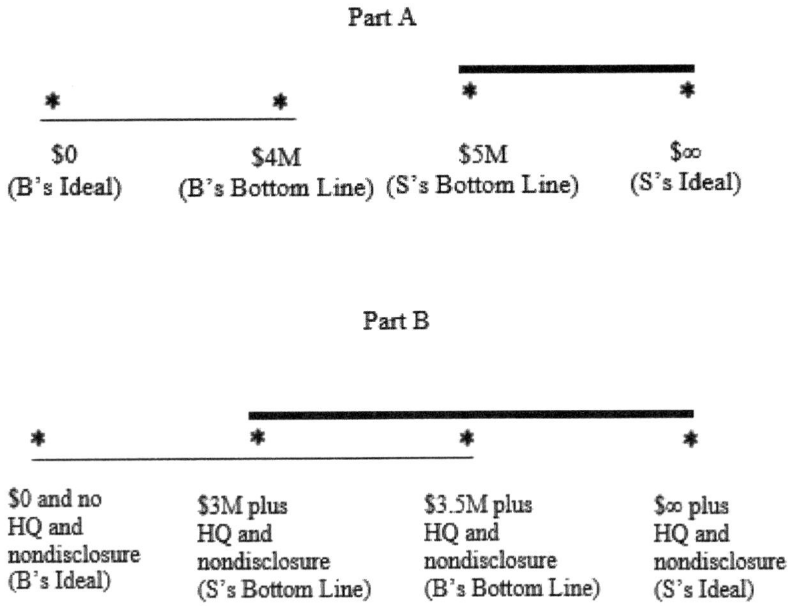


Part A shows that for a deal in which Seller receives only money, the parties' bottom lines do not overlap, so no deal is possible. There is no Zone of Possible Agreement (ZOPA). In contrast, Part B shows a ZOPA for a deal in which Buyer promises to keep the business's headquarters in Seller's hometown for at least five more years and promises not to disclose certain information Buyer learned about Seller while investigating the business. This is an example of how positive-sum negotiation can create a ZOPA that would not otherwise exist.

As this example shows, if a party considers multiple issues, that party can see its bottom line in multiple ways.[45] For example, Seller in Diagram 1-6 can see her bottom line as either "$5M with no promises" or "$3M plus the promises about the headquarters and nondisclosure." Perhaps Seller can also see her bottom line as "$4M plus the promise about the headquarters," or "$4.1M plus the promise of nondisclosure." The more issues a party considers, the more different ways it can see its bottom line. In other words, the more issues a party considers, the more possible agreements that party will find acceptable, that is, better than one way to express its bottom

[45] John S. Murray, Alan Scott Rau & Edward F. Sherman, Processes of Dispute Resolution: The Role of Lawyers 89 (2d ed. 1996) ("Bottom lines are no longer single figures, but a series of settlement packages that for the offering party represent the same utility value.").

line. And the more possible agreements a party finds acceptable, the more likely at least one of them will also be acceptable to the other side (better than its bottom line). In sum, the more issues parties consider, the more likely they are to create a Zone of Possible Agreement. So, lawyers counseling or negotiating on behalf of parties often help their clients, and sometimes other parties, to consider additional issues with an eye to creating a ZOPA that would not otherwise exist.

Nevertheless, positive-sum negotiation, like zero-sum negotiation, occurs within the constraints of bottom lines. And positive-sum negotiation poses the additional challenge of converting multiple goals (such as maintaining a headquarters' location or nondisclosure) into a single measure of value. That measure is often money, but it does not have to be.

## § 1.11 Barriers to Agreement

### *(a) No Zone of Possible Agreement*

A common reason negotiation does not result in an agreement is that it shouldn't. If the negotiators try to find an agreement better for each party than its best alternative (BATNA, § 1.5), but cannot find such an agreement, that may be because no such agreement exists. In other words, the parties' bottom lines (§ 1.6) do not overlap to create a Zone of Possible Agreement (ZOPA, § 1.7). Under such circumstances, forming an agreement would, for at least one party, be "the most basic negotiating mistake—agreeing to a deal when [that party] would have been better off walking away from the table with no agreement."[46]

In contrast, when a ZOPA exists because some set of agreement terms seems to each party better than its BATNA, and thus its bottom line, failure to form an agreement on such terms is a failure of the negotiating parties to help themselves. Causes of this failure are discussed next.

### *(b) Ignorance of the ZOPA's Existence or Boundaries*

The existence of a Zone of Possible Agreement means that an agreement is possible, that is, the negotiators *might* reach an agreement, not that they *will* reach an agreement. For example, in Part B of Diagram 1-6 (§ 1.10(f)), the range between $3M (Seller's bottom line when making promises regarding the headquarters and nondisclosure) and $3.5M (Buyer's bottom line when receiving those

[46] Russell Korobkin, A Positive Theory of Legal Negotiation, 88 Geo. L.J. 1789, 1797 (2000).

promises) is the ZOPA, but the negotiators might be unable to agree on a price within that range for a number of reasons.

First, the negotiators may not even realize that a zone of agreement exists. Negotiators typically conceal their bottom lines from each other and often try to make their bottom lines appear tougher than they really are (§ 1.15).[47] This sort of bluffing may lead each side to conclude that no ZOPA exists. In other words, each negotiator may conclude that no possible agreement is better for their side than that side's bottom line, so the parties should stop wasting time trying to negotiate a deal with each other and pursue other options instead.

### (c) *Dividing the Value Created by Agreement, Including the Game of "Chicken"*

Even if both negotiators discover that a ZOPA exists, and learn its precise boundaries, they still may not reach agreement. For example, an agreement on the sale depicted in Part B of Diagram 1-6 (§ 1.10(f))—with the promises about the headquarters and non-disclosure—at a price between $3M and $3.5M will create $500,000 in value. That is because, given the promises Buyer also makes, Buyer values the business at $3.5M while Seller, given those promises, values the business at only $3M. But who gets how much of that $500,000 new value depends on where the price falls in the zone between $3M and $3.5M. If the parties agree to $3,000,001 then Buyer captures nearly all the new value created by agreement. Seller is barely made better off by the agreement. Conversely, if the parties agree to $3,499,499 then Seller captures nearly all the value created by agreement, and Buyer is barely made better off.

The negotiators may spend much time and money negotiating within the Zone of Possible Agreement. Indeed, each negotiator may be so determined to capture the potential value from a settlement that they never reach a deal.[48] Buyer may say to Seller "We will not pay more than $3,000,001. You should agree to it because it is better for you than no agreement at all." Seller may say to Buyer "I will not

---

47 See Michaela Keet, Litigation Risk Assessment: A Tool to Enhance Negotiation, 19 Cardozo J. Conflict Resol. 17, 20 (2017) ("Except in the most open and collaborative negotiations, neither party will be aware of the other's reservation value").

48 Herein lie the transaction costs of the bilateral monopoly that is settlement negotiation. See § 1.3. See also Richard A. Posner, Economic Analysis of Law 779 (9th ed. 2014) ("Settlement negotiations are a classic example of bilateral monopoly. The plaintiff can settle only with the defendant and the defendant only with the plaintiff, and each party is eager to engross as much as possible of the surplus that settlement will generate over litigation. Indeed, the larger the settlement range, the more the parties will stand to gain from hard bargaining and the likelier (it may seem) the parties are to end up litigating because they cannot agree on how to divide the available surplus.").

take less than $3,499,999. You should agree to it because it is better for you than no agreement at all." These negotiators are playing the game of "chicken."

> The story behind this game comes . . . from an earlier time. Two teenagers drive cars headlong at each other. A driver gains stature when that driver drives headlong and the other swerves. Both drivers die, however, if neither swerves. Each player's highest payoff comes when that player drives head on and the other swerves; the second highest comes when that player swerves and the other [swerves] as well; and the third highest comes when that player swerves and the other drives. The lowest payoff results when both drive.[49]

As with the teenage drivers, so with negotiators. When negotiating within the Zone of Possible Agreement, whoever yields first loses. But if neither yields, then both lose even worse. Going without a deal is like crashing the cars because going without a deal is worse for each party than accepting the other side's offer within the ZOPA.[50] Whoever yields first, by accepting the other side's offer within the ZOPA, fails to capture most of the value created by agreement, but does capture a sliver of it, which is better than none at all. And if neither side yields by accepting the other side's offer within the ZOPA, then neither party gets any of the value—not even a sliver of the value—that could have been created by agreement.[51]

## C. APPROACHES TO NEGOTIATION

### § 1.12 Three Broad Approaches to Negotiation

An "approach" to negotiation encompasses both the negotiator's mindset or attitude and the negotiator's behavior, including specific tactics. Approaches to negotiation are as varied as negotiators themselves, so any attempt to categorize approaches to negotiation must generalize in ways that do not always hold true. Another challenge is that different negotiation theorists use different labels to describe similar approaches to negotiation.[52] No single set of labels

---

[49] Douglas G. Baird, Robert H. Gertner & Randall C. Picker, Game Theory and the Law 44 (1994).

[50] Going without a deal is worse for both parties when examined at the time they are deciding whether to make a deal. Of course, the result may turn out such that, with the benefit of hindsight, we see that one party was made better off by going without a deal.

[51] For tactics to win the game of chicken, see §§ 1.13–1.18.

[52] Andrea Kupfer Schneider, Teaching A New Negotiation Skills Paradigm, 39 Wash. U. J.L. & Pol'y 13, 21 (2012) (a "problem with existing labels, particularly in style, is the sheer number of labels that appear to say the same thing. For problem-solving, we have integrative, principled, or interest-based. Competitive is also hard

to describe the major approaches to negotiation has gained a consensus. So, this book uses common labels to describe three negotiation approaches: (1) Adversarial/Competitive, (2) Cooperative, and (3) Problem-Solving.[53]

Dividing negotiation approaches into these three concisely captures the two main distinctions among approaches: the distinction between creating value and distributing value (§ 1.10(a)), and the distinction between competing for value and sharing value. The problem-solving approach aims to create value and thus orients toward *positive-sum* negotiation. In contrast, both the adversarial/competitive and cooperative approaches aim to distribute value and thus orient toward *zero-sum* negotiation. The adversarial/competitive approach tries to distribute value toward the party using it, while the cooperative approach tries to share value more equally or fairly among the parties.

You can use any of the three approaches in any kind of negotiation, but as Section 1.3 explains, settlement negotiation tends to be more adversarial than transactional negotiation. In both settlement and transactional negotiation, skilled negotiators often use different approaches at different stages of the same negotiation, so you should be prepared to adjust your approach during negotiation (§ 1.32). Some negotiation experts go so far as to describe stages of a negotiation—such as a "value creation" stage followed by the "value claiming" stage—with a different approach suited to each stage.[54]

## 1. THE ADVERSARIAL/COMPETITIVE APPROACH

### § 1.13 Introduction to the Adversarial/Competitive Approach

The adversarial/competitive approach orients toward *zero-sum* negotiation (§ 1.9), which distributes value rather than creating it. Moreover, the adversarial/competitive approach orients toward

---

bargaining, adversarial, or distributive. Accommodating is also sharing, soft bargaining, or cooperative.").

[53] Accord Donald G. Gifford & Robert J. Rhee, Legal Negotiation: Theory and Practice 18 (3d ed. 2017). See also Carrie J. Menkel-Meadow, Lela Porter Love, Andrea Kupfer Schneider & Michael Moffitt, Dispute Resolution: Beyond the Adversarial Model 85 (3d ed. 2019) (similarly describing three approaches); Roger Fisher, William Ury & Bruce Patton, Getting to Yes: Negotiating An Agreement Without Giving In (2d ed. 1991) (discussing three approaches: hard bargaining, soft bargaining, and principled bargaining); Andrea Kupfer Schneider, Shattering Negotiation Myths: Empirical Evidence on the Effectiveness of Negotiation Style, 7 Harv. Negot. L. Rev. 143, 152 (2002) (distinguishing "Cooperative . . . willingness to split the pie" from problem-solving/integrative "focus on making [the pie] larger" and from the adversarial/competitive "hard bargainer").

[54] Charles B. Craver, Effective Legal Negotiation and Settlement ch. 6–7 (9th ed. 2020).

claiming (taking) the value distributed in negotiation rather than sharing it equally or fairly with other parties.

As Section 1.3 explains, settlement negotiation is more likely than transactional negotiation to be zero-sum (§ 1.9), which is one reason the adversarial/competitive approach is more common in settlement negotiation than in transactional negotiation. In addition, as Section 1.3 also explains, parties litigating against each other tend to be displeased with each other and less interested than parties in transactional negotiation in continuing their relationship after the negotiation. These characteristics of settlement negotiation tend toward the adversarial/competitive approach, as does the fact that settlement negotiation tends to be a bilateral monopoly in which the disputing parties are stuck with each other for at least as long as it takes to resolve the dispute (§ 1.3).

Because the adversarial/competitive approach orients toward claiming (taking) value in zero-sum negotiation, a negotiator using the adversarial/competitive approach during some or all of a negotiation treats that portion of the negotiation as a contest against the opposing party and its negotiator. A big victory in this contest would be getting the opposing party to offer an agreement at its *bottom line* (§ 1.6.) And even better if during the course of the negotiation the negotiator using the adversarial/competitive approach persuaded the opponent to soften its bottom line, so an offer at the opponent's new bottom line gives away even more value than an offer at the opponent's earlier bottom line would have.

If you succeed in getting your counterpart to offer an agreement at its bottom line, you and your client should nevertheless reject this offer if it is worse for your client than its own bottom line (§ 1.6). On the other hand, if this offer is better for your client than its bottom line, then you should accept it as the best you can do in zero sum negotiation because, by definition, your opponent will not offer you more than your opponent's bottom line. ("Opponent" is how an adversarial/competitive negotiator views their counterpart.)

## § 1.14 Information as Power in the Negotiation Contest

### *(a) Information as a Weapon*

All approaches to negotiation recognize the tremendous power of information. The approaches sharply differ, though, in how they harness the power of information.[55]

[55] Compare §§ 1.19–1.21 (discussing cooperative approach) and §§ 1.22–1.26 (discussing problem-solving approach).

In the adversarial/competitive approach, information is a weapon.[56] The better your information, the stronger you are.[57] "In an important sense, the competitive negotiator plays negotiation as an information game. In this game, the object is to get as much information from the other party as possible while disclosing as little information as possible."[58] So, a negotiator planning to use the adversarial/competitive approach prepares for negotiation (§§ 1.29–1.33) by trying to learn the other party's interests, bottom line, and specific goals. And how to exploit them. The more you know about a party's wants and needs, and their urgency or priority, the more you can get from them in negotiation.

Learning your opponent's bottom line is so important to the adversarial/competitive negotiator that it gets its own subsection, but first we consider learning about your opponent's interests and priorities. How will you do this? In litigation, discovery possibilities in the United States include depositions and document requests. Outside of litigation, including in transactional negotiation, you can pursue "informal discovery" such as:

- internet searches, including social media,
- searches of court and other government records,
- reports from credit reporting agencies and corporate bond-rating agencies,
- inquiries to the other party's neighbors, employers, or business associates, and even
- hiring an investigator to spy on the other party.

Your counterpart representing the other party in negotiation may similarly be trying to learn about your client's interests and priorities. You do not want your counterpart to succeed if you plan to use the adversarial/competitive approach or want to reserve the option to use it. To deprive your counterpart of information, you may resist or narrowly construe discovery requests by your counterpart and advise your client on ways to avoid inadvertently revealing

---

[56] Gary Goodpaster, A Primer on Competitive Bargaining, 1996 J. Disp. Resol. 325, 342–43 (1996) ("In an important sense, the competitive negotiator plays negotiation as an information game. In this game, the object is to get as much information from the other party as possible while disclosing as little information as possible.").

[57] "Negotiation literature teaches that knowledge is power." Ronald F. Wright, Jenny Roberts & Betina Cutaia Wilkinson, The Shadow Bargainers, 42 Cardozo L. Rev. 1295, 1331 (2021).

[58] Gary Goodpaster, A Primer on Competitive Bargaining, 1996 J. Disp. Resol. 325, 342–43 (1996).

information. The adversarial/competitive negotiator tries to keep her cards hidden until it is time to play them.

What a lawyer should not do, even when pursuing the adversarial/competitive approach, is lie. In addition to the lawyer's conscience, other constraints on lying are reputation (§ 1.20(b)) and law. If a fraudulent or material misrepresentation induces the other party to form a contract, that contract is voidable at the option of the other party, and a misrepresentation may also lead to tort liability for fraud (§ 1.40(c)(2)). Finally, Model Rule of Professional Conduct 4.1 provides that a lawyer shall not knowingly

(a) make a false statement of material fact or law to a third person; or

(b) fail to disclose a material fact to a third person when disclosure is necessary to avoid assisting a criminal or fraudulent act by a client, unless disclosure is prohibited by rule 1.6 [which deals with the lawyer's obligation to keep client confidences].[59]

So, a lawyer can be reprimanded, suspended from practice, or even disbarred for the lawyer's misrepresentations in negotiations.[60]

While the aforementioned factors deter misrepresentations, one cannot be sure that everything her counterpart says in negotiations is true.[61] The adversarial/competitive negotiator remains suspicious of her counterpart's truthfulness.

### *(b) Information About Bottom Lines*

In the adversarial/competitive approach, information is a weapon, and the nuclear weapon is information about *bottom lines* (§ 1.6). The adversarial/competitive negotiator is especially alert to anything that might reveal the other party's bottom line, and she is

---

59 Model Rules of Prof'l Conduct R.4.1 (2019).

60 See Matter of Disciplinary Proc. Against Scholz, 950 N.W.2d 793, 803 (Wis. 2020) (imposing a two-year suspension on an attorney for, among other acts of misconduct, lying to "the mediator and opposing counsel regarding whether [the attorney] could disburse any of the disputed funds"); Off. of Disciplinary Couns. v. DiAngelus, 907 A.2d 452, 453, 458 (Pa. 2006) (imposing a five-year suspension on an attorney with a history of misconduct for lying to a prosecutor during plea deal discussion); Disciplinary Couns. v. Furth, 754 N.E.2d 219, 231, 232 (Ohio 2001) (permanently disbarring attorney for "intentionally misle[ading] the insurance company during negotiations by falsely asserting that [his client] suffered psychological injuries" and multiple other counts of misconduct). See also Ausherman v. Bank of America Corp., 212 F. Supp. 2d 435 (D. Md. 2002) (counsel's misrepresentation of material fact during settlement negotiations would be referred to court's disciplinary committee).

61 James J. White, Machiavelli and the Bar: Ethical Limitations on Lying in Negotiation, 1980 Am. B. Found. Res. J. 926, 935 (1980).

especially careful to prevent the opposing negotiator from learning anything that might shed light on her own client's bottom line.[62]

> The information the competitive negotiator seeks is the other party's bottom line. How much he will maximally give or minimally accept to make a deal. On the other hand, the competitive negotiator wants to persuade the other side about the firmness of the negotiator's own asserted bottom line. The competitive negotiator works to convince the other party that it will settle only at some point that is higher (or lower, as the case may be) than its actual and unrevealed bottom line.[63]

As this passage suggests, deception plays a big role in the adversarial/competitive approach. Deception feeds misinformation to the opposing negotiator and her client. Deception matters because information matters.

The importance of information and misinformation about bottom lines can be illustrated with an example. Assume that Defendant's bottom line is $200,000 and Plaintiff's bottom line is $150,000. The *settlement zone* (§ 1.39), which is the *Zone of Possible Agreement* (§ 1.8) in settlement negotiation, is from $150,000 to $200,000. These assumptions are reflected in Diagram 1-7, in which the thin line represents possible settlements acceptable to Defendant and the thick line represents possible settlements acceptable to Plaintiff.

**Diagram 1-7**

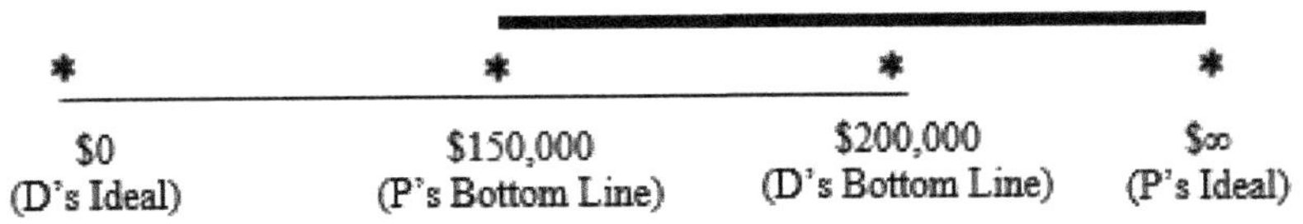


Suppose Plaintiff's lawyer knows Defendant's bottom line, but Defendant's lawyer is ignorant of Plaintiff's bottom line. If Defendant's lawyer learns that Plaintiff's bottom line is $150,000, then settlement may occur anywhere within the zone between

---

62 See, e.g., Hal Abramson, Fashioning an Effective Negotiation Style: Choosing Between Good Practices, Tactics, and Tricks, 23 Harv. Negot. L. Rev. 319, 326 (2018) (listing as a common negotiating tactic "Exaggerating a bottom line by using various techniques such as conveying misleading clues and shading information to influence the other side's perception of your bottom line").

63 Gary Goodpaster, A Primer on Competitive Bargaining, 1996 J. Disp. Resol. 325, 342–43 (1996).

$150,000 and $200,000. But if Defendant's lawyer comes to believe that Plaintiff's bottom line is $190,000, Defendant's lawyer will believe the settlement zone is only between $190,000 and $200,000. This is reflected in Diagram 1-8 in which the thick dashed line represents possible settlement terms that *Defendant's lawyer believes* are acceptable to Plaintiff.

**Diagram 1-8**

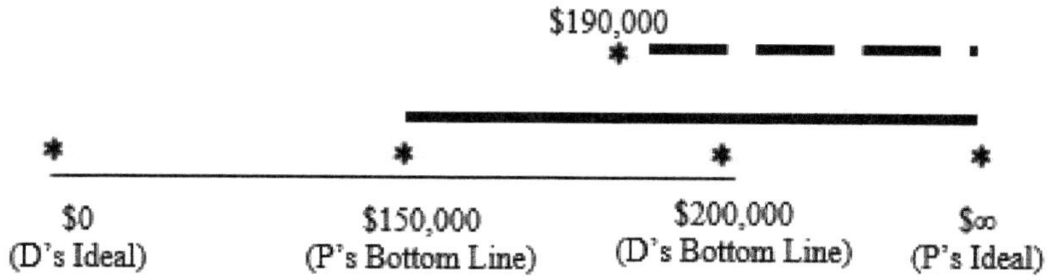


Defendant's lawyer's belief that Plaintiff will settle for no less than $190,000 helps Plaintiff. It ensures that any settlement will be near the high end of the real settlement zone.

The important practical question is how Defendant's lawyer came to believe that Plaintiff's bottom line was $190,000. Perhaps Defendant's lawyer reached that belief without any help from Plaintiff's lawyer. More likely though, Plaintiff's lawyer tried to convince Defendant's lawyer that Plaintiff's bottom line was higher than it really was. This is a standard practice of the adversarial/competitive approach and can involve many of the tactics discussed in the following pages.

## § 1.15 Misinformation About One's Bottom Line

### *(a) Misrepresenting One's Bottom Line*

To make her client's bottom line appear tougher than it really is, an adversarial/competitive lawyer may misrepresent it. For example, in the negotiation depicted in Diagram 1-8 (§ 1.14(b)), Plaintiff's lawyer might say "$190,000 is as low as we can go," even though she has been authorized by her client to go down to $150,000.

This sort of misrepresentation probably does not violate the Model Rules of Professional Conduct. Rule 4.1 (which is quoted in § 1.14(a)) only prohibits false statements of *material* fact, and Comment 2 to this Rule says, "a party's intentions as to an acceptable settlement of a claim" is not ordinarily taken as a statement of material fact.[64] Thus, "the comment defines away, as not material,"[65] representations about one's bottom line, even though one's bottom line is perhaps the most material information.[66] Misrepresenting bottom lines can be hard to distinguish from bluffing, which is generally considered "fair play" in negotiation,[67] so few lawyers are naïve enough to accept uncritically a counterpart's representation about the counterpart's bottom line, also known the counterpart's "reservation value."[68]

Understanding this, the adversarial/competitive lawyer seeks more imaginative ways to mislead opposing counsel. The most common way is to project confidence in one's alternatives to this negotiation and thus one's lack of pressure to reach an agreement in this negotiation.

### (b) Projecting Confidence in One's BATNA and Lack of Urgency to Reach Agreement in This Negotiation

A negotiator using the adversarial/competitive approach exudes confidence. Whether she believes it or not, she acts as though her client has very attractive alternatives to reaching an agreement in this negotiation. The best of those alternatives is a party's BATNA, or Best Alternative to a Negotiated Agreement (§ 1.5). "Perception is reality," because "it is not the actual, objective quality of the negotiator's BATNA that determines his degree of bargaining power,

---

64 Model Rules of Prof'l Conduct R.4.1, cmt. 2 (2019) ("Under generally accepted conventions in negotiation, certain types of statements ordinarily are not taken as statements of material fact. Estimates of price or value placed on the subject of a transactions and a party's intentions as to an acceptable settlement of a claim are ordinarily in this category . . . ."). But see American Bar Association Comm. on Ethics and Professional Responsibility, Formal Op. 93–370 (1993) ("a party's actual bottom line or the settlement authority given to a lawyer is a material fact.").

65 Carrie Menkel-Meadow, Ethics, Morality and Professional Responsibility in Negotiation in Dispute Resolution Ethics 131–39 (2002).

66 Art Hinshaw & Jess K. Alberts, Doing the Right Thing: An Empirical Study of Attorney Negotiation Ethics, 16 Harv. Negot. L. Rev. 95, 103 (2011) (Comment 2 "provides examples of statements that ordinarily fall into this immaterial fact category, including estimates of price or value and a party's intentions as to an acceptable settlement of a claim, arguably the two most material matters during bargaining interactions").

67 See Edward Brunet, Charles B. Craver & Ellen Deason, Alternative Dispute Resolution: The Advocate's Perspective 197 (5th ed. 2016) ("disingenuous behavior is indigenous to most legal negotiations and could not realistically be prevented due to the nonpublic nature of most bargaining interactions.") James J. White goes so far as to make the following assertion. "To conceal one's true position, to mislead an opponent about one's true settling point, is the essence of negotiation." James J. White, Machiavelli and the Bar: Ethical Limitations on Lying in Negotiation, 1980 Am. B. Found. Res. J. 926, 928 (1980).

68 Michaela Keet, Litigation Risk Assessment: A Tool to Enhance Negotiation, 19 Cardozo J. Conflict Resol. 17, 20 (2017) ("Except in the most open and collaborative negotiations, neither party will be aware of the other's reservation value").

but what the counterpart believes that the negotiator believes about the quality of his BATNA."[69]

In *settlement negotiation* (§§ 1.34–1.43), a party's Best Alternative to a Negotiated Agreement (§ 1.5) is usually further litigation or arbitration of the case, so the lawyer using the adversarial/competitive approach to negotiation expresses confidence in her case on the merits. She acts as though she relishes the idea of litigating or arbitrating the case to conclusion and goes out of her way to show that she has little or no desire to settle. She will not propose meeting to discuss settlement and may reject the idea if raised by her counterpart. If she is brought to the negotiation table, she is quick to storm out of the room if her counterpart is not acceding to all her demands. Why should she waste time talking about a deal that will give her anything less than the total victory she is sure she will win in court or arbitration?

One common way to project confidence in one's case is to overstate its strength on the law and the facts. Adversarial/competitive lawyers often overstate the strength of their cases on the law. For example, Plaintiff's lawyer may say to Defendant's lawyer "We both know the court will agree with my argument that the *Jones* case is a closely analogous precedent," even though Plaintiff's lawyer worries the court will distinguish *Jones*. Plaintiff's lawyer tries to convince Defendant's lawyer that the law compels a ruling for Plaintiff or, at least, that Plaintiff's lawyer *believes* the law compels a ruling for Plaintiff. Even if Defendant's lawyer thinks Plaintiff's lawyer misunderstands the relevant cases and statutes, Plaintiff's lawyer succeeded in convincing Defendant's lawyer that Plaintiff's bottom line is higher than it really is. Plaintiff's lawyer failed if Defendant's lawyer realizes that Plaintiff's lawyer knows the *Jones* case is easily distinguishable. Defendant's lawyer realizes that Plaintiff's lawyer is just bluffing or posturing.

What has just been said about overstating the strength of a case on the law applies as well to overstating the strength of a case on the facts. Plaintiff's lawyer will try to convince Defendant's lawyer that Plaintiff's lawyer thinks the jury will be outraged by documents Defendant created, even though Plaintiff's lawyer worries that the jury will not be interested in them. Plaintiff's lawyer will try to convince Defendant's lawyer that Plaintiff's lawyer thinks her client will perform marvelously on the witness stand, even though Plaintiff's lawyer expects her client to be a shaky witness. In short,

---

[69] Russell Korobkin, Bargaining Power As Threat of Impasse, 87 Marq. L. Rev. 867, 869 (2004).

Plaintiff's lawyer will act as though she has much greater confidence in her case than she really does.

While in settlement negotiation a party's BATNA is usually further litigation or arbitration of the case, BATNAs in transactional negotiation are more varied, as discussed in Section 1.5. But whatever a party's BATNA, that party's adversarial/competitive negotiator exudes confidence about how good it is. For example, if the adversarial/competitive negotiator and her counterpart have been through many grueling hours of negotiation on the sale of a business and are only a few thousand dollars apart, her counterpart may be excited about the prospect of a deal, psychologically invested in it, and nervous that some last-minute disagreement might kill the deal that is starting to gel. In contrast, the adversarial/competitive negotiator approach remains coolly uninterested in reaching a deal. She nonchalantly acts as though it would not bother her or her client in the least to walk away from this negotiation, which almost reached a deal, to pursue a deal with another party instead. The adversarial/competitive negotiator patiently waits for her counterpart to make the last few concessions necessary to form a deal at last. (See § 1.16(c)).

## § 1.16 Positional Tactics to Project Confidence

### *(a) Positions*

Sections 1.14–1.15 explain why adversarial/competitive negotiators try to make their client's bottom line appear tougher than it really is by projecting confidence in the client's BATNA and thus the negotiator's lack of pressure to reach an agreement in the negotiation under consideration. Among the many tactics to project confidence are several relating to the positions the negotiator takes. *Positions* are what the negotiator suggests as terms of a deal (§ 1.23). For instance, a seller or plaintiff may demand a particular sum of money from the buyer or defendant, who may then respond by offering a lower sum of money. (While plaintiffs often "demand" money, these "demands" are typically offers to settle, that is, offers to sell their claims for whatever sum of money they are "demanding" (§ 1.2(b)). So, when the defendant responds by offering a lower amount of money to settle the case, the defendant is making a counteroffer.)

### *(b) Opening Offers*

An adversarial/competitive negotiator's opening offer proposes terms that are extremely favorable to her client, rather than proposing terms that are "fair" or "reasonable."[70] Such extremely selfish opening offers have important advantages, as much experimental research shows a significant correlation between opening offers and the terms of an eventual deal.[71] An extreme opening offer allows the offeror room to later grant concessions, while still reaching a favorable settlement.

Any offer you make tells your counterpart something about your bottom line. For example, Seller's offer (or "ask") of $300,000 tells Buyer that Seller's bottom line is less than or equal to $300,000. The more extreme Seller's offer ($500,000, $1,000,000, . . .), the less it tells Buyer about Seller's bottom line. Suppose that, until hearing Seller's opening offer of $300,000, Buyer was willing to pay up to $400,000. Upon hearing Seller's opening offer of $300,000, Buyer's willingness to pay should immediately drop to $300,000 or lower, so Seller's opening offer cost Seller $100,000 or more. The more selfish the opening offer, the less likely this sort of "give away" is to occur. An extremely selfish opening offer better conceals the offeror's bottom line (§ 1.15(a)).

However, the danger of an extreme opening offer is that it may lead the other party and its negotiator to conclude that the parties are simply too far apart to reach a deal (§ 1.11(b)). So, the other party may stop negotiating with the party who made the extreme opening offer to pursue other options instead (§ 1.5). This result is harmful to both parties in cases with a *Zone of Possible Agreement* (§ 1.8) because the parties are forgoing an agreement that both believe would have made them both better off than they are with any alternative. And even when extreme opening offers do not kill a deal, they tend to delay the deal, making the negotiation process more costly and stressful for negotiators and clients (§ 1.11(c)).

Adversarial/competitive negotiators often believe it is disadvantageous to make the first offer, that is, for your opening offer to precede your counterpart's opening offer. The risk of making the first offer is revealed by the above example of Seller who "gave away" at least $100,000 by opening with $300,000. Had Seller been able to elicit the first offer from Buyer, that offer might have been high enough to encourage Seller to make his opening offer above $300,000, thus reducing or eliminating the "give away." The risk of a "give

---

[70] See, e.g., Hal Abramson, Fashioning an Effective Negotiation Style: Choosing Between Good Practices, Tactics, and Tricks, 23 Harv. Negot. L. Rev. 319, 326 (2018) (listing as a common negotiating tactic "Making inflated or deflated proposals to anchor the other side toward an upper or lower range").

[71] Dan Orr & Chris Guthrie, Anchoring, Information, Expertise, and Negotiation: New Insights from Meta-Analysis, 21 Ohio St. J. on Disp. Resol. 597, 621 (2006) (meta-analysis of bargaining experiments finds "that every one dollar increase in an opening offer is associated with an approximate fifty-cent increase in the final sale price.").

away" leads most adversarial/competitive negotiators to refrain from making the first offer.

Also, if your counterpart makes the first offer, you can try "The Flinch." When you hear your counterpart's opening offer, you visibly flinch at its obvious inadequacy. Then you express your disappointment and look expectantly at your counterpart. If your counterpart falls for this, he will then make another offer that moves in your client's direction. You will indicate that this second offer is "a step in the right direction but still insufficient," and if you are very successful, you may generate three or four offers from your counterpart before you finally make one.[72] This counterpart is "bidding against himself," a weakness elaborated in the following subsection on concessions in the adversarial/competitive approach.

While the previous paragraphs counsel against making the first offer, you may want to make the first offer if you think it likely to influence your counterpart. Perhaps you can make your first offer the focus of subsequent negotiation and *anchor* (§ 1.38(b)) discussion around it.

> Research has shown that individuals often use a salient piece of information as an anchor on which to base their future judgments. Regardless of the level of the anchor, adjustments tend to be insufficient. Thus, different opening offers (anchors) will result in final outcomes which are biased in the direction of that offer.[73]

The advantages of making the first offer tend to be greater when you are confident that your counterpart's bottom line "lies in a small range," while the disadvantages of making the first offer tend to be greater when you are "quite uncertain" about your counterpart's bottom line.[74]

### *(c) Few, Small, and Slow Concessions*

When you make an offer less favorable to your client than your opening offer was, you have made a *concession*. The bigger your concessions, the worse for your client any deal will be. Accordingly, the adversarial/competitive negotiator makes as few concessions as possible and makes them as small as possible.

---

72 Charles B. Craver, Effective Legal Negotiation and Settlement 185–86 (9th ed. 2020).

73 Laurie R. Weingart et al., Tactical Behavior and Negotiation Outcomes, 1 Intl. J. of Conflict Mgt. 7, 9–10 (1990).

74 David A. Lax & James K. Sebenius, The Manager as Negotiator: Bargaining for Cooperation and Competitive Gain 132–34 (1986).

On the other hand, few significant agreements are reached without concessions. If you reached such an agreement without making any concessions from your opening offer, then your opening offer was probably not ambitious enough. You probably could have gotten a better deal than you did. So, you do want to make some concessions after an appropriately ambitious opening offer, but you do not want to concede too much. The adversarial/competitive approach's guidelines for concessions are discussed in the following paragraphs.

When you make your first concession, you admit to your counterpart that you can be moved. You lead your counterpart to doubt your tenacity. Your counterpart may believe that you are on the slippery slope toward further concessions. After all, if you did not stick with your first position, why should your counterpart believe that you will stick with your second position?

To avoid this sort of thinking, when you make a concession, you may want to give your counterpart a "positional commitment," that is, a reason why you are not conceding more. Your determination to concede nothing more can be substantiated by linking your concession to:

- a principle ("I'm offering you the same terms as other similar agreements in our city"),
- your personal reputation ("If I go any higher, I'll be known as a soft touch"), or
- a threat of ending negotiations ("This is my final offer").

Even better, you do not give away a concession. Instead, you extract something in exchange for your concession. You can say to your counterpart, "I'll give up my demand for X if you give up your demand for Y." In this manner, your side's concession is contemporaneously exchanged for the opposing side's concession. This may, even if unintentionally, accomplish the value-creating *logrolling* discussed in § 1.10(c).

Concessions can also be exchanged sequentially. For example, the parties may make offers in the following order: Seller opens at $900,000, Buyer opens at $600,000, Seller offers $800,000, Buyer offers $700,000, Seller offers $750,000 and Buyer accepts. This process of taking turns conceding is a common way agreements are reached.

Suppose Seller opens at $900,000 and then Buyer opens at $600,000. If Seller then offers $800,000, Seller should make no further concessions until Buyer offers more than $600,000. If, after

Seller's $800,000 offer, Buyer sticks at $600,000 and Seller offers, say, $750,000 then Seller is "bidding against himself," rewarding Buyer for her intransigence. This reward likely makes Buyer even more intransigent, hoping that Seller will continue to bid against himself. An adversarial/competitive negotiator will not bid against herself and will try to get her counterpart to bid against himself, as in The Flinch, discussed in Section 1.16(b).

The adversarial/competitive approach also generally advises that each of your concessions be smaller than the last.[75] If, as the Seller's negotiator, you previously dropped your demand from $900,000 to $800,000, then your next concession should keep your position above $700,000. By conceding $100,000, and then conceding less than $100,000, you try to give the impression that you are rapidly approaching your *bottom line* (§ 1.6), the point at which you will concede no more, even if that impression is false. Through this misimpression, you may succeed in persuading the Buyer's negotiator that your bottom line is higher than it really is (§ 1.15).

If negotiators are exchanging concessions sequentially, how quickly should the concessions come? The adversarial/competitive negotiator generally likes to make her own concessions more slowly than her counterpart's. Suppose Seller made her most recent offer June 1 and Buyer made its most recent offer June 5. Seller should, according to the adversarial/competitive approach, probably wait until after June 9 before making her next offer. This delay conveys to Buyer:

> "I am in less of a rush to make a deal than you are. That means my best alternative to a deal with you (BATNA) is good, so if you want a deal with me you will need to move a lot closer to my position."

The adversarial/competitive negotiator does not want to seem thirsty for an agreement, so she signals that she is in no rush to reach a deal. If she receives an encouraging offer, but one not good enough to accept, she does not reply right away. She leaves the other party on read. She waits—to induce anxiety in the other party. Conversely, when the other party seems to be rushing toward an agreement, the adversarial/competitive negotiator smells blood and thus pauses confidently. She demands large concessions and offers little or no concessions in return.

If negotiators are exchanging concessions either contemporaneously or sequentially, the adversarial/competitive negotiator wants her concession to be smaller than the concession for

---

[75] Howard Raiffa, The Art and Science of Negotiation 128 (1982).

which it is exchanged. The size of a concession is not, however, always easily measured. One might think Buyer raising its offer from $100,000 to $150,000 concedes less than Seller lowering its demand from $300,000 to $200,000 because Buyer conceded $50,000, while Seller conceded $100,000. But the size of concessions should be assessed against the opening offer. Perhaps Seller's opening offer of $300,000 was extremely high, while Buyer's opening offer of $100,000 was reasonable. Given these opening offers, Seller might have expected that Buyer's concessions would only be one-tenth the dollar amount of Seller's. When Buyer's concession turned out to be one-half the dollar-amount of Seller's concession, Seller was pleasantly surprised.

#### *(d) The Backward Step*

While many lawyers consider the above concession tactics within the bounds of good faith and fair dealing, that may not be true of the "backward step." This is when a negotiator makes a concession but then retracts it. For example, in negotiation on a voice call, Plaintiff's lawyer might go down from $300,000 to $200,000, while Defendant's lawyer goes up from $100,000 to $200,000. Defendant is reasonably pleased to have a deal at $200,000. But then the next day, plaintiff refuses to sign a release for anything less than $250,000. Plaintiff's lawyer—who planned it all this way—tells Defendant's lawyer: "your side revealed its willingness to pay at least $200,000. Surely, you can move to $250,000 to make this case go away." There is not likely to be much evidence of the oral settlement agreement,[76] and even if there is, a writing may be required for enforceability (§ 1.40(c)(3)).

A rare case to impose liability for the backward step is *Hoffman v. Red Owl Stores, Inc.*[77] Red Owl was a chain of grocery stores and Hoffman wanted to be a Red Owl franchisee. Hoffman said he had $18,000 to invest and Red Owl assured him that this would be enough money to acquire a franchise.[78] Red Owl advised Hoffman to do several things to gain experience in the grocery business, and Hoffman did them.[79] Red Owl kept raising more demands of Hoffman before it would sell him the franchise. Red Owl finally insisted that his contribution be $34,000, instead of the originally promised $18,000.[80] Hoffman sued Red Owl and won on a theory of promissory

[76] Before negotiating by voice, you might learn your state's law on recording such communications without the other party's consent.

[77] 133 N.W.2d 267 (Wis. 1965).

[78] Id. at 268–69.

[79] Id. at 269–70.

[80] Id. at 271.

estoppel.[81] According to the court, Red Owl made promises to Hoffman and Hoffman reasonably relied on those promises.

### (e) Rare Duty to Negotiate in Good Faith

The *Hoffman* case just discussed remains a rarity; few courts impose liability for negotiating "in bad faith." The one significant exception in the U.S. is negotiation between labor unions and employers because the National Labor Relations Act imposes on these parties a duty to negotiate in good faith.[82] Outside the collective bargaining context, however, there is generally no duty to negotiate in good faith.[83] In settlement negotiations, especially, the parties should be keenly aware that neither owes a fiduciary duty to the other (they are negotiating "at arm's length"), so courts should be especially reluctant to impose any good faith requirement in this context.[84]

### (f) "Oh, by the Ways"

A potentially more nuanced tactic similar to the *backward step* (§ 1.16(d)) is introducing a new issue late in negotiation, just as an agreement seems to be emerging. Consider negotiation of a patent-infringement case in which the only issue discussed over months of difficult negotiation sessions was the scope of the technology Defendant would refrain from exploiting. These negotiations were long and difficult as lawyers and businesspeople struggled over scientific concepts and terminology. Just as the parties agreed on these matters, Plaintiff's lawyer demanded that Defendant make a cash payment of $50,000 and told Defendant's lawyer: "you wouldn't want to squander all this work reaching a deal for a mere $50,000, would you?"

While this sort of bald demand for money may be a late addition to some negotiations, more common is the subtle introduction of a new issue just as an agreement seems to be emerging. These are "Oh,

---

81 Id. at 247. See Restatement (Second) of Contracts § 90 (1981) ("A promise which the promisor should reasonably expect to induce action or forbearance on the part of the promisee or a third person and which does induce such action or forbearance is binding if injustice can be avoided only by enforcement of the promise. The remedy granted for breach may be limited as justice requires.").

82 29 U.S.C. § 158(a)(5), (b)(3) & (d). See, e.g., N.L.R.B. v. General Electric Co., 418 F.2d 736 (2d Cir. 1969) ("Boulwareism," that is, take-it-or-leave-it bargaining, prohibited), cert. denied, 397 U.S. 965 (1970).

83 See, e.g., Restatement (Second) of Contracts § 205 (limiting duty of good faith and fair dealing to contract's "performance and enforcement", as distinguished from its formation). Section 2.30(d) of this book discusses the duty of good faith participation in mandatory mediation.

84 See Robert S. Adler & Elliot M. Silverstein, When David Meets Goliath: Dealing With Power Differentials in Negotiations, 5 Harv. Negot. L. Rev. 1, 28–32 (2000).

by the ways" masquerading as mere details that hopefully will not attract too much attention from the fatigued counterpart who just wants to finish the negotiation and get the settlement signed.[85]

### *(g) False Concessions*

One way to keep your concessions "smaller" than your counterpart's is to concede only on those issues you do not really care about.[86] The adversarial/competitive negotiator often begins negotiations by raising such issues.[87] For example, assume that Seller cares only about how much money it can get from Buyer. If Seller's negotiator is using the adversarial/competitive approach, Seller's negotiator might open negotiations by saying "We'll sell for $700,000, plus Buyer's promise to keep Seller's brother employed in his current role at his current salary for at least five more years." Seller does not value this promise because Seller's brother is ready to retire, but Seller's lawyer knows keeping Seller's brother employed would be costly to Buyer. So early in negotiation, Seller's negotiator pretends that her client strongly wants his brother to remain employed. But later in negotiation, Seller's negotiator agrees, with a great show of reluctance, to forgo the brother's employment in exchange for Buyer raising its cash offer. Seller gets a concession it cares about, money, by giving up something Seller never really wanted anyhow. Generally, the more convincingly you insist upon a particular demand early in negotiation, the larger the concession you can ultimately obtain for dropping it.[88] A danger of this false-concession tactic though, especially if both parties use it for too long, is that it produces a deal that gives the parties what they said they wanted while posturing, instead of what they really want (§ 1.24(c)).

While many lawyers consider false concessions within the bounds of good faith and fair dealing, that may not be true of sneaky

---

[85] Larry L. Tepley, Legal Negotiation in a Nutshell 313–14 (4th ed. 2023).

[86] Compare *logrolling*, discussed in Section 1.10(c).

[87] See, e.g., Hal Abramson, Fashioning an Effective Negotiation Style: Choosing Between Good Practices, Tactics, and Tricks, 23 Harv. Negot. L. Rev. 319, 326 (2018) (listing as a common negotiating tactic "Asserting a false demand for something unimportant, and then giving it up in return for something important; and Exploiting the Reciprocity Norm—Exploiting the reciprocity norm by making an unimportant concession to manipulate the other side into making a concession. This is a variation of a false demand in which a negotiator might make several demands, including a false one, and then concede the false demand. The false concession may then spur the other side to make a reciprocal concession").

[88] This is related to the well-documented psychological phenomenon of "reactive devaluation," which is "the tendency of a party to devalue a settlement proposal simply because it originated with the other side. . . . [A] compromise or concession made unilaterally by a party is often valued less highly than one that is initially withheld and subsequently extracted through reciprocal proposals or concessions." G. Nicholas Herman & Jean M. Cary, Legal Counseling and Negotiation: A Practical Approach 146 (2d ed. 2009).

drafting. In a patent-infringement case, for example, Plaintiff's lawyer's initial draft settlement agreement might, in clear and concise language, prohibit Defendant from exploiting certain technology. Plaintiff's lawyer might then delete this language in exchange for a monetary concession from Defendant, while simultaneously adding new language to the draft agreement that, in a convoluted and complex way, also prohibits Defendant from exploiting the same technology. If Defendant's lawyer is not alert, Plaintiff's lawyer may succeed in "sneaking in" this nullification of his side's concession.

## § 1.17 Psychological Warfare

Negotiation causes stress and anxiety in almost all people. To exploit this stress and anxiety, psychological warfare is part of the adversarial/competitive approach. The variety of tactics along these lines is endless and some of the most common are discussed next.

### *(a) Anger, Threats, Ridicule, Accusation, and Intimidation—or Silence*

Anger, threats, ridicule, accusation, and intimidation may undermine your counterpart's confidence in their positions and in their judgment. While "proficient negotiators almost never lose their tempers," "they use carefully orchestrated anger that is designed to intimidate anxious opponents."[89] If you have an anxious counterpart lacking confidence, an aggressive style may work to soften your counterpart's position and push them closer to their *bottom line* (§ 1.6). In contrast, if your counterpart is strong, she will look at you as she looks at "petulant children,"[90] and she will yield to you as little as a strong parent yields to a child throwing a fit.

In contrast to the aggressive style of the previous paragraph, a nearly opposite approach that may have the same effect on an anxious counterpart is silence, "one of the most potent, yet frequently overlooked, power bargaining techniques."[91]

> Many less competent negotiators fear silence. They are afraid that they will lose control of the interaction if they stop talking, and they remember the awkwardness they have experienced in social settings during prolonged pauses. Thus they feel compelled to speak. When they do, they tend to disclose, both verbally and nonverbally,

---

89 Charles B. Craver, Effective Legal Negotiation and Settlement 187 (9th ed. 2020).

90 Id. at 188.

91 Id. at 144.

information they did not intend to divulge. They often find themselves making unintended concessions.[92]

You can avoid falling into this trap by having a plan that, if a silence starts to feel uncomfortable, you will look down at your papers or device and re-read some material pertinent to the matter you are negotiating. And then when you have regained your poise, you can ask your counterpart an open-ended question, like "What do you think about that?"

### *(b) Negotiate on Your Own Turf*

Face-to-face negotiation should, according to the adversarial/competitive approach, occur in your office or some other place that is yours, so you will feel more comfortable than your counterpart. You hosting the negotiation may put your counterpart at a psychological disadvantage "because he has had to come to you."[93] Also, "the guest-host relationship may subtly influence the negotiators to take on dominant-subordinate roles in which the host is more assertive and the guest more deferential than would occur at a neutral site. Magnanimously making the visiting negotiator comfortable—offering coffee or arranging for food, for example—has the advantage of subtly highlighting the host negotiator's power."[94]

In addition to this psychological advantage, negotiating on your own turf can also give you a physical advantage. You can adjust the seating and thermostat, so your counterpart is uncomfortable, while you sit in your favorite chair and dress for the extreme temperature you choose. While some suggest "[p]eople who are physically uncomfortable are less likely to be agreeable,"[95] others suggest that fatigue tends to reduce negotiators' willpower to stick to their positions and hold firm against concessions.[96]

### *(c) Outnumber Your Counterparts*

Negotiation is hard work. Having more negotiators on your side than on the other side makes it more likely that you will be able to control the flow of discussion and remain sharp and energetic while the other side tires. Having multiple negotiators on your side also allows you to divide responsibilities. For example, you can do the

---

[92] Id. at 144–45.

[93] Michael Meltsner & Philip G. Schrag, Negotiating Tactics for Legal Services Lawyers, 7 Clearinghouse Rev. 259, 259 (1973).

[94] Larry L. Tepley, Legal Negotiation in a Nutshell 188 (4th ed. 2023).

[95] Id. at 192.

[96] Baumeister, Simpson, Ware & Weber, The Glucose Model of Mediation, 15 Pepp. Disp. Resol. L.J. 377, 410 (2015) ("people who are hungry, exhausted, or highly stressed tend to have less willpower than those who are well-fed, well rested, and relatively stress-free")

talking while your teammate carefully observes you (to intervene if you are about to inadvertently reveal anything) and your counterpart (to pick up information you may miss).[97]

Having multiple negotiators on your side also enables you to do the "Good Cop, Bad Cop" routine. This is where one negotiator on your side is warmly cooperative with the counterpart while the other negotiator on your side standoffishly demands an extremely one-sided deal. While the unreasonable negotiator is out of the room, the cooperative negotiator apologizes for his colleague and says that with a few more concessions from the other side he thinks he can persuade the unreasonable negotiator to calm down and go along with the deal.[98]

However, those who negotiate in teams must be careful in how they communicate with each other to avoid revealing confidential information to the other side.

### *(d) Negotiate When You Have Time and Your Counterpart Does Not*

Opposing negotiators may be under the same time pressure, for example a trial date that induces them to settle on the courthouse steps the morning a trial would have begun, or even during the trial.[99] But if your counterpart feels a time pressure you do not feel, then their time pressure is vulnerability you can exploit because time pressures induce concessions (§§ 1.15, 1.16(c)). For example, if "they are handling an expansive number of cases" and so are not able "to devote a substantial amount of their time to any one dispute," you quickly scheduling "all pertinent depositions" and demanding that your counterpart produce an extensive array of documents may cause your counterpart "to look more favorably upon settlement proposals in an effort to alleviate the inordinate time pressure associated with [your] particular case."[100]

---

97 Edward Brunet, Charles B. Craver & Ellen Deason, Alternative Dispute Resolution: The Advocate's Perspective 47 (5th ed. 2016).

98 See, e.g., Hal Abramson, Fashioning an Effective Negotiation Style: Choosing Between Good Practices, Tactics, and Tricks, 23 Harv. Negot. L. Rev. 319, 329 (2018) (listing as a "trick" that "can be viewed as unethical": "Teaming up on one side whereby one member of the team performs the role of the good guy to psychologically assert pressure to settle by apologizing and protecting the victim (other side) from the hostile treatment of the other team member, who performs the role of the bad guy. In appreciation for the protection, the victim may feel inclined to concede").

99 See, e.g., Catching Up With Delaware's Chancery Court, Law360 (July 21, 2025) ("Last week at the Delaware Court of Chancery, a major settlement between Meta Platforms Inc. and its investors reached on the proverbial courthouse steps during day two of a trial ended an $8 billion-plus suit accusing the company's directors and officers of breaching privacy regulations and corporate fiduciary duties").

100 Charles B. Craver, Effective Legal Negotiation and Settlement 12 (9th ed. 2020).

"Studies indicate that the less time pressure felt by negotiators, the better they tend to do".[101] For example, if your counterpart has traveled to you and needs to leave for the airport in an hour or else find a hotel in your city, they may be willing to concede what's needed to get a deal done before the evening's last flight home. In contrast, you wouldn't mind if negotiations continue until tomorrow because, however the rest of today's negotiating goes, you will be comfortably home for the night as usual.

### *(e) Lack of Authority*

A negotiator may begin negotiating by saying that he will have to get his client's approval for any agreement.[102] When he and his counterpart reach a deal, he calls his client who (as planned from the start) refuses to sign the deal unless the other side makes a few additional concessions. This is a variant of the general tactic in which the adversarial/competitive negotiator attempts to squeeze concessions out of a counterpart who, after working hard to achieve a deal, feels invested in it (§ 1.16(c-f)).

If your counterpart announces that he lacks authority to agree on behalf of his client, you might try one of three responses. One is to simply refuse to negotiate until the other side sends someone with authority to reach a deal. The second is to say that you, too, lack authority. The third is to keep some concessions in reserve when you reach a deal, the first deal, with the negotiator. That way, when the negotiator says his client will not sign unless you make further concessions, you can concede something you had planned to concede all along.

Negotiators frequently say, "my client has only given me authority to settle above/below" a specific monetary amount. Sometimes this is true, but it may not be.[103] The negotiator with (true

---

[101] Larry L. Tepley, Legal Negotiation in a Nutshell 293 (3d ed. 2016).

[102] See § 1.41 (without a grant of authority from the client, a lawyer cannot bind the client to a deal). See, e.g., Hal Abramson, Fashioning an Effective Negotiation Style: Choosing Between Good Practices, Tactics, and Tricks, 23 Harv. Negot. L. Rev. 319, 328 (2018) (listing as a "trick" that "can be viewed as unethical": "Arriving to the negotiation with purposely insufficient settlement authority for the likely settlement range of the dispute. A lawyer claims he cannot accept the offer because it is more than his client has authority to accept and pay. The lawyer purposely arrived with insufficient settlement authority so that he can make the claim in order to pressure the other side to concede within an unreasonable settlement range. This trick might breach a local rule that requires the negotiator to appear with settlement authority, unless he can demonstrate that the level of authority was sufficient for the amount in dispute").

[103] See Model Rules of Prof'l Conduct R.4.1, cmt.2 (2019) (quoted in Section 1.14(a)); Patrick Emery Longan, Ethics in Settlement Negotiations: Forward, 52 Mercer L. Rev. 807, 813–14 (2001) ("comment 2 to Model Rule 4.1 defines statements about settlement authority not to be material. Technically, therefore, the lawyer should feel free to lie about his or her authority. Another strategy, however, and one

or false) "limited authority" is trying to bias the negotiation in his favor by making "out of bounds" certain outcomes favorable to the other side. Responses to this tactic parallel the responses to the "lack of authority" tactic.

### *(f) Locked into Position*

The *game of chicken*, discussed in Section 1.11(c), is when negotiators believe a Zone of Possible Agreement exists, because a deal will create value compared to no deal, and each side is trying to capture all of that value for itself. So, neither concedes and each tries to show that it has the greater confidence in its BATNA (§ 1.15(b))) and thus greater willpower to resist the temptation to concede.

To raise pressure on your counterpart to yield in the game of chicken, you can lock yourself into your position. For example, in a case followed by the news media, a lawyer can announce to the television cameras "we will pursue this litigation until we get an end to the pollution." Then in negotiation with his counterpart, the lawyer can credibly say that he cannot accept a settlement that does not end the pollution because, if he did, he would be publicly embarrassed and would lose his professional credibility. Putting professional credibility at stake though, is a high-risk tactic. Wise lawyers don't make threats they aren't willing to backup with action.

### *(g) Feign Irrationality*

As emphasized in Sections 1.15 and 1.16, adversarial/competitive negotiators routinely project confidence in their BATNAs (their client's best alternative to the negotiation under consideration). The tactic of feigning irrationality takes this to the extreme. By seeming irrational, a negotiator hopes to convince his counterpart to accept his one-sided demands because the only alternative is no deal. The feigning-irrationality negotiator hopes his counterpart will think "there is no reasoning with this irrational person toward a mutually beneficial agreement, so my choice is to accept a deal around my *bottom line* (§ 1.6) or both sides will lose a deal that would be mutually advantageous."

Few successful lawyers convincingly portray themselves as irrational, but some convincingly portray their clients as irrational, which accomplishes the same goal and which resembles the "Good

---

that may be more effective in the long run, is simply to deflect any questions of authority with statements such as, 'You know neither one of us can discuss our authority-let's talk about a fair settlement of this case.' ").

cop, Bad cop" tactic (§ 1.17(c)).[104] The feigned irrationality tactic is particularly useful in winning the *game of chicken* (§ 1.11(c)).

### *(h) Wolf in Sheep's Clothing*

Perhaps the most effective form of psychological warfare is to use none of the psychological tactics listed above, or at least not to use them in a way that allows your counterpart to realize that you are using them. If your counterpart discovers that you are engaging in the tactics listed above, your counterpart will probably realize that you are taking an adversarial/competitive approach. For reasons discussed below (§§ 1.18–1.21), your adversarial/competitive approach is likely to be more effective if your counterpart does not realize you are using it. If you appear to be using either the *cooperative* (§ 1.19) or the *problem-solving* (§§ 1.22–1.24) approach, while actually using the adversarial/competitive approach, you are likely to be quite effective in advancing your client's interests.[105]

To pursue this wolf-in-sheep's-clothing strategy, you should be courteous and pleasant.[106] You might also try some of the following tactics. But you cannot be too obvious in your use of them, or you will be unmasked as the wolf you are.

One tactic is to flatter your counterpart and thus build her confidence. The rationale for this tactic is that negotiators are more likely to make concessions when they feel competent.[107] You might tell your counterpart, with a sense of frustration and respect in your voice, what a hard deal she is driving. If you can lead her to think she

---

[104] See Larry L. Tepley, Legal Negotiation in a Nutshell 232 (4th ed. 2023) (referring to "the impossible client game, in which a lawyer claims to understand the other side's position and would like to meet its apparently reasonable demands—except that the impossible client will not let the negotiator do it.")

[105] Because some wolves may succeed in disguising themselves as sheep, researchers cannot know whether lawyers' descriptions of their counterparts' approaches to negotiation are accurate. See Jay Folberg, Dwight Golann, Thomas J. Stipanowich, Jennifer Reynolds & Amy J. Schmitz, Resolving Disputes: Theory, Practice, and Law 66 (4th ed. 2021). For studies surveying lawyers on their counterparts in negotiation, see Andrea Kupfer Schneider, Shattering Negotiation Myths: Empirical Evidence on the Effectiveness of Negotiation Style, 7 Harv. Negot. L. Rev. 143 (2002); Gerald R. Williams & Charles B. Craver, Legal Negotiation and Settlement 12–57 (2007). On the limitations of survey data relying on perceptions, see Schneider, 7 Harv. Negot. L. Rev. at 190–96.

[106] Charles B. Craver, The Impact of Negotiator Styles on Bargaining Interactions, 35 Am. J. Trial Advoc. 1, 10 (2011) ("many persons who are characterized by their opponents as effective cooperative problem-solving negotiators are actually wolves in sheep's skin. They behave as if they are employing an open and cooperative style, but they subtly work to obtain competitive objectives"); id. ("They are thoroughly prepared; conduct themselves in an honest and ethical manner; are perceptive readers of opponent verbal leaks and nonverbal cues; are analytical, realistic, and convincing; and observe the customs and courtesies of the bar").

[107] Jeffrey Rubin, Negotiation: An Introduction to Some Issues and Themes, 27 Am. Behavioral Scientist 135, 138–44 (Nov.–Dec. 1983).

is succeeding, while you are actually taking most of the value created by a deal, then you are more likely to achieve a similarly good result the next time she is your counterpart. You may also be able to "generate greater concessions through disingenuous appeals to [your counterpart's] reputation for reasonableness and fair dealing."[108] In short, you may be able to exploit your counterpart's sense of guilt or shame. And even better if she tells her client that they got a great deal, because "People who think they have been treated fairly are more likely to accept the final terms and carry out their contractual obligations."[109]

## § 1.18 Drawbacks of the Adversarial/Competitive Approach

The adversarial/competitive approach orients to *zero-sum* negotiation (§ 1.9). Using only this approach in a negotiation is likely to waste any available *positive-sum* opportunities (§ 1.10). And even if no such opportunities exist because the situation is zero-sum, the adversarial/competitive approach still has its drawbacks, such as its tendency to foster deadlocks.

As discussed in Sections 1.14–1.17, many adversarial/competitive tactics aim to mislead your counterpart into thinking your *bottom line* is tougher than it really is. If these tactics work, the terms of a deal will be far better than your bottom line even if the terms are close to what your counterpart believes is your bottom line. But these tactics can work too well. Suppose Plaintiff's bottom line is $150,000 and Defendant's bottom line is $200,000, as in Diagram 1-7 (§ 1.14(b)). Plaintiff's lawyer's tactics work if they convince Defendant's lawyer that Plaintiff's bottom line is $190,000. But they work too well if Plaintiff's lawyer convinces Defendant's lawyer that Plaintiff's bottom line is $250,000. If the latter happens, Defendant's lawyer will believe no settlement is possible because Defendant is only willing to pay $200,000. Defendant's lawyer will give up on settlement negotiations and pursue litigation as the only option. This result is harmful to both parties because they are forgoing an agreement (anywhere between $150,000 and $200,000) that both believe would have made them better off than they are by continued litigation (§§ 1.6–1.8). Plaintiff's lawyer has outsmarted herself.

The chance of this failure occurring is even greater when Defendant's lawyer, as well as Plaintiff's lawyer, is trying to mislead her counterpart into thinking her *bottom line* is tougher than it really

---

108 Edward Brunet, Charles B. Craver & Ellen Deason, Alternative Dispute Resolution: The Advocate's Perspective 27 (4th ed. 2011).

109 Charles B. Craver, Effective Legal Negotiation and Settlement 13 (9th ed. 2020).

is. If Plaintiff's lawyer succeeds in convincing Defendant's lawyer that Plaintiff's bottom line is $190,000, and Defendant's lawyer succeeds in convincing Plaintiff's lawyer that Defendant's bottom line is $160,000, then neither lawyer has succeeded at all because they have convinced each other that a deal is not possible, even though a deal would create $50,000 of value compared to no deal.

This is reflected in Diagram 1-9 in which the thin line represents possible settlements acceptable to Defendant and the thick line represents possible settlements acceptable to Plaintiff. Moreover, a thin dashed line represents possible settlements *Plaintiff's lawyer believes* are acceptable to Defendant, and a thick dashed line represents possible settlement terms that *Defendant's lawyer believes* are acceptable to Plaintiff.

**Diagram 1-9**

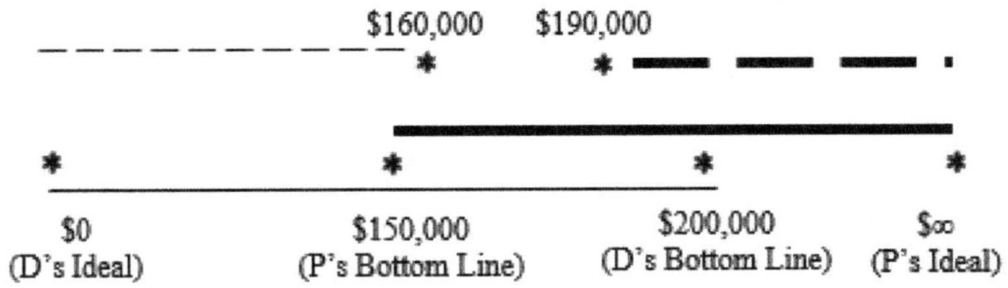


Each party has succeeded in bluffing the other, so no agreement occurs. This result is less desired by each party than any agreement between $150,000 and $200,000.

In sum, adversarial/competitive negotiators are less likely than other negotiators to reach agreement. For example, lawsuit defendants who make " 'zero offers' (i.e., they offer absolutely nothing)" tend to "increase the percentage of cases taken to trial by plaintiffs who are angered by such offensive bargaining behavior and see no possible gain through non-adjudication alternatives."[110] This result is harmful to both parties in situations with a *Zone of Possible Agreement* (§ 1.8) because the parties forgo an agreement that both believe would have made them better off than they are without a deal.

Even if an opposing pair of negotiators using the adversarial/competitive approach do reach an agreement, they are likely to spend lots of time and effort in doing so. By constantly trying to mislead and intimidate each other, adversarial/competitive negotiators end up

110 Id. at 15.

delaying resolution of their clients' matters, costing their clients extra legal fees and causing stress to all concerned.[111]

Another drawback of the adversarial/competitive approach is its tendency to make enemies. A negotiator may use the adversarial/competitive approach to achieve a one-sided agreement by "defeating" a counterpart who is not using the adversarial/competitive approach. But what about the next time the "victor" faces the same counterpart? Her counterpart will then be likely to use the adversarial/competitive approach, (§ 1.20). The counterpart may be vengeful, fighting on every issue and refusing to extend even routine professional courtesies. This danger of making adversaries out of future counterparts faces the adversarial/competitive negotiator even if she never again crosses paths with the same counterpart again. People talk. A negotiator's reputation as adversarial/competitive may be known to people she has not even met. The danger of having such a reputation is discussed in Section 1.20.

## 2. THE COOPERATIVE APPROACH AND THE PRISONER'S DILEMMA

### § 1.19 The Cooperative Approach

Many negotiators depart from the *adversarial/competitive* approach discussed in Sections 1.13–1.18.[112] Rather than make an extreme opening offer, they make a reasonable one. Rather than strongly resisting concessions, they make concessions fairly easily. Rather than aiming for a one-sided agreement, they aim for one that is objectively fair or reasonable. Rather than engage in deception and psychological warfare, they are forthcoming and civil. They are using the *cooperative* approach to negotiation. They do so, perhaps, because they believe it is the ethical or decent approach. Or they do so because they believe it is best suited to advancing the interests of their clients. The cooperative approach, like the adversarial/competitive approach, orients toward *zero-sum* (distributive) negotiation (§ 1.9), and thus should be distinguished from the *problem-solving* approach

---

[111] See, e.g., Hal Abramson, Fashioning an Effective Negotiation Style: Choosing Between Good Practices, Tactics, and Tricks, 23 Harv. Negot. L. Rev. 319, 326 (2018) ("Aggressively belittling the opposing offeror, acting insulted by the offer, and walking out of a negotiation and later returning, while perhaps not unusual tactics, promote an adversarial tone and pose a higher risk of corroding trust, impairing the relationship, and ultimately hindering progress").

[112] See Gerald R. Williams & Charles B. Craver, Legal Negotiation and Settlement, 14–19 (2007) (65% of surveyed lawyers use cooperative approach); Andrea Kupfer Schneider, Shattering Negotiation Myths: Empirical Evidence on the Effectiveness of Negotiation Style, 7 Harv. Negot. L. Rev. 143 (2002) (updating Williams study and continuing to find majority of lawyers depart from adversarial/competitive approach).

discussed in Section 1.22–1.26, which orients toward *positive-sum* (integrative) negotiation (§ 1.10).

If both negotiators are cooperative rather than adversarial/competitive, both parties tend to gain. In situations with a *Zone of Possible Agreement* (ZOPA § 1.8), an agreement is more likely to be achieved if both negotiators are cooperative than if they are adversarial/competitive. In other words, a deal that should be made—because it appears better for each party than its Best Alternative to a Negotiated Agreement (BATNA § 1.5)—is more likely to be made when both sides are cooperative rather than adversarial/competitive. Many situations with a Zone of Possible Agreement nevertheless do not result in deals because the adversarial/competitive negotiators conceal their bottom lines so they don't realize a zone exists, or because each negotiator stubbornly tries to capture more of the value that would be created by a deal and neither gives in (§§ 1.11, 1.18). So, both parties lose by walking away from a negotiation in which both believe they would have been better off with a deal within the same range—compared to no deal. The mutually disadvantageous result of no deal is far more likely to happen with adversarial/competitive negotiators than cooperative ones because cooperative negotiators are more willing to make concessions and are more candid about their BATNAs and their bottom lines.

Not only are deals that should be made more likely to be made when all sides are cooperative, these deals are likely to be reached more quickly and inexpensively.[113] As the cooperative negotiators build mutual trust, they can dispose of the costly and time-consuming tactics adversarial/competitive negotiators use to mislead and intimidate each other.[114] This cooperative advantage also applies to situations that should not result in a deal, that is, situations without a Zone of Possible Agreement (ZOPA). Two cooperative negotiators tend to discover the lack of a ZOPA faster and cheaper than two adversarial/competitive negotiators would. The cooperative negotiators will still end their negotiation, but without wasting as much time and money before doing so. Finally, whether an agreement is reached or not, each negotiator using the cooperative

[113] For example, observing cooperative negotiating behavior by lawyers with high caseloads of criminal matters, Andrea Kupfer Schneider observes that "to focus on the cases that will be proceeding to trial," and "to actually go home at night, criminal lawyers need to move the bulk of their cases quickly to the plea bargaining stage in order to get to the next one." Andrea Kupfer Schneider, Cooperating or Caving in: Are Defense Attorneys Shrewd or Exploited in Plea Bargaining Negotiations?, 91 Marq. L. Rev. 145, 157–58 (2007). "Because adversarial behavior during the plea bargaining will likely add more time to the plea bargaining itself, criminal lawyers on both sides have incentives to be more cooperative and move quickly to resolution." Id.

[114] See §§ 1.13–1.18 (discussing these tactics).

approach will likely have built goodwill with the other and enhanced her reputation for the future (§ 1.20(b)).

When opposing cooperative negotiators reach an agreement, the agreement's terms are likely to be fair and reasonable, rather than one-sided. Cooperative negotiators use "objective" standards of fairness or reasonableness such as market value, precedent, professional standards, established moral standards, tradition, equal treatment, principles of reciprocity, scientific judgment, and efficiency.[115]

The danger, of course, for a negotiator using the cooperative approach is a counterpart who is using the adversarial/competitive approach. When these two negotiate, the cooperative negotiator makes a reasonable opening offer, but her counterpart responds with an extreme one. The cooperative negotiator makes concessions, but her counterpart does not. The result is a one-sided agreement in which the cooperative negotiator quickly agrees to terms right at his client's bottom line. The adversarial/competitive negotiator celebrates her smashing victory and is rewarded for her choice of the adversarial/competitive approach. The cooperative negotiator rightly feels like a loser and likely has a displeased client.

Section 1.20 discusses incentives to cooperate and Section 1.21 discusses tactics for a cooperative negotiator with an adversarial/competitive counterpart.

## § 1.20 The Prisoner's Dilemma and Reputation as an Incentive to Cooperate

### *(a) The Prisoner's Dilemma*

Section 1.19 suggests that, considering only a single negotiation, you and your client fare best if you use the adversarial/competitive approach while your counterpart uses the cooperative approach. Your second-best result is for both negotiators to use the cooperative approach. Your third-best result is for both negotiators to use the adversarial/competitive approach. And your worst result is if you use

---

115 Roger Fisher, William Ury & Bruce Patton, Getting to Yes: Negotiating An Agreement Without Giving In 85 (2d ed., 1991). The "objectivity" of such criteria is critiqued in Robert J. Condlin, Bargaining in the Dark: The Normative Incoherence of Lawyer Dispute Bargaining Role, 51 Md. L. Rev. 1, 31–34 (1992). See also Russell Korobkin, A Positive Theory of Legal Negotiation, 88 Geo. L.J. 1789 (2000).

> Calling such criteria "objective" is a misnomer because (1) any such criteria will benefit one party over the other as compared to a different criteria and (2) none can be conclusively established by logical argument to be justifiable ways to divide the cooperative surplus. Nonetheless, they are critical concepts in legal negotiation because they facilitate the parties' agreement on a single deal point that both can perceive as fair.

Id. at 1826.

the cooperative approach while your counterpart uses the adversarial/competitive approach. This is depicted in Diagram 1-10.

Diagram 1-10

| | **Your counterpart uses Cooperative Approach** | **Your counterpart uses Adversarial/ Competitive Approach** |
|---|---|---|
| **You use Cooperative Approach** | Your 2d-best result | Your 4th-best (worst) result |
| **You use Adversarial/ Competitive Approach** | Your best result | Your 3d-best result |

This "payoff matrix" encourages you to use the adversarial/ competitive approach because it is better for your client than the cooperative approach, no matter what your counterpart does. If your counterpart cooperates then your choice to be adversarial/competitive gives your client its best result, rather than its second-best result. And if your counterpart is adversarial/competitive then your choice to be adversarial/ competitive gives your client its third-best result, rather than its fourth-best (worst) result.

The problem is that the same analysis applies to your counterpart's choice between the adversarial/competitive and cooperative approaches. Just as you should choose the adversarial/competitive approach, so should your counterpart. But if you and your counterpart each choose the adversarial/competitive approach, each get side gets its third-best result. In contrast, if you and your counterpart both used the cooperative approach, then each side would get its second-best result. What is best for the two sides in the aggregate is cooperation, for reasons discussed in Section 1.19, but each party's incentive is to advance itself by outcompeting the other. This quandary is an example of the Prisoner's Dilemma.

> The name comes from the story that was first told in the 1950s to illustrate the following strategic interaction: Two criminals are arrested. They both have committed a serious crime, but the district attorney cannot convict either of them [of the serious crime] without extracting at least one confession. The district attorney can, however, convict them both on a lesser offense without the cooperation of either. The district attorney tells each prisoner that if neither confesses, they will both be convicted of the lesser offense. Each will go to prison for two years. If, however, one of the prisoners confesses and the other does not, the former will go free and the latter will be tried for the serious crime and given the maximum penalty of ten years in prison. If both confess, the district attorney will prosecute them for the serious crime but will not ask for the maximum penalty. They will both go to prison for six years.
>
> Each prisoner wants only to minimize time spent behind bars and has no other goal. Moreover, each is indifferent to how much time the other spends in prison.[116]

The Prisoner's Dilemma just described resembles opposing negotiator's choices of whether to use the adversarial/competitive or cooperative approach. The prisoners' fewest combined years in prison results from them cooperating with each other by withholding confessions, but each prisoner's individual incentive is to be adversarial/competitive toward the other prisoner by being the first to confess.

### *(b) Reputation as an Incentive to Cooperate*

The solution to the Prisoner's Dilemma is to change each individual prisoner's incentives to discourage adversarial behavior toward the other prisoner. While this is not possible if, as stated above, "each prisoner wants only to minimize time behind bars," an actual prisoner might also want their family members outside of prison to be safe. So, an organized gang of criminals might teach its members that if they confess crimes committed with other gang members—that is, engage in adversarial/competitive behavior toward their fellow gang members—then terrible harm will come to the family of the gang member who confessed. In other words, the gang encourages cooperative behavior among its members by showing them that snitching—that is, succumbing to the temptation to benefit oneself at the expense of the group (gang)—will not pay off

[116] Douglas G. Baird, Robert H. Gertner & Randall C. Picker, Game Theory and the Law 33 (1994).

in the long run because the gang will punish that selfish behavior in the future.

Similarly, that emphasis on the future is key in encouraging negotiators to be cooperative, rather than adversarial/competitive, with each other. This is not possible if the negotiator cares only about the single negotiation in which the negotiator is choosing to be adversarial/competitive or cooperative. Such a negotiator's incentive is, as explained in and around Diagram 1-10 (§ 1.20(a)), to be adversarial/competitive. But most negotiators care about the future. They care not only about this negotiation, but also about future negotiations and their reputations more generally. A negotiator who cares about the future has some incentive to be cooperative now because cooperating now builds a reputation as a cooperative negotiator. A reputation as a cooperative negotiator leads to rewards in the following way.

Before you begin negotiating, you are likely to consider your counterpart's reputation, and your counterpart is likely to consider your reputation (§ 1.29). When either "is known to be adversarial and have a competitive approach to negotiations, negotiators share less information, waste more time talking around the subject, and achieve less beneficial and creative outcomes."[117] On the other hand, if you and your counterpart both have firmly established reputations as cooperative negotiators, then you are both likely to use the cooperative approach in the zero-sum (distributive) part of this negotiation because that will save you both time and money compared to what will happen if you both use the adversarial/competitive approach (§ 1.19).[118]

Through this process, cooperative negotiators repeatedly negotiating with each other provide their clients with better and cheaper results than adversarial/competitive negotiators repeatedly negotiating with each other. Negotiators using the cooperative approach get the corner office and the vacation home, while negotiators using the adversarial/competitive approach have to scrap and hustle to pay their bills.

Whether this reputational incentive outweighs the short-term incentive to be adversarial/competitive in the current negotiation depends on how much the negotiator values the future compared to how much she values success in the current negotiation. The more

[117] Cynthia Alkon & Andrea Kupfer Schneider, Negotiating Crime: Plea Bargaining, Problem Solving, and Dispute Resolution in the Criminal Context 236 (2019).

[118] See generally Ronald J. Gilson & Robert H. Mnookin, Disputing Through Agents: Cooperation and Conflict Between Lawyers in Litigation, 94 Colum. L. Rev. 509 (1994).

important the future, the greater the incentive to be cooperative now, while the more important the current negotiation, the greater the incentive to be adversarial/competitive in it.

When you start negotiating with a counterpart with whom you expect to be negotiating many times in the future, some experts say your best long-term strategy is "Tit for Tat." This is the strategy of cooperating in the first negotiation and then, in future negotiations, doing whatever your counterpart did in the previous negotiation.[119] If your counterpart cooperated in the first negotiation, then you cooperate in the second negotiation. If your counterpart used the adversarial/competitive approach in the first negotiation, then you use that approach in the second negotiation. Before cooperating in the first negotiation, you tell your counterpart that you are about to cooperate and that if he fails to cooperate, you will use the adversarial/competitive approach the next time you meet.

> The reasons for the success of Tit for Tat are many: It avoids unnecessary conflict as long as the other person cooperates; it responds immediately and firmly to provocation so that one is not exploited; it gives the other person an incentive to cooperate after you retaliate because he knows you will cooperate in response; and it adopts a clear, long-term strategy that elicits an easily understood and stable responsive pattern.[120]

The incentive to cooperate becomes even greater in light of the fact that one's approach to a particular negotiation will affect one's reputation not only with that counterpart but also with other future counterparts who are part of the same community or profession. For instance, lawyers talk with each other about other lawyers.

To the extent reputations matter, the more adversarial/competitive you have been in the past, the more likely you are to face an adversarial/competitive counterpart in the future. And the more cooperative you have been in the past, the more likely you are to face a cooperative counterpart in the future (§ 1.21).

---

[119] See generally Robert Axelrod, The Evolution of Cooperation 20 (1984).

[120] John S. Murray, Alan Scott Rau & Edward F. Sherman, Processes of Dispute Resolution: The Role of Lawyers 161 (2d ed. 1996). But see Stephen B. Goldberg, Frank E.A. Sander, Nancy H. Rogers & Sarah Rudolph Cole, Teacher's Manual, Dispute Resolution: Negotiation, Mediation, and Other Processes 2 (4th ed. 2003).

> One problem with using the Tit-for-Tat strategy in face-to-face negotiations is that strategy of punishing one's opponent for varying from a value-creating approach may lead to retaliation based on emotions that the computer does not possess. Your opponent may feel that his value-claiming approach was justified by his legitimate fears that you would engage in value claiming first, so that you were wrong to punish him, and he will react by continuing in a value claiming mode regardless of what you do thereafter.

Id.

Having cooperative counterparts enables you to provide your clients with better and cheaper results than if you had adversarial/competitive counterparts,[121] so a negotiator who cares about the future has an incentive to be cooperative.

Of course, an ordinarily cooperative negotiator will use the adversarial/competitive approach when faced with a counterpart known to be adversarial/competitive (§ 1.21). This targeted use of the adversarial/competitive approach should not hurt the reputation of the ordinarily cooperative negotiator among her fellow cooperatives, because they should recognize that she is just doing what is necessary under the circumstances. When she again negotiates with fellow cooperatives, she and they will all take the cooperative approach and enjoy its benefits.

In this regard, one can analogize negotiators with reputations for using the cooperative approach to members of a club that won't let just anyone join. When negotiating with each other, club members cooperate because not cooperating would destroy one's reputation and thus reduce one's future success. But these bonds of reciprocal cooperation extend only to fellow members of the cooperatives club. Negotiators with reputations for using the adversarial/competitive approach (who are sometimes called "junkyard dogs"[122]), are not treated to the cooperative approach. Memberships in the club, and the benefits of cooperation that flow from them, go only to applicants who build a reputation through a track-record of engaging in the right sort of behavior—cooperation.

This story presumes negotiators' reputations are clearly defined and widely known, which may be true among lawyers in a small town with few enough lawyers that each lawyer has a clearly defined reputation known by all the other lawyers in town. But this is clearly not true in larger cities with many lawyers, so we would expect big-city lawyers to be generally less cooperative negotiators.[123] It is more

---

[121] This raises an ethical issue. In some situations, your current client would benefit if you used an adversarial/competitive approach, but your future clients would benefit if you used a cooperative approach on behalf of your current client. You face a conflict between what is good for your current client and what is good for your future clients. For reactions to this conflict, see Rodney J. Uphoff, The Criminal Defense Lawyer as Effective Negotiator: A Systematic Approach, 2 Clinical L. Rev. 73, 90–94 (1995).

[122] See, e.g., Larry Hance, The Good Lawyer, the Junkyard Dog, and why Collaborative may just be your Answer, Calabrese Budner, https://calabresebudner.com/blog/2017/01/2017-01-the-good-lawyer-the-junkyard-dog-and-why-collaborative-may-just-be-your-answer-by-larry-hance/ ("Many clients make life-altering decisions from an unconscious place of fear: their need for 'protection' becomes primary. Many of these folks, to their own detriment, equate the best lawyer with the 'meanest' or 'toughest'—the junkyard dog mentality.")

[123] Michael Meltsner & Philip G. Schrag, Negotiating Tactics for Legal Services Lawyers, 7 Clearinghouse Rev. 259, 259 (1973) ("The more 'tricky' [negotiation] ploys

rational to take the adversarial/competitive approach when your future counterparts will not know what approach you have taken in the past than if they will know.

However, the importance of reputation is not determined only by the size of a city. Even in the biggest cities, a community of repeat negotiators may develop. For instance, a lawyer may find herself interacting with the same handful of other lawyers over and over again because they share a specialized practice. If, for example, you specialize in defending securities fraud claims, you may find that your counterpart is invariably one of the relatively few lawyers who specialize in asserting securities fraud claims. If you specialize in international commercial arbitration, you may find that your counterpart is invariably one of the relatively few lawyers who also specialize in international commercial arbitration. This sort of repeated interaction among a small group of negotiators creates a small town in the big city. Reputation, in short, matters more among *repeat players* than *one-shotters*.[124] If a small group of negotiators—even if they are separated by several time zones—repeatedly interact among themselves, their reputations in the group will be important to them, so they have strong incentives to take a cooperative approach to negotiation.[125]

## § 1.21 Tactics for a Cooperative Negotiator with an Adversarial/Competitive Counterpart

A negotiator who regularly uses the cooperative approach will eventually have a counterpart using the adversarial/competitive approach. The result may be a one-sided agreement in which the cooperative negotiator quickly reaches his client's bottom line (§ 1.19, Diagram 1-10). The cooperative negotiator can avoid this by quickly identifying that his counterpart is using an adversarial/competitive

---

are used most commonly in urban centers, where lawyers are not likely to be negotiating repeatedly with the same adverse attorneys who will eventually recognize their favorite tactics. Lawyers who have to deal with each other in case after case are more likely to conduct an open, straightforward discussion than those who may never negotiate with each other again.").

[124] See, e.g., Jason Scott Johnston & Joel Waldfogel, Does Repeat Play Elicit Cooperation? Evidence from Federal Civil Litigation, 31 J. Legal Stud. 39 (2002) (finding that lawyers who litigated against each other frequently were more likely than others to settle their cases and to do so more quickly). For another distinction between repeat players and one-shotters, see § 1.37, discussing risk-aversion and diversification.

[125] Andrea Kupfer Schneider, Cooperating or Caving in: Are Defense Attorneys Shrewd or Exploited in Plea Bargaining Negotiations?, 91 Marq. L. Rev. 145, 157 (2007) ("In criminal law, the geographic area of practice is narrow and the population of prosecutors and criminal lawyers is also limited. Criminal lawyers deal with each other repeatedly."); id. ("So, given the small population of criminal lawyers, the likelihood of ongoing relationships, clear communication, and problem-solving behavior could be understood to occur as a result of repeat play among the lawyers.")

approach and then withholding cooperation until his counterpart's approach becomes cooperative.

The first step for the cooperative negotiator is realizing that he is dealing with an adversarial/competitive counterpart. This may be harder than it seems because an adversarial/competitive negotiator is not necessarily abrasive or unpleasant. Adversarial/competitive negotiators have a variety of personal styles, as do cooperative negotiators. Do not be fooled by your counterpart's courteous or pleasant style into assuming that your counterpart has adopted a cooperative approach. Your counterpart may be a wolf in sheep's clothing (§ 1.17(h)).

A risky way to determine if you have an adversarial/competitive counterpart is to begin negotiations with a concession and see if your counterpart reciprocates with a concession of their own. If you choose this approach, and your counterpart does not reciprocate your concession, then you should stop making concessions until your counterpart catches up with concessions of their own. A safer way to determine if you have an adversarial/competitive counterpart is to begin negotiations with a disclosure of information and see if your counterpart reciprocates with a disclosure of their own.[126] If your counterpart does not reciprocate your disclosure, then you should stop making disclosures until your counterpart catches up with disclosures of their own.

In sum, once you, the ordinarily cooperative negotiator, realize you have a counterpart using the adversarial/competitive approach, you should stop cooperating.[127] You should punish your counterpart for taking an adversarial/competitive approach and offer the reward of further cooperation if your counterpart adopts a cooperative approach. In short, you should adopt the strategy of Tit for Tat (§ 1.20(b)).

Essentially, the ordinarily cooperative negotiator should convert a single *prisoner's dilemma* (§ 1.20(a)) into a repeated one. You should treat the negotiation of this transaction or dispute, not as one single event, but as a series of events, one after the other. Your counterpart's adversarial/competitive approach in an early event is punished by you in the following event. If your counterpart cooperates in a later event, then you reward that cooperation in a

---

[126] Charles B. Craver, Effective Legal Negotiation and Settlement 17 (9th ed. 2020).

[127] Cooperative negotiators "are forced to assume a more competitive posture to avoid the exploitation that would probably result if they were too open and accommodating with their manipulative and greedy opponents." Edward Brunet, Charles B. Craver & Ellen Deason, Alternative Dispute Resolution: The Advocate's Perspective 30 (4th ed. 2011).

still-later event. The Tit-for-Tat strategy for multiple negotiations can be adapted and applied to the negotiation of a single deal or case. Notice, however, that it works only if you, the cooperative negotiator, discover that your counterpart is using the adversarial/competitive approach before you have made too many disclosures and concessions. So, you must keep your disclosures and concessions small early in negotiation until you are confident that your counterpart is reciprocating with a cooperative approach of their own.

Tit for Tat may not succeed in inducing your counterpart to switch to the cooperative approach. Your counterpart may remain adversarial/competitive. If so, your client and you can do one of three things. One is to switch to the adversarial/competitive approach. Another is to simply stop negotiating and instead devote your efforts to your BATNA, whether that is winning your case in litigation or pursuing a transaction with a different counterpart. And the final option for the cooperative negotiator is to offer to settle at your client's bottom line. If that offer is rejected, of course, you—the cooperative lawyer—should stop negotiating and devote your efforts to your BATNA.

## 3. THE PROBLEM-SOLVING APPROACH AND THE NEGOTIATOR'S DILEMMA

### § 1.22 Overview of Problem-Solving: Positive-Sum

Unlike the *adversarial/competitive* (§§ 1.13–1.18) and *cooperative* (§§ 1.19–1.21) approaches, which orient toward *zero-sum* (distributive) negotiation (§ 1.9), the *problem-solving* approach orients toward *positive-sum* (integrative) negotiation (§ 1.10). Positive-sum negotiation finds those possible settlement terms that are better for both parties than other possible settlement terms.[128]

Achieving this is not always possible (§ 1.10(e)). The parties' interests may be so diametrically opposed that their negotiation must be zero-sum, no matter how sincerely they seek to find a positive-sum aspect to it. On the other hand, the parties' interests may present opportunities for positive-sum negotiation that go unexploited because the negotiators do not find them. In such a case, a zero-sum negotiation occurs in a positive-sum situation. To put it another way, positive-sum situations can yield either positive-sum or zero-sum

---

128 See Robert H. Mnookin, Scott R. Peppet & Andrew S. Tulumello, Beyond Winning: Negotiating to Create Value in Deals and Disputes 12 (2000) ("The Goal: Creating Value Through Problem-Solving Negotiation."); id. ("When we talk about creating value, we typically mean reaching a deal that, when compared to other possible *negotiated* outcomes, either makes both parties better off or makes one party better off without making the other party worse off." (emphasis in original)).

negotiations, while zero-sum situations can yield only zero-sum negotiations. A zero-sum negotiation in a positive-sum situation is not necessarily a failure because the value created by exploiting a positive-sum opportunity may be lower than the value of the time and effort required to find it.

Problem-solving negotiators generally treat negotiation as collaboration by the parties and their negotiators to solve their shared challenge of identifying positive-sum opportunities and using them to create additional value beyond the value created by a deal better for each party than its bottom line (§ 1.4) and BATNA (§ 1.5). Creating this additional value usually requires the negotiators to consider multiple issues (§ 1.10(c)). Positive-sum negotiation almost never occurs if only one issue is considered, especially if that issue is the amount of money a buyer or defendant will pay a seller or plaintiff. The parties' interests are almost certain to be diametrically opposed on the issue of money, as the seller wants to receive as much as possible, while the buyer wants to pay as little as possible. In contrast, considering issues other than money raises the possibility of finding an issue on which the parties' interests coincide (§ 1.10(d)) or which the parties prioritize differently so they can engage in *logrolling* (§ 1.10(c)).

To exploit positive-sum opportunities, problem-solving negotiators generally:

- focus, not on the parties' positions, but on their underlying interests and priorities,
- identify the other party's interests and priorities through questions and attentive listening,
- openly communicate their side's interests and priorities, and
- invent and explore a wide variety of potential solutions.

These tactics of the problem-solving negotiator are discussed in Sections 1.23–1.25.

## § 1.23 Interests, Not Positions

### *(a) Distinguishing Interests from Positions*

The parties' underlying interests and priorities are central to the problem-solving approach to negotiation. *Interests* should be contrasted with *positions*.[129] Examples of a negotiator's positions

[129] Art Hinshaw et al., Negotiation and Lawyers 16 (2021) ("Understanding the difference between interests and positions is the most fundamental skill a negotiator can learn.")

include: "I demand that Defendant stop releasing chemicals into the lake," and "I offer $30,000 to buy this car." In these examples, the party's interests are the reasons *why* the party wants to stop chemical release or obtain the car. "Your positions are what you want. Your interests are why you want them."[130] "Interests are needs, desires, concerns, fears—the things one cares about or wants. They underlie people's positions—the tangible items they say they want."[131]

One who knows only the parties' positions on various issues can rarely determine how strongly each party cares about each issue, that is, each party's priorities. If a recently fired employee demands $50,000 and his job back, the former employer cannot tell how important each item is to the former employee. Would the employee be just as happy with $50,000 and a different job, perhaps with a different employer? Or is the employee so focused on getting his old job back that to get it he will accept much less than $50,000 as part of a settlement that restores him to his old job?

Positive-sum negotiation typically requires identifying issues about which one party cares more strongly than the other party does, so the negotiators can engage in the *logrolling* of trading away what a party values a little in exchange for that party receiving what it values a lot (§ 1.10(c)). Consequently, positive-sum negotiation typically requires negotiators to identify what is behind each party's positions. What underlying interests motivate the party to take a particular position? Those interests may reveal a party's priorities, that is, which issues are of great importance to a party, and which issues are less important.

The former employee demanding $50,000 and his job back may have no family or friends other than his co-workers at that job. His job was his social life, a source of great joy, as well as a way to earn a living. He really wants that particular job, so another job, even at higher pay, will not satisfy his interests. Central to the problem-solving approach of exploring underlying interests is the recognition that people are diverse with different preferences, not standardized copies of each other with identical goals. Some other former employee

---

130 Stephen B. Goldberg, Frank E.A. Sander, Nancy H. Rogers & Sarah Rudolph Cole, Dispute Resolution: Negotiation, Mediation, and Other Processes 21 (5th ed. 2020). See also Leonard L. Riskin et al., Dispute Resolution and Lawyers 9 (6th ed. 2019) ("A position is what someone says she wants or is entitled to have . . . . An interest is the need or motive that underlies the position.")

131 William L. Ury, Jeanne Brett & Stephen Goldberg, Getting Disputes Resolved 5 (1988). See also Michaela Keet, Heather Dianne Heavin & John Lande, Litigation Interest and Risk Assessment: Help Your Clients Make Good Litigation Decisions xix (2020) ("Parties' interests are their fundamental goals and concerns in a situation, which often are based on deep hopes and fears about the conflict," while positions are what parties "demand in litigation or negotiation.")

would have been more concerned about money than spending the workweek with those particular co-workers.

Identifying the interests and priorities of the particular parties to a particular dispute is crucial to the problem-solving approach. You can and should identify your client's interests before you begin negotiation (§ 1.30). You will typically be less able to learn the other party's interests prior to negotiation (§ 1.31). So, you may try to learn more about them during negotiation, which is discussed next.

### *(b) Active Listening*

When her counterpart states a position, the problem-solving negotiator neither accepts nor rejects it. Rather, she seeks to understand the interests behind it. She takes what her counterpart says and "reframe[s] it as an attempt to deal with the problem."[132] One way to do this is to ask direct questions. The questions most likely to be effective are broad and open-ended. "Why?" questions are a common example: "Why are you concerned about pollution in the lake?" or "Why do you pick $30,000 as your offer for this car?" Sometimes more indirect questions elicit more telling information. If the discharged employee was asked about his life outside of work, for example, "what are your hobbies?", he might well reveal that his friendships all revolved around the job he wants back.

Eliciting information is also as much about how you ask a question as the content of the question. For example, you might preface your question with a phrase like, "Help me understand where you are coming from," which signals a collaborative rather than adversarial posture, and "you want to use a tone" of voice "that expresses genuine curiosity and is not condescending or tinged with sarcasm."[133]

In seeking to understand the other party's interests, the main point is that you do not learn as much while you are talking as you do while your counterpart or his client is talking. The longer you can keep them talking, the more likely you are to notice clues to their interests.

> A good listener uses follow-up questions to probe for additional details: "Can you tell me a bit more about that?" A good listener also uses follow-up questions to clarify that she has understood what the speaker has said: "So, you've said that . . . Have I got that right?" Such questions indicate to the speaker that the listener has heard him, verify the listener's understanding, and invite any necessary

---

132 William Ury, Getting Past No: Dealing With Difficult People 144 (1991).

133 Damali Peterman, Negotiating While Black 117 (2024).

> clarification or elaboration. Such active listening motivates speakers to continue.[134]

"Listening connotes respect and caring, and people are more likely to trust those who they believe listen to them."[135]

In addition to listening for the answers to your questions, "[y]ou also have to listen for what someone omits from an answer, for answers that are not answers or that deflect the question, for hesitations and vagueness in the responses that you get."[136] People who do not want to give responsive answers to a question sometimes answer only a part of it, or their answer departs from the level (specific or general) of the question, or they answer a different question. In addition to being alert to these evasions, you should be alert to any non-verbal signals your counterpart may, intentionally or not, be conveying. Facial expressions and body language can be significant.[137] Overall, be patient and do not rush the process of gathering information if you are seriously trying to solve problems by *logrolling*.

In identifying the other side's interests, do not forget to distinguish between negotiator and client. Negotiators have interests, too. For example, lawyer-negotiators do not like to appear weak or foolish in the eyes of their clients or other lawyers. The lawyer with whom you are negotiating may stand in the way of a deal that advances his client's interests if that deal, or the way it is generated, threatens his ego. For example, making your first offer "take-it-or-leave-it" may prevent acceptance from your counterpart who feels a need to "wring concessions out of you" to satisfy his own ego and to show his client how skilled he is. Finally, you should remember that your counterpart may have a financial incentive that diverges from his client's interests (§ 1.36).

## § 1.24 Communicating Your Side's Interests

The problem-solving negotiator communicates to her counterpart more than her client's positions. She also communicates the underlying interests motivating those positions. In fact, she may not take any positions until late in the negotiation. She will keep the

---

134 Jennifer K. Robbennolt & Jean R. Sternlight, Psychology for Lawyers: Understanding the Human Factors in Negotiation, Litigation, and Decision Making 161–63 (2012).

135 Art Hinshaw et al., Negotiation and Lawyers 191 (2021).

136 Melissa L. Nelkin, Understanding Negotiation 71 (2001).

137 See Edward Brunet, Charles B. Craver & Ellen Deason, Alternative Dispute Resolution: The Advocate's Perspective 46–60 (5th ed. 2016); Donald G. Gifford & Robert J. Rhee, Legal Negotiation: Theory and Practice 137–43 (3d ed. 2017).

negotiators' focus on the interests she needs advanced by any settlement.

For instance, a problem-solving lawyer representing the discharged employee in the previous section will not begin with a demand for $50,000 plus reinstatement. The problem-solving lawyer will tell her client's story:

> Here is a man with no family or friends other than his co-workers at the job he lost. Here is a guy whose job was his social life, a source of great joy, as well as a way to earn a living. He really wants that job back, so any settlement must prioritize that.

The problem-solving lawyer is honest and forthcoming with information, even her client's most important information. She asks her counterpart to be similarly honest and forthcoming about the other party's interests. If neither side deceives or conceals, then everyone's interests and priorities can be laid bare for all to see. This allows both sides to identify issues on which the parties' interests coincide (§ 1.10(d)), and it allows for *logrolling,* in which each party trades away its lower priority to get its higher priority (§ 1.10(c)).

Logrolling can occur without previously laying bare everyone's interests and priorities, but such logrolling may not be positive sum. Even where negotiators consider multiple issues simultaneously and trade concessions, they may make the wrong trades. If Seller cares a lot about Issue A and Buyer cares a lot about Issue B, then value is created when Seller concedes on Issue B in exchange for Buyer's concession on Issue A. In contrast, value is not necessarily created, and may even be destroyed, if Seller concedes on Issue B in exchange for Buyer's concession on Issue C, D, or E. And value is certainly destroyed if Seller concedes on Issue A (his high-priority issue) in exchange for Buyer's concession on Issue B (her high-priority issue). Negotiators risk making these "wrong trades"—trades that miss opportunities to create value and may even destroy value—if they have not revealed to each other their side's underlying interests and priorities.

## § 1.25 Variety of Solutions

The problem-solving negotiator is in no rush to take positions, that is, to begin the exchange of offers and counteroffers (§§ 1.23–1.24). The problem-solving negotiator defers such talk until both sides have thoroughly explored the underlying interests and priorities of all parties. Only then is it time to "generate solutions." The problem-solving negotiator thinks in terms of "solutions," rather than "offers." While they may amount to the same thing, the term "solutions" implies that determining the best terms of a deal is a shared problem to be solved jointly.

The problem-solving negotiator seeks to generate not just one but many solutions that advance both parties' interests. Designing such solutions typically requires simultaneously considering numerous issues (§ 1.22) and thus is difficult under the pressure of negotiation. Accordingly, problem-solving negotiators may set aside a designated time for brainstorming.[138] You can brainstorm with your client in private, or with all parties and negotiators present. The problem-solving negotiator encourages each party to generate many possible solutions before assessing any of them. The crucial point is to separate the inventive phase of generating possible solutions from the evaluative phase of assessing the merits of those possibilities.[139]

When the time comes to assess the possible solutions, the problem-solving negotiator judges them by how well they advance the interests of both parties. And when the problem-solving lawyer finally takes a position, that is, suggests a particular solution to his counterpart, he justifies it by explaining how well it satisfies the interests of both parties.

## § 1.26 The Negotiator's Dilemma and Collaborative Lawyering

### *(a) The Drawbacks of Problem Solving and the Collaborative Law Response*

The drawbacks of the problem-solving approach are similar to the drawbacks of the cooperative approach, which is discussed in Sections 1.19–1.21. The primary danger to a negotiator using the problem-solving approach is a counterpart using the adversarial/competitive approach. The result may be unfortunate in two respects. First, no problem-solving occurs, that is, the negotiators have a zero-sum negotiation in a positive-sum situation.[140] Second, the outcome of that zero-sum negotiation is a one-sided deal at or near the problem-solving negotiator's bottom line.

---

[138] Roger Fisher, William Ury & Bruce Patton, Getting to Yes: Negotiating An Agreement Without Giving In 60–65 (2d ed. 1991).

[139] Id. On the other hand, "people often have great difficulty selecting the value-maximizing option when multiple options are on the table; that is, the very presence of multiple options has a tendency to induce people to make suboptimal decisions." Chris Guthrie, Panacea or Pandora's Box?: The Costs of Options in Negotiation, 88 Iowa L. Rev. 601, 605 (2003).

[140] Having a zero-sum negotiation in a positive-sum situation, that is, declining to problem-solve, may have been the sensible thing for the lawyers to do. The value created by exploiting a positive-sum opportunity may be lower than the value of the time and effort required to find it.

Attempting to avoid this result, some lawyers have formed agreements that essentially require each side to use the problem-solving, rather than adversarial/competitive, approach. These agreements are formed by members of the *Collaborative Law* movement, which has grown more in family law than in other fields. At the outset of a negotiation, both sides' lawyers and clients sign a four-way "participation agreement" committing to use an interests-based or problem-solving approach, including full disclosure of all relevant information.[141] The agreement also typically provides that each lawyer is disqualified from representing the clients if the negotiation fails to resolve the matter, so the case is litigated. This disqualification agreement provides an incentive to resolve the case in negotiation rather than litigation. However, the Colorado Bar Association Ethics Committee found the disqualification agreement violates Model Rule of Professional Responsibility 1.7(a)(2), which prohibits a lawyer from representing a client if the client's representation may be "materially limited by the lawyer's responsibilities to . . . a third person."[142] In contrast, other states have found the collaborative-law disqualification agreement consistent with the rules of professional responsibility.[143] The Uniform Collaborative Law Act has been enacted by 26 states.[144]

### *(b) The Negotiator's Dilemma*

In the absence of a collaborative law agreement, how should the problem-solving negotiator deal with a counterpart using the adversarial/competitive approach? The standard view is that the problem-solving negotiator should use many of the same tactics available to a cooperative negotiator confronted with an adversarial/competitive counterpart (§ 1.21). The lessons of the *Prisoner's Dilemma* (§ 1.20) apply to the interaction of the adversarial/competitive and problem-solving approaches, much as they do to the interaction of the adversarial/competitive and cooperative approaches. When confronted with an adversarial/competitive counterpart, the problem-solving negotiator should quickly identify that his counterpart is using an adversarial/competitive approach (§ 1.21). Then he should stop those

---

[141] See John Lande, Possibilities for Collaborative Law: Ethics and Practice of Lawyer Disqualification and Process Control in a New Model of Lawyering, 64 Ohio St. L.J. 1315, 1318–28 (2003); Steven Keeva, Working It Out Amicably: Collaborative Lawyers Agree Up Front to Settle Disputes Out of Court, A.B.A. J., June 2003, at 66.

[142] Colo. Ethics Op. 115 (2007).

[143] Ky. Ethics Op. E-425 (2005); N.J. Ethics Op. 699 (2005). See generally Charles B. Craver, Effective Legal Negotiation and Settlement 22 (9th ed. 2020).

[144] Collaborative Law Act, Uniform Law Comm'n (Apr. 8, 2026), https://www.uniformlaws.org/committees/community-home?CommunityKey=fdd1de2f-baea-42d3-bc16-a33d74438eaf.

problem-solving tactics that are vulnerable to an adversarial/competitive counterpart.

Importantly, the very features of the problem-solving approach that make it effective in positive-sum negotiation make it vulnerable in zero-sum negotiation. Negotiation tactics aimed at "creating value are vulnerable to tactics for claiming value."[145] Thus, what is often called the *Negotiator's Dilemma*: "There is a central, inescapable tension between cooperative [problem-solving] moves to create value jointly and competitive moves to gain individual advantage."[146]

> One of the most fundamental features of negotiation is what is known as the Negotiator's Dilemma, which at its essence is how negotiators must engage in two separate but complementary negotiation tasks—claiming or distributing value, often described as "dividing the pie," and potentially creating new value from the opportunities that the negotiation presents, often described as "expanding the pie."[147]

To honestly disclose one's interests and priorities, and reveal information, especially information about bottom lines, makes one vulnerable to an adversarial/competitive negotiator,[148] but those disclosures are what enable negotiators to exploit positive-sum opportunities.

Accordingly, some theorists recommend reserving the problem-solving approach until after zero-sum negotiation.[149] Once the parties have reached tentative agreement on zero-sum issues, according to these theorists, the parties can begin problem-solving. More specifically, these theorists recommend that negotiation unfold in several stages: a value-creating (information) stage of negotiation before a value-claiming (competitive/distributive) stage, and then a

---

145 David A. Lax & James K. Sebenius, The Manager as Negotiator: Bargaining for Cooperation and Competitive Gain 32–35 (1986).

146 Id. at 29–41. See also Russell Korobkin, Negotiation Theory and Strategy ch. 7 (4th ed. 2024).

147 Art Hinshaw et al., Negotiation and Lawyers 29 (2021).

148 See, e.g., Robert H. Mnookin, Why Negotiations Fail: An Exploration of Barriers to the Resolution of Conflict, 8 Ohio St. J. on Disp. Resol. 235, 240 (1993); Donald G. Gifford, A Context-Based Theory of Strategy Selection in Legal Negotiation, 46 Ohio St. L.J. 41, 70 (1985).

149 Edward Brunet, Charles B. Craver & Ellen Deason, Alternative Dispute Resolution: The Advocate's Perspective 141 (5th ed. 2016) ("negotiators should be careful to ensure the presence of a minimal Competitive/Distributive Stage and usually a Closing Stage *before* they permit transition to the Cooperative/Integrative Stage."); Howard Raiffa, Post-Settlement Settlements, 1 Neg. J. 9 (1985) (negotiators search for positive-sum potential after tentative agreement is reached; negotiators agree to adhere to tentative agreement unless both agree to particular revised agreement).

closing stage to reach agreement, followed finally by a problem-solving (integrative or "value maximizing") stage to improve upon that agreement.[150] "During the Information Stage, negotiators focus primarily upon the needs, interests, and objectives of their *counterparts*."[151] This process hopefully enables negotiators to identify the "items that may be divided between them. Once this basic informational objective is achieved, the focus of the discussions usually changes from what the different parties hope to achieve to what the negotiators must obtain for their *own* clients."[152]

If, however, the negotiators use the adversarial/competitive approach for zero-sum negotiation prior to engaging in problem-solving, their opportunities for positive-sum negotiation may have been reduced because adversarial/competitive tactics often conceal or distort the underlying interests and priorities that must be laid bare for problem-solving to work.[153] So, it is difficult and perhaps impossible to fully employ the adversarial/competitive and problem-solving approaches in the same negotiation. "The tension between creating and distributing value . . . *cannot be resolved*. It can only be managed."[154]

Nevertheless, a leading legal-negotiation theorist says, "Most successful negotiators are able to combine the most salient traits associated with the cooperative/problem solving and the competitive/adversarial styles."[155] These "competitive problem-solvers":

> are quite open with respect to underlying client interests to enable the parties to look for areas of possible joint gain, but they frequently over- or under-state the degree to which their clients actually want the various items to enable them to obtain more of the joint surplus than they give to their opponents. If they think their adversaries really want

---

150 Charles B. Craver, Effective Legal Negotiation and Settlement Ch. 6–9 (9th ed. 2020).

151 Id. at 119.

152 Id.

153 David A. Lax & James K. Sebenius, The Manager as Negotiator: Bargaining for Cooperation and Competitive Gain 34 (1986).

154 Robert H. Mnookin, Scott R. Peppet & Andrew S. Tulumello, Beyond Winning: Negotiating to Create Value in Deals and Disputes 11, 27 (2000). Given this tension, some suggest that a negotiator should be more open to disclosure about her interests than her bottom line. Gerald B. Wetlaufer, The Limits of Integrative Bargaining, 85 Geo. L.J. 391 (1996) ("an opportunity for integrative bargaining will present an occasion for a certain amount of truthtelling with respect to one's relative interest in various issues (or one's projections about the future or aversion to risk) without also presenting even a weak argument for truthtelling with respect to one's reservation price.")

155 Charles B. Craver, Effective Legal Negotiation and Settlement 18 (9th ed. 2020).

> several issues their side does not value highly, they may exaggerate their interest in those terms, making it appear that they are conceding more than they actually are. If their side really desires specific items they believe the opposing party does not consider important, they may understate their actual interest in those terms enabling them to obtain these items in exchange for less significant concessions.[156]

This hybrid competitive problem-solving approach has been aptly "characterize[d] as: 'WIN-win: big win for your side, little win for theirs.' "[157]

While the just-discussed combination of adversarial/competitive and problem-solving approaches may be difficult to manage fully, the cooperative and problem-solving approaches can more easily be combined because the problem-solving lawyer faces less danger from a cooperative counterpart than from an adversarial/competitive one. That said, the problem-solving lawyer should not mistake her counterpart's cooperativeness for problem-solving. The counterpart may be thinking in entirely zero-sum terms. The problem-solving negotiator may need to teach her counterpart about positive-sum negotiation, that is, opportunities for expanding the pie, rather than just dividing a fixed pie in a fair or reasonable way. Teaching your counterpart about positive-sum negotiation is, however, a delicate matter because:

> pedantic lecturing to a more experienced attorney on the virtues of a new type of negotiation—whether termed "problem-solving" or "principled"—is likely to be ineffective. Implicit in such assertions are a thinly veiled sense of moral superiority and a rejection of how the other negotiator has operated during his professional life. At best, such proselytizing behavior is ineffective and looks silly or naive; at worst, it is offensive.[158]

A more effective way of trying to stimulate problem-solving is to ask the sort of interest-revealing questions discussed in Section 1.23, such as "Why are you concerned about pollution in the lake?" or "Why do you pick $30,000 as your offer to buy this car?"

---

156 Charles B. Craver, The Impact of Negotiator Styles on Bargaining Interactions, 35 Am. J. Trial Advoc. 1, 10–14 (2011).

157 Id. (quoting Ronald M. Shapiro & Mark A. Jankowski, The Power Of Nice: How To Negotiate So Everyone Wins—especially you! 5 (rev. ed. 2001)).

158 Donald G. Gifford & Robert J. Rhee, Legal Negotiation: Theory and Practice 76–77 (3d ed. 2017).

# 4. GENDER, CULTURE, AND RACE

## § 1.27 Gender

Many studies compare women and men negotiating.[159] A 1998 meta-analysis of such studies concluded that "the proposition that females bargain more cooperatively than males received some, though limited, support."[160] It went on to note that,

> [i]n simulations of explicit bargaining, where face-to-face communication is usually permissible and participants enact elaborate role-plays, women behaved less competitively than men. In contrast, the average effect of gender differences was essentially zero in experiments involving matrix games [such as the prisoner's dilemma (§ 1.20)] in which bargainers have little contact with one another and negotiating usually proceeds through a series of "offers" or choices to compete or cooperate.[161]

As to specifics, some evidence suggests that men tend to be more confident in negotiation,[162] set higher goals,[163] and be more comfortable making decisions quickly,[164] taking risks,[165] and "employing deceptive tactics,"[166] while women tend to be better than

---

[159] See, e.g., Andrea Kupfer Schneider, What's Sex Got to Do with It: Questioning Research on Gender & Negotiation, 19 Nev. L.J. 919 (2019) (examining the negotiation and gender literature).

[160] Amy Walters et al., Gender and Negotiator Competitiveness: A Meta-Analysis, 76 Organizational Behav. and Hum. Decision Processes 1, 20 (1998).

[161] Id. at 20–21. "[W]hen participants are given some opportunity to communicate in matrix games (thus providing a less restrictive, more realistic interaction) stereotypic gender difference become much larger." Id. at 21.

[162] Sandra R. Farber & Monica Rickenburg, Under-Confident Women and Over-Confident Men: Gender and Sense of Competence in a Simulated Negotiation, 11 Yale J.L. & Feminism 271, 283 (1999).

[163] Linda Babcock & Sara Laschever, Women Don't Ask: Negotiation and the Gender Divide 137–43 (2003).

[164] Andrea Kupfer Schneider, What's Sex Got to Do with It: Questioning Research on Gender & Negotiation, 19 Nev. L.J. 919, 943 (2019) ("Studies have found that women take longer to make decisions than men.").

[165] Amy J. Schmitz, Sex Matters: Considering Gender in Consumer Contracting, 19 Cardozo J.L. & Gender 437, 447 (2013) (women "tend to be more risk-averse than men in negotiation studies."); Susan Fisk, Who's on Top? Gender Differences in Risk-Taking Produce Unequal Outcomes for High-Ability Women and Men, 8 Soc. Psychol. Q. 185 (2018); Claire B. Wofford, The Effect of Gender and Relational Distance on Plaintiff Decision Making in the Litigation Process, 51 Law & Soc'y Rev. 966, 970 (2017).

[166] Charles B. Craver & David W. Barnes, Gender, Risk Taking, and Negotiation Performance, 5 Mich. J. Gender & L. 299, 317 (1999) (citing studies). See also Andrea Kupfer Schneider, What's Sex Got to Do with It: Questioning Research on Gender & Negotiation, 19 Nev. L.J. 919, 939–40 (2019) (citing studies suggesting women tend to be more ethical and trustworthy, less likely to engage in unethical negotiation tactics, and more disapproving of the use of deception).

men at reading and using nonverbal signals,[167] empathizing and building rapport,[168] and consulting multiple opinions.[169] More broadly, some evidence suggests that men tend to focus on "maximiz[ing] their own side's return," while women tend to "emphasize the maintenance of relationships."[170] In short, some evidence suggests that men more than women tend toward the adversarial/competitive approach, while women more than men tend toward the cooperative and problem-solving approaches.

To the extent these generalizations are accurate, they are just that, generalizations—with presumably numerous counterexamples of men who avoid the adversarial/competitive approach and women who rely on it.[171] And the presence or absence of gender differences may be related to the situation or type of negotiation.[172] For example, gender differences in negotiation may be less likely in a formal, professional situation than in a social or family situation. For this reason, among others, there is reason to believe that gender differences in negotiation are less pronounced among lawyers engaged in professional negotiation than among other people engaged in other sorts of negotiations.[173] Lawyers negotiating on

---

[167] Andrea Kupfer Schneider, What's Sex Got to Do with It: Questioning Research on Gender & Negotiation, 19 Nev. L.J. 919, 929–31 (2019).

[168] Id. at 932–35.

[169] Id. at 943 ("Studies of women and men in leadership roles show that women are more likely to consult and get multiple opinions before deciding").

[170] Amy Walters et al., Gender and Negotiator Competitiveness: A Meta-Analysis, 76 Organizational Behav. and Hum. Decision Processes 1, 4–5, 22 (1998); Charles B. Craver & David W. Barnes, Gender, Risk Taking, and Negotiation Performance, 5 Mich. J. Gender & L. 299, 315 (1999) (citing studies). See also Claire B. Wofford, The Effect of Gender and Relational Distance on Plaintiff Decision Making in the Litigation Process, 51 Law & Soc'y Rev. 966, 971–72 (2017) (although the "connection thesis"—"the notion that relationships with others are fundamental to women and women's lives"—"has been widely criticized as essentialist, it has shown empirical grounding in studies of conflict resolution and negotiation" (citations omitted)).

[171] Nevertheless, perceptions may have an impact even if those perceptions are inaccurate. See Carol M. Rose, Bargaining and Gender, 18 Harv. J. L. & Pub. Pol'y 547 (1995) (women are believed to value cooperation more than men do, so men negotiating with women can demand a disproportionate share of the value created by cooperation. The man can more credibly threaten deadlock because he is, or is thought to be, more tolerant of confrontation.)

[172] "[R]ecent research suggests there may be some truth in some of the stereotypes [e.g., men are competitive, while women are cooperative,] at least under certain conditions." Carrie Menkel-Meadow, Teaching About Gender and Negotiation: Sex, Truths, and Videotape, 16 Neg. J. 357, 358–59 (2000).

[173] Edward Brunet, Charles B. Craver & Ellen Deason, Alternative Dispute Resolution: The Advocate's Perspective 69 (5th ed. 2016) ("Formal education diminishes the presence of gender-based verbal differences. When individuals receive specific training, male-female communication distinctions are largely eliminated. This factor would explain why male and female lawyers tend to employ similar language when endeavoring to persuade others."); Andrea Kupfer Schneider et al., Likeability v. Competence: The Impossible Choice Faced by Female Politicians, Attenuated by Lawyers, 17 Duke J. Gender L. & Pol'y 363, 380–81 (2010) ("Women entering law

behalf of clients may be even less prone to gender differences than lawyers negotiating for themselves.[174]

All that said, "negotiations may unfold differently depending on the identity of the parties. That is to say, issues of systemic or individual bias may play a significant role in shaping outcomes."[175]

> For example, in 1995, Ian Ayres and Peter Siegelman sent individuals into car dealerships to assess whether men and women and white and African American individuals would be presented with different opening offers for their purchase of the same car. For the initial offers, the range of profit that would accrue to the dealer varied widely depending on the sex and race of the purported purchaser. The salesmen gave white men an offer that, on average, would provide $1019 in profit to the dealer, while white women received an offer that provided $1127 in profit to the dealer. In contrast, offers to African American purchasers provided $1337 (women) and $1954 (men) profit to the dealer.[176]

## § 1.28 Culture and Race

Although each individual negotiator is different, broad cultures matter for negotiation. For example, one cross-cultural negotiation authority distinguishes three categories of cultures with respect to negotiation: "dignity" cultures (generally North American and

---

school may have already been screened so that they are no more caring or cooperative than the males in law school, and the women likely possess many of the same attributes as men because both sexes were driven enough to enter law school to begin with. Additionally, women may also take on the view that when they are in a male-dominated profession, they will do as the males do."); Steven Hartwell et al., Women Negotiating: Assertiveness and Relatedness, in Constructing and Reconstructing Gender 53, 56 (Linda Perry et al. eds. 1992) (hypothesizing that "law school socialization serves to make women, as a group, more assertive," after finding female law students significantly more competitive than female undergraduates, while finding no significant difference between male law students and male undergraduates).

[174] See Hannah Riley Bowles et al., Constraints and Triggers: Situational Mechanics of Gender in Negotiation, 89 J. of Personality & Soc. Psych. 951, 959 (2005) (study data supporting prediction that "[a]s opposed to being held back when negotiating for themselves, . . . women would be particularly energized in negotiations in which they felt a personal responsibility or obligation to represent the interests of another person.")

[175] Rebecca Hollander-Blumoff & Matthew T. Bodie, The Market as Negotiation, 96 Notre Dame L. Rev. 1257, 1282 (2021).

[176] Id. at 1282–83 (citing Ian Ayres & Peter Siegelman, Race and Gender Discrimination in Bargaining for a New Car, 85 Am. Econ. Rev. 304, 305–07 (1995)).

European), "face" cultures (generally Asian), and "honor" cultures (generally Middle Eastern, North African, and Latin American).[177]

> In dignity cultures, people strive to manage conflict rationally and directly while avoiding strong emotional reactions, research finds. Because dignity cultures typically are supported by an effective system of law and strong markets, members tend to trust others automatically and engage in mutually enhancing trades rather than behaving in a selfless, altruistic manner. This analytic, trusting mind-set leads members of dignity cultures to prefer a collaborative approach to negotiation. They explore one another's interests and priorities by engaging in questions and answers.[178]

In face cultures, "norms encourage people to save face and preserve harmony by avoiding direct confrontation, suppressing negative emotions, and deferring to authority."[179]

> A lack of trust, which characterizes face cultures, often leads negotiators to take an indirect approach to exploring the other side's interests. Instead of directly probing their interests through Q&A, as members of dignity cultures tend to do, they take turns making and substantiating offers and judging one another's reactions. Negotiators from face cultures are just as effective at negotiating joint gains through this exchange of offers as negotiators who rely on Q&A, research shows. Overall, this research suggests that when trust between negotiators is low, you may achieve more by exchanging offers and backing them up than by directly trading information about your priorities and preferences.[180]

Finally, honor cultures include "a strong defense of oneself and one's family, reliance on a code of honor, and close family ties. Members tend to view insults and other conflicts as direct challenges to their status and to respond boldly and even aggressively to slights."[181] Some evidence suggests that people from honor cultures are more "reluctant to trust their counterparts for fear of being betrayed," so "it may be particularly important to spend time

---

[177] Jeanne M. Brett, Negotiating Globally: How to Negotiate Deals, Resolve Disputes, and Make Decisions Across Cultural Boundaries 2 (3d ed. 2014).

[178] Harvard Law School Program on Negotiation, Overcoming Cultural Barriers in Negotiation 11 (2019).

[179] Id. at 12.

[180] Id.

[181] Id. at 12–13.

building trust and managing conflict when negotiating with members of honor cultures."[182]

> The observations of cultural differences that seem to be the most consistent across studies—and therefore that are the most likely to accurately reflect true cultural variation and result in widely held stereotypes—are those between negotiators from Western and Eastern cultures. The former category is usually exemplified by the United States, Canada, Great Britain, and Western Europe, while the latter category is often, but not exclusively, exemplified by Japan and China. The oft-observed cultural differences can be viewed as reflecting the Western focus on the individual, problem solving, and material progress, and the Eastern emphasis on the collective good and preserving social structures.[183]

One might initially think that, to use phrases just quoted, "Western focus on the individual" would lead to more competitive negotiation than "Eastern emphasis on the collective good." "Cultural psychology has long been highlighting the idea that people in East Asia attune to a collective self," while "Westerners tend to focus on an individual self . . . . Much literature on competition and cooperation tends to associate collectivism with cooperation and individualism with competition."[184] However, a 2021 study reports that "accumulating empirical evidence has suggested otherwise. Compared to people in individualistic cultures, people in collectivistic cultures place just as much importance on the role of competition [and] are more likely to subscribe to zero-sum beliefs."[185] In a series of studies, researchers had people from 10 cultures negotiate the same business deal. Compared to negotiators from individualistic cultures of the United States, Germany, Israel, and Sweden, "participants from traditionally collectivistic cultures Japan, Hong Kong, India, and Thailand shared far less information with their counterpart." This negotiation "had win-win tradeoffs that participants could find if they shared information about their true priorities. Because they had a harder time gathering this

---

182 Id.

183 Russell Korobkin, Negotiation Theory and Strategy 254 (4th ed. 2024).

184 Kaidi Wu & Thomas Talhelm, Hide a Dagger Behind a Smile: A Review of How Collectivistic Cultures Compete More Than Individualistic Cultures in The Oxford Handbook of the Psychology of Competition (Stephen Garcia et al. eds. 2021).

185 Id. "Researchers tested people's zero-sum beliefs in over 40 countries. They found that people in collectivistic cultures and lower-income nations were more likely to endorse zero-sum beliefs." Id. (citing J. Różycka-Tran, et al., Belief in a zero-sum game as a social axiom: A 37-nation study, 46 J. of Cross-Cultural Psych. 525–548 (2015)).

information, cultures that withheld information won fewer points on average."[186]

Importantly for negotiation, communication in eastern cultures tends to be more contextual than in western cultures.[187] In low-context cultures like the United States, communicators tend to convey their meaning directly and explicitly. By contrast, "[i]n high-context cultures, this direct approach is disfavored—negotiators are more likely to rely on indirect cues."[188] "For example, negotiators from the United States usually do not have any trouble saying 'no.' In contrast, a Japanese negotiator might say 'that would be difficult' to mean the same thing."[189] If you are used to low-context communication and find yourself negotiating with someone from a high-context culture with which you are not familiar, you will lack the knowledge to make those inferences so you may find it very difficult to develop an understanding of your counterpart's interests.[190]

In preparing for negotiation (§§ 1.29–1.33), you may want to learn about your counterpart's culture and how it might affect your counterpart's approach.[191] Some employers hire risk management companies that provide culturally sensitive negotiation advice to their employees heading overseas. For example, before this book's author traveled to Turkey, such a company advised:

- "Negotiations may be slow, be prepared to meet several times before the negotiation stage."
- "Exchange business cards once the introductions are complete. It is important to take time to read the cards you have received."

---

186 Id. (citing B. C. Gunia, et al. Paying a price: Culture, trust, and negotiation consequences, 96 J. of Applied Psych. 774–789 (2011)).

187 See, e.g., Pat K. Chew, The Pervasiveness of Culture in Conflict, 54 J. Leg. Educ. 60, 62–63 (2004); William B. Gudyknunst & Stella Ting-Toomey, Culture and Interpersonal Communication 43 (1988); Amy J. Cohen, Debating the Globalization of U.S. Mediation: Politics, Power, and Practice in Nepal, 11 Harv. Negot. L. Rev. 295, 330 & n.121 (2006) (contrasting national cultures of Chinese and Japanese with those of North Americans, Swiss-Germans, and Scandinavians); Ilhyung Lee, The Law and Culture of the Apology in Korean Dispute Settlement (With Japan and the United States in Mind), 27 Mich. J. Int'l L. 1, 10 & n.57 (2005) ("the United States is considered a low-context culture"; "[s]ocieties with long social histories, shared experiences, and free from foreign intervention tend to be high-context cultures. Both Korea and Japan would fit this description.")

188 Russell Korobkin, Negotiation Theory and Strategy 266 (4th ed. 2024).

189 See Larry L. Tepley, Legal Negotiation in a Nutshell 240 (4th ed. 2023).

190 Id. at 298–299.

191 Alan Scott Rau, Edward F. Sherman & Scott R. Peppet, Processes of Dispute Resolution 217–22 (4th ed. 2002).

- "Greet both males and females with a handshake. Never use the first name on its own, always add in Ms or Mr to your given name."
- "Business dress is conservative, with men expected to wear a suit and tie, and women smart professional outfits."
- "Certain gestures and body language can be interpreted as rude or insulting, including: standing with your hands on your hips or in your pockets, pointing at someone with your finger, showing the soles of your feet, making the 'OK' sign with your hand."

Of course, these sorts of superficial observations only go so far. Learning a culture well, like learning a language well, takes more time, which you may not have, so you may want to bring onto your negotiation team someone already immersed in your counterpart's culture and language. A translator can help bridge cultural as well as linguistic gaps, and a translator on your team may help you more than relying on someone from your counterpart's team to do all the translating.

Once you learn about your counterpart's culture, you can think about whether to adapt your approach to negotiation accordingly. For example, one study of Chinese and American business students found that "Chinese subjects within our sample were more vulnerable to being influenced by the other party's opening offers than were American subjects,"[192] but a subject's "extraversion and agreeableness did not enhance the risk of being influenced by opening offers among Chinese as they did among American subjects."[193]

Cultures may vary on two topics discussed in Section 1.17: whether to negotiate solo or as a team, and negotiators who say they lack authority to make a deal without first getting approval from those who the negotiators represent. A team of co-authors from the relatively individualistic Dutch and British cultures contrast "communitarian cultures" which "prefer plural representation," of negotiating teams who, "in the face of unexpected demands" "will wish to confer with those back home." And these co-authors say that in communitarian cultures, "unaccompanied people" "are assumed to lack status. If there is no one to take notes for you or help you carry

[192] Leigh Anne Liu et al., "Ren Qing" versus the "Big Five": The Role of Culturally Sensitive Measures of Individual Difference in Distributive Negotiations, 1 Mgmt. & Org. Rev., 225, 241 (2005).

[193] Id.

bags you cannot be very important."[194] This may disincline your counterpart from dealing with you if their ascriptive-oriented culture "must be assured that your organization has great respect for you and that you are at or near the top."[195] So they advise negotiators from individualist cultures to "show patience," and recognize the "high status" of your counterpart "surrounded by helpers."[196] Relatedly, they note that in many cultures status often correlates with age, so "sending whiz kids" who "spout knowledge as if it were a kind of ammunition" against "people 10 or 20 years their senior often insults" negotiating teams from cultures that defer to their wise "éminence grise."[197]

More broadly, when people from the United States negotiate abroad they may be much more likely to encounter an approach that: "lays particular stress on long-term and affective aspects of the relationship between the parties; is preoccupied with considerations of symbolism, status and face; and draws on highly developed communications strategies for evading confrontation."[198] Negotiators accustomed to this approach may not react well to (stereo)typical Americans who think of themselves as direct and efficient, but who may come across as blunt, aggressive, impatient, and insensitive. Indeed, for affective cultures, "the entire negotiation is typically focused on you as persons, not so much on the object or proposition being discussed,"[199] according to the Dutch and British co-authors quoted above.

Even within the United States, negotiating approaches may tend to differ among various cultural, racial, or ethnic groups.[200] For example, some studies have found that Black Americans tend to negotiate more cooperatively than white Americans, while other studies have found no significant differences among members of

---

194 Fons Trompenaars & Charles Hampden-Turner, Riding the Waves of Culture: Understanding Diversity in Global Business 74 (2021).

195 Id. at 126.

196 Id. at 82.

197 Id. at 123–24.

198 Raymond Cohen, Negotiating Across Cultures: Communication Obstacles in International Diplomacy 153–54 (1991).

199 Fons Trompenaars & Charles Hampden-Turner, Riding the Waves of Culture: Understanding Diversity in Global Business 93 (2021).

200 See, e.g., Hazel Rose Markus & Leah R. Lin, Conflictways: Cultural Diversity in the Meanings and Practices of Conflict, in Cultural Divides: Understanding and Overcoming Group Conflict 302, 303 (Deborah A. Prentice & Dale T. Miller eds., 1999) (contrasting "understandings and practices of conflict in four overlapping yet still somewhat different cultural contexts: European American, Asian American, Mexican American, and African American.").

various racial groups.[201] And as noted in Section 1.27, there is evidence of continuing discrimination on the basis of race (and gender) in negotiation.[202] Relatedly, it may be illuminating to place any race and gender differences in negotiation within the context of broader power differentials in society. Perhaps "high-power negotiators tend to compete whereas low-power negotiators tend to cooperate,"[203] regardless of race and gender. And perhaps "when adversaries are members of the same race, they bargain more cooperatively with one another."[204]

On the other hand, Section 1.27 notes reason to believe that gender differences in negotiation are less pronounced among lawyers negotiating for their clients than among other people engaged in other sorts of negotiations. Similarly, "extrapolating from the findings of studies that examine the impact of race from research in nonprofessional settings to legal practice . . . may lead to false conclusions. African American, Latino, and Asian American attorneys share a common professional culture with other attorneys."[205] As a result of that culture, two experts on legal negotiation write, "[t]he power dynamics for the attorney of color participating in legal negotiations are far more likely to be determined by the facts of her case or the alternatives that she has to an agreement with her negotiating counterpart than by her

---

[201] See Jeffrey Z. Rubin & Bert R. Brown, The Social Psychology of Bargaining and Negotiation 163 (1975); Charles Craver, The Impact of Gender on Clinical Negotiating Achievement, 6 Ohio St. J. on Disp. Resol. 1, 17 n.81 (1990).

[202] See also Donald G. Gifford & Robert J. Rhee, Legal Negotiation: Theory and Practice 295 (3d ed. 2017) (noting "a 2005 survey of a diverse group of Texas attorneys found that over 93% of the respondents perceived that race had a played a role in the negotiations in which they had participated" (citing Josefina M. Rendón, Under the Justice Radar?: Prejudice in Mediation and Settlement Negotiations, 30 T. Marshall L. Rev. 347, 363 (2005))); Morela Hernandez et al., Bargaining While Black: The Role of Race in Salary Negotiations, 104 J. Applied Psychol. 581 (2018) ("Black job seekers are expected to negotiate less than their White counterparts and are penalized in negotiations with lower salary outcomes when this expectation is violated; especially when they negotiate with an evaluator who is more racially biased"); Michael Z. Green, Negotiating While Black in The Negotiator's Desk Reference 563, 563–581 (Christopher Honeyman & Andrea Kupfer Schneider, eds. 2017).

[203] Carol Watson, Gender Versus Power as a Predictor of Negotiation Behavior and Outcomes, 10 Neg. J. 117, 119 (1994).

[204] Cynthia R. Mabry, African Americans "Are Not Carbon Copies" of White Americans-the Role of African American Culture in Mediation of Family Disputes, 13 Ohio St. J. on Disp. Resol. 405, 420 (1998). "Same-race disputants are more cooperative because they trust each other more easily than they trust people of different racial groups. In contrast, intercultural adversaries endeavor to 'maintain a certain face or posture in the eyes of someone different.' " Id. (quoting Charles B. Craver, Effective Legal Negotiation and Settlement, in Negotiation: Winning Tactics and Techniques 81, 126 (PLI Litig. & Admin. Practice Course Handbook Series No. 347, 1988)).

[205] Donald G. Gifford & Robert J. Rhee, Legal Negotiation: Theory and Practice 294 (3d ed. 2017).

race."[206] This is just one example of the broader point that "individuals belong to multiple groups and therefore carry multiple cultures," so most any "encounter between two individuals is likely to be a multicultural encounter since each participant can draw on more than one culture to make sense of the situation."[207]

## D. PREPARING FOR NEGOTIATION

### § 1.29 Introduction

Whichever negotiation approach, or mix of approaches, you choose, preparation is essential.[208] Well-prepared negotiators do not begin negotiation until they have:

- thoroughly considered their client's *interests* (§ 1.23) and priorities,
- identified their client's BATNA (§ 1.5) and *bottom line* (§ 1.6) and specific goals for negotiation,
- researched the other party's interests and priorities,
- made an educated guess about the other party's BATNA, bottom line, and specific goals for negotiation,
- anticipated what negotiation approach(es) (§ 1.12) their counterpart is likely to use,
- decided what negotiation approach(es) to use, and
- considered the desired time, place, and method (in person, voice call, Zoom, etc.) for the negotiation.[209]

Thorough preparation provides several benefits. A poorly prepared negotiator may fail to advance her client's interests simply because she does not know what they are.[210] A well-prepared negotiator has a clear understanding of not only her own client's interests, but also the other party's interests, because all approaches to negotiation

---

206 Id.

207 Jayne Seminare Docherty, Culture and Negotiation: Symmetrical Anthropology for Negotiators, 87 Marq. L. Rev. 711, 715 (2004).

208 Charles B. Craver, Effective Legal Negotiation and Settlement Ch. 4 (9th ed. 2020) ("People who carefully prepare for a negotiation generally achieve more beneficial results than those who do not" (citing studies)). Preparing for plea bargaining is discussed in Cynthia Alkon & Andrea Kupfer Schneider, Negotiating Crime 210–34 (2019).

209 For a more detailed discussion, see Jay Folberg, Dwight Golann, Thomas J. Stipanowich, Jennifer Reynolds & Amy J. Schmitz, Resolving Disputes: Theory, Practice, and Law 73–77 (4th ed. 2021).

210 Robert H. Mnookin, Scott R. Peppet & Andrew S. Tulumello, Beyond Winning: Negotiating to Create Value in Deals and Disputes 179–80 (2000) (lawyers often fail to learn their clients' interests because lawyers wrongly assume they already know or would feel foolish asking).

build from the insight that knowing your counterpart's goals helps you to achieve your own goals. Also, a negotiator whose preparation gives her a good sense of her own client's bottom line, and her counterpart's, has a better sense of when to take the other side's offer, when to push for a better deal, and when to turn from negotiation to one's Best Alternative to a Negotiated Agreement (BATNA § 1.5).

## § 1.30 Identifying Your Client's Interests, Bottom Line, and Specific Goals

"At the core of an attorney's ability to advise her client effectively is an understanding of the client's interests."[211] Identifying your client's interests may take some time and effort. Representing clients would be easier if all clients quickly told you—in a clear, organized manner—all relevant information and provided you with all relevant documents and materials. But clients rarely do this, and clients may, for a variety of reasons, hold back some of what you need to know. For example, a divorcing client may say he most wants custody of the children because he is embarrassed to say what he really wants, which is to keep his spouse from getting any money.[212] "Clients often provide lawyers with self-serving, optimistic, and incomplete information in the initial discussions to avoid embarrassment and persuade the lawyers to represent them."[213] Clients also may fail to consider all available alternatives. For instance, a client may tell her lawyer that she wants to sue for lots of money, because that is what she thinks lawyers do, when what she really wants is an equitable remedy like an injunction, or even just an apology from the defendant. Sometimes a client will lie to his lawyer because the client is engaged in illegal or unethical activities and does not want the lawyer (or anyone else) to know about it.

To identify their clients' interests, lawyer-negotiators should learn to interview their clients in a way that makes the client comfortable telling the lawyer the whole truth and nothing but the truth.[214] And forthright communication should go in the other

---

211 Michael Moffitt, Settlement Malpractice, 86 U. Chi. L. Rev. 1825, 1858 (2019).

212 Charles B. Craver, Effective Legal Negotiation and Settlement 11 (9th ed. 2020) ("Seemingly objective discussions of alimony, child custody and visitation privileges, and property rights may mask a strong urge for emotional retribution.")

213 Michaela Keet, Heather Dianne Heavin & John Lande, Litigation Interest and Risk Assessment: Help Your Clients Make Good Litigation Decisions 10 (2020).

214 Books on the subject of interviewing and counseling include: David A. Binder, Paul Bergman, Paul R. Tremblay & Ian S. Weinstein, Lawyers As Counselors: A Client-Centered Approach (4th ed. 2019); Robert F. Cochran, Jr., John M.A. DiPippa & Martha M. Peters, The Counselor-at-Law: A Collaborative Approach to Client Interviewing and Counseling (3d ed. 2014); G. Nicholas Herman & Jean M. Cary, Legal Counseling and Negotiation: A Practical Approach (2d ed. 2009); Oscar J. Salinas, A Short & Happy Guide to Effective Client Interviewing and Counseling (2016).

direction, too. The Model Rules of Professional Conduct state that "[a] lawyer shall explain a matter to the extent reasonably necessary to permit the client to make informed decisions regarding the representation."[215]

A lawyer and client may disagree about what the client's interests are. While some lawyers quickly defer to any client as the best judge of the client's interests, other lawyers try to persuade some clients that what they initially think would be in their interests really would not be. Or at least that these alleged interests should be lower priorities.

Once you and your client identify your client's interests, you and your client can formulate a *bottom line*. As Section 1.6 explains, determining a client's bottom line begins with identifying the client's Best Alternative to a Negotiated Agreement (§ 1.5) and then valuing the differences between what the client would get from its BATNA with what it can get in this negotiation. Once lawyer and client determine their side's bottom line, they should use it as a constraint preventing them from agreeing to a deal worse than that bottom line.

As important as it is for the lawyer-negotiator and client to translate the client's interests into a specific bottom line, it may be even more important to translate those interests into a specific goal. This goal, or "aspiration level," is the specific target for which you are aiming in negotiation. Keeping your eye on this target, rather than on your bottom line, can be a very helpful tactic to achieve a better deal for your side. "[H]umans have a limited capacity for maintaining focus in complex, stressful situations such as negotiations. Consequently, once a negotiation is under way, we gravitate toward the single focal point that has the most psychological significance for us."[216] Better that focal point be your goal than your bottom line.

> Once most people set a firm bottom line in a negotiation, that becomes their dominant reference point as discussions proceed. They measure success or failure with reference to their bottom line . . .
>
> To avoid falling into the trap of letting your bottom line become your reference point, be aware of your absolute limits, but do not focus on them. Instead, work energetically on formulating your goals—and let your bottom line take care of itself. . . .

---

215 Model Rules of Prof'l Conduct R. 1.4(b) (2019).

216 G. Richard Shell, Bargaining for Advantage: Negotiation Strategies for Reasonable People 29 (1999).

> Orient firmly toward your goal in the planning and initial stages of negotiation, then gradually reorient toward a bottom line as that becomes necessary to close the deal.[217]

In other words, reach for the stars while keeping your feet firmly on the ground.

## § 1.31 Identifying Other Party's Interests, Bottom Line, and Specific Goals

As difficult as it may be to learn thoroughly your client's interests, bottom line, and specific goals, that is usually easier than gaining a similarly thorough understanding of the other party's interests, bottom line, and specific goals. To inquire about the other party's interests, you can ask your client.[218] In litigation in the United States, as Section 1.14 noted, you can use discovery, such as depositions and document requests. You can also use "informal discovery" such as:

- internet searches, including social media,
- searches of court and other government records,
- reports from credit reporting agencies and corporate bond-rating agencies,
- inquiries to the other party's neighbors, employers, or business associates, and even
- hiring an investigator to spy on the other party.

During negotiation, you can obtain further information that may shed light on the other party's interests, bottom line, and goals (§§ 1.14, 1.23.)

## § 1.32 Adjusting During Negotiation

### *(a) Adjusting Approaches During Negotiation*

Preparing for negotiation includes anticipating the negotiation approach(es) your counterpart will use. You may have repeatedly negotiated with this counterpart before and know that she always uses the same approach (§ 1.20). Or you may not have negotiated

---

[217] Id. See also Russell Korobkin, Aspirations and Settlement, 88 Cornell L. Rev. 1, 4 (2002) (compared to litigants with low aspirations, litigants with high aspirations are less likely to settle—even when settlement is in both sides' interests—but, when they do settle, more likely to get a favorable deal).

[218] This may not occur because "[a] lawyer may assume that his client doesn't care about the other side's interests, that discussing such interests will raise doubts about the lawyer's loyalty, or that understanding the other side might weaken the clients' resolve." Robert H. Mnookin, Scott R. Peppet & Andrew S. Tulumello, Beyond Winning: Negotiating to Create Value in Deals and Disputes 180–82 (2000).

with this counterpart before, so you may contact others to learn what you can about her approach to negotiation.

While you will have decided what negotiation approach(es) to use as part of your preparation, you should be prepared to adjust your approach during negotiation. Because "negotiation involves interacting with others, both *analysis* (conceptualizing the issues being negotiated) and *behavior* are dynamic works-in-progress and must be revised before, during, and after engagements and processing of new information."[219] "[M]ost effective negotiators will moderate their behavior as needed (respond in kind or respond to change the situation, ask questions to get information or ask questions to build rapport, etc.) throughout the course of the negotiation."[220] In this regard, "some have analogized negotiation to jazz. Jazz, like negotiation, relies on some measure of intuition and improvisation."[221] For example, if you planned to use the cooperative or problem-solving approach because you expected your counterpart to do likewise, you may want to switch quickly to the adversarial/competitive approach if you discover that your counterpart is using it (§§ 1.21, 1.26). On the other hand, you may want to abandon your planned adversarial/competitive approach if you see that it seems to be wasting positive-sum opportunities, jeopardizing important relationships, or just making the negotiation unnecessarily slow and painful (§§ 1.18–1.19).

### *(b) Adjusting Your Bottom Line During Negotiation*

While you should be open to adjusting your negotiating approach during negotiation, you should be leery of adjusting your bottom line during negotiation. As a negotiator acquires more information in negotiation or otherwise, she and her client should reconsider their side's bottom line (§ 1.35(d)). Toughening your bottom line is a sensible response to new information revealing problems with your counterpart's BATNA (§ 1.5). Conversely, softening your bottom line is a sensible reaction to new information revealing problems with your BATNA. But you should be very cautious about softening your bottom line in the presence of your counterpart or soon after receiving communications from your counterpart. Your counterpart wants you to soften your bottom line (§ 1.13) and may be engaging in deception and psychological warfare to try to get you to soften your bottom line (§§ 1.15, 1.17).

---

219 Carrie Menkel-Meadow, Negotiation: A Very Short Introduction 3 (2022).

220 Andrea Kupfer Schneider, Teaching A New Negotiation Skills Paradigm, 39 Wash. U. J.L. & Pol'y 13, 23 (2012).

221 Michael Moffitt, Settlement Malpractice, 86 U. Chi. L. Rev. 1825, 1848 (2019).

Don't fall for it! If your counterpart has you doubting your BATNA or bottom line, take a break from negotiating. Walk away from your counterpart or end the phone call. Give yourself time to think without pressure. Ask yourself, your client, or (while protecting attorney-client privilege) a trusted confidant: are you tempted to soften your bottom line because of your counterpart's tactics? Or has something importantly relevant to valuing your case really changed since you previously determined your bottom line?

## § 1.33 Specific Preparations

You can make more specific preparations for your negotiation after you and your client have researched both parties' interests and priorities, formulated your side's BATNA, bottom line, and specific goals, made an educated guess about your counterpart's BATNA, bottom line, and specific goals, and anticipated both negotiators' approaches to negotiation. Your specific preparations relate to questions like:

- What information do you to seek to obtain? How?
- What information will you disclose? When?
- What will be your opening offer/position? When will you communicate it?
- How will you defend your opening offer/position, that is, what are the arguments on behalf of it?
- What counter-arguments do you expect?
- When will you make concessions? How big will they be?
- What are the principled arguments for making your planned concessions but not conceding further? and
- Do you want or anticipate that negotiation will be in-person meetings, video conferences, voice calls, emails, or text messages?[222]

While all these specific preparations are valuable, even a thoroughly prepared negotiator will not likely be able to force the negotiation to follow her script. An overly scripted negotiator will be less successful than one who easily adjusts as the negotiation develops. As noted above, negotiation—like jazz—relies on some measure of intuition and improvisation.

---

[222] See Noam Ebner, Negotiating via Email, and Noam Ember, Negotiating via Videoconferencing, in The Negotiator's Desk Reference 116 & 155 (Christopher Honeyman & Andrea Kupfer Schneider, eds., 2017).

# E. SETTLEMENT NEGOTIATION

## § 1.34 Settlement Negotiation in the Shadow of the Law Revisited

Section 1.2 defines *settlement negotiation* as the negotiation of disputes that are already in binding adjudication (litigation or arbitration) or are likely to go there if negotiation does not result in agreement. Thus, a *settlement* is an agreement resolving a dispute and thus preventing or ending litigation or arbitration. Some settlements address multiple claims each party has against the other, or many parties' claims but first consider settling one claim a plaintiff or potential plaintiff (P) has against the defendant or potential defendant (D). In that context, a settlement is the sale of a claim by P to D,[223] and the sales price is whatever D pays or promises to pay P, which is typically but not necessarily money.

Perhaps more controversially, Section 1.2(b) suggests that we might think similarly of *plea bargaining* (settlement negotiation of criminal cases) as the prosecuting government's "sale" of a charge with the "price" to be paid by the defendant often expressed in months of incarceration rather than in dollars.[224]

While settlement negotiation is negotiation about the sale of a claim (or perhaps a criminal charge) to the defendant, claims differ from other sell-able things in the legal consequences that follow when the negotiators do not agree on a sale price. If a car, for example, is not sold because the negotiators do not agree on a price, the potential buyer will keep his money, and the potential seller will keep her car. Nobody will force a sale. In contrast, if a claim is not sold because the negotiators do not agree on a price, the plaintiff or prosecution can force a sale through litigation. The court's judgment will transfer (or "sell") the claim from Plaintiff to Defendant and will set the price Defendant is obligated to pay.[225]

---

[223] Keith N. Hylton, Selling Out: An Instrumentalist Theory of Legal Ethics, 34 Geo. J. Legal Ethics 19, 54 (2021) ("A settlement occurs when the defendant, the violator of the plaintiff's right, purchases the claim from the plaintiff."); id. ("As is well known in the literature on settlement, the plaintiff and the defendant are likely to arrange a transaction where the plaintiff sells the claim to the defendant when the expected net reward to the plaintiff is less than the expected payout by the defendant, or equivalently, when the expected judgment differential is less than the joint litigation cost"); D. Theodore Rave, Tort Claims As Property Rights, 69 DePaul L. Rev. 587, 591 (2020) ("there are several ways in which tort claims are alienable. Most fundamentally, the plaintiff can sell the claim to the defendant in a settlement").

[224] Frank H. Easterbrook, Criminal Procedure as a Market System, 12 J. Legal Stud. 289, 308 (1983) ("Plea bargaining establishes the price for most crimes. It establishes price in the same way as bargaining in the market for goods and services.").

[225] Robert J. Rhee, A Price Theory of Legal Bargaining: An Inquiry into the Selection of Settlement and Litigation Under Uncertainty, 56 Emory L.J. 619, 670 (2006) ("A plaintiff asserts a legal claim, which may be 'bought' by a defendant either

This impending "forced sale" looms over settlement negotiation, casting what is widely known as the "shadow of the law."[226] Settlement negotiation is conducted "in the shadow of the law" because the negotiators' expectations about the results of litigation or arbitration (the "law" determining the price at the forced sale) shape the negotiators' attitudes toward various possible settlement terms.[227] Negotiators' expectations about the "price" of a forced sale, should it come to that, influence the price at which they will agree to settle.[228] In other words, litigating further is typically the only, and therefore best, alternative to a negotiated agreement (BATNA § 1.5) of a party engaged in settlement negotiation.[229]

## § 1.35 Valuing a Civil Case

### *(a) Litigation as BATNA*

The previous section explains that the Best Alternative to a Negotiated Agreement (§ 1.5) of a party in settlement negotiation is further litigation. So, formulating a party's *bottom line* (§ 1.6) in settlement negotiation requires determining the expected result (§ 1.7) of further litigation and then valuing the differences between what the party would get from that expected result of litigation with what the party can get in settlement negotiation. This is an example of Section 1.6's observation that your *bottom line* in negotiation "should be tied to" your BATNA because agreeing in a negotiation to something worse than your best alternative to it would be "the most

---

voluntarily or by forced purchase"); id. at 675 ("It is often said that a defendant is a buyer of the plaintiff's claim.")

226 Robert H. Mnookin & Lewis Kornhauser, Bargaining in the Shadow of the Law: The Case of Divorce, 88 Yale L.J. 950 (1979); In re OHT Hawk AS, No. 21-60796, 2022 WL 1486778, at *2 (5th Cir. May 11, 2022) ("To borrow a phrase, settlements are negotiated 'in the shadow of the law' "); United States v. Khattak, 273 F.3d 557, 562 n.6 (3d Cir. 2001) ("criminal sentences in most cases are, at least in part, bargained for; that is, they are negotiated between the defendant and the government. In this sense, the sentencing regime has come to resemble the negotiation of civil settlements, also conducted in the shadow of the law.")

227 See Robert H. Mnookin & Lewis Kornhauser, Bargaining in the Shadow of the Law: The Case of Divorce, 88 Yale L.J. 950, 968 (1979) ("the outcome that the law will impose if no agreement is reached gives each [party] certain bargaining chips—an endowment of sorts.")

228 As noted above, the "price" of a claim (or criminal charge), whether agreed to in settlement or imposed by litigation, is not necessarily an amount of money. The price includes whatever the plaintiff (or prosecuting government) receives in exchange for the claim (or charge).

229 Alan Scott Rau, Edward F. Sherman & Scott R. Peppet, Processes of Dispute Resolution 89 n.3 (4th ed. 2002) ("In litigation, both parties usually share the same alternative to negotiating a resolution of their dispute: proceeding to court."). See also Paul F. Kirgis, Bargaining with Consequences: Leverage and Coercion in Negotiation, 19 Harv. Negot. L. Rev. 69, 99 (2014) ("Negotiation texts commonly refer to litigation as a BATNA because settlement and litigation are the alternative ways for the plaintiff to receive compensation for his injuries").

basic negotiating mistake—agreeing to a deal when [you] would have been better off walking away from the [negotiation] table with no agreement."[230]

The process of determining the expected result of litigation (the BATNA in settlement negotiation) is often known as the process of "valuing a case."[231] Case valuation is often difficult for several reasons, including the fact that the results of litigation can be highly uncertain.

Clients ask their lawyers for help valuing a case when clients ask how a court is likely to rule. Lawyers often resist making such predictions. Lawyers know that the results of litigation are difficult to predict,[232] especially when one "rolls the dice" by going to trial.[233] Many lawyers are understandably cautious about giving their clients predictions about the results of litigation.[234]

> Lawyers typically use imprecise or qualitative language when advising clients on their chances of success. For example, some lawyers tell clients that they have a

---

230 Russell Korobkin, A Positive Theory of Legal Negotiation, 88 Geo. L.J. 1789, 1797 (2000).

231 See, e.g., Laura A. Kaster, Cognitive Barriers to Valuing Your Case for Settlement or Mediation: Improving Your Risk Assessment, N.J. Law., April 2011, at 43, 44 ("How can we actually improve the accurate assessment of the value of a case in order to assure that the settlement, whether reached through negotiation or mediation, represents a better alternative for the client than actually trying the case?"); Peter Toll Hoffman, Valuation of Cases for Settlement: Theory and Practice, 1991 J. Disp. Resol. 1 (1991) ("Trial lawyers frequently talk about the value of their cases when they are counseling clients, negotiating with opposing counsel, or conversing with their fellow attorneys. The term 'value' may have several definitions when referring to cases, but most attorneys intend it to mean the amount at which they expect a case to settle").

232 See, e.g., Roger Haydock, Negotiation Practice § 2.3 (1984) (widely divergent valuations of simulated personal injury case by 30 experienced personal injury lawyers); Douglas E. Rosenthal, Lawyer and Client: Who's in Charge? 200–08 (1974) (survey of experienced lawyers reviewing identical case files revealing widely varying estimates of settlement value); Gerald R. Williams & Charles B. Craver, Legal Negotiation and Settlement 4–6, 111–15 (2007).

233 The uncertainty of trial can be reduced with a "high-low" agreement, which guarantees the plaintiff a particular dollar amount, even if the court's verdict is lower and caps the defendant's liability, even if the court's verdict is higher. See Molly McDonough, High-Lows' Ups and Downs, A.B.A. J. Aug. 2005, at 12.

234 On the other hand, some lawyers are insufficiently cautious. See, e.g., Sauer v. Flanagan & Maniotis, P.A., 748 So. 2d 1079 (Fla. Dist. Ct. App. 2000). Sauer, the client who ultimately lost the case, stated that her lawyer, Maniotis, told her that it was going to be "an open and shut case" and that "[t]here was no way I was going to lose this case." "The only time he said anything different, he said there's always that slight percentage that something screwy is going to go on so I can't put it down in writing but I guarantee you this right now I'm ninety-nine percent sure that this case is going to be won." She testified that Maniotis told her that there was no reason to accept the [million dollar] offer since they were going to win the case at trial and that there was no potential downside in rejecting the offer.

Id. at 1080.

> "good," "arguable," or "challenging" case. They vaguely allude to risks, saying things like "there are no guarantees" or "it's impossible to predict what a judge or jury will do." . . .
>
> Lawyers often use the phrase that clients have a "good chance of winning at trial." At a training session, [researchers] asked lawyers how to define "good chance" as a percentage, and the answer ranged from 51% to 80%, a huge range. When lawyers provide vague assessments such as this, clients are uninformed and especially subject to the [cognitive] biases [discussed in § 1.38].[235]

The Model Rules of Professional Conduct state that, "A client is entitled to straightforward advice expressing the lawyer's honest assessment. Legal advice often involves unpleasant facts and alternatives that a client may be disinclined to confront."[236] A client thinking about making a settlement offer or accepting one made by the other side cannot make an informed decision without realistic expectations about the results of further litigation.[237]

Because further litigation is each party's BATNA in settlement negotiation, lawyers helping their clients value cases should want to know:

- What is the likelihood the case will be dismissed before trial?
- If it does go to trial, what is the likelihood of a plaintiff's verdict?
- If the plaintiff does win a verdict, what remedy will the court order?

---

235 Michaela Keet, Heather Dianne Heavin & John Lande, Litigation Interest and Risk Assessment: Help Your Clients Make Good Litigation Decisions 13 (2020).

236 Model Rules of Prof'l Conduct R. 2.1, cmt.1 (2019).

237 Michael Moffitt, Settlement Malpractice, 86 U. Chi. L. Rev. 1825, 1830 (2019) ("Supporting clients' autonomy—their ability to make informed choices between different litigation and settlement paths—demands at least three separate tasks of lawyers. Competent lawyers must, in this context, understand their clients' interests, compare the implications of any proposed settlement against those interests, and articulate the risks and opportunities associated with continued litigation. Each of these may appear obvious, and each finds support in existing articulations of professional ethical obligations."); Stephanos Bibas, Designing Plea Bargaining from the Ground Up: Accuracy and Fairness Without Trials As Backstops, 57 Wm. & Mary L. Rev. 1055, 1075–76 (2016) ("At bottom, what [criminal] defendants really need is an informed forecast of the expected conviction and sentence (including collateral consequences), how they compare to those received by other defendants, and the risks and benefits of holding out or walking away. Defense lawyers try to communicate their best estimates to their clients, but they may not be able to do much investigation and discovery, may not have enough time to counsel their clients and weigh options, and may even 'meet 'em and plead 'em' at the initial appearance").

- How much money is the judge or jury expected to award?
- What is the likelihood that any award of damages will be paid?
- What is the likelihood of a reversal upon appeal?

All these questions should be considered by the lawyer advising a client about a settlement offer.[238]

These questions, however, are not enough. Valuing a case (determining the expected result of further litigation) includes valuing what will happen on the way to that result. Litigating further will cost the client additional time and, usually, additional legal fees.[239] And the costs of litigating further often go beyond time and money.[240] Further litigation may involve a grueling two-day deposition of the client by hostile lawyers, or a trial in which the client's family secrets are exposed to the public. In short, the process of litigation can be very stressful for a client.[241] All those process factors should be a part of case valuation.

---

[238] See G. Nicholas Herman & Jean M. Cary, Legal Counseling and Negotiation: A Practical Approach 207–09 (2d ed. 2009). See also Michaela Keet, Litigation Risk Assessment: A Tool to Enhance Negotiation, 19 Cardozo J. Conflict Resol. 17, 23–24 (2017) ("a simple, practical framework for litigation risk analysis, which includes the following basic stages and steps."); id. ("The first stage develops the projection of litigation outcome, initially by weighing the likelihood that a breach of law will be established. . . . The second step in Stage One of the analysis is the calculation of damages.")

[239] Michael Moffitt, Settlement Malpractice, 86 U. Chi. L Rev. 1825, 1874–75 (2019) ("calculating the value associated with a case and its resolution may be relatively straightforward: a case's settlement value equals the litigation value of a case, plus or minus the anticipated risk-adjusted transaction costs associated with continued litigation. This is familiar, indeed foundational, to much of the classic economic analysis of the settlement of litigated cases. Transaction costs, fully understood, include both direct, easily quantifiable transaction costs such as attorneys' fees and less direct opportunity costs such as the time and attention litigation consumes, depriving people of the ability to otherwise be engaged in productive activities.")

[240] Michaela Keet, Litigation Risk Assessment: A Tool to Enhance Negotiation, 19 Cardozo J. Conflict Resol. 17, 25 (2017) ("a simple, practical framework for litigation risk analysis" "develops the projection of litigation costs. . . . [L]awyers tend to focus first on legal fees and expenses—the client's tangible out-of-pocket costs. A multi-dimensional assessment of process costs includes much more. Which client interests are engaged or put at risk in continued litigation and trial?"); id. ("Internal impacts must be considered, including human and organizational energy (time, emotional energy, psychological strain); the internal environment of the family or organization; and issues of identity and reputation. External impacts must also be explored—on relationships (family, business, community) and on larger individual or commercial networks; third parties, direct or indirect; and opportunities (the advancement of life or organizational goals)."); id. ("clients should be encouraged to assign monetary values to drains on their psychological, emotional, social, and financial resources.")

[241] Michaela Keet, Heather Dianne Heavin & John Lande, Litigation Interest and Risk Assessment: Help Your Clients Make Good Litigation Decisions 30–42 (2020).

On the other hand, pursuing litigation to its conclusion can bring great satisfaction to the client. Some clients care less about the money that can be exchanged in settlement and more about the public vindication that comes from a favorable verdict.[242] Relatedly, some clients—from insurance companies to ideological organizations seeking social change—avoid settling strong cases they hope will produce landmark judicial decisions that serve as precedents to guide future cases.[243] And businesses worried about getting sued often may avoid settling to develop a reputation among plaintiffs' lawyers "for scorched earth, delay, and fight-to-the-end tactics"[244] that make plaintiffs' lawyers and their clients think twice about suing these tough business defendants in the future.[245] Finally, a few clients avoid settling because they just have litigious personalities that enjoy the process of litigating more than settling. All these factors also should be a part of case valuation.

Considering all these factors—as well as the more routine factors of time and money—can make the process of case valuation quite complex and uncertain.

### *(b) Examples of Case Valuation*

The case-valuation process introduced in Section 1.35(a) is often called "litigation risk analysis," and is a specific application of

---

[242] Barella v. Exchange Bank, 84 Cal.App.4th 793, 801 (2000) ("[T]he value to a particular plaintiff of public vindication (or, conversely, the negative value of confidentiality) is so highly subjective and elusive that no court can determine its monetary worth.").

[243] Jeffrey W. Stempel, Hard Battles over Soft Law: The Troubling Implications of Insurance Industry Attacks on the American Law Institute Restatement of the Law of Liability Insurance, 69 Clev. St. L. Rev. 605, 667–68 (2021) (insurers can " 'pick their battles' in litigation. . . . When a given lawsuit involves bad facts . . ., the insurer can settle such cases, perhaps even 'overpaying' as necessary to avoid risking unfavorable precedent or generating adverse publicity."); id. ("By contrast, when a case involves favorable facts, less competent or effective counsel, or a sympathetic judge or jury, insurers can make their stand on this ground, hoping to generate favorable precedent."); Ben Depoorter, The Upside of Losing, 113 Colum. L. Rev. 817, 825 (2013) ("Similarly, public law litigation focuses on the strategic pursuit of favorable case outcomes on the basis of individual verdicts. The civil rights, women's rights, and New Deal labor movements are generally remembered for providing landmark victories and creating new rights where none existed before. By selecting disputes carefully, choosing venues wisely, and timing certain claims accurately, social movements could gradually win cases and ultimately reform entire areas of law.")

[244] Fred Einbinder, Mass Torts: Dispute Resolution in France and the United States-the Vioxx and Mediator Cases Compared, 29 Wash. Int'l L.J. 575, 647 (2020).

[245] John K. Villa, Billing—Alternative billing arrangements: Their genesis, utility and limitations, 1 Corporate Counsel Guidelines § 4:7 (2022) ("the corporation's reputation for 'scorched earth' litigation may dissuade other potential litigants from suing the corporation and ultimately result in unquantifiable savings to the corporation.")

decision analysis,[246] which in turn is an application of rational choice theory.[247] This rational analysis of case valuation continues in the rest of Sections 1.35–1.37. Then Section 1.38 discusses biases leading parties to depart from it.

A rational litigant facing the settlement/litigation choice would behave like a rational person facing any choice—by assessing the costs and benefits of each option and then choosing the one with the highest *expected value* (§ 1.7). The expected value of further litigation is the best alternative (BATNA, § 1.5) to a settlement agreement, and thus the value a party should compare with a settlement offer. Two examples follow.

Suppose a rational plaintiff owns lakefront property and sues to stop (enjoin) Defendant's pollution of the lake. Time involved in the case is Plaintiff's only cost of litigating because her lawyer is working without pay (pro bono). Plaintiff's lawyer's best estimate is that there is a ten percent chance of obtaining the injunction and a ninety percent chance of a defendant's verdict. Assume that no other results are possible from litigation and that Defendant is certain to comply with an injunction. Assume also that Plaintiff is *risk-neutral* (§ 1.37).

Suppose Defendant offers Plaintiff $100,000 to settle the case. To decide whether to accept this offer, our rational Plaintiff must convert to dollars the values she places on:

- the time she will have to spend on the case to complete litigation, and
- ending the pollution.

If Plaintiff values the time she will have to spend on the case to complete litigation at $20,000 and ending the pollution at $800,000, then Plaintiff should accept the settlement offer because:

$$100{,}000 > (800{,}000 \times .1) - 20{,}000$$

$$100{,}000 > 80{,}000 - 20{,}000$$

$$100{,}000 > 60{,}000$$

The benefit to Plaintiff from settling is the $100,000 payment. The benefit to Plaintiff of not settling is an end to the pollution (which

[246] See, e.g., Michaela Keet, Heather Dianne Heavin & John Lande, Litigation Interest and Risk Assessment: Help Your Clients Make Good Litigation Decisions (2020); Marjorie Corman Aaron, Risks & Rigor: A Lawyer's Guide to Decision Trees for Assessing Cases and Advising Clients (DRI 2018); Howard Raiffa, The Art and Science of Negotiation 128 (1982); David P. Hoffer, Decision Analysis as a Mediator's Tool, 1 Harv. Negot. L. Rev. 113 (1996).

[247] See generally Howard Raiffa, Decision Analysis: Introductory Lectures on Choices Under Uncertainty (1968) (providing a nontechnical account of the rational choice model).

Plaintiff values at $800,000) multiplied by the probability of attaining this result (.1) and then subtracting the time she will have to spend to attain this result (worth $20,000). As the calculations show, the benefit to Plaintiff of litigating is only $60,000. As that is less than the $100,000 benefit of settling, Plaintiff should settle.

In this example, Plaintiff values her BATNA (§ 1.5) at $60,000 and thus her *bottom line* (§ 1.6) in settlement negotiation is $60,000. As noted above, the bottom line is the worst deal a party will accept and it should be determined by the party's BATNA. Plaintiff's bottom line is determined by her valuation of the case because her best alternative to negotiating an agreement with Defendant is to continue litigating the case.[248]

Because the BATNA of a party in settlement negotiation is continued litigation of the case, the bottom line of that party in settlement negotiation (like Plaintiff in the lake-pollution example) should be the value that party places on continued litigation of the case.[249] In short,

Case Valuation = BATNA = Bottom Line[250]

---

[248] Alan Scott Rau, Edward F. Sherman & Scott R. Peppet, Processes of Dispute Resolution 89 n.3 (4th ed. 2002) ("In litigation, both parties usually share the same alternative to negotiating a resolution of their dispute: proceeding to court."); Paul F. Kirgis, Bargaining with Consequences: Leverage and Coercion in Negotiation, 19 Harv. Negot. L. Rev. 69, 99 (2014) ("Negotiation texts commonly refer to litigation as a BATNA because settlement and litigation are the alternative ways for the plaintiff to receive compensation for his injuries").

[249] See, e.g., Michaela Keet, Litigation Risk Assessment: A Tool to Enhance Negotiation, 19 Cardozo J. Conflict Resol. 17, 19 (2017) ("When litigation is underway, the best option short of a settlement agreement is usually to continue to litigate. A detailed understanding of the 'litigation alternative' becomes the point of comparison—how the negotiator knows when to stay or leave the negotiation table."); id. ("Building on this, how a lawyer views her client's 'best alternative to a negotiated agreement' ('BATNA') will be how she defines the walkaway point in any negotiation"); Ronald F. Wright, Jenny Roberts & Betina Cutaia Wilkinson, The Shadow Bargainers, 42 Cardozo L. Rev. 1295, 1319 (2021) ("In criminal cases, where alternatives to a negotiated plea agreement are limited, determining the BATNA requires a calculation of the likelihood of conviction and the likely sentence after a conviction"). This is simply a reiteration of the point that settlement negotiation is conducted in the shadow of the law. See § 1.34.

[250] Other negotiation scholars make the same point in different language. See, e.g., Russell Korobkin, A Positive Theory of Legal Negotiation, 88 Geo. L.J. 1789 (2000).

> If Goliath's [plaintiff's] research leads to an estimate that he has a 75% chance of winning a jury verdict, and the likely verdict if he does prevail is $100,000, then using a simple expected value calculation ($100,000 × .75) would lead him to value his BATNA at $75,000.
>
> . . . Goliath might determine, for example, that a $50,000 settlement would have the equivalent value to him of a jury verdict with an expected value of $75,000, because pursuing a jury verdict would entail greater tangible and intangible costs such as attorneys' fees, emotional strain, inconvenience, and the

If a party's valuation of the case changes, then the party's bottom line should change. Two examples of this follow.

If the assumptions from the preceding lake-pollution example hold except that Plaintiff values ending the pollution at $1,500,000, then Plaintiff should continue litigating, rather than accept the $100,000 settlement offer, because:

$$100{,}000 < (1{,}500{,}000 \times .1) - 20{,}000$$

$$100{,}000 < 150{,}000 - 20{,}000$$

$$100{,}000 < 130{,}000$$

Because Plaintiff now values ending the pollution at $1,500,000 (rather than the previous $800,000), Plaintiff now values her case at $130,000.[251] In other words, her BATNA is now worth $130,000 to her, so her bottom line in settlement negotiation is now $130,000, which is $30,000 more than the settlement offer, so she should turn down the offer.

If these assumptions hold, except that Plaintiff values the time she will have to spend on the case to complete litigation at $60,000, then Plaintiff should accept the $100,000 settlement offer because:

$$100{,}000 > (1{,}500{,}000 \times .1) - 60{,}000$$

$$100{,}000 > 150{,}000 - 60{,}000$$

$$100{,}000 > 90{,}000$$

Because Plaintiff now values the time to complete litigation at $60,000 (rather than the previous $20,000), Plaintiff now values her case at $90,000. In other words, her BATNA is now worth $90,000 to her, so her bottom line in settlement negotiation is now $90,000, which is $10,000 less than the settlement offer, so she should accept the offer.

For another example of case valuation, consider a personal injury case in which a court will only hold the defendant liable if it holds that

(1) the plaintiff did not assume the risk of injury, and

(2) the defendant violated the standard of care.

---

risk of losing the case altogether. If so, Goliath would set his RP ["reservation price" or bottom line] at $50,000. . . .

Id. at 1796. Korobkin accounts for factors such as the attorney's fees and emotional strain of trial when converting BATNA into RP (bottom line), while this book accounts for such factors earlier, in a more complete valuation of the case, which then serves (without further adjustments) as the BATNA and bottom line. But the bottom line, so to speak, of each method is the same.

[251] Recall that Plaintiff values the time it will take her to complete litigation at $2000 and does not have to pay her lawyer, who is working pro bono.

If plaintiff has a 70% chance of defeating the assumption-of-the-risk defense and an 85% chance of proving the defendant violated the standard of care, then the plaintiff has a 59.5% chance of establishing the defendant's liability because $.7 \times .85 = .595$.[252]

The examples just provided are case valuation by a rational plaintiff. Rational defendants should similarly value a case, but the values will be expected losses rather than expected gains. For example, a defendant may ask its lawyer how much it should expect to pay the plaintiff after a court rules and how much will Defendant have to pay you (its lawyer) to get to that ruling? Defendant may think of paying its lawyer as one of several "transaction costs" of further litigation. As the Supreme Court said, using the language of litigation risk analysis, "Most defendants are unlikely to settle unless the cost of the predicted judgment, discounted by its probability, plus the transaction costs of further litigation, are greater than the cost of the settlement package."[253]

### *(c) Additional Valuation Factors in Many Cases*

Expected value calculations get more complicated as more factors are added. The previous subsection's lake-pollution example is extraordinarily simple because it assumes only two possible rulings by the court: injunction or defendant's verdict. In much litigation, by contrast, the possible judicial rulings are many. For example, if the plaintiff seeks money damages for pain and suffering or future medical expenses, precise calculations will have to assign a probability that the court will award $1, a probability that the court will award $2, a probability that the court will award $3, and so on, all the way up to billions of dollars. Of course, such elaborate calculations would be silly because the time spent doing them would yield little additional accuracy.

On the other hand, sometimes money damages can be predicted with great confidence as in a simple collection action for money owed by a customer who did not pay for goods or services rendered. And even in cases where the amount of money damages is more speculative or debatable, case valuation does require an estimate of the likely dollar amount of a verdict, and the chance of a verdict amount far from the likely verdict.[254] Asking the chance of a verdict amount far from the likely verdict is something like asking "How

---

[252] Michaela Keet, Heather Dianne Heavin & John Lande, Litigation Interest and Risk Assessment: Help Your Clients Make Good Litigation Decisions 72 (2020).

[253] Evans v. Jeff D., 475 U.S. 717, 734 (1986).

[254] Michael Moffitt, Settlement Malpractice, 86 U. Chi. L. Rev. 1825, 1863 (2019) ("A client who is told simply that his case is 'worth $1,500,000' has no sense of the shape of the distribution curve leading to this probabilistic conclusion, and even no sense of the likelihood of a $0 recovery or some other extreme outcome").

steep is the (presumably-bell-shaped) curve of expected verdicts?" This question is, because of risk aversion (§ 1.37), sometimes almost as important a question as the amount of the expected verdict.

Lawyers often estimate money damages by talking with each other and reading reports of similar cases. For example, "using Westlaw's Litigation Analytics tools or Lex Machina (a Lexis-Nexis product), damages and awards for certain case types are available in an accessible, charted format."[255] In the personal-injury field, lawyers can obtain published reports showing in great detail the facts and the dollar amounts of verdicts in various categories of cases.[256]

In addition to avoiding the challenges of estimating money damages, the lake-pollution example's simplicity is also achieved by assuming away questions about:

- attitudes toward risk (§ 1.37),
- discounting to *present value*,[257]
- legal fees (§ 1.36(b)), including possibly having to pay some of the opposing side's legal fees,[258]

---

[255] Jacqueline Perrotta and Frank Proscia, Use of Quantitative Data in ADR, 40 Alternatives to High Cost Litig. 24 (2022). See also Lex Machina, LexisNexis, https://www.lexisnexis.com/en-us/products/lex-machina.page [http://perma.cc/3YE2-7Y76]; Westlaw Case Evaluator, https://store.legal.thomsonreuters.com/law-products/westlaw-legal-research/case-evaluator [http://perma.cc/CU83-867U].

[256] Personal injury verdicts appear in publications such as the Personal Injury Valuation Handbooks and Personal Injury Verdict Reviews. Thompson Reuters, Personal Injury Valuation Handbooks, https://www.westlaw.com/Browse/Home/JuryVerdictsSettlements/PersonalInjuryValuationHandbook?transitionType=Default&contextData=(sc.Default)&VR=3.0&RS=cblt1.0 (last visited Mar. 9, 2026); Thompson Reuters, Personal Injury Verdict Reviews, https://www.westlaw.com/Browse/Home/SecondarySources/LegalNewspapersNewsletters/PersonalInjuryVerdictReviews?transitionType=Default&contextData=(sc.Default)&VR=3.0&RS=cblt1.0 (last visited Mar. 9, 2026). ALM Verdict Search Reporter created a website for the legal professionals to be able to search various verdicts and settlements, covering both plaintiff and defense information. ALM Intelligence, Verdict Search, www.verdictsearch.com (last visited Aug.16, 2022).

[257] Jeffrey J. Haas, Corporate Finance ch. 4 (2021) ("If future value lies on one side of the valuation coin, then present value (PV) lies on the other. PV is simply a lump sum of money to be received or paid in the future valued in today's dollars. . . . In determining PV, we move backward in time—from a future date back to today—through the process of discounting.")

[258] Adding to the complexity financial costs pose for the settlement/litigation choice is Federal Rule of Civil Procedure 68, which has many state counterparts and variants. Rule 68 provides that a plaintiff who rejects the defendant's settlement offer and then receives a judgment "not more favorable than the offer" must pay the defendant's court costs and fees incurred after the offer. See, e.g., Marek v. Chesney, 473 U.S. 1 (1985) (civil rights plaintiff's statutory right to attorney's fees lost when amount of Rule 68 offer was higher than eventual judgment for damages but lower than judgment for damages plus otherwise-recoverable attorney's fees); Gurule v. Land Guardian, Inc., 912 F.3d 252, 260 (5th Cir. 2018) (affirming reduction in plaintiff's award of attorney fees from defendant because plaintiff rejected defendant's offer of judgement in the amount of $3,133.44, but the jury returned an award for only

- costs of litigating, other than money and time, such as stress or lost privacy (§ 1.35(a)),
- benefits of litigating, such as a favorable precedent or an imposing reputation (§ 1.35(a)), and
- reconsidering the settlement/litigation choice at different times in the litigation process (§ 1.35(d)).

Each of these topics is an additional factor that must be added to the rational litigant's calculation (§ 1.35(b)). The rational litigant must, at least implicitly, place a numerical value on each. The numerical value will not necessarily be expressed in terms of money because not all tradeoffs involve money. There may be a tradeoff between, for example, plaintiff's time spent on a defamation case and the reputational improvements the case brings. So, the rational plaintiff must determine where to strike the balance: how much time is worth how much reputational improvement? The rational litigant must, at least implicitly, quantify the value she places on both time and reputational improvement.

### *(d) Changes in Case Valuation During Litigation*

The previous subsection considers the many difficult predictions lawyers must make to help their clients value a case. Making these predictions at the start of litigation, when "uncertainty is great,"[259] may lead to a different case valuation than the valuation that results from answering these questions months or years into litigation (or arbitration) of a case. Litigation's pleadings, discovery, and pre-trial rulings may change a lawyer's prediction about the likely results of litigation.[260] For example, a court's denial of a defendant's motion to

$1,131.39); Wichita Firemen's Relief Ass'n v. Kansas City Life Ins. Co., 737 F. App'x 865, 872 (10th Cir. 2018) (affirming award of post-settlement costs to defendant after its settlement offer of $101,000 was rejected by plaintiff who then won jury award of $100,000).

[259] Robert J. Rhee, A Price Theory of Legal Bargaining: An Inquiry into the Selection of Settlement and Litigation Under Uncertainty, 56 Emory L.J. 619, 674 (2006).

[260] Tim A. Baker, Sizing Up Settlement: How Much Do the Merits of A Dispute Really Matter?, 24 Harv. Negot. L. Rev. 253, 269–70 (2019) ("The settlement value for a case varies over the course of the life cycle of a dispute or a lawsuit [due to] factors such as: (a) favorable witness testimony in a deposition, (b) obtaining helpful admissions found in the opposing party's document production, (c) defeating a Daubert motion where one side sought to exclude the other's expert witness, (d) the court's ruling on discovery and dispositive motions, and (e) the court's ruling on motions in limine governing the introduction or exclusion of witnesses and/or documents as exhibits."); Hayward v. Superior Ct., 206 Cal. Rptr. 3d 102, 141 (Ct. App. 2016) ("It is virtually a truism that parties considering settlement after a lengthy period of litigation take into consideration the court's rulings to that point; those rulings tell the parties where they stand on whatever issues have been determined, providing some basis for assessing the strengths and weaknesses of their respective cases and anticipating the outcome of further rulings").

dismiss not only raises the chance of an eventual plaintiff's verdict but may in the U.S. also enable the plaintiff to engage in extensive discovery, imposing production costs on the defendant far above discovery's costs to plaintiff. Both the rising chance of a plaintiff's verdict and the uneven rise in discovery costs should raise the value each party places on the case because each is a reason the defendant should be willing to pay more to resolve the case.[261]

Moreover, the weight or confidence with which lawyers can predict litigation outcomes tends to rise during litigation. So even if a lawyer expects the same outcome years into litigating as she did at the start of a case, the lawyer and her client may have needed those years of additional information generated by litigation's pleadings, discovery, and pre-trial rulings to feel sure enough about what settlement gives up (the option to keep litigating[262]) to settle. So, in many cases that settle, "litigation is not a waste, but rather an essential ingredient of the dispute resolution process."[263]

In addition, the passage of time during litigation may change the client's attitude toward the opposing party or the dispute. Some parties get worn down or distracted, while others become more committed to victory. So, the case's value should be considered anew in light of such developments. Whether to make or accept a particular settlement offer should be considered, and reconsidered, throughout litigation because the answer may change during litigation.

The choice of whether to make a settlement offer (and if so, what offer?) or to accept an offer made by the other side can be a difficult judgment call. Lawyers and clients may agonize over the settlement/litigation choice. Sometimes the results of litigation lead to regret: "we should have taken their settlement offer" or "we should have made them a better offer." Conversely, when one does settle, one never knows for sure what would have happened had litigation

---

261 J. Maria Glover, The Federal Rules of Civil Settlement, 87 N.Y.U. L. Rev. 1713, 1731 (2012) ("access to discovery is granted without limitation once a motion to dismiss is denied, enabling claimants to impose significant, asymmetric production costs on the opposing party"); Bell Atl. Corp. v. Twombly, 550 U.S. 544, 559 (2007) ("the threat of discovery expense will push cost-conscious defendants to settle even anemic cases before reaching those proceedings.")

262 Because the settlement/litigation choice is not a single choice at one point in time, but rather a series of choices over the course of litigation, one can think of plaintiff's claim as a particular sort of asset, a series of options. See, e.g., Christopher R. Drahozal, Arbitration Costs and Contingent Fee Contracts, 59 Vand. L. Rev. 729, 764 n.175 (2006). "[T]he option value of a case will never be lower, and may well be higher, than its expected value." Id. at 763. See also Joseph A. Grundfest & Peter H. Huang, The Unexpected Value of Litigation: A Real Options Perspective, 58 Stan. L. Rev. 1267 (2006).

263 Robert J. Rhee, A Price Theory of Legal Bargaining: An Inquiry into the Selection of Settlement and Litigation Under Uncertainty, 56 Emory L.J. 619, 677–78 (2006).

continued. In this sense, "settlement can be as much of a gamble as trial."[264]

Plaintiffs always face the settlement/litigation choice. At any time—from before a complaint is drafted until a judgment is satisfied[265]—the plaintiff can drop the case (sell the claim) in exchange for whatever consideration the defendant is willing to pay. Defendants, on the other hand, cannot unilaterally end litigation. Settlement requires the plaintiff's consent. But the defendant always has the option of making a more generous offer to the plaintiff. This option faces the defendant from the moment it learns of the dispute until the defendant complies with a judgment against it. In short, settlement options are ever present for both parties.

This is so widely appreciated by lawyers who handle large, time-consuming cases that the process of settlement negotiation—from the first offer through many counteroffers back and forth and then finally to an offer that is accepted—may take years. As one lawyer put it,

> It is all negotiation from the time suit is filed. You are constantly negotiating or setting up the negotiation. It doesn't just happen. You are negotiating from the outset, .... Negotiations don't occur in a week or a month. They occur in the entire time of the lawsuit. If anyone tells you they aren't negotiating, they really are. Every step in the [litigation] process is a negotiation. You don't call it negotiation but in effect, that's what it is.[266]

Settlement negotiation throughout the litigation process is so common in the U.S. that it has spawned its own word combining the two processes, "litigotiation," which is "the strategic pursuit of a settlement through mobilizing the court process."[267] With lawyers realizing that most cases settle, lawyers understand that each stage of litigation—such as a particular deposition—is an opportunity not only to strengthen their side at trial but also to strengthen their side

---

264 Id. at 624.

265 Settlement can occur after a court has rendered judgment, but this is unlikely to nullify the precedential effect of that judgment, or any opinion written by the court. Compare U.S. Bancorp Mortg. Co. v. Bonner Mall Partnership, 513 U.S. 18 (1994); Re Memorial Hospital of Iowa County, Inc., 862 F.2d 1299 (7th Cir. 1988) ("the judicial system ought not allow the social value of that precedent, created at cost to the public and other litigants, to be a bargaining chip in the process of settlement .... If the parties want to avoid stare decisis and preclusive effects, they need only settle before the district court renders a decision, an outcome our approach encourages."), with Neary v. Regents of University of California, 10 Cal. Rptr.2d 859 (Cal. 1992) (allowing parties to stipulate to reversal of trial court's judgment).

266 John Lande, Good Pretrial Lawyering: Planning to Get to Yes Sooner, Cheaper, and Better, 16 Cardozo J. Conflict Resol. 63, 66 (2014).

267 Marc Galanter, Worlds of Deals: Using Negotiation to Teach About Legal Process, 34 J. Legal Educ. 268, 268 (1984).

in settlement negotiation. Because further litigation is the BATNA (§ 1.5) in settlement negotiation, strengthening one's chances in further litigation simultaneously strengthens one's position in negotiation. An unexpectedly good or bad deposition may well be reflected in the next settlement offer.

## § 1.36 The Lawyer-Client Relationship in Valuing a Case

### *(a) Professional Responsibility*

Section 1.35 shows why valuing a case is often complex and highly uncertain. This complexity and uncertainty can add challenges to the lawyer-client relationship, which is introduced in Section 1.1. Sometimes the client is overly optimistic about the expected results of litigation, so the lawyer tries to serve as an "agent of reality" who brings the client's expectations down to earth.[268] Conversely, in other cases the client benefits from disregarding the lawyer's advice to settle. And in a third group of cases the client settles against the lawyer's advice to keep litigating.

When lawyer and client disagree on the settlement/litigation choice, the lawyer must, as a matter of professional responsibility, defer to the client. The Model Rules of Professional Conduct require a lawyer to disclose to her client all settlement offers received from the other side,[269] and to provide whatever information is "reasonably

---

[268] Marjorie Corman Aaron, Client Science: Bad News and the Fully Informed ADR Client, 32 Alternatives to High Cost Litig. 167, 169 (2014) ("The most challenging and important bad news for a lawyer to convey is a prediction that the other side's arguments or evidence are likely to prevail. Because negative predictions arise in contexts where the client is more likely to have choices and a decision to make, the lawyer's success in conveying them matters most. If the client understands and accepts the bad news prediction, he will carefully consider settlement options and, presumably, make a wise and informed decision"); Jill Schachner Chanen, Reality Checks, 83 ABA J. 60, 64 (November 1997) (quoting lawyer saying, "Lawyers to need to be assertive, to stand up to clients and give them the bad news or tell them the real facts and the real law. But that assertiveness has to be tempered with the objective of trying to solve clients' problems"); Anne MacArthur, Effective Advocacy at Mediation of Personal Injury Cases, Wis. Law., June 2025, at 22, 24–25 (the personal injury "plaintiff's counsel walks a delicate line in supporting the client through the process while also having to control client expectations."); id. ("counsel should discuss the client's expectations while explaining counsel's valuation analysis. Other issues to discuss include the strength of the respective parties' evidence on liability when disputed, the claims being made and in what amount, potential merits-based defenses such as failure to mitigate, and valuation"); id. ("In some cases, clients plan to use claim proceeds for a specific purpose—buying a home, for example. In those instances, the value of what the plaintiff seeks in compensation bears no relationship to claim value."); id. ("From a plaintiff's perspective, these cases are personal and emotional, especially when serious injuries or death result or when the defendant's conduct in causing the occurrence is highly negligent."); id. ("Plaintiffs experience the litigation process as invasive, often feeling as though they are on trial.").

[269] Model Rules of Prof'l Conduct R.1.4, cmt. 2 (2019) ("a lawyer who receives from opposing counsel an offer of settlement in a civil controversy or a proffered plea bargain in a criminal case must promptly inform the client of its substance unless the client has previously indicated that the proposal will be acceptable or unacceptable or has

necessary to permit the client to make informed decisions."[270] The Model Rules also provide that "[a] lawyer shall abide by a client's decision whether to settle a matter."[271] Lawyers, especially litigators, sometimes need to be reminded that the client is the boss. Legally, the relationship between client and lawyer is one of principal and agent. Unless the principal has given the agent authority to make settlement decisions, the agent cannot do so (§ 1.41).

Ultimately, lawyer-client disagreement over the settlement/litigation choice may lead a client to switch lawyers or a lawyer to stop working for the client. However, the lawyer must be aware of limits on the circumstances under which a lawyer may end representation of a client.[272] Lawyer-client disagreement over the settlement/litigation choice may continue even after the client has

authorized the lawyer to accept or to reject the offer.") See, e.g., In re Disc. Proc. Against Pfefer, 344 P.3d 1200, 1207 (Wash. 2015) (lawyer suspended from practice for six months and conditioned reinstatement on payment of restitution because lawyer failed to communicate settlement offer with client); In re Ballew, 695 S.E.2d 573, 576 (Ga. 2010) (lawyer accepted settlement offer without client knowledge and was subsequently disbarred); In re Steele, 868 A.2d 146, 154–56 (D.C. App. 2005) (lawyer suspended from practice for three years and ordered to pay restitution because, among other disciplinary incidents, lawyer failed to inform client of initial settlement offer); In re Cardenas, 791 P.2d 1032, 1033 (Ariz. 1990) (lawyer suspended from practice and ordered to pay client restitution because, among other things, lawyer "failed to inform [client] of settlement offers received from the Defendants, including a settlement offer in the amount of $20,000.00 or to consult with [client] prior to rejecting the same.")

[270] Model Rules of Profl Conduct R.1.4(b) (2019).

[271] Id. R.1.2(a). Anne MacArthur, Effective Advocacy at Mediation of Personal Injury Cases, Wis. Law., June 2025, at 22, 24–25 (personal injury plaintiff's "Counsel must explain the implications of the offer and document the file if the client, against the lawyer's advice, does not agree to settle.")

[272] See Model Rules of Profl Conduct R.1.16 (2020); Byrd v. District of Columbia, 271 F. Supp. 2d 174 (D.D.C. 2003) (denying lawyer's motion to withdraw). Compare In re Petition for Distribution of Attorney's Fees between Stowman L. Firm, P.A., 870 N.W.2d 755, 766 (Minn. 2015) ("the refusal of a client to accept a settlement offer in a civil case does not constitute good cause to withdraw"), with McKenna v. Ass'n of Apt. Owners of Elima Lani, 148 Hawai'i 233, 236 (2020) (allowing lawyer to withdrawal after client told court that client agreed to terms of settlement but then refused to sign written agreement reflecting those terms); Barros v. Natl. R.R. Passenger Corp., No. 18 Civ. 3394, 2020 WL 6581184, at *5 (S.D.N.Y. Nov. 10, 2020) (allowing attorney to withdraw where attorney and client "were in conflict about the nature of the case," client refused to accept settlement offer as suggested by attorney, and client questioned attorney's "ability to pursue the case and . . . they had disagreements on how to proceed with the case, especially as to discovery and the value of a further settlement offer." "Under New York law, good cause for withdrawal exists where there are irreconcilable differences with respect to the proper course to be pursued in the litigation [and] where the client flatly challenged counsel's loyalty and professional integrity[.]" (internal citations omitted)). Compare Haines v. Liggett Group, Inc., 814 F. Supp. 414, 427 (D.N.J. 1993) (denying contingent-fee plaintiffs' law firm's motion to withdraw); In re L.J.B., No. 21CA2007, 2023 WL 12057373, at *8 (Colo. App. Apr. 27, 2023) (attorney not allowed to withdraw with insufficient time for client "to find another attorney to represent him in the settlement conference."), with Smith v. R.J. Reynolds Tobacco Co., 630 A.2d 820 (N.J. Super. Ct. App. Div. 1993) (granting motion to withdraw by similarly-situated law firm).

settled. Some clients have sued their lawyers for malpractice in negotiating the settlement.[273]

A lawyer's obligation to defer to the client about the settlement/litigation choice remains even when the client's decision harms the lawyer. An example comes from the Supreme Court case of *Evans v. Jeff D.*,[274] which involved a claim under a statute providing that prevailing plaintiffs are entitled to have their attorneys' fees paid by the defendant. The defendants' settlement offer provided virtually all the relief plaintiffs had sought in their complaint, but defendants conditioned this offer on a waiver by the plaintiffs of their right to have their attorneys' fees paid by the defendant.[275] The plaintiffs followed the recommendation of their lawyer to accept the settlement offer but then asked the court to order the defendants to pay the plaintiffs' legal fees anyhow. The Supreme Court denied that request. Plaintiffs contended that their lawyer faced an "ethical dilemma" when defendants offered "relief greater than that which he could reasonably have been expected to obtain for his clients at trial (if only he would stipulate to a waiver of the statutory fee award)."[276] The Court rejected this contention:

---

[273] Compare Muhammad v. Strassburger, McKenna, Messer, Shilobod and Gutnick, 587 A.2d 1346 (Pa. 1991) (immunizing lawyer from malpractice claim of negligence in negotiating settlement); id. at 1348 ("we will not permit a suit to be filed by a dissatisfied plaintiff against his attorney following a settlement to which that plaintiff agreed, unless that plaintiff can show he was fraudulently induced to settle the original action. An action should not lie against an attorney for malpractice based on negligence and/or contract principles when that client has agreed to a settlement. Rather, only cases of fraud should be actionable"), with Khalil v. Williams, 278 A.3d 859, 861 (Pa. 2022) (*Muhammad* "held that a plaintiff may not sue his attorney on the basis of the adequacy of a settlement to which the plaintiff agreed, unless the plaintiff alleges the settlement was the result of fraud"); id. at 872 (reversing dismissal of complaint "not merely challenging the amount of her settlement" but rather alleging that her lawyer "provided incorrect legal advice regarding the scope and effect the Travelers Release," so "*Muhammad*'s bar on lawsuits based on the adequacy of a settlement is not implicated in this case."); White v. Jungbauer, 128 P.3d 263, 265 (Colo. App. 2005) ("We are not persuaded that fear of malpractice suits will make lawyers reluctant to settle cases, nor are we persuaded that prohibition of such suits in settled cases is necessary to encourage settlements."); id. ("Malpractice lawsuits arising out of settlement have proceeded before Colorado courts in the past, and we see no reason to bar such suits at this time"); Grayson v. Wofsey, Rosen, Kweskin and Kuriansky, 646 A.2d 195 (Conn. 1994) (affirming judgment against lawyer on such a malpractice claim); Wassall v. DeCaro, 91 F.3d 443 (3d Cir. 1996) (plaintiffs could maintain malpractice action against attorney after agreeing to dismissal, based on failure to prosecute, of defamation action in which he represented them); Meyer v. Wagner, 429 Mass. 410, 419, 709 N.E.2d 784, 791 (1999) (adopting *Grayson*'s rule that "where a client establishes that his or her attorney, in advising on the settlement of a divorce action, has failed to exercise the degree of skill and care of the average qualified lawyer, and that the failure has resulted in loss or damage to the client, the client is entitled to recover even if the settlement has received judicial approval")

[274] 475 U.S. 717 (1986).

[275] Id. at 722.

[276] Id. at 727.

> we do not believe that the "dilemma" was an "ethical" one in the sense that Johnson [the plaintiffs' lawyer] had to choose between conflicting duties under the prevailing norms of professional conduct. Plainly, Johnson had no ethical obligation to seek a statutory fee award. His ethical duty was to serve his clients loyally and competently. Since the proposal to settle the merits was more favorable than the probable outcome of the trial, Johnson's decision to recommend acceptance was consistent with the highest standards of our profession.[277]

The *Evans* case is just one example of a lawyer's financial interests differing from their client's interests with respect to the settlement/litigation choice. Other examples are discussed next.

### *(b) Legal Fees*

#### *(1) Hourly Billing*

Lawyers who bill by the hour are sometimes thought to resist settlement early in litigation.[278] Pleadings, discovery, and motion practice can generate lots of billable hours and settling early in the case deprives the lawyer of this income. Of course, a lawyer can only work and bill so many hours. So, an early settlement may not reduce the income of a lawyer who has other cases, because the hours she would have worked and billed on the settling case she, instead, works and bills on another case. But this fails to account for firm structure. Most lawyers who bill by the hour are not solo practitioners; they are owners (members, partners, or shareholders) or employees (associates, of counsel, staff attorneys) of a law firm. While an individual lawyer can only bill so many hours, the number of hours a firm can bill is nearly limitless because the firm can continue to add lawyers. A law firm then seems to have a financial incentive to avoid early settlement when billing by the hour.

---

277 Id. at 727–28. See also Willis v. Gov't Accountability Off., 448 F.3d 1341, 1346 (Fed. Cir. 2006) ("*Evans* establishes that only the prevailing party and not the attorney has the right to assert a claim for attorney's fees under the statute") (settlement condition waived attorney's fees); Staton v. Boeing Co., 327 F.3d 938, 972 (9th Cir. 2003) ("in a class action involving both a statutory fee-shifting provision and an actual or putative common fund, the parties may negotiate and settle the amount of statutory fees along with the merits of the case, as permitted by *Evans*. . . . Alternatively, the parties may negotiate and agree to the value of a common fund (which will ordinarily include an amount representing an estimated hypothetical award of statutory fees) and provide that, subsequently, class counsel will apply to the court for an award from the fund, using common fund fee principles. In those circumstances, the agreement as a whole does not stand or fall on the amount of fees. Instead, after the court determines the reasonable amount of attorneys' fees, all the remaining value of the fund belongs to the class rather than reverting to the defendant.").

278 Edward Brunet, Charles B. Craver & Ellen Deason, Alternative Dispute Resolution: The Advocate's Perspective 27 (5th ed. 2016).

However, a constraint on a firm that seeks to prolong litigation to increase billable hours is competition from other lawyers. Clients who believe their law firms are needlessly prolonging litigation can switch to another firm. This switch can occur during a single case or before the next case. Clients who litigate frequently, such as insurance companies, are particularly adept at setting law firms against each other to keep legal fees down.[279] Clients who litigate rarely seem to be more vulnerable to lawyers who prolong litigation to increase their billable hours because such clients probably cannot easily obtain reliable information about the cost-effectiveness of various law firms. However, many clients who litigate rarely avoid these issues of hourly billing because they hire a lawyer on a contingent fee or fixed fee.

*(2) Contingency Fees*

Contingent fees "are common in a variety of settings, such as consumer protection, personal injury, and civil rights."[280] Suppose Plaintiff's fee agreement entitles her lawyer to receive a contingency fee of one-fourth of the recovery, however that recovery is obtained. Also suppose that Plaintiff's lawyer must bear the expenses of litigation (such as travel, fees charged by courts, investigators, expert witnesses, etc.), regardless of the outcome of litigation. These costs will be higher if litigation continues through trial than if a settlement is obtained before trial. Thus, Plaintiff's lawyer has a financial incentive to settle, even at an amount somewhat less than the expected result of trial. In other words, Plaintiff's lawyer has an incentive to settle at a lower price than is in her client's interest.

---

[279] See, e.g., Joseph M. Schreiber, Alternative Fee Structures: When Breaking the Mold Makes Sense, 57 Hous. Law. 22 (March/April 2020) ("[L]arge defendant[s] (such as an insurance company or Fortune 500 defendant) with market power—because that defendant has lots of legal work—will negotiate down the list rate."); Herbert M. Kritzer, The Commodification of Insurance Defense Practice, 59 Vand. L. Rev. 2053, 2055 (2006) ("insurance companies have come to view the more routine work of insurance defense as something to be purchased in a marketplace where there are a large number of interchangeable providers. Loyalty between buyer and seller, to the extent that it had been an important element of the relationship, has faded. Today, insurance companies frequently shop for the best deal").

[280] Wiley v. Portfolio Recovery Assocs., LLC, No. 20-CV-00737, 2022 WL 903207, at *5 (D. Minn. Mar. 28, 2022). See also In re Domestic Drywall Antitrust Litig., No. 13-MD-2437, 2018 WL 3439454, at *20 (E.D. Pa. July 17, 2018) ("Under many precedents, the general rubric in this geographical area is that a 1/3 attorneys' fee is often the standard in contingent fee cases in 'routine' personal injury and product liability cases, plus reimbursement to counsel for expenses."); David Goguen, Lawyers' Fees in Your Personal Injury Case, ALLLAW, https://www.alllaw.com/articles/nolo/personal-injury/lawyers-fees.html [https://perma.cc/B6QF-RAC7] (indicating that contingency fee pricing structures for legal fees are common in personal injury suits, and that such fees often range from 33% to 40% of the amount the attorney secures in settlement).

Consider a simple example.[281] Plaintiff's lawyer "expects" the case to yield a $100,000 judgment because she predicts a fifty-percent chance of a $200,000 judgment and a fifty-percent chance of a judgment for Defendant. If Plaintiff's lawyer's fee agreement entitles her to one-fourth of any recovery, then she expects to earn $25,000 if she pursues litigation. Suppose Defendant offers $80,000 to settle the case. Assuming that Plaintiff is *risk-neutral* (§ 1.37) and ignoring the *time-value of money* (§ 1.10(b)), Plaintiff's interests would not be served by accepting this offer. Plaintiff would rather have three-fourths of $100,000 ($75,000) than three-fourths of $80,000 ($60,000). However, accepting the settlement offer would be in the interest of Plaintiff's lawyer if the cost of litigating further is expected to be, for example, $10,000. By settling, Plaintiff's lawyer will get one-fourth of $80,000 ($20,000). By litigating further, Plaintiff's lawyer expects to get one-fourth of $100,000 ($25,000) but will have to pay $10,000 in litigation costs. That leaves $15,000, which is less than the $20,000 the lawyer gets by settling.

The Model Rules of Professional Conduct permit lawyers to pay the expenses of litigation only for indigent clients.[282] But, no matter who the client, "a lawyer may advance court costs and expenses of litigation the repayment of which may be contingent on the outcome of the matter."[283] Accordingly, many plaintiffs' contingency fee agreements provide that the lawyer shall bear the costs of litigation if there is no recovery but that any recovery shall be applied first to reimburse the lawyer for expenses, then the rest is divided according to a formula, such as three-fourths for the client and one-fourth for the lawyer.[284] Such an arrangement also gives the plaintiff's lawyer

---

[281] See § 1.35 (discussing more complicated and realistic models).

[282] Model Rules of Professional Conduct R.1.8(e) (2020) ("A lawyer shall not provide financial assistance to a client in connection with pending or contemplated litigation, except that: . . . (2) a lawyer representing an indigent client may pay court costs and expenses of litigation on behalf of the client. . .").

[283] Id. R.1.8(e)(1). This "advance" is, in practice, rarely repaid in the absence of a recovery. See Lester Brickman, Effective Hourly Rates of Contingency-Fee Lawyers: Competing Data and Non-Competitive Fees, 81 Wash. U. L.Q. 653, 735 (2003) ("many firms make no effort to seek reimbursement of expenses if there is no recovery"); Christopher R. Drahozal, Arbitration Costs and Contingent Fee Contracts, 59 Vand. L. Rev. 729, 768 (2006) ("A common practice in contingent fee cases is for the claimant's attorney to advance on behalf of the client the costs of litigating the case. If the claimant prevails, the attorney obtains repayment of the advances from the judgment or award. If the claimant does not prevail, the attorney rarely if ever seeks to recover the advance."); Samuel R. Gross & Kent D. Syverud, Getting to No: A Study of Settlement Negotiations and the Selection of Cases for Trial, 90 Mich. L. Rev. 319, 349 n.71 (1991) ("In practice, attorneys rarely attempt to collect expenses from personal injury clients, both because it would be impractical and because such a practice might drive away future clients").

[284] Such an arrangement is known as a "net fee" contract because the lawyer's percentage is applied to the recovery net of expenses. More favorable to the lawyer is the "gross fee" contract, which applies the lawyer's percentage to the gross recovery

an incentive to settle at a lower price than is in the client's interest,[285] but this divergence of interests is less pronounced than in the situation of an indigent plaintiff whose lawyer pays the expenses of litigation even if the plaintiff recovers from the defendant.

While the contingent fee agreements discussed thus far give the plaintiff's lawyer an incentive to settle at a lower price than is in the client's interest, this divergence of interests can be narrowed with a contingency fee agreement that gives the lawyer a higher percentage if the recovery is obtained through trial than if it is obtained through settlement. Accordingly, many contingency agreements give the lawyer a higher percentage of trial proceeds than of settlement proceeds.[286]

*(3) Retainers and Other Fixed-Fees*

Some lawyers agree to handle a particular case (or even all the client's litigation during a certain time period) for a fixed payment.[287] Such flat fee "retainer" arrangements give the lawyer an incentive to settle and the client an incentive to shun settlement.

---

and then requires the client to reimburse the lawyer for expenses out of the client's portion of the gross recovery.

285 In the example in the text, assume that Plaintiff's lawyer "expects" a $100,000 judgment because she predicts a fifty-percent chance of a $200,000 judgment and a fifty-percent chance of a judgment for Defendant. If Plaintiff wins, her lawyer will get one-fourth of $190,000 ($47,500—because the first $10,000 of the $200,000 judgment is applied to the expenses of litigating—and if Plaintiff loses her lawyer will lose $10,000. As each of these outcomes is equally likely to occur, the expected value to Plaintiff's lawyer of litigating is (47,500/2) + (–10,000/2), which equals $18,750. That is less than the one-fourth of $80,000 ($20,000) Plaintiff's lawyer will get from a settlement, although not as much less as in the example in the text.

286 Fernandez v. Victoria Secret Stores, LLC, No. CV 06-4149-MMM(SHx), 2008 WL 8150856, at *16 n.59 (C.D. Cal. July 21, 2008) (fees representing one-third of the recovery are justified based on study showing that standard contingency fee rates are 33% if the case settles before trial, 40% if a trial commences, and 50% if trial is completed); Herbert M. Kritzer, Seven Dogged Myths Concerning Contingency Fees, 80 Wash. U. L. Rev. 739, 757 n.60 (2002) ("Standard contingency fees are typically at least one-third, forty and even fifty percent in cases settled before trial and often more than fifty percent [of the net recovery] in cases which go to trial.")

287 Alan S. Gutterman, Business Transactions Solutions § 2.25 (Sept. 2022) ("Another group of alternative fee arrangements falls under the category of 'flat fee' models. The most common example is a fixed fee arrangement that calls for payment of a set fee for an entire engagement, or a defined project. The fee is payable regardless of the number of hours spent on the matter by the attorney. A variation of this theme is a retainer arrangement that calls for the attorney or firm to perform a defined set of services for an agreed period of time for a fixed fee."); Form Flat-Fee Agreement, Colorado Judicial Branch, https://www.coloradojudicial.gov/sites/default/files/2024-06/Form%20Flat%20Fee%20Agreement%20for%2011-4-16%20meeting.pdf (last visited Mar. 9, 2026) (This is a flat fee arrangement. Client will pay Lawyer [or Firm] $_______________ for Lawyer's [or Firm's] performance of the Services described . . . .").

### *(4) Legal Fees Paid Through Liability Insurance*

In many civil cases, the defendant has liability insurance. An insured defendant has generally contracted to have its insurer pay to defend the claim and also to pay any settlement or judgment against the defendant up to the amount of the insurance policy. However, the typical liability insurance policy gives the insurer control over settlement and litigation.[288] The insurer hires the defense lawyer and, importantly, the lawyer's client may thus be not only the defendant, but also the defendant's insurer.[289]

In cases where the claims made against an insured defendant are claims of the type that would be within the coverage of a liability policy, even if the total liability exposure may exceed the policy limit, the insurer has the responsibility for the defense and the right to control the defense. If, however, the defendant's exposure exceeds the policy limit, the insurer will generally permit the defendant's private counsel to participate in an advisory capacity.[290] Within broad limits, the insurer decides whether to make settlement offers and, if so, at

---

[288] See, e.g., 14A Couch on Ins. § 203:3 (3d ed. 2022) ("A provision which grants the insurer the right to make such investigation, negotiation, and settlement of any claim or suit as it deems expedient is generally recognized as valid and vests the insurer with the exclusive control over settlement negotiations and defense of litigation. Such exclusive control must be exercised within the boundaries of good faith, but depending on the language of the policy, the insurer may be permitted to settle within policy limits without regard for whether the underlying claim was meritorious or whether the settlement will damage the reputation of the insured"); John F. Dobbyn & Christopher C. French, Insurance Law in a Nutshell 389 (6th ed. 2021) ("Under many lines of liability insurance, it is customary for an insurer to include a clause in the policy that provides the insurer with a right and an obligation to defend any action brought by a third party against the policyholder on any cause of action that potentially falls within coverage under the policy, 'even if any of the allegations of the suit are groundless, false or fraudulent.' It is accordingly possible that the insurer could be called upon to defend an action with respect to which there would be no obligation to pay an indemnity amount. This is because the obligation to defend arises whenever an action is filed against the policyholder in which the allegations of the third party, if successful, would bring the claim within policy coverage, while the indemnity obligation arises only if the policyholder ultimately has an actual legal obligation to pay a claim covered by the policy.").

[289] James M. Fischer et al., Keeton, Widiss and Fischer's Insurance Law: A Guide to Fundamental Principles, Legal Doctrines, and Commercial Practices 702 (2d ed. 2016) ("Much ink has been spilt over the issue whether insurer-retained defense counsel represents the insured and the insurer or only the insured. The general consensus is that the insured is defense counsel's client, the debate is over whether the insurer is also a client. The often-stated view is that the insurer is also a client, but the cases are mixed." (footnotes omitted)).

[290] John F. Dobbyn & Christopher C. French, Insurance Law in a Nutshell 401 (6th ed. 2021) ("In cases in which the only claims pressed against the policyholder are claims of the type that would be within coverage of a liability policy, even if the total possible exposure of the policyholder exceeds the policy limit, the insurer has both the responsibility for the defense and the right to control the defense. An insurer will, however, generally permit the policyholder's private counsel to participate in an advisory capacity where the policyholder's exposure exceeds the policy limit.").

what amount.[291] This arrangement can create a divergence between the interests of Defendant and its insurer.[292]

Suppose, for example, that the limit of the insurance policy is $150,000 and Defendant and its insurer each "expect" a $100,000 judgment because each predicts a fifty-percent chance of a $200,000 judgment and a fifty-percent chance of a judgment for Defendant. In this case, the insurer's incentive is to offer Plaintiff at most $100,000 (the expected value of the claim) and probably much less than that to strengthen the insurer's reputation as a fierce litigator.[293] While the insurer's incentive is to offer at most $100,000, Defendant's incentive is for its insurer to offer $150,000, the policy limit. The more money offered by the insurer, the more likely Plaintiff is to accept, and offering $150,000 does not cost Defendant any more than offering $100,000 because it is its insurer's money. By contrast, Defendant does pay its own money if its insurer's refusal to make a high settlement offer causes Plaintiff to go to trial and Plaintiff wins a judgment above $150,000. Defendant is personally liable for the excess. This sort of divergence between the interests of Defendant and those of its insurer can create troubling incentives for the lawyer who was hired by the insurer and likely hopes to be hired again by the insurer. In some cases, this sort of conflict of interests between insurer and insured "will require the insurer to cede control of the defense to the insured; yet the insurer will remain responsible for the cost of the defense.".[294]

## § 1.37 Risk Aversion and Diversification in Case Valuation

### *(a) Risk Aversion*

An important factor influencing case valuation (§ 1.35), and thus a party's *bottom line* (§ 1.6) in settlement negotiation, is risk aversion. *Risk aversion* is the willingness to pay for increased certainty. Consider a choice between:

---

291 Steven Plitt et al., 14A Couch on Insurance § 203 (3d ed. 2022). Id. § 203:14 ("An insurer's right to settle claims against its insured must be exercised in good faith and that duty of good faith requires the insurer to act reasonably in protecting the insured from liability in excess of the policy limits. The implied covenant of good faith and fair dealing requires an insurer to settle where appropriate even if the duty is not expressly imposed in the terms of the policy.").

292 Id. § 203:1 ("One of the most complex postloss issues in the realm of third-party insurance involves the question of the relative rights of the insurer and the insured in determining when to settle a claim or suit against the insured. The interests of the two parties are not identical and may often be at variance.").

293 The insurer is very much a *repeat player* litigant, so it benefits from a reputation that intimidates future adversaries (§ 1.35(c)).

294 James M. Fischer et al., Keeton, Widiss and Fischer's Insurance Law: A Guide to Fundamental Principles, Legal Doctrines, and Commercial Practices 780 (2d ed. 2016).

(A) receiving one million dollars, or

(B) flipping a coin and receiving two million dollars if it comes up heads and receiving nothing if it comes up tails.

Choosing (A) reveals risk-aversion. The *expected value* (§ 1.7) of each choice is one million dollars because choice (B) entails a fifty-percent chance of receiving two million dollars and a fifty-percent chance of receiving nothing. So, a risk-neutral person would find choices (A) and (B) equally appealing.

If choice (A) was $900,000, a *risk-neutral* person would choose (B) with its higher expected value of one million dollars. Yet many people would choose a certain $900,000 over a fifty-percent chance of two million dollars, that is, many people would pay for increased certainty. Risk-aversion manifests itself in countless ways. People reveal their risk-aversion when they buy insurance, or when they invest in bonds rather than stocks. The same person who is risk-averse in some contexts may be *risk-seeking* in other contexts. Risk-seeking behavior, such as gambling, is the willingness to pay for decreased certainty.

The more risk-averse you are, the more you are willing to pay for the increased certainty of a settlement over the uncertainty of further litigation. Consider the unrealistically simple case of a plaintiff who, after consulting her lawyer, believes she has a fifty-percent chance of a verdict awarding her two million dollars and a fifty-percent chance of a defendant's verdict. Accepting a settlement offer of one million dollars would allow Plaintiff to increase certainty without paying anything because the expected value of the claim she releases (.5 × $2,000,000) is equal to the money she receives. But how much less than one million dollars would Plaintiff accept in settlement? That is the amount Plaintiff is willing to pay to increase certainty in this situation. And that amount is higher than it would be if determined by someone less risk-averse. To put it another way, all else equal, the more risk-averse a plaintiff is, the less a defendant needs to offer in settlement to win the plaintiff's acceptance. Conversely, all else equal, the more risk-averse a defendant is, the more a plaintiff can get in settlement. In either direction, risk-aversion is a vulnerability opposing parties can exploit.

Psychological research gives reason to believe that plaintiffs tend to be more risk-averse than defendants because "people tend to make risk-averse decisions when choosing among options that appear to be gains and risk-seeking decisions when choosing among options that appear to be losses."[295] From the plaintiff's perspective,

---

[295] Charles B. Craver, Effective Legal Negotiation and Settlement 32–33 (9th ed. 2020); Maya Steinitz, How Much Is That Lawsuit in the Window? Pricing Legal

the settlement/litigation choice generally appears to be a choice among gains (because the plaintiff gets something from either choice), while from the defendant's perspective, the settlement/litigation choice generally appears to be a choice among losses (because the defendant loses something from either choice).[296]

### *(b) Diversification, Including Assigning and Financing Claims*

Risk, and thus risk-aversion, can be reduced through diversification. Consider two types of plaintiffs: parties who are plaintiffs only once in their lives, such as an individual injured in a car accident, and parties who are frequently plaintiffs, such as a credit card company that brings many debt-collection actions. The one-time plaintiff tends to be more risk-averse than the repeat plaintiff because the repeat plaintiff benefits from *diversification.*

Recall the choice between a certain $900,000 and a fifty-percent coin-flip chance of two million dollars. Now, imagine that this choice is broken down into a million separate choices, each one a choice between ninety cents and a fifty-percent coin-flip chance of two dollars. Many people who would take the certain $900,000 in the first scenario would, in the second scenario, choose the coin flip in each of their million choices. This is a rational response to diversification. Risk is highest when "all of one's eggs are in the same basket." That is the position of the one-time plaintiff who has an enormous stake in one case and no other cases for diversification. In contrast, the repeat plaintiff is faced with something closer to the second scenario of a million coin-flips. The repeat plaintiff has a portfolio of cases, much like a diversified investor has a portfolio of stocks,[297] and thus is likely to be less risk-averse than the one-time plaintiff.

---

Claims, 66 Vand. L. Rev. 1889, 1924 (2013) ("plaintiffs often choose between options that appear to represent gains, while defendants often choose between options that appear to represent losses. As such, plaintiffs are more likely to prefer settlement, the risk-averse option, while defendants are more likely to prefer trial, the risk-seeking option" (citing Chris Guthrie et al., Inside the Judicial Mind, 86 Cornell L. Rev. 777, 794–95 (2001))). Interestingly, the greater risk-aversion when choosing among gains than losses may be reversed when the gain or loss has a very low probability, as in "lawsuits in which the plaintiff's chance of prevailing is very low—lawsuits that are often thought of as 'frivolous'." Russell Korobkin, Negotiation Theory and Strategy 81 (3d ed. 2014) (citing Chris Guthrie, Framing Frivolous Litigation: A Psychological Theory, 67 U. Chi. L. Rev. 163 (2000)).

[296] For experimental evidence indicating that framing a settlement offer as a gain rather than a loss increases the willingness of people (except for lawyers) to accept that offer, see Russell Korobkin & Chris Guthrie, Psychology, Economics, and Settlement: A New Look at the Role of the Lawyer, 76 Tex. L. Rev. 77, 96 (1997).

[297] Robert J. Rhee, A Price Theory of Legal Bargaining: An Inquiry into the Selection of Settlement and Litigation Under Uncertainty, 56 Emory L.J. 619, 686 (2006) ("The practical implication of risk aversion is that repeat players tend to be risk

The paradigm repeat plaintiffs—engaged in "assembly-line litigation"—are "financial services companies attempting to collect on contracts that they have directly with consumers or suits by third-party debt collectors attempting to collect consumer debts that they have purchased from other companies."[298] Such repeat plaintiffs often sue unrepresented defendants, who do not contest the case, which results in a default judgment. When the defendant does appear in court, the settlement "negotiations between debt-collector attorneys and pro se defendants often take the form of hallway conferences. I have witnessed these myself, with a debt-buyer attorney often cornering a defendant—who may not even speak English—in the courtroom hallway and urging them to settle."[299] Eviction cases may similarly involve repeat landlord-plaintiffs' lawyers engaging unrepresented tenant-defendants in hallway negotiations.[300] "Rent court, more than most other courts, is a theater of class conflict in which businesses and their hirelings constitute a class of professional claimants exercising significant advantages over the individual defendants whom they bring before the court, who are poor and poorly situated with respect to the attributes that garner respectful hearing in court rooms."[301]

So-called "debt buyers," who are actually claims buyers, buy claims against debtors.[302] For example, a debt buyer might buy several hospitals' claims for unpaid medical bills, thus pooling those

---

neutral, allowing a portfolio approach toward risk management, a luxury that most people lack.")

[298] Daniel Wilf-Townsend, Assembly-Line Plaintiffs, 135 Harv. L. Rev. 1704, 1709 (2022).

[299] Nina Lea Oishi, Judging Debt: How Judges' Practices in Consumer-Credit Court Undermine Procedural Justice, 133 Yale L.J. Forum 271, 294 (2023).

[300] Erica L. Fox, Alone in the Hallway: Challenges to Effective Self-Representation in Negotiation, 1 Harv. Negot. L. Rev. 85, 111 (1996) ("In the Boston Housing Court, tenant negotiators do not exercise self-agency effectively."); id. at 93 ("With few exceptions, tenants negotiate directly with a landlord's lawyer, occasionally with their landlord also participating. Nevertheless, many tenants do not perceive that they play an active role in the process"); id. at 92 ("Groups in the hallway are stratified by socio-economic class and authority with the court. In addition to visible discrepancies such as style of dress and color of skin, other palpable distinctions exist between those with more and less privilege").

[301] Barbara Bezdek, Silence in the Court: Participation and Subordination of Poor Tenants' Voices in Legal Process, 20 Hofstra L. Rev. 533, 557 (1992).

[302] See, e.g., Consumer Fin. Prot. Bureau, Fair Debt Collection Practices Act: CFPB Annual Report 2015, at 1, 7–8 (2015), https://files.consumerfinance.gov/f/201503_cfpb-fair-debt-collection-practices-act.pdf (reporting that debt buyers account for close to a third of the debt-collection industry's revenue with earnings over $4 billion dollars); Hannah Lieberman, Uncivil Procedure: How State Court Proceedings Perpetuate Inequality, 35 Yale L. & Pol'y Rev. 257, 262 (2016) ("Debt collection cases start when a lender sells a portfolio of hundreds—sometimes thousands—of delinquent accounts to a third-party debt collector, who buys the portfolio for a fraction of its value. These portfolios may be sold repeatedly. Debt buyers typically work with specialized laws firms that file collection lawsuits in bulk—also hundreds at a time.")

claims together and achieving greater diversification. This is possible because most breach-of-contract claims are assignable.[303] This assignability frees the hospital plaintiff from the *bilateral monopoly* (§ 1.3) of most settlement negotiations in which the plaintiff can only sell its claim to the defendant because the hospital can sell its claim to the debt buyer. But the ultimate settlement negotiation remains a bilateral monopoly because any settlement agreement must be between Defendant and whoever currently owns the claim against Defendant—whether that is the original owner of the claim (the hospital) or an assignee of the claim, like the debt buyer.

While breach of contract claims are generally assignable, many statutory claims and most tort claims for injury to the person or reputation are not assignable.[304] But this restraint on a plaintiff's freedom to sell her claim is partially overcome by the *contingency fee* contract in which the plaintiff sells part of her claim to her lawyer who pays for it with legal services rather than money.[305]

A contingency fee is a way for a plaintiffs' lawyer to sell insurance to her clients. The clients shift some risk to the lawyer in exchange for giving the lawyer a greater payout from a successful case than the lawyer would likely earn charging by the hour. In contrast to the risk averse one-time plaintiff with all his litigation

---

303 See Restatement (Second) of Contracts § 317(2) (1981). Anthony Sebok, Going Bare in the Law of Assignments: When Is an Assignment Champertous?, 14 FIU L. Rev. 85, 86 (2020) ("While the early common law rejected all assignments of a cause of action, regardless of whether it was based in contract or tort, that restriction eventually shrank until courts could state the modern rule was that 'assignability of things [in action] is now the rule; non-assignability, the exception; and this exception is confined to wrongs done to the person, the reputation, or the feelings of the injured party.' ")

304 John Glenn, 6 Am. Jur. 2d Assignments § 46 (Aug. 2022) ("Although choses in action are generally assignable, public policy still invalidates assignments of certain types of choses in action, including personal torts, . . . the right to apply for attorney's fees as the prevailing party in a civil rights case, the right to recover payments made as preferences in bankruptcy proceedings, in some cases, the right to collect a statutory penalty."); id. ("damages for injury to commercial credit and reputation are personal and unassignable, and, depending on the circumstances of the case, economic damages may be purely personal in nature thus precluding assignment. Exceptions to the general rule of assignability are choses in action for wrongs done to the person, the reputation, or the feelings of the injured party, and to contracts of a purely personal nature").

305 See § 1.36(b)(2). Nathaniel Donahue & John Fabian Witt, Tort As Private Administration, 105 Cornell L. Rev. 1093, 1113–14 (2020) ("The contingent fee contract is the most famous type of contract for ownership stakes in the claim. This arrangement, too, has not always been enforceable in American law. Many American jurisdictions in the early nineteenth century viewed contingent fees as champertous and thus prohibited. Only toward the end of the century did these prohibitions give way to the pressure of a growing number of indigent victims of industrial accidents, to the demands for justice among the injured, and to the practical difficulty of regulating lawyers' fees. But since then, the contingent fee contract has allowed plaintiffs to use equity in their claim to gain the services of repeat-play lawyers in the tort claims market.")

eggs in one basket (one case), the plaintiff's lawyer has a portfolio of cases and thus is likely to be less risk-averse than the one-shot client. This is especially true if the lawyer, rather than practicing solo, is part of a firm that spreads risk among its lawyers. This greater risk tolerance of the plaintiffs' lawyer than her average client may be enhanced by the lawyer's desire for trial experience. The plaintiff's lawyer may prefer a million-dollar verdict to a million-dollar settlement because the verdict will help the lawyer's career more or at least provide better stories for her to tell her grandchildren.

Contingency fees permit a plaintiff's lawyer to finance a lawsuit. Other lawsuits are financed by the third-party litigation funding industry. Such a funder lends the plaintiff money the plaintiff is obligated to repay (with interest) only if the plaintiff "ultimately receives compensation for her underlying legal claim."[306]

The previous paragraphs on diversification focus on plaintiffs. Going further to consider both parties to a case allows one to compare the relative diversification of opposing parties. For instance, compounding the challenge for the risk-averse one-time plaintiff is the likelihood that their opponent is a repeat defendant with a portfolio of cases it defends over the years.

> In personal injury, employment, civil rights, and other contexts, . . . defendants often face repeating claims over the same or related conduct. Distributing thousands of products, supervising thousands of employees, or employing policies that affect thousands of people can create a significant volume of litigation. Plaintiffs, on the other hand, are typically in a one-off situation, litigating a single case over a single injury (though their attorneys may have multiple similar cases).[307]

In other words, the risk tolerance of a one-time plaintiff is likely much lower than that of its repeat defendant adversary, which tends to make the plaintiff less willing to "roll the dice" on trial and thus willing to pay more (by reducing the settlement payment they demand) for the certainty of a settlement.[308] And all of that increases

---

[306] Ronen Avraham et al., The MDL Revolution and Consumer Legal Funding, 40 Rev. Litig. 143, 149–50 (2021). "This fact is critical to understanding why such funding has not historically been held to be a 'loan' which is subject to state usury laws. This exemption enables funders to charge higher interest and fees than would be permitted if these advances were ordinary consumer loans." Id.

[307] Dustin B. Benham, Foundational and Contemporary Court Confidentiality, 86 Mo. L. Rev. 211, 214 (2021).

[308] Robert J. Rhee, A Price Theory of Legal Bargaining: An Inquiry into the Selection of Settlement and Litigation Under Uncertainty, 56 Emory L.J. 619, 686 (2006) ("Risk-neutral parties, like insurance companies, will obtain a greater share of any settlement because they can extract yield from the differences in both risk preferences and risk discount. Likewise, if most corporations are repeat players, this

the incentives for such plaintiffs and their lawyers to use the diversification techniques discussed above.

## § 1.38 Cognitive Biases in Case Valuation

Section 1.35 explains how a hypothetical rational litigant, with input from her lawyer, values a case. The extent to which many actual litigants behave like our hypothetical rational litigant is an important question. Cognitive psychological research indicates that many, perhaps nearly all, people make several recurring departures from the rational-choice model.[309] The following biases in judgment and decision-making may affect how a particular litigant or lawyer values a case.

### *(a) Availability Bias*

In thinking about previous cases, people tend to give more weight to the memorable ones, such as those covered by the media, than to more bland and forgettable cases. "[W]hen making predictions, people often fail to compensate for the gap between what is memorable and what is typical."[310]

### *(b) Anchoring Bias*

When some piece of information is the starting point in a person's thinking, that starting point—even if it is totally random—can exert undue influence on the person's subsequent thinking. Many people have a

> tendency to anchor on a salient number and make insufficient adjustments in response to individuating details of the case at hand. For example, if a recent court award for a similar case comes to mind, people may be unduly influenced by this value in their assessment of the present case. Research shows that even when a focal number is not particularly relevant, it can exert a bias on judgment under uncertainty.[311]

*Anchoring* is also discussed in Section 1.16(b).

---

fact has significant implications for whether corporate defendants in tort actions are appropriately deterred by tort law and its remedies.")

309 For discussions of cognitive psychological research and its implications for negotiation, see Robert H. Mnookin, Why Negotiations Fail: An Exploration of Barriers to the Resolution of Conflict, 8 Ohio St. J. on Disp. Resol. 235, 243–47 (1993); Chris Guthrie, Better Settle Than Sorry: The Regret Aversion Theory of Litigation Behavior, 1999 U. Ill. L. Rev. 43, 54–59.

310 Richard Birke and Craig R. Fox, Psychological Principles in Negotiating Civil Settlements, 4 Harv. Negot. L. Rev. 1, 9 (1999).

311 Id. at 10. See also Russell Korobkin, Negotiation Theory and Strategy 60–63 (4th ed. 2024).

### *(c) Egocentric (Self-Serving) Biases*

"[P]eople have great difficulty divorcing themselves from their idiosyncratic role sufficiently to take an objective view of disputes in which they are involved."[312] "Even when negotiators possess complete and shared information, they tend to assess the strength of their case in a self-interested (or 'egocentric') manner."[313] As a result, parties (and their lawyers) tend to be overly optimistic about the strength of their cases. This bias is compounded by the tendency of people to "seek information that confirms rather than discredits their hypotheses, . . . to assimilate data in ways that are consistent with their prior views."[314]

### *(d) Overconfidence Bias*

The tendency toward over-optimism in case valuation is further compounded by "people's tendency to overestimate their ability to control outcomes that are determined by factors outside of their control."[315] This may cause a lawyer to overestimate her ability to influence the outcome of litigation in a way favorable her client by, for example, writing an especially persuasive brief or delivering a stirring closing argument.[316]

---

[312] Richard Birke & Craig R. Fox, Psychological Principles in Negotiating Civil Settlements, 4 Harv. Negot. L. Rev. 1, 14 (1999). See also Russell Korobkin, Negotiation Theory and Strategy 51–57 (4th ed. 2024) (discussing how widespread is the self-serving bias).

[313] Richard Birke & Craig R. Fox, Psychological Principles in Negotiating Civil Settlements, 4 Harv. Negot. L. Rev. 1, 14 (1999).

[314] Id. at 16. See also Michaela Keet, Heather Dianne Heavin & John Lande, Litigation Interest and Risk Assessment: Help Your Clients Make Good Litigation Decisions 9 (2020) ("People often look for, focus on, analyze, and remember information to confirm their preconceptions. Lawyers and parties are especially prone to view data as supporting their cases and undermining the other side's cases.")

[315] Richard Birke & Craig R. Fox, Psychological Principles in Negotiating Civil Settlements, 4 Harv. Negot. L. Rev. at 16. Charles B. Craver, Effective Legal Negotiation and Settlement 36 (9th ed. 2020).

[316] While a lawyer's tendency toward over-optimism is an impediment to accurately valuing a case, over-optimism may be an advantage in negotiating a favorable settlement if it helps the lawyer to project confidence in her case. See § 1.15(b); Oren Bar-Gill, The Evolution and Persistence of Optimism in Litigation, 22 J.L. Econ. & Org. 490, 491 (2006) ("The adaptive force of optimism derives from its function as a commitment device in the pretrial bargaining stage. Optimistic lawyers, by credibly threatening to resort to costly litigation, succeed in extracting more favorable settlements. Therefore, market-selection forces and cultural transmission dynamics dictate an equilibrium with a positive level of optimism.")

## § 1.39 Why Do Most Civil Cases in the U.S. Settle?

### *(a) Case Valuations Determine Bottom Lines, Which Determine Settlement Zones*

Civil litigation in the U.S. usually ends in a settlement, rather than proceeding to a trial verdict or other conclusive ruling by the court.[317] Why do litigants typically settle, rather than pursue litigation to completion? As Section 1.4 notes, agreements occur because, at the time parties make them, each party thinks that making the agreement is better than that party's alternatives. This means, in the context of civil litigation, that settlement agreements occur when each party (Plaintiff and Defendant) believes it will be better off with the settlement than litigating further.[318] The same point applies to settling disputes in arbitration, as those settlements occur when each party (Claimant and Respondent) believes it will be better off with the settlement than arbitrating further. And it applies to settling disputes not yet in litigation or arbitration but likely to go to one of those binding processes of adjudication if the parties do not settle. The following paragraphs speak in terms of a case already in litigation, and the reader can translate them to a case in arbitration or a case likely to go to litigation or arbitration if the parties do not settle.

To reiterate, cases settle only when each party believes it will be better off with the settlement than litigating further. In other words, litigating further is typically the only, and therefore best, alternative to a negotiated agreement (BATNA, § 1.5) of a party engaged in

---

317 While there are difficulties with data collection and classification, in the U.S. generally about two-thirds of civil cases filed in court settle and most of the rest are resolved through non-trial adjudication. See, e.g., J.J. Prescott & Kathryn E. Spier, A Comprehensive Theory of Civil Settlement, 91 N.Y.U. L. Rev. 59, 143 (2016) ("Roughly 19 million civil cases were filed in state courts in 2010. While settlement rates vary by type of case and jurisdiction, generally less than 3% of filed cases reach trial verdict. This figure does not include the countless number of disputes that are resolved without a complaint ever being filed. In a study of 385,000 automobile and general liability insurance claims, approximately 12% were filed as lawsuits or involved insurer litigation costs and approximately 0.6% went to trial or arbitration" (citations omitted)); Jay Tidmarsh, Opting Out of Discovery, 71 Vand. L. Rev. 1801, 1809 (2018) ("in the last fiscal year, only 0.9 percent of federal civil cases reached trial. Perhaps three percent of federal civil cases are dismissed in whole or part on a Rule 12 motion to dismiss. The vast bulk of the remaining civil cases (or remaining claims, in the case of a partial dismissal) end on a Rule 56 motion for summary judgment or with a settlement"); id. at n.44 ("available evidence suggests that summary judgment is granted in ten percent or less of all federal civil cases, meaning that somewhere in the neighborhood of sixty to seventy percent of cases settle."); Lynn Langton & Thomas H. Cohen, Bureau of Justice Statistics, Special Report: Civil Bench and Jury Trials in State Courts, 2005, at 1 (2008), http://bjs.ojp.usdoj.gov/?content/pub/pdf/cbjtsc05.pdf.

318 Richard A. Posner, Economic Analysis of Law 779 (9th ed. 2014) ("As with any contract, a necessary condition for [settlement] negotiations to succeed is that there be a price at which both parties would conclude that agreement would increase their welfare.")

settlement negotiation.[319] Accordingly, Section 1.35 explains, formulating a party's *bottom line* (§ 1.6) in settlement negotiation requires that party to determine the expected result (§ 1.7) of further litigation and then value the differences between what the party would get from that expected result of litigation with what the party can get in settlement negotiation. This is an example of Section 1.6's observation that your *bottom line* in negotiation "should be tied to" your BATNA because agreeing in a negotiation to something worse than your best alternative to it would be "the most basic negotiating mistake—agreeing to a deal when [you] would have been better off walking away from the [negotiating] table with no agreement."[320]

The fact that any agreement must be at least as good for each party as its bottom line means that some, but not all, negotiations will have, even if it is not fully known to the parties, a Zone of Possible Agreement (§ 1.8). The ZOPA is the range of possible deals that are better for each party than its bottom line. Any deal must be within this range. The ZOPA in settlement negotiation is the *settlement zone*.

In contrast, cases lacking a settlement zone are cases in which settlement cannot occur because there is no possible deal each party believes is better for it than the value it places on the case, i.e., further litigation. Suppose, for example, that Plaintiff values the case (§ 1.35) at $600,000 and thus is unwilling to settle for anything less than $600,000, while Defendant values the case at $400,000 and thus is unwilling to settle for anything more than $400,000. Plaintiff's bottom line is $600,000 and Defendant's bottom line is $400,000. No settlement can occur because no possible settlements are acceptable to both parties; no *settlement zone* exists. If this case settles, it will be because one or both of the parties changes its bottom line in a way that creates a settlement zone, for example by Plaintiff dropping her case valuation to $300,000.

---

[319] Alan Scott Rau, Edward F. Sherman & Scott R. Peppet, Processes of Dispute Resolution 89 n.3 (4th ed. 2002) ("In litigation, both parties usually share the same alternative to negotiating a resolution of their dispute: proceeding to court."). See also Paul F. Kirgis, Bargaining with Consequences: Leverage and Coercion in Negotiation, 19 Harv. Negot. L. Rev. 69, 99 (2014) ("Negotiation texts commonly refer to litigation as a BATNA because settlement and litigation are the alternative ways for the plaintiff to receive compensation for his injuries").

[320] Russell Korobkin, A Positive Theory of Legal Negotiation, 88 Geo. L.J. 1789, 1797 (2000).

### (b) Similar Predictions About Litigation Usually Create Settlement Zones

Consider what happens if the parties on opposing sides of a case each reach (with help from their lawyer) the same answers to the questions in Section 1.35(a):

- What is the likelihood the case will be dismissed before trial?
- If it does go to trial, what is the likelihood of a plaintiff's verdict?
- If the plaintiff does win a verdict, what remedy will the court order?
- How much money is the judge or jury expected to award?
- What is the likelihood that any award of damages will be paid?
- What is the likelihood of a reversal upon appeal?
- How much money will litigation cost for each party?
- How much time will litigation cost for each party?
- How will litigation affect the parties' reputations?
- Will litigation, for each party, be traumatic, vindicating, or both?

In other words, consider what happens when each side makes the same predictions about the results of litigation.

These parties, with the help of their lawyers, will probably formulate their bottom lines in a way that creates a settlement zone. For example, suppose both Plaintiff and Defendant recognize a range of possible outcomes from litigation, including a range of possible damage awards. But after doing the calculations suggested by Section 1.35, each party "expects" (in the *expected value* sense explained in § 1.7) that litigation will result in Defendant paying $600,000 to Plaintiff after each party spends significant time, money, and aggravation on litigation.

If neither party highly values something that can be provided by a court's judgment but not by settlement (such as a favorable precedent for the future, § 1.35(a)), then each party would prefer settling at the *present value* (§ 1.10(b)) of $600,000 to completing litigation. That is because settlement enables each party to save the time, money, and aggravation that would otherwise be spent on litigation, and because most parties are at least to some extent *risk averse* (§ 1.37(a)).[321] As the Supreme Court has recognized, "The parties' desire to avoid litigation costs, to reduce uncertainty, and to maintain ongoing commercial relationships is sufficient to ensure nontrial dispositions in the vast majority of cases."[322]

This is reflected in Diagram 1-11 in which the thin line represents possible settlements acceptable to Defendant and the thick line represents possible settlements acceptable to Plaintiff. While both parties expect a $600,000 judgment to result from litigation, neither party values the case at $600,000 because each party wants to avoid the time, money, risk, and aggravation of (further) litigation. So, Plaintiff is willing to accept less than $600,000 to settle and Defendant is willing to pay more than $600,000 to settle.

Diagram 1-11

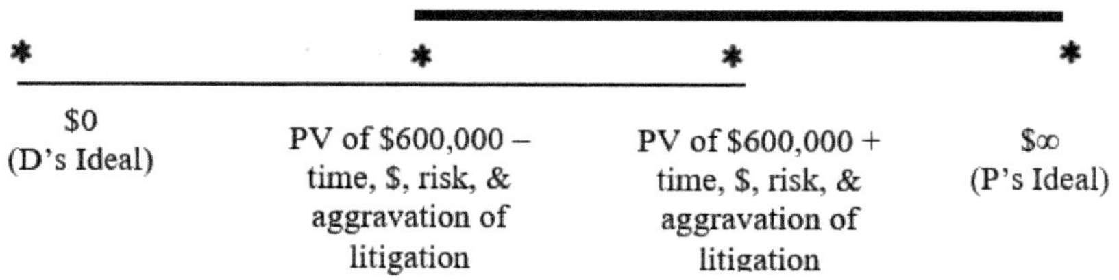


The result of each party wanting to avoid the time, money, risk, and aggravation of (further) litigation is that each party's bottom line is less demanding than the (present value of) $600,000 they each expect from litigation. This is what creates a settlement zone.

In short, settling helps both parties if they settle on the same outcome a court would have reached if, as is usually the case, the process of litigating is less attractive to the parties than the process of settling.[323] Given the same result, most parties would prefer to reach that result through a settlement (which typically is quick, cheap, private, and certain) than through litigation (which typically is slow, expensive, public, and uncertain).

---

[321] J.J. Prescott & Kathryn E. Spier, A Comprehensive Theory of Civil Settlement, 91 N.Y.U. L. Rev. 59, 60–61 (2016) ("If the two parties to a litigation largely agree about the likely outcome of a trial and both are well informed (i.e., each party has a good sense of what the other knows), full settlement is extremely likely, at least so long as the costs of litigation are nontrivial or at least one of the parties is somewhat sensitive to risk.")

[322] McDermott, Inc v. AmClyde, 511 U.S. 202, 215 (1994).

[323] Michael Moffitt, Settlement Malpractice, 86 U. Chi. L. Rev. 1825, 1874–75 (2019) ("the simple prospect of avoiding transaction costs makes settlement Pareto dominant [econ-speak for 'beneficial to both sides'] over litigation in many conditions.")

In exceptional cases, though, at least one of the parties seeks something from a trial that, unlike money, cannot be provided by settlement. As discussed in Section 1.35(c), some parties care about the public vindication that comes from a favorable verdict, want to "make law" with a favorable precedent, or develop a reputation for being fierce litigators in order to intimidate future adversaries. In these exceptional cases, opposing sides may not set their bottom lines in a way that creates a settlement zone even if they make the same predictions about the results of litigation. Outside these exceptional cases though, opposing sides set their bottom lines in a way that creates a settlement zone when they each make the same predictions about the results of litigation.

Rarely do both sides of a case make exactly the same predictions about the results of litigation. For example, rarely will both Plaintiff and Defendant expect (§ 1.35) exactly a $600,000 verdict. The likelihood that both sides will have identical expectations is quite low in most sorts of litigation. But settlement zones occur not just in cases in which both sides have identical expectations but also in cases in which Plaintiff expects a less pro-Plaintiff result than Defendant expects. If, for example, the assumptions of the previous example hold except that Plaintiff expects a $550,000 verdict, while Defendant expects a $600,000 verdict, then Plaintiff will set its bottom line approximately $50,000 lower than when Plaintiff expected a $600,000 verdict.[324] This *increases* the size of the settlement zone, making settlement *more* likely than if each side made the same predictions about the results of litigation. So, settlement zones usually occur in cases in which both sides make the same predictions about the results of litigation and in cases in which Plaintiff expects a less pro-Plaintiff result than Defendant expects. Indeed, settlement zones are present in all such cases, other than the exceptional cases discussed in the previous paragraph.

To reiterate, other than the exceptional cases in which a party seeks something from litigation that cannot be provided by a settlement, settlement zones exist in all cases in which Plaintiff expects a less pro-Plaintiff result from litigation than Defendant expects and all cases in which both sides expect the same result. These settlement zones exist even if the parties' expectations are wrong. Settlement zones are created by beliefs, regardless of the accuracy of those beliefs. Moreover, these settlement zones exist even if the parties and their lawyers publicly deny that they exist. In a case where both sides expect a $600,000 verdict, Plaintiff's lawyer may be telling everyone that he expects a $9 million verdict, while

[324] The difference may not be exactly $50,000 because of the *time value of money*. See § 1.10(b).

Defendant's lawyer may be telling everyone that she expects a verdict for Defendant (§§ 1.15–1.17). Regardless of what the negotiators tell each other and the public about their expectations, if they both really expect a $600,000 verdict then a settlement zone exists, except in the rare cases in which a party seeks something from litigation that cannot be provided by a settlement.

### *(c) Over-Optimism as a Barrier to Settlement*

Other than the exceptional cases in which a party seeks something from litigation that cannot be provided by settlement, the only cases lacking a settlement zone are those in which Plaintiff expects a more pro-Plaintiff result than Defendant expects. If we revise the previous example, so now Plaintiff expects a $850,000 verdict, while Defendant expects a $600,000 verdict, then the settlement zone shrinks by approximately $250,000 when compared to the settlement zone created by both parties expecting a $600,000 verdict. That $250,000 shrinkage may well cause the settlement zone to disappear.[325] These cases in which Plaintiff expects a more pro-Plaintiff result than Defendant expects can be called cases of over-optimism. If Plaintiff expects a verdict of $850,000 and Defendant expects a verdict of $600,000, then at least one of the parties is overly optimistic about its likely success at litigation.

This is reflected in Diagram 1-12 which adds to the previous diagram Plaintiff's new bottom line of $850,000 minus the time, money, risk, and aggravation of (further) litigation which is represented by the thick dashed line.

[325] Whether it disappears turns on how the two sides value the costs and benefits of the two processes: settlement and litigation. It may, for example, be that litigation is so costly that both sides are better off settling at any one of many possible settlement terms than they are litigating even though Plaintiff expects a higher verdict than Defendant expects.

Diagram 1-12

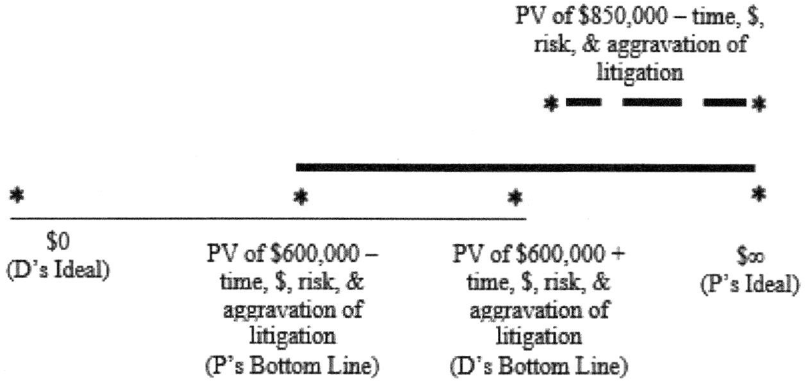


These cases lacking a settlement zone are cases in which at least one of the parties is in for a disappointment at the end of litigation. So, encouraging settlement, which many courts want, calls for reducing parties' over-optimism. Chapter 2 discusses some ways courts try to reduce parties' over-optimism (§§ 2.30–2.36).

### *(d) Ignorance of the ZOPA's Existence or Boundaries*

The existence of a settlement zone does not mean that the negotiators *will* reach an agreement, only that they *might* reach an agreement. First, the negotiators may not even realize that a settlement zone exists (§ 1.11(b)). Negotiators typically conceal their bottom lines from each other and often try to make their bottom lines appear tougher than they really are (§ 1.15). This sort of bluffing may lead each side to conclude that no possible settlement is better for each side than that side's bottom line, so they should stop wasting time trying to negotiate a settlement and instead focus on winning the case in litigation (§ 1.18).

### *(e) Dividing Value as a Barrier to Settlement*

Even if both negotiators discover that a settlement zone exists, and even if they learn its precise boundaries, they still may not reach agreement because they cannot agree on how to divide the value created by settling (§ 1.11(c)). For example, suppose that Plaintiff's bottom line is $150,000, while Defendant's bottom line is $200,000. This is depicted in Diagram 1-13.

Diagram 1-13

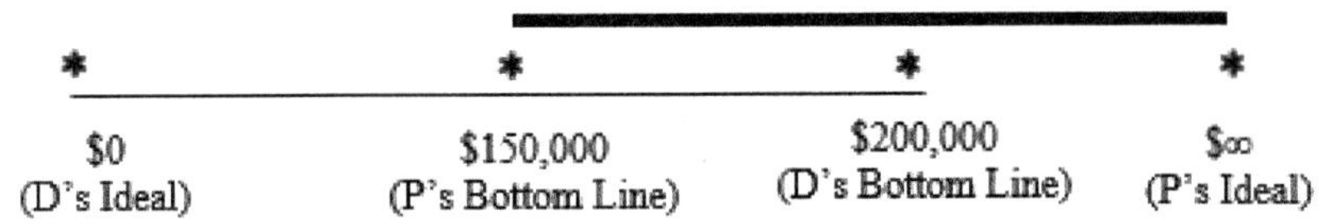


The thin line represents possible settlement terms acceptable to Defendant. The thick line represents possible settlement terms acceptable to Plaintiff. The possible settlement terms from $150,000 to $200,000 comprise the settlement zone. Settlement cannot occur outside this zone because any settlement must be at least as good for each party as its bottom line. A party's bottom line is the worst deal that party will accept.[326]

A settlement of the case depicted in Diagram 1-11 will create $50,000 in value compared to non-settlement.[327] But who gets how much of that value depends on where the price falls in the zone between $150,000 and $200,000. If the parties settle at $150,001 then Defendant captures virtually all the value created by settling. Plaintiff is barely made better off by the settlement.

The negotiators may spend much time and money negotiating within the settlement zone. Indeed, each negotiator may be so determined to capture the potential value from a settlement that they never reach a deal.[328] Defendant's lawyer may say to Plaintiff's lawyer "We will not pay more than $150,001. You should agree to it because it is better for your client than continuing litigation."

---

[326] If a party announces its bottom line and then accepts a deal worse than that, either the party has changed its bottom line since the announcement or the party's announcement misstated that party's actual bottom line. Changing one's bottom line during negotiation is discussed in § 1.32(b), and misinformation about one's bottom line is discussed in § 1.15.

[327] Settlement creates $50,000 in value because settlement transfers from Plaintiff to Defendant an asset (the claim) Plaintiff values at $150,000 and Defendant values at $200,000. Claims, like other assets, have no intrinsic value. Value is subjective so total value increases when assets are sold by those who value them less to those who value them more.

[328] Herein lie the transaction costs of the *bilateral monopoly* that is settlement negotiation. See § 1.3. See also Richard A. Posner, Economic Analysis of Law 779 (9th ed. 2014) ("Settlement negotiations are a classic example of bilateral monopoly. The plaintiff can settle only with the defendant and the defendant only with the plaintiff, and each party is eager to engross as much as possible of the surplus that settlement will generate over litigation. Indeed, the larger the settlement range, the more the parties will stand to gain from hard bargaining and the likelier (it may seem) the parties are to end up litigating because they cannot agree on how to divide the available surplus.")

Plaintiff's lawyer may say to Defendant's lawyer "We will not take less than $199,999. You should agree to it because it is better for your client than continuing litigation." These lawyers are playing the game of "chicken" discussed in § 1.11(c).

### *(f) Why are Settlement Rates Especially High in the U.S.?*

Section 1.39 began by noting that civil litigation in the U.S. usually ends in a settlement, rather than proceeding to a trial verdict or other conclusive ruling by the court.[329]

> Common law countries, such as the U.S., U.K., and Australia, tend to have the highest settlement rates. Countries with legal systems based on French civil law, such as France and Belgium, tend to have the lowest settlement rates. Countries with legal systems in the German or Nordic civil law families, such as Germany, China, and Sweden, tend to have middling settlement rates.[330]

These variations may be due to several factors, including a basic difference between litigation in common law systems and in civil law systems, which tends to make the latter much less costly. "What common lawyers think of as a trial in civil proceedings does not exist in the civil law world."[331] While a trial in the United States brings together the parties, lawyers, judge, and jury in a single, concentrated event, civil law systems use "an entirely different approach" with "no such thing as a trial in our [common law] sense; there is no single, concentrated event. The typical civil proceeding in a civil law country is actually a series of isolated meetings of and written communications between counsel and the judge, in which evidence is introduced, testimony is given, procedural motions and rulings are made, and so on."[332]

> Why this major difference between common law and civil law systems? "The reason is that the right to a jury in civil actions, traditional in the common law world, has

---

[329] See § 1.39(a).

[330] Yun-chien Chang & Daniel Klerman, Settlement Around the World: Settlement Rates in the Largest Economies, 14(1) Journal of Legal Analysis 80–175, https://doi.org/10.1093/jla/laac006 (11 April 2023). See also Nofit Amir & Michal Alberstein, From Transplant to Disintegration? A Comparative Study of the Judicial Role, 37 Ohio St. J. on Disp. Resol. 555, 564–65 (2022) ("The vanishing trial is apparent in many common law systems. . . .Civil law judges, on the other hand, commonly decide cases on their merits, as settlement is not as embedded in the legal culture as in common law jurisdictions.")

[331] John Henry Merryman & Rogelio Perez-Perdomo, The Civil Law Tradition 113 (3d ed. 2007).

[332] Id.

> never taken hold in the civil law world." Following the civil law approach of a series of isolated meetings at which some, but not all, evidence is introduced would not be practical with a jury because the "lay jury cannot easily be convened, adjourned, and reconvened several times in the course of a single action without causing a great deal of inconvenience." So in common law systems a trial must be a single, concentrated event. In contrast, civil law systems can spread out the case over several appearances with each involving the examination of only one witness or the introduction of "only one or two pieces of material evidence."[333]

This "lack of concentration" in civil law systems "explains the lesser importance of discovery"; "Discovery is less necessary because there is little, if any, tactical or strategic advantage to be gained from the element of surprise."[334] In most civil law jurisdictions, "[e]vidence-taking is largely controlled by the court and the parties have no (or virtually no) right to demand relevant materials from one another or from witnesses."[335]

In sum, the cost of discovery—including paying lawyers to do it and fight over it—can be much higher in the U.S. and other common law countries than in much of the rest of the world. And as we saw in § 1.35 and § 1.39(b), the more money and time and aggravation that can be saved by settling, the more likely settlement is to occur. So perhaps settlement is especially common in the U.S. because litigation in the U.S. is especially expensive, time-consuming, and aggravating.

The exemplar of high litigation costs facilitating frequent settlements in the U.S. may be so-called "settlement mills" of plaintiffs' lawyers who represent people injured in auto accidents and slip-and-fall against typically insurance company defendants.

> Partly traceable to small claim size (which, at least in the short run, makes it cheaper for the insurer to pay something as opposed to contesting liability), and partly traceable to repeat-play dynamics (since settlement mills' high case volumes ensure [their frequent interactions with insurance adjusters]), even cases with serious liability issues are often amicably resolved. Insurers will offer

---

333 Stephen J. Ware & Ariana R. Levinson, Principles of Arbitration Law § 58(a) (2d ed. 2023) (quoting Merryman & Perez-Perdomo at 113–14).

334 Merryman & Perez-Perdomo, at 116.

335 Gary B. Born, International Commercial Arbitration 2344–45 (2d ed. 2014).

something (as opposed to an outright denial) for nearly every claim.

. . .

[S]ettlement values are also relatively predictable. Settlement mills tend to settle cases for formulaic "going rates"—i.e., values worked out over time between the settlement mill and insurance adjuster, often calculated based on the medical bills the claimant has accumulated. Guided by going rates, according to one settlement mill negotiator, "you know going in and [the adjusters] know going in about the value of this case."[336]

## F. LAW GOVERNING CIVIL SETTLEMENT

### § 1.40 Releases and Settlement Agreements

#### *(a) Releases as Sales*

Suppose Sykes rear-ends Epstein on Lake Shore Drive, so Epstein threatens to bring a tort suit against Sykes.[337] To settle this dispute, Sykes might pay Epstein to complete, sign, notarize, and deliver the following document after the parties fill in its blank spaces with names, dates, and dollar amounts.

**GENERAL RELEASE**

To all whom these presents shall come or may concern, greeting: know ye, that _______ for and in consideration of the sum of _______ dollars ($_______) to _______ in hand paid, the receipt whereof is hereby acknowledged, have remissed, released, and forever discharged, and by these presents do for _______ heirs, executors and administrators and assigns, remise, release and forever discharge _______, his successors and assigns, and/or his, her, their, and each of their associates, heirs, executors and administrators, and any and all other persons, associations and corporations, whether herein named or referred to or not, of and from any and every claim, demand, right, or cause of action, of whatsoever kind or nature, either in law or in equity, arising from or by reason of any bodily and/or personal injuries known or unknown sustained by me, and/or damage to property, or otherwise, as the result of a certain accident which happened on or about the ___ day of _______, 20__ for which I have claimed the said _______ to be legally liable, but this release shall not be construed as an admission of such liability.

---

[336] Nora Freeman Engstrom, Sunlight and Settlement Mills, 86 N.Y.U. L. Rev. 805, 827–28 (2011).

[337] This example is inspired by a Torts class taught by Alan O. Sykes at the University of Chicago Law School in 1987.

In Witness Whereof _______ have hereunto set _______hand and seal the _______ day of _______ in the year two thousand_______

Sealed and delivered in the presence of

_________________________ _________________________

(Seal)

(Witness)

_________________________ _________________________

(Seal)

(Witness)

State of

} ss.

County of

On this ____ day of _______, 20 ___ before me personally appeared _______ to me known, and known to me to be the same person described in and who executed the within instrument and _______ acknowledged to me that _______ executed the same.

_________________________

_________________________

(Official Title)

This document is commonly known as a *release* because, by signing it, Epstein "releases" (sells, § 1.2(b)) his claim. The effect of the release is to discharge Sykes' legal duties to Epstein arising out of the alleged tort.[338] If, after signing the release, Epstein sues Sykes for damages arising out of the Lake Shore Drive collision, Sykes would attach the release to his answer or motion, and the court would dismiss Epstein's case.[339]

338 66 Am. Jur. 2d Release § 1 (2024) ("A release . . . gives up or abandons a claim or right to the person against whom the claim exists or the right is to be enforced or exercised. In other words, a release is a discharge of a claim or obligation and a surrender of a claimant's right to prosecute a cause of action.")

339 See, e.g., N.Y. Civil Practice Law and Rule 3211(a)(5) ("A party may move for judgment dismissing one or more causes of action asserted against him on the ground that . . . the cause of action may not be maintained because of . . . [a] release"); Carew v. Baker, 109 N.Y.S.3d 205, 207 (App. Div. 2019) (quoting N.Y. Civ. P. L. & R. 3211, and dismissing claim because plaintiff had signed a release); Cal. Civ. Code § 1541 ("An obligation is extinguished by a release therefrom given to the debtor or the released party by the creditor or releasing party, upon a new consideration, or in writing, with or without new consideration."); Winet v. Price, 6 Cal. Rptr. 2d 554, 561 (Ct. App. 1992) (Plaintiff signed a general release leading to dismissal of the claim); Shine v. Williams-Sonoma, Inc., 233 Cal. Rptr. 3d 676, 682 (Ct. App. 2018) (dismissing

Releases are used to prevent or end litigation of many sorts of claims, ranging from personal-injury tort claims from an accident,[340] to claims by a former employee against their former employer.[341]

---

claims because they were previously released in a class action settlement agreement); Tex. R. Civ. P. 94 ("[i]n pleading to a preceding pleading, a party shall set forth affirmatively accord and satisfaction, . . . release . . . and any other matter constituting an avoidance or affirmative defense"); Ellis v. Woods, 453 S.W.2d 509, 510 (Tex. Civ. App. 1970) (affirming a take-nothing judgment in personal injury case because plaintiff had agreed to release a drilling company "and other persons, firms or corporations . . . from any and all known and unknown personal injuries and property damage resulting or to result" from the accident in question); In re Com. Credit Grp. Inc., No. 05-21-00115-CV, 2021 WL 1884657, at *4 (Tex. App. May 11, 2021) ("if a claim falls within the plain language of the release, the claim should be dismissed."); Fla. R. Civ. P. 1.110(d) ("[i]n pleading to a preceding pleading, a party must set forth affirmatively: accord and satisfaction, . . . release . . . and any other matter constituting an avoidance or affirmative defense"); Biscoe v. Evans, 181 So. 2d 564, 565 (Fla. Dist. Ct. App. 1966) (granting summary judgment because defendant properly pleaded release, attached proof of the release, and plaintiff did not rebut defendant's defense of release); Yassan v. J.P. Morgan Chase & Co., 708 F.3d 963, 975 (7th Cir. 2013) (affirming grant of motion to dismiss, thus enforcing release; "Because Chase attached a copy of the release to its motion to dismiss, and because Yassan's complaint repeatedly referenced the release, it was proper for the district court to consider the text of the release in dismissing this case"); Alternative Energy, Inc. v. St. Paul Fire & Marine Ins. Co., 267 F.3d 30, 34, 36 (1st Cir. 2001) (affirming grant of motion to dismiss, thus enforcing release; "the district court properly took into consideration the 1998 Settlement Agreement in ruling on defendant's motion to dismiss"; "the district court properly granted appellee's motion to dismiss under Rule 12(b)(6) based on the unambiguous language of the 1998 Settlement Agreement releasing appellee from liability."); Kraus v. Wells Fargo Sec., LLC, 721 S.E.2d 408 (N.C. Ct. App. 2012) (affirming grant of motion to dismiss, thus enforcing release; "the Release Agreement provides a complete defense to Plaintiff's claims, and the trial court did not err by granting Defendant's motion to dismiss"); National Union Fire Ins. Co. v. Walton Ins. Ltd., 696 F. Supp. 897, 901 (S.D.N.Y. 1988) ("[i]t is well-settled that a valid release constitutes a complete bar to an action on a claim which is the subject of the release."); Conley v. Harry J. Whelchel Co., 410 So.2d 14 (Ala. 1982).

340 Jonathan M. Purver, Representing Automobile Accident Victims, 58 Am. Jur. Trials 283, §§ 169–71 (2025) ("Since the release often serves as the settlement agreement, counsel for both sides must take care to ensure that the release accurately recites the terms of the settlement"; "defense counsel (or the insurance adjuster) typically prepares the release, since the defense is keenly interested in ensuring that the proper parties are released."); Kendrick v. Barker, 15 P.3d 734, 741 (Wyo. 2001) ("[plaintiff] bargained away all of her rights against Barker when she accepted the settlement offer. In light of these facts and available protections under the law, we do not find it necessary to adopt a rule providing for special treatment of releases for personal injuries."); Long v. Brown, 1995 CarswellSask 290 (Holding claim released against both defendants: "A release is a contract once the consideration is paid."); id. ("The plaintiff did not read the document but did know that he was signing a release. He did not exercise reasonable care as against the defendant driver, who relied on it in good faith and for value. The plaintiff was bound by his release.")

341 Hope Brinn, Note, Improving Employer Accountability in A World of Private Dispute Resolution, 118 Mich. L. Rev. 285, 291–92 (2019) ("Scholars and policymakers also struggle to gather concrete data on the use of prelitigation settlements in labor and employment litigation. No laws require disclosure of prelitigation settlements in labor and employment litigation, and the circumstances surrounding the agreements are typically secret. These settlements typically arise when an employee sends a demand letter to an employer regarding potential claims. In response, the employer offers a paid settlement in exchange for the employee releasing all claims and promising to not disparage the employer. . . . Although precise figures are hard to

Releases are used to resolve disputes not yet in litigation, as well as disputes already in litigation. Prelitigation releases produce no public record, unless introduced in court to defeat a claim, so data about their frequency is largely anecdotal. Prelitigation releases may with some frequency be signed by unrepresented parties under circumstances of ignorance or pressure that may implicate the grounds for non-enforcement discussed in Section 1.40(c). In contrast, for disputes already in litigation, releases are often drafted or read by a client's lawyer before the client signs. To end litigation, the defendant likely will insist on a stipulated dismissal of the litigation (with prejudice) as well as a signed release,[342] with only the dismissal filed in court and thus public (§ 1.43(d)).

Releases are used not only in the U.S. but also in other common law countries, such as England, Canada, and Australia.[343]

A release may contain no promises and thus not be a contract. Such a release is more like a deed or bill of sale, effecting or memorializing a present transfer of property (the claim), rather than obligating one or more parties to do anything more in the future. In

---

obtain given the private nature of these settlements, data from plaintiffs' attorneys suggest that approximately four out of five claims settle before a lawsuit is ever filed."); Carew v. Baker, 109 N.Y.S.3d 205, 207 (N.Y. App. Div. 2019) ("plaintiff agreed to retire from his employment with NYCHA and to release NYCHA and its employees 'from all claims or causes of action he may have or claim to have . . . including any and all claims in any way arising out of, or related to, his employment with NYCHA, or his separation from that employment.' "); BCCI v. Ali [2001] UKHL 8 at [9] (releases given by employees pursuant to terminating their employment); Seidler v. University of New South Wales, [2011] FCA 830 (judgement for respondent employer dismissing claims of former employee, Seidler, because "the very width of the terms of the release manifest an intention of the parties that the subject matter of the release was a release from all liability arising out of Ms Seidler's association with the University and her employment.")

[342] See, e.g., Marco Destin, Inc. v. Levy, 111 F.4th 214, 216 (2d Cir. 2024) ("The parties ultimately entered into a stipulated order of settlement and dismissal in 2011 (the 'Stipulated Judgment'), under which Marco Destin was required to pay L&L $3.5 million and cease using the 'Wings' mark. The settlement also included releases that precluded Marco Destin from bringing any action against L&L based on the 'Wings' mark or the License Agreement.")

[343] BCCI v. Ali [2001] UKHL 8 at [9] ("[t]he law cannot possibly decline to allow parties to contract that all and any claims, whether or not known, shall be released"); Alexandra Urbanski, Interpreting Releases: The Supreme Court of Canada Clarifies the Correct Approach, July 29, 2021 ("most commercial settlements are contingent on releases"); Corner Brook (City) v. Bailey, Supreme Court of Canada, July 23, 2021 (the Baileys "release[d] and forever discharge[d] the City. . . from all actions, suits, causes of action. . . foreseen or unforeseen. . . and claims of any kind or nature whatsoever arising out of or relating to the accident"); Jeffrey Goldberger, Drafting Effective Releases (Norton Rose Fulbright, Australia, May 2021), https://www.nortonrosefulbright.com/en-au/knowledge/publications/0964fa6a/drafting-effective-releases ("Legal advisers are frequently called upon to document the terms of a settlement reached between disputing parties often after lengthy and complex negotiations. Settlement deeds typically incorporate releases which may be unilateral but are often mutual. There is now a significant body of case law dealing with the principles governing the construction and interpretation of releases").

contrast, a *settlement agreement,* discussed next, does contain promises of future performance.

### *(b) Settlement Agreements*

#### *(1) Settlement Agreements as Contracts: Accord and Satisfaction*

In the hypothetical Lake Shore Drive collision just discussed, the release purported to be (and probably was) the end of the interaction between the parties. Other settlements, in contrast, involve promises to perform in the future. The documents memorializing these promises to settle are commonly known as *settlement agreements,* rather than *releases.* Lawyers in the U.S. often use the word "release" to describe a document in which the plaintiff releases (sells, § 1.2(b)) a claim in exchange for consideration received from the defendant when plaintiff signs the release. In contrast, lawyers often use the phrase "settlement agreement" to describe a contract in which the plaintiff promises to release (sell) a claim in the future and the defendant promises to provide some consideration in the future.[344]

Suppose, for example, Plaintiff alleged Defendant's negligence caused an auto accident and Plaintiff sued Defendant for $800,000. At some point during litigation, the parties agreed in writing to settle the claim for $300,000 payable in three annual installments of $100,000 each, plus another $75,000 to Plaintiff's lawyer. The writing signed by the parties may resemble the following document with, of course, the blanks filled in.

Agreement made _______, 20__, between _______, of _______ [*address*], City of _______, County of _______, State of _______, referred to as plaintiff and _______, of _______ [*address*], City of _______, County of _______, State of _______, referred to as defendant.

---

[344] Palavan v. McCulley, 498 S.W.3d 134 (Tex. App. Houston 1st Dist. 2016) (by filing an appeal from an agreed judgment, tenant breached a settlement agreement with the defendants that formed the basis of the agreed judgment, pursuant to which the tenant agreed to a judgment dismissing the complaint against the defendants with prejudice, in exchange for a payment of $1,200, in complete satisfaction of any and all claims, pled or not pled, arising out of or related to claims for damages alleged in the complaint.)

A third term, *covenant not to sue,* is sometimes still used. See Pro Done, Inc. v. Basham, 210 A.3d 192, 195 (N.H. 2019) (distinguishing covenant not to sue from release and recognizing a cause of action for breach of contract based upon breach of a covenant not to sue); id. at 196 ("Unlike a release, a covenant not to sue does not relinquish a right or claim, or extinguish a cause of action. A covenant not to sue constitutes an agreement or promise of future forbearance from suing the other party on certain claims. The party making the covenant not to sue agrees only not to assert any right or claim based upon the obligation. Thus, instead of extinguishing a claim, a covenant not to sue recognizes the continuation of the obligation or liability." (internal quotations omitted)).

RECITALS

A. On ________, 20__, plaintiff suffered ________[*specify, such as:* personal injuries and damage to property as a result of an automobile accident at the intersection of ________ (*street*) and ________ (*street*) in the City of ________, County of ________, State of ________, involving plaintiff's automobile and an automobile owned and operated by defendant]. The damages suffered by plaintiff are listed in a schedule, marked Exhibit ____ and attached and made a part of this instrument.

B. On account of the occurrence described in Paragraph A, an action for the recovery of damages in the total amount of ________ Dollars ($___) was filed by plaintiff against defendant in ________ [*court*] as civil action No. _____, entitled ________v________.

C. Plaintiff contends that the sole cause of the occurrence described in Paragraph A was defendant's negligence, in that defendant ________ [*set forth alleged negligence of defendant*]. On the other hand, defendant contends that it is not liable to plaintiff because ________ [*set forth defense of defendant*].

D. Plaintiff and defendant are willing to compromise and settle their differences in the litigation at present pending between them.

AGREEMENT

In consideration of the mutual covenants set forth, the parties agree as follows:

SECTION ONE

PURPOSE

This agreement is made and executed for the sole purpose of settling between plaintiff and defendant the litigation at present existing between them arising from the occurrence described above and to terminate any controversy or claims for injuries or damages of any nature, whether now known or hereafter known, resulting from such occurrence, so that, by the execution of this agreement and the acceptance of the payments provided, plaintiff shall be barred completely and forever from making any further claims or bringing any other actions or suits in connection with such occurrence.

The execution of this agreement by defendant does not constitute an admission of negligence or liability to plaintiff as a result of the described occurrence.

SECTION TWO

TERMS OF SETTLEMENT

a. Payment for property damage. Defendant agrees to pay plaintiff on the execution of this agreement the amount of ________ Dollars ($________) as compensation for the damages to plaintiff's automobile.

b. Payment for personal injuries. Defendant agrees to pay to plaintiff as compensation for plaintiff's personal injuries the following:

(1) The amount of _______ Dollars ($_______) for the medical, hospital, and nursing expenses of plaintiff resulting from the described occurrence.

(2) The amount of _______ Dollars ($_______) per year, beginning with the year 20__ and continuing up to and including the year 20__, such annual payments to be made on or before the _______ day of _______ [*specify month*] of each year.

c. Payment for litigation expenses. Defendant agrees to pay to plaintiff the amount of _______ Dollars ($_______) as reimbursement for actual litigation expenses, other than attorney fees, incurred by plaintiff.

d. Payment for attorney fees. Defendant agrees to pay to plaintiff's attorney the amount of _______ Dollars ($_______) as and for claimant's attorney fees. Such payments shall be made as follows: _______ [*specify manner of payment*].

e. Death of plaintiff before receiving all payments. In the event plaintiff dies before receiving all the payments to which plaintiff is entitled as specified above, payment shall be made to _______ [*specify, such as:* plaintiff's executor or administer or _______ (*beneficiary)*].

SECTION THREE

RELEASE OF DEFENDANT

In consideration of the payments agreed to be made, plaintiff for plaintiff, and legal representatives, successors, and beneficiaries of plaintiff, agrees to release and discharge defendant, and heirs, and legal representatives of defendant, from any and all claims, damages, causes of action of any kind, for personal injuries or property damage suffered by plaintiff in connection with the described occurrence, whether now known or hereafter known, and whether existing or subsequently arising. Plaintiff further agrees to file a dismissal of the legal action against defendant now pending in _______ [*court*] on the happening of all of the following:

a. On receipt by plaintiff of the amounts agreed on to be paid as provided in Section Two, Paragraphs a, b, and c of this agreement.

b. On receipt by plaintiff's attorney of the amount agreed on to be paid by defendant as attorney fees as provided in Section Two, Paragraph d of this agreement.

SECTION FOUR

WAIVER

No waiver of any of the terms of this agreement shall be valid unless in writing and signed by all parties to this agreement. The failure of plaintiff to enforce at any time any of the provisions of this agreement, or to require at any time performance by defendant of any of the provisions, shall not be construed to be a waiver of such provisions, or the right of plaintiff to thereafter enforce each and every such provision. No waiver of any breach of this agreement shall be held to be a waiver of any other or subsequent breach.

In witness whereof, the parties have executed this agreement at ________ [*place of execution*] the day and year first above written.

*[Signatures]*

*[Acknowledgment]*

In addition to this settlement agreement, the defendant likely will insist on a stipulated dismissal of the litigation with prejudice.[345] In the U.S. only the stipulated dismissal typically needs to be filed in court and thus public (§ 1.43(d)), so the terms of settlement can be kept confidential unless later litigation alleges breach of the settlement agreement.

This settlement agreement, like many others, is technically an *accord*.[346] Its most basic terms are Defendant's promise to pay, and Plaintiff's promises to dismiss the suit and to "release and discharge" Defendant. The legal effect of this accord, in contrast to a release (§ 1.40(a)), is not to discharge Defendant's underlying tort-law duty, but merely to suspend it. To discharge that duty, Defendant must perform the accord; that is, pay three annual installments of $100,000 each, plus $75,000 to Plaintiff's lawyer.[347] Performance of an accord is called *satisfaction*.

Instead of performing the accord, Defendant may breach it by failing to pay an installment when due. The legal effect of Defendant's material breach is to give Plaintiff a choice of suing in

---

345 See, e.g., Fed. R. Civ. P. 41(a)(1)(A)(ii) ("the plaintiff may dismiss an action without a court order by filing . . . a stipulation of dismissal signed by all parties who have appeared."); id. ("Unless the notice or stipulation states otherwise, the dismissal is without prejudice."); Kan. Stat. § 60–241 ("the plaintiff may dismiss an action without a court order by filing . . . a stipulation of dismissal signed by all parties who have appeared. When the dismissal is by stipulation, the clerk of the court must enter an order of dismissal as a matter of course"); id. ("Unless the notice or stipulation states otherwise, the dismissal is without prejudice.")

346 See 1 Am. Jur. 2d Accord and Satisfaction 523 (2005) ("An 'accord' is a contract by which parties agree to settle an existing duty, obligation, debt or dispute or is an agreement in which parties discharge or settle a preexisting contract, claim, obligation or agreement by giving and accepting a substituted consideration or performance."); Scipio v. Sony Music Ent't, Inc., No. 05-5134, 2006 WL 527062, at *7 (6th Cir. 2006) ("An accord is an agreement whereby one of the parties undertakes to give or perform, and the other to accept in satisfaction of a claim, liquidated or in dispute, and arising either from contract or from tort, something other than or different from what he is or considers himself entitled to; and a satisfaction is the execution of such agreement.")

347 See Restatement (Second) of Contracts § 281(1) (1981).

contract for breach of the accord or in tort on Defendant's underlying duty.[348] Recall that the underlying tort-law duty had been suspended rather than discharged by the accord. That duty is revived by Defendant's breach of the accord.[349] In contrast, as long as Defendant's underlying tort-law duty remains suspended because Defendant has not (yet) breached the accord, any suit to enforce that duty will be dismissed.[350] Such a dismissal enforces Plaintiff's duty to perform the accord.

Breach of contract suits for breaches of settlement agreements may involve any of the issues that arise in other breach of contract cases. These include contract formation,[351] terms,[352] interpretation,[353] breach,[354] defenses (§ 1.40(c)), liquidated

---

[348] See id. § 281(2). Toppy v. Passage Bio, Inc., 285 A.3d 672, 686–7 (Pa. Super. 2022) ("when a settlement contract is breached, the plaintiff has two coexistent but inconsistent remedies available: he may treat the compromise agreement as rescinded and sue on the original tort, or he may sue on the contract. The plaintiff may not, however, prosecute one of these remedies to judgement and then sue on the other.") (quoting Smith v. Brink, 561 A.2d 1253 (Pa. Super. 1989)).

[349] By contrast, a substituted contract (including a novation) "discharges the original duty and breach of the substituted contract by the obligor does not give the obligee a right to enforce the original duty." Restatement (Second) of Contracts § 279(2) (1981).

[350] Clark v. Elza, 286 Md. 208, 219, 406 A.2d 922, 928 (1979) (enforcing a settlement agreement against injured plaintiff because the "circuit court should not have permitted the plaintiffs to proceed with the underlying tort action in violation of their settlement agreement" and explaining that until "there is a breach of the accord or a justifiable change of position based upon prospective non-performance, the original cause of action is suspended.")

[351] In re Motors Liquidation Co., 580 B.R. 319, 351–52 (Bankr. S.D.N.Y. 2018) (no settlement agreement formed because some parties did not execute the Settlement Agreement document, "which clearly specifies that the settlement 'shall become effective and binding on the parties on the date on which this Agreement is fully executed by each of the Parties.' "); Philip Chong & Elizabeth Tout, United Kingdom in John Fellas, Transnational Litigation § 29:86 (2024) (formation of a settlement is by "the general requirements of English contract law (offer, acceptance, consideration, due capacity, and an intention to create legal relations).").

[352] Mason v. United States, 126 Fed. Cl. 149, 159 (2016) ("the Settlement Agreement includes a merger clause. ('This Stipulation of Settlement and Order contains the entire agreement between the parties and supersedes any and all previous agreements, whether written or oral, between the parties relating to this subject matter.'). Therefore, Plaintiff's use of parol evidence to establish that the Settlement Agreement required the Navy to allocate contributions as Plaintiff desired is inadmissible."), aff'd sub nom. Franklin-Mason v. United States, 692 F. App'x 633 (Fed. Cir. 2017).

[353] Ivy v. Calais Co., Inc., 397 P.3d 267, 278 (Alaska 2017) ("we interpret settlement agreements as contracts, and the objective of contract interpretation is to determine and enforce the reasonable expectations of the parties"; "the parties expected that Calais would pay Ivy within 225 days of the execution of the Agreement—i.e. by January 7, 2010. The parties did not expect six more years of litigation to resolve this dispute. Given these facts, we cannot say that awarding Ivy post-judgment interest beginning in July 2010 would do an injustice.")

[354] Madison Ave. Diamonds LLC v. KGK Jewelry LLC, 39 N.Y.S.3d 18 (App. Div. 2016) (wholesaler sued manufacturer for breach of settlement agreement, manufacturer counterclaimed for payment for goods sold; judgment for manufacturer

damages,[355] and calculating damages, including pre and post judgment interest.[356]

*(2) Settlement Agreements as Court Orders: Agreed Judgments and Consent Decrees*

Enforcing a settlement agreement (accord) by suing for its breach, as just discussed, can be slow and expensive because it takes two steps. First, the plaintiff from the underlying settled action starts a new suit (presumably last in line on the court's docket) for breach of the settlement agreement,[357] seeking the remedy of specific performance—a court order that the defendant do what defendant promised in the settlement agreement. If the plaintiff wins that order and then the defendant still does not comply, the plaintiff "can enforce the specific performance decree through a contempt proceeding."[358] So, if the defendant still does not do what the

---

defeating plaintiffs' claim for breach of settlement agreement and awarding manufacturer damages on counterclaim).

[355] MBR Contracting, Inc. v. Atakhanian, 25 N.Y.S.3d 287, 288 (App. Div. 2016) ("The parties entered into a stipulation of settlement (hereinafter the stipulation) dated February 12, 2014, pursuant to which the plaintiff was to receive $10,000 from the defendants in five monthly installment payments of $2,000 each. The first installment payment was due by February 15, 2014. The stipulation also provided that if the defendants failed to pay the installment payments within the time provided, they consented to the plaintiff entering a judgment against them in the amount of $50,508.06, upon five days' written notice. The plaintiff did not receive the first installment by February 15, 2014. On February 20, 2014, the plaintiff's counsel sent, via email, to the defendants' counsel a notice of default. On February 26, 2014, a clerk's judgment in the amount of $50,508.06 was entered against the defendants.")

[356] JSC Transmashholding v. Miller, No. CV 17-20 (RBW), 2017 WL 7279396, at *1 (D.D.C. Nov. 14, 2017) ("the Court issued a Memorandum Opinion and Order granting the plaintiff's motion for summary judgment in this breach of settlement agreement case. The Court determined that the defendant owed the plaintiff a total principal amount of $599,282.56, plus prejudgment interest at a rate of 8.0% per annum, and directed the plaintiff to file on the docket an additional affidavit calculating the amount of prejudgment interest due as of the date of this judgment" (internal citations omitted)).

[357] D. Patrick, Inc. v. Ford Motor Co., 8 F.3d 455, 460 (7th Cir. 1993) ("Standing alone, a settlement agreement is nothing more than a contract; the imprimatur of an injunction is required to render it a consent decree enforceable through contempt."); Robles v. Gov't of Virgin Islands, No. CV 2012-069, 2014 WL 2503757, at *2 (D.V.I. June 3, 2014) ("a settlement agreement that has been validly entered into is just another contract to be enforced the usual way, that is, by a fresh suit. . . . Accordingly, the Court will deny Plaintiff's "Motion to Enforce Settlement Agreement." (internal quotations omitted)).

[358] Anthony DiSarro, Six Decrees of Separation: Settlement Agreements and Consent Orders in Federal Civil Litigation, 60 Am. U.L. Rev. 275, 282–83 (2010) ("Where they are part of a contract, settlement terms can only be enforced via the breach-of-contract route. This entails a two-step process. First, the party seeking enforcement will have to commence a plenary action to obtain a decree of specific performance. Then, the party can enforce the specific performance decree through a contempt proceeding. The two-step enforcement process is lengthier and consumes more judicial resources" than contempt of a settlement which has been entered as a court order).

defendant promised in the settlement agreement, the court can fine or even jail the defendant to compel performance. This two-step process is necessary if the dispute was never in litigation or was the basis for a case the court dismissed pursuant to a stipulated dismissal the parties signed along with their settlement, as is common on in the U.S.

In contrast, the enforceability of a settlement agreement can—if the dispute is already in litigation—be expedited by having the court retain jurisdiction over the case. Then the agreement can be enforced on a motion in that existing case without need for a new suit.[359] For example, a California rule of civil procedure allows a court, if jointly requested by the parties, to "enter judgment pursuant to the terms of the settlement" and "retain jurisdiction over the parties to enforce the settlement until performance in full of the terms of the settlement."[360] In Texas, one "agreed judgment" provided

> After considering the issues of the case with the Judge, the parties announced they reached a settlement in the case as to all claim[s] of plaintiff, as to any parties to the litigation, or otherwise. TBW Development LLC, Boulevard Realty, LLC, and Brian McCulley are dismissed with prejudice from this litigation. Plaintiff accepts the

---

[359] Ingrid M. Evans, Holding Defendants to Their Word, Trial, April 2020, at 20, 22 ("In various jurisdictions, it is possible to have the court enforce the settlement when the agreement specifies that the court has retained jurisdiction over the matter. It is much easier to ensure a court has continued jurisdiction over the matter rather than being forced to file a new case for breach of contract to enforce the settlement. If you have to return to court to enforce the settlement or if it blows up completely, leaving you back at square one, the retention of jurisdiction means you do not have to start over."). See also McKenna v. Ass'n of Apartment Owners of Elima Lani, 148 Haw. 233, 241, 470 P.3d 1110, 1118 (2020) (treat motions to enforce settlement as motions for summary judgment); Infinite Sec. Solutions, L.L.C. v. Karam Props. II, Ltd., 37 N.E.3d 1211 (Ohio 2015) (a trial court may enforce a settlement on motion if dismissal expressly retained jurisdiction for that purpose); Stricklin v. Flavel, 43 P.3d 1116 (Or. Ct. App. 2002) (trial court retained jurisdiction to enforce the settlement agreement terms); Barber v. Ohana Military Cmtys., LLC, 728 Fed. Appx. 749, 750–751 (9th Cir. 2018) (noting that the district court "retained jurisdiction to adjudicate any purported violations of the settlement agreement brought to its attention" "during the six-month window of jurisdiction the court created.")

In contrast, a federal court otherwise lacks jurisdiction to enforce a settlement agreement from a case it dismissed. Hendrickson v. United States, 791 F.3d 354, 358 (2d Cir. 2015) ("to retain ancillary jurisdiction over enforcement of a settlement agreement," "a district court's order of dismissal must either (1) expressly retain jurisdiction over the settlement agreement, or (2) incorporate the terms of the settlement agreement in the order." (citing Kokkonen v. Guardian Life Insurance Co. of America, 511 U.S. 375, 381 (1994))).

[360] See, e.g., Cal. Civ. Proc. Code § 664.6 ("If parties to pending litigation stipulate, in a writing signed by the parties outside the presence of the court or orally before the court, for settlement of the case, or part thereof, the court, upon motion, may enter judgment pursuant to the terms of the settlement. If requested by the parties, the court may retain jurisdiction over the parties to enforce the settlement until performance in full of the terms of the settlement.")

> settlement of $1,200 as complete satisfaction of all claims or causes of action, pled or otherwise, which arise out of or relate to the claims for damages as alleged in this Litigation. TBW Development LLC's claims against any contractor for the sums paid under the settlement shall not be released or affected by this settlement. The $1,200 shall be paid by counsel for Defendants Brian McCulley and/or TBW Development LLC to Shea Palavan by April 19, 2014. Based upon the settlement this court ORDERS:
>
> All claims of [plaintiff] Shea Palavan against all Defendants in this Litigation are hereby dismissed with prejudice.[361]

While customary practice varies from place to place, parties are more likely to ask courts to convert settlements into judgments when the parties expect to have a post-settlement relationship beyond the immediate payment of money. Examples include divorce settlements,[362] where parties may have ongoing issues about child custody or support payments, and litigation against government entities such as prisons and schools, where parties expect to have ongoing issues about compliance with the settlement.

While some courts use the terms "agreed judgment," "consent judgment," and "consent decree" interchangeably,[363] others allege distinctions among them.[364] A judgment incorporating the terms of a settlement agreement is often called a "consent decree" when the agreed remedy is equitable, rather than legal, in nature.[365] That is, the phrase "agreed judgment" seems more common in suits for money, while "consent decree" seems more common when equitable remedies are involved, particularly if they require ongoing judicial oversight. Consent decrees are common in federal government actions enforcing environmental,[366] and antitrust law, and in actions

---

361 Palavan v. McCulley, 498 S.W.3d 134, 137 (Tex. App. 2016).

362 See, e.g., Lewis v. Lewis, 603 P.2d 650, 652 (Kan. Ct. App. 1979) ("all separation agreements which are found to be fair, just and equitable by the trial court are merged into the divorce decree and become a judgment of the court.")

363 Branch Banking & Tr. Co. v. Mellow Mushroom Three Peat, Inc., No. 4:19-CV-00346-P, 2020 WL 532256, at *2 n.4 (N.D. Tex. Feb. 3, 2020).

364 See, e.g., Brooks v. City of Kankakee, Illinois, 7 F.4th 649, 661 (7th Cir. 2021) (city argued that referring to the Agreed Judgment Order as a consent decree was damaging to the police department, as consent decrees are generally the result of investigations of civil rights violations by the Department of Justice).

365 See Judith Resnik, Procedure as Contract, 80 Notre Dame L. Rev. 593, 630 (2005) (referring to "the linguistical and normative puzzle of whether consent decrees, consent judgments, consent orders, and settlements are or ought to be all the same. The term 'decree' comes from equity practice whereas the term 'judgment' comes from law.")

366 Tracy Hester, Consent Decrees As Emergent Environmental Law, 85 Mo. L. Rev. 687, 691 (2020) ("The value of environmental remedies compelled by consent

to reform a prison, public school district, or other instrumentality of state or local government.[367]

Entering judgment on a settlement agreement effectively converts it from a private contract to a judgment of the court. Settlement terms that are part of a consent decree may be enforced in a single step because the consent decree includes an injunction ordering each party to do what it promised in the settlement agreement. "A consent decree is a judgment or order that reflects the settlement terms agreed to by the parties, and that contains an injunction."[368]

> If the parties agree to compose their differences by a settlement agreement, [ ] the only penalty for failure to abide by the agreement is another suit. Litigants, therefore, have sought to reinforce their compromise and to obtain its more ready enforceability by incorporating it into a proposed consent decree and seeking to have the court enter this decree.
>
> A consent decree, although founded on the agreement of the parties, is a judgment. It has the force of res judicata, protecting the parties from future litigation. It thus has greater finality than a compact. As a judgment, it may be enforced by judicial sanctions, including citation for contempt if it is violated.[369]

If the defendant breaches the consent decree, the plaintiff can quickly enforce it by simply filing "a motion to hold the violator in contempt of court. Some district courts will even permit a party seeking to hold

---

decrees in U.S. Environmental Protection Agency ('EPA') civil enforcement actions exceeded $4.5 billion in the first six months of 2019"); id. ("Some federal statutes, regulations, and policies . . . explicitly require the United States to use consent decrees lodged in federal courts to settle certain types of environmental claims").

[367] Maimon Schwarzschild, Public Law by Private Bargain: Title VII Consent Decrees and the Fairness of Negotiated Institutional Reform, 1984 Duke L.J. 887, 888 (1984) ("Consent decrees first became prominent in antitrust cases, and are now common in every variety of lawsuit over public policy, including environmental cases, litigation over the rights of the institutionalized, school and housing desegregation suits, and equal employment litigation.").

[368] Anthony DiSarro, Six Decrees of Separation: Settlement Agreements and Consent Orders in Federal Civil Litigation, 60 Am. U. L. Rev. 275, 277 (2010). See also Charles Alan Wright & Mary Kay Kane, Law of Federal Courts § 98 n. 1851 (8th ed. 2017) ("A consent judgment or consent decree is a settlement that includes an injunction, or some other form of specific relief, and that is formally entered by the court and enforceable by contempt."); Russell L. Weaver & Michael B. Kelly, Principles of Remedy Law 32 (4th ed. 2022) ("The primary function of civil contempt is to benefit the plaintiff either by coercing defendant into complying with a court order, or compensating him for noncompliance.")

[369] United States v. City of Miami, Fla., 664 F.2d 435, 439–40 (5th Cir. 1981) (Rubin, J., concurring).

another in contempt to proceed by way of an expedited procedure known as an 'order to show cause' or 'rule to show cause,' which will set a more abbreviated briefing schedule than is typical for motions."[370] By removing the need for a separate breach of contract suit, a consent decree "enables the party seeking enforcement to avoid the court's docket queue and obtain sanctions more quickly than if a new lawsuit had to be filed."[371]

Section 1.40(c)(4) explains that while most courts routinely dismiss litigation pursuant to settlements without critically assessing the terms of settlement, this sort of "rubber stamp" is less likely with respect to agreed judgments and especially with respect to federal consent decrees.

*(3) Settlement Agreements and Tax Law*

The settlement agreement discussed in Section 1.40(b)(1) is known in tax law as a "structured settlement" because it provides for a series of installment payments, rather than one single payment.[372] This example of three installment payments of $100,000 each (plus $75,000 for Plaintiff's lawyer) is unusually simple. Structured settlements can be quite complicated and subject to important considerations of tax law.[373] Structured settlements usually provide that, rather than making a series of payments directly to the plaintiff, the defendant will make a single payment to an insurance company or other financial institution which will then pay plaintiff a series of payments. This is the defendant buying an "annuity" for the plaintiff.[374]

***(c) Grounds for Non-Enforcement***

Grounds to rescind a settlement agreement or release resemble grounds to rescind other contracts and sales. These grounds include duress, unconscionability, misrepresentation, mistake, the

---

370 Anthony DiSarro, Six Decrees of Separation: Settlement Agreements and Consent Orders in Federal Civil Litigation, 60 Am. U.L. Rev. 275, 282–83 (2010) ("The contempt route fulfills the 'need for speed' by enabling a party to use a single-step enforcement process. The party seeking enforcement simply files a motion to hold the violator in contempt of court. Some district courts will even permit a party seeking to hold another in contempt to proceed by way of an expedited procedure known as an 'order to show cause' or 'rule to show cause,' which will set a more abbreviated briefing schedule than is typical for motions").

371 Larry Kramer, Consent Decrees and the Rights of Third Parties, 87 Mich. L. Rev. 321, 325 (1988).

372 See Structured settlements, generally, 5 Mertens Law of Fed. Income Taxation § 24A:27 (2022) ("A structured settlement is simply a settlement providing for periodic payments, as opposed to a lump sum.")

373 See generally id., §§ 24A:27–24A:31.

374 Id. § 24A:28.

requirement of a writing (Statute of Frauds), and public policy.[375] However, courts are generally reluctant to rescind settlements, and they may apply some of these grounds more narrowly to settlements than they do to other contracts. For instance, several courts have held that even if unilateral mistake is sometimes a ground for rescinding other contracts, only a mutual mistake suffices to rescind a settlement (§ 1.40(c)(2)).

*(1) Duress, Incapacity, Undue Influence, and Unconscionability*

In Section 1.40(a)'s example of the Lake Shore Drive collision, if Epstein signed the release while Sykes pointed a gun at Epstein, a court's finding of duress would allow Epstein to rescind the settlement. Or if a severely-injured-and-desperate-for-cash Epstein signed the release in exchange for only twenty dollars, a court might find the settlement unconscionable. While settlements have been rescinded due to duress,[376] unconscionability,[377] and related grounds, these findings are uncommon, and they are especially rare outside the context of divorce and other family actions.

*(2) Misrepresentation and Mistake*

Settlements in a wide variety of contexts are challenged on grounds of misrepresentation and mistake. Many common negotiation tactics at least border on misrepresentation (§§ 1.13–1.17). A settlement induced by a material misrepresentation is

---

[375] See, e.g., Ryberg v. Landsiedel, 956 N.W.2d 749, 753 (N.D. 2021) ("A settlement will not be set aside absent a showing of fraud, duress, undue influence, or any other grounds for rescinding a contract."); Lodhi v. Stewart's Shops Corp., 861 N.Y.S.2d 160, 162 (N.Y. 2008) ("A party is bound by his or her signature on a release containing language that is clear and unambiguous, unless cause exists sufficient to invalidate a contract, such as duress, illegality, fraud or mutual mistake"); Industrial Commercial Elec., Inc. v. McLees, 101 P.3d 593, 597 (Alaska 2004) ("settlement agreements and releases, like any other contracts, are susceptible to attack for mistake, fraud, misrepresentation, and duress."); Watson v. Sadiq [2013] EWCA Civ 822 at [49] ("The customary basis upon which such a contract compromising litigation can be set aside are those upon which any ordinary contract can be set aside, i.e. for misrepresentation, fraud, undue influence, duress and the like."); Daniele Bertolini, Releasing the Unknown: Theoretical and Evidentiary Challenges in Interpreting the Release of Unanticipated Claims, 48 Queen's Law Journal 61 n.1 (2023) (referring to duress, unconscionability, and mistake as "grounds upon which the validity of a release can be challenged").

[376] See, e.g., Holler v. Holler, 612 S.E.2d 469 (S.C. Ct. App. 2005); Duncan v. Hensley, 248 Ark. 1083 (Ark. 1970); Service Fire Ins. Co. v. Reed, 72 So.2d 197 (Miss. 1954).

[377] Compare, e.g., In re Marriage of Moran, 483 N.E.2d 580, 586–87 (Ill. App. Ct. 1985) (divorce settlement "manifestly unfair and unconscionable when considering the parties' relative circumstances and station in life"; also misrepresentation, duress and coercion), with In re Marriage of Bielawski, 764 N.E.2d 1254, 1261 (Ill. App. Ct. 2002) (enforcing settlement; "The fact that an agreement merely favors one party over another does not make it unconscionable. To rise to the level of being unconscionable, the settlement must be improvident, totally one-sided or oppressive.")

voidable by the party relying on the misrepresentation.[378] Fraud may also give rise to tort liability.[379]

Similarly, rescission may be available where both parties made a material mistake as to a basic assumption of the settlement.[380] In the example of the Lake Shore Drive collision, Epstein might make such an argument if his personal injuries turn out to be much more severe than anyone thought at the time of settlement.[381] Anticipating such an argument, Sykes' lawyer may have tried to draft the release Epstein signed to allocate to Epstein the risk of unexpectedly severe injuries. For example, the sample release in Section 1.40(a) refers to "injuries known or unknown sustained by me."

Several courts have held that even if unilateral mistake is sometimes a ground for rescinding other contracts, only a mutual

---

[378] See, e.g., Hoyt Properties, Inc. v. Prod. Res. Grp., L.L.C., 736 N.W.2d 313 (Minn. 2007) (action to rescind settlement agreement based on alleged misrepresentation by lawyer negotiating it); Dice v. Akron, C. & Y.R.Co., 342 U.S. 359 (1952); Barrett v. United States, 660 F. Supp. 1291 (S.D.N.Y. 1987); Quinn v. City of Kansas City, Kan., 64 F. Supp. 2d 1084, 1096 (D. Kan. 1999) ("the Court rescinds the settlement agreement and orders plaintiff to repay the $100,000 settlement amount which he has received."); Diagnostic Imaging Ctr. Assocs. v. H & P, 815 P.2d 865 (Alaska 1991).

[379] See, e.g., Slotkin v. Citizens Casualty of New York, 614 F.2d 301 (2d Cir. 1979) (in suit to recover damages for misrepresentation as to insurance coverage in prior medical malpractice action, measure of damages was difference in settlement value of prior action before and after discovery of such fraud); Cresswell v. Sullivan & Cromwell, 668 F. Supp. 166 (S.D.N.Y. 1987) ("under New York law, a second action for damages rather than for rescission of the judgment or settlement may be brought when a state court judgment or settlement is allegedly procured by fraud."); Fire Insurance Exchange v. Bell, 643 N.E.2d 310 (Ind. 1994) (misrepresentation of insurance policy limits); Raymark Industries, Inc. v. Stemple, 714 F. Supp. 460, 468 (D. Kan. 1988).

[380] Rice v. Denley, 944 P.2d 497, 500 (Alaska 1997) ("Rice asks that this court hold that no contract was formed, or if we conclude that a settlement agreement was reached . . ., that we grant him rescissionary relief on the basis of either Rice's unilateral mistake as to a material term, or void the agreement on the basis of the parties' mutual mistake. . . . Based on our study of the record, we think that Rice has made out a strong case").

[381] Keller v. Liberty Nw., Inc., 2010 MT 279, ¶ 31, 358 Mont. 448, 457 (remanding cases to district court because "even if the parties were mutually aware of the contents of Keller's medical records. . . it is entirely possible that they entered into the settlement agreements under a mistaken impression as to the nature and extent of Keller's injuries."); Taylor v. Chesapeake & Ohio Railway Co., 518 F.2d 536 (4th Cir. 1975) (denying summary judgment because "it is possible to conclude from the plaintiff's testimony that at the time he executed the release both he and the railroad agent assumed, on the basis of Dr. Vaziri's advice, that the plaintiff had no serious, permanent injury" and that "the issue of the invalidity of the release on account of mutual mistake was for the jury."); Oliver v. Clark, 537 N.W.2d 635 (Neb. 1995) ("Nebraska has long followed the majority rule that a settlement agreement which purports to release any and all claims for accident-related damages may be set aside on grounds of mutual mistake where there are injuries of a serious character wholly unknown to the parties which were not taken into consideration when the release was executed.")

mistake suffices to rescind a settlement.[382] But occasionally a court voids a settlement due to unilateral mistake.[383]

*(3) The Requirement of a Writing*

Whether a dispute is in litigation or not, a settlement of it can be embodied in a signed writing. When a dispute is in litigation, however, it is common in some jurisdictions for settlement agreements to be reached orally and then made legally-binding by stating them on the record in open court.[384] In some states, settlements of disputes in litigation are not enforceable unless they are in writing or made in open court.[385] By contrast, a few cases from

---

[382] Henley v. Cuyahoga Cnty. Bd. of Mental Retardation & Developmental Disabilities, 141 F. App'x 437, 443 (6th Cir. 2005) (If the parties reached agreement on all material terms, then existing precedent "dictates that only the existence of fraud or mutual mistake can justify reopening an otherwise valid settlement agreement."); Brown v. Cnty. of Genesee, 872 F.2d 169, 174 (6th Cir. 1989) ("the district court erroneously concluded that since a mutual mistake of material fact would suffice to warrant reformation of a settlement agreement, a unilateral mistake also constituted permissible reason to do so. Existing precedent, however, dictates that only the existence of fraud or mutual mistake can justify reopening an otherwise valid settlement agreement."); Cheyenne-Arapaho Tribes of Indians of Oklahoma v. United States, 671 F.2d 1305, 1311 (Ct. Cl. 1982) ("If a mistake was made in the present case, it was made by the defendant alone. Unlike a mutual mistake, a unilateral mistake is not sufficient to allow the mistaken party to limit or avoid the effect of an otherwise valid settlement agreement.")

[383] Compare Brown v. Richard A. Murphy, Inc., 862 P.2d 406 (Mont. 1993) (injured worker may rescind settlement with state worker's compensation fund on grounds of unilateral mistake of law and fact because of confusion regarding a subrogation clause with the state fund); Devon Energy Prod. Co., L.P. v. Line Finders, LLC, No. 21-6119, 2022 WL 4232404, at *3 (10th Cir. Sept. 14, 2022) ("A unilateral mistake of fact as to a material term of a contract may be grounds for rescission. But a unilateral mistake rarely warrants recission unless the mistake goes to a material term of the agreement itself—that is, when the language of the contract contains a latent ambiguity and one of the parties is in fact assenting to something different from what the other party agrees to." (internal quotations and citations omitted), with Simmons v. Blauw, 635 N.E.2d 601, 603 (Ill. Ct. App. 1994) ("[a] unilateral or self-induced mistake is not sufficient to void a clear and unambiguous release. The mistake of fact must be mutual, . . .")).

[384] Nieborak v. W54-7 LLC, 163 N.Y.S.3d 526, 528 (App. Div. 2022) ("Stipulations of settlement are favored by the courts and not lightly cast aside. This is all the more so in the case of 'open court' stipulations within CPLR 2104, where strict enforcement not only serves the interest of efficient dispute resolution but also is essential to the management of court calendars and integrity of the litigation process."); Matter of K.K., 2021 OH Ct. App. 3338, ¶ 13 ("When parties voluntarily enter into an oral settlement agreement in the presence of the court, the agreement constitutes a binding contract."); Cohen v. Cohen, 629 So. 2d 909, 910 (Fla. Dist. Ct. App. 1993) ("[W]e expressly approve of oral settlement agreements announced in open court.")

[385] See, e.g., N.Y.C.P.L.R. 2104 ("An agreement between parties or their attorneys relating to any matter in an action, other than one made between counsel in open court, is not binding upon a party unless it is in a writing subscribed by him or his attorney or reduced to the form of an order and entered."); Tex. R. Civ. P. 11 ("Unless otherwise provided in these rules, no agreement between attorneys or parties touching any suit pending will be enforced unless it be in writing, signed and filed with the papers as part of the record, or unless it be made in open court and entered of record."); Neasbitt v. Warren, 105 S.W.3d 113, 115, 116 (Tex. App. 2003) (affirming the

other states indicate that oral agreements to settle disputes in litigation are enforceable even if the oral agreements are not made in open court.[386] Even in these states, enforceability may require a settlement to be in writing if its subject matter is within the Statute of Frauds, like an interest in land[387] or a promise that cannot be performed within a year.[388]

### *(4) Public Policy: Court Approval Required for Kids, Class Actions, Bankruptcies, & Environmental Enforcement*

Each of the above discussed grounds for non-enforcement of settlement agreements allows a party to win a suit for rescission of a settlement but proving to a court the absence of these grounds is not

---

enforcement of the settlement agreement) ("The parties, through counsel, agreed in open court to settle the case and recited the terms of the agreement on the record. . . . According to [Texas Rules of Civil Procedure] Rule 11, no agreement between the parties or their attorneys shall be enforceable unless the agreement is either (1) in writing, signed by the parties, and filed as part of the record or (2) made orally in open court and entered as part of the record."); Elyaoudayan v. Hoffman, 129 Cal. Rptr. 2d 41, 42 (Ct. App. 2003) ("Under Section 664.6 of the [California] Code of Civil Procedure, a trial court may enforce a settlement agreement made during pending litigation if the parties entered into the agreement either orally before the court or in writing outside the presence of the court.")

[386] Devon Energy Prod. Co., L.P. v. Line Finders, LLC, No. 21-6119, 2022 WL 4232404, at *2 (10th Cir. Sept. 14, 2022) (enforcing settlement agreement signed by only one party because the other party accepted it orally; "Under Oklahoma law, '[a] settlement agreement is an oral or written contract' "); K4 Enterprises, Inc. v. Grater, Inc., 914 N.E.2d 617, 620–21 (Ill. App. 2009) (affirming enforcement of oral settlement agreement, "brokered" by trial judge, in judge's chambers); Quint v. A.E. Staley Mfg. Co., 246 F.3d 11, 14–15 (1st Cir. 2001); Zimmerman v. McColley, 826 N.E.2d 71, 76 (Ind. Ct. App. 2005); Murray v. State, 737 P.2d 1000, 1001 (Utah 1987) ("Plaintiffs have not at any time argued that an agreement was not reached and, in fact, at oral argument, conceded such an agreement.")

[387] See, e.g., Waddle v. Elrod, 367 S.W.3d 217 (Tenn. 2012) (statute of frauds' requirement that contracts for sale of real property be in writing applied to settlement agreement pursuant to which niece agreed to convey her one-half interest in real property back to owner, but e-mail exchange between attorneys for owner and niece confirming that settlement agreement had been reached, which identified material terms with sufficient specificity was "writing" signed by party to be charged, in compliance with statute of frauds); Omaha Nat'l Bank v. Mullenax, 320 N.W.2d 755, 758 (Neb. 1982); Byblos Corp. v. Salem Farm Realty Trust, 692 A.2d 514, 517 (N.H. 1997) ("when a settlement agreement includes the transfer of an interest in land, it necessarily implicates the statute of frauds. Therefore, the agreement must be in writing and signed by the party to be charged, or by some person authorized by him. We continue to adhere to the view that settlements that involve land conveyances are excepted from the statute when they are finalized under court supervision.")

[388] See, e.g., Sherman v. Haines, 652 N.E.2d 698, 701 (Ohio 1995) ("In this case, the alleged oral agreement provided that appellant would 'pay the $3,000.00 debt in monthly installments of $25.00.' By its express terms, the agreement necessarily required one hundred twenty months (or ten years) of installment payments. These terms are neither indefinite nor based upon a contingency. The agreement made no provision for the possibility of an early payoff. Having been entirely oral, the agreement violated R.C. 1335.05 [Ohio's Statute of Frauds]. Thus, the trial court was correct in denying appellees' motion for leave to file an amended complaint alleging a breach of this oral agreement.").

necessary to make a settlement. "Settlements ordinarily require no judicial approval, as they are simply private agreements between parties concerning the release of a claim."[389]

In contrast, some settlements do require judicial approval. For instance, if parties seeking a divorce reach a settlement agreement involving child custody, the court is not likely to grant the divorce until the court determines that the settlement adequately serves the interests of children and, to a lesser extent, both spouses.[390] Similarly, many jurisdictions require court approval of some settlements involving minor plaintiffs to ensure the agreements serve the best interests of the minors.[391]

In class actions, the court is not likely to approve a settlement ending the claims of absent class members until the court determines

---

[389] Howard M. Erichson & Ethan J. Leib, Class Action Settlements As Contracts?, 102 N.C. L. Rev. 73, 79 (2023).

[390] See, e.g., Goss v. Goss, 2021 WL 4163778, No. 1 CA-CV 20-0565 FC, at *2 (Ariz. Ct. App. Sept. 14, 2021) ("the court is not bound to enforce an agreement between parties involving custody matters if the court is not convinced the agreement will advance the best interests and welfare of the children"); id. ("above all else, the primary consideration in custody determinations is the best interests of the children, and any attempt, through agreement or otherwise, which circumvents this paramount consideration requires a closer look"); Copple v. Swindle, 112 N.E.3d 205, 211 (Ind. Ct. App. 2018) ("the principles of freedom of contract that govern property settlements do not apply to child support and child custody because of the 'overriding policy concern [to] protect[ ] the welfare and interests of children.' "); Albins v. Elovitz, 791 P.2d 366, 368–69 (Ariz. Ct. App. 1990) ("a custodial parent can waive child support payments" and "surrender visitation rights. . . . However, any such agreement is not binding on the court and will be enforced only so long as the interest of the child is not adversely affected."); Lewis v. Lewis, 603 P.2d 650, 653 (Kan. Ct. App. 1979) ("if a trial court finds that a separation agreement is not just and equitable . . . it is free either to reject or make reasonable adjustments to the agreement . . . provided it does so before entering a final judgment that merges the separation agreement into a divorce decree."); Unif. Marriage and Divorce Act § 306(a)–(c) (1982); id. § 306(b) ("[T]he terms of the separation agreement, except those providing for the support, custody, and visitation of children, are binding upon the court unless it finds, after considering the economic circumstances of the parties and any other relevant evidence produced by the parties, on their own motion or on request of the court, that the separation agreement is unconscionable."); Homer H. Clark Jr. & Sanford N. Katz, The Law of Domestic Relations in the United States 903 (3d ed. 2021) ("Agreements between parents as to custody of their children, usually made as part of their separation agreement are usually encouraged by the courts and therefore enforced, so long as they appear to serve the child's interests. Although the courts are free to disregard such contracts when they find that the child's interests are not being served, as a practical matter the courts are only too happy to enforce the contracts and avoid litigating custody").

[391] Tenn. Code Ann. § 29–34–105(a)(1) ("In any tort claim settlement involving a minor, the court shall conduct a hearing at which the minor and legal guardian are present if the tort claim settlement: (A) Is a settlement of ten thousand dollars ($10,000) or more; (B) Is a structured settlement; or (C) Involves a minor who is not represented by an attorney licensed to practice in this state.")

that the proposed settlement adequately serves the interests of those absent class members.[392]

> What binds class members to the settlement is not that they agreed to it—they didn't—but rather that a court entered a judgment giving binding effect to the terms of the agreement reached between the defendant and class counsel. A court enters such a judgment only upon finding that the matter is fit for resolution as a class action, that the lawyer is fit to serve as class counsel, and that the proposed terms for resolving the dispute are "fair, reasonable, and adequate."[393]

In bankruptcy cases, the debtor is typically insolvent, so the more money one creditor recovers from the debtor, the less money other creditors will recover. So, settling one creditor's claim requires bankruptcy court approval, with the court looking out for the interests of other creditors.[394]

Finally, when government is the plaintiff enforcing environmental law, court approval of the settlement—typically a consent decree (§ 1.40(b)(2))—is often required. "Some federal statutes, regulations, and policies . . . explicitly require the United States to use consent decrees lodged in federal courts to settle certain types of environmental claims."[395]

Minor children, absent class members, absent creditors in bankruptcy, and members of the public served by federal enforcement of environmental law are effectively governed by

---

[392] See, e.g., Fed. R. Civ. P. 23(e) ("The claims, issues, or defenses of a certified class—or a class proposed to be certified for purposes of settlement—may be settled, voluntarily dismissed, or compromised only with the court's approval."); Jay Tidmarsh & Roger H. Transgrud, Complex Litigation and Its Alternatives 424–25 (2d ed. 2018) ("the court must decide 'whether the interests of the class are better served by the settlement than by further litigation.' . . . The central question is whether the settlement is a good value for the class"). Whether courts are sufficiently rigorous in ensuring that settlements protect absent class members is the subject of debate. See, e.g., John Bronsteen, Class Action Settlements: An Opt-In Proposal, 2005 U. Ill. L. Rev. 903 ("The outcome of a class action binds all class members except the few who take the trouble to opt out. This default rule enables plaintiffs' lawyers and defendants to settle class lawsuits on mutually beneficial terms that exploit class members. Judges approve such settlements because, among other things, they have a strong incentive to clear their dockets.")

[393] Howard M. Erichson & Ethan J. Leib, Class Action Settlements As Contracts?, 102 N.C. L. Rev. 73, 76 (2023).

[394] Fed. R. Bankr. P. 9019(a) ("after notice and a hearing, the court may approve a compromise or settlement. Notice must be given to: all creditors;"); id. (b)(2) ("After a hearing on such notice as the court may order, the court may: . . . authorize the trustee to compromise or settle controversies within the class or classes without further hearing or notice.")

[395] Tracy Hester, Consent Decrees As Emergent Environmental Law, 85 Mo. L. Rev. 687, 691 (2020).

settlements made by others, so the court looking out for their interests is the rationale for requiring court approval of such settlements.[396] And the environmental law example generalizes to some degree because courts scrutinize settlements more critically before entering judgment on them, especially if the judgment goes beyond money to equitable remedies the court will have to supervise.[397]

In most other contexts, by contrast, courts in the U.S. are fine with settling parties looking out for their own interests, and thus are generally happy to dismiss litigation pursuant to the parties' settlement without inquiring about its terms.[398] "Courts regularly rely on negotiated settlements for disposition of cases and nearly as regularly incorporate these negotiated settlement terms into agreed judgments, stipulated judgments, and consent judgments—and most of the time, they do this without any significant review."[399] "This is particularly true in state courts, even though there is some variation in the showing required before these courts issue consent decrees,

[396] For example, "the Tunney Act requires that consent decrees that resolve antitrust enforcement actions must serve the 'public interest.' " Tracy Hester, Consent Decrees As Emergent Environmental Law, 85 Mo. L. Rev. 687, 697 (2020). See 15 U.S.C. § 16(e)(1). ("Before entering any consent judgment proposed by the United States under this section, the court shall determine that the entry of such judgment is in the public interest").

[397] United States v. City of New Orleans, 731 F.3d 434, 439 (5th Cir. 2013) (explaining "Consent decrees cannot be approved without due consideration by the district court and, once approved, have the force of a legal judgment. . . . 'Even if all of the litigants were in accord, it does not follow that the federal court must do their bidding. . . . The entry of a consent decree is more than a matter of agreement among litigants. It is a judicial act.' " (internal citations omitted)). United States v. City of Miami, Fla., 664 F.2d 435, 441 (5th Cir. 1981) (Rubin, J., concurring) ("Because the consent decree does not merely validate a compromise but, by virtue of its injunctive provisions, reaches into the future and has continuing effect, its terms require more careful scrutiny. Even when it affects only the parties, the court should, therefore, examine it carefully to ascertain not only that it is a fair settlement but also that it does not put the court's sanction on and power behind a decree that violates Constitution, statute, or jurisprudence.")

[398] See, e.g., Mars Steel Corp. v. Continental Illinois Nat'l Bank, 834 F.2d 677, 681 (7th Cir. 1987) ("The fairness of a settlement of a legal dispute is like the adequacy of the consideration supporting a contractual promise: a matter best left to negotiation between the parties."); Janus Films, Inc. v. Miller, 801 F.2d 578, 581–82 (2d Cir. 1986) (explaining "Lawsuits ended by agreement may either be dismissed by stipulation, Fed.R.Civ.P. 41(a)(1)(ii), or may culminate in a judgment. If dismissed by stipulation, the judge normally plays no role whatever, standing 'indifferent' to the terms the parties have agreed to."); Walters v. Wal-Mart Stores, Inc., 703 F.3d 1167, 1172 (10th Cir. 2013) (finding "the 'Settlement Terms' document signed by Walters patently evidences the parties' intent to effectuate a defined settlement. The fact that certain formalities remained—namely, the drafting of a final, formal document—does not undermine Walters' acceptance of Wal-Mart's offer of compromise. Thus, Walters was not in a position to repudiate the agreement even if he was later unhappy with its terms" without analyzing the merits of agreement provisions.).

[399] Nancy A. Welsh, Drive-By Mediation and Other Opportunistic Distortions of Process, 67 Ariz. L. Rev. 773, 817 (2025).

consent judgments, agreed judgments, or stipulated judgments that incorporate parties' settlement terms."[400] In sum, with respect to settling litigation, courts say, the law "favors compromise,"[401] and leading scholars suggest that "[b]ecause settlements conserve resources and make less work for the courts, they are highly favored by judges."[402]

However, in some cases settling parties looking out for their own interests is overridden or by public policy voiding particular terms of settlement agreements. For example, public policy may void some settlement terms requiring confidentiality (§ 1.43) or prohibiting a lawyer from later representing clients with claims similar to the one being settled.[403]

### *(d) Beyond the U.S.*

#### *(1) Common Law and Civil Law Systems*

The previous paragraphs explain how U.S. courts enforce settlement agreements. Similar law generally governs in other nations with similar legal systems. English law, for example, treats "a settlement [a]s merely an agreement or contract to end a dispute," and thus applies "the general requirements of English contract law (offer, acceptance, consideration, due capacity, and an intention to create legal relations)."[404] As in the U.S., in England "[i]f litigation has not commenced, the settlement agreement usually operates as a contract between the parties, thereby requiring fresh proceedings to

---

[400] Id.

[401] Vildibill v. Palmer Johnson of Savannah, Inc., 244 Ga. App. 747, 748, 536 S.E.2d 779, 781 (2000). See also Meyer v. Ten Mile Island Condo. Ass'n, No. 1:22-CV-02042-SKC-KAS, 2025 WL 2720545, at *3 (D. Colo. Sept. 24, 2025) ("The law favors compromise and settlement"); Krantz v. Univ. of Kansas, 271 Kan. 234, 241, 21 P.3d 561, 567 (2001) ("It is an elemental rule that the law favors compromise and settlement of disputes").

[402] Sarah R. Cole, Craig A. McEwen, Nancy H. Rogers, James R. Coben, Peter N. Thompson & Nadja M. Alexander, Mediation: Law, Policy, & Practice § 7:2 (2024).

[403] See Model Rules of Prof'l Conduct R. 5.6(b) (2019), which bars lawyers from participating in the making of "an agreement in which a restriction on the lawyer's right to practice is part of the settlement." A lawyer's confidentiality agreement, if written broadly enough, can be "tantamount" to an agreement not to sue the same defendant on behalf of a later client with a substantially related claim. Stephen Gillers & Richard W. Painter, Free the Lawyers: a Proposal to Permit No-Sue Promises in Settlement Agreements, 18 Geo. J. Legal Ethics 291, 294 (2005) (arguing that such no-sue agreements should be enforceable).

[404] Philip Chong & Elizabeth Tout, United Kingdom in John Fellas, Settlement and compromise of proceedings—Kinds of settlement and effect on litigation, Transnational Litigation § 29:86 (2024). "As a settlement agreement is a contract, it can be challenged as any other contract. Thus, it could be found to be void on grounds of concepts such as mistake, frustration, fraud and illegality. It could also be set aside on grounds of misrepresentation, duress and undue influence." Donald Lambert, Mediation in United Kingdom, Lexology (Sept. 9, 2019), https://www.lexology.com/library/detail.aspx?g=02ee5416-79ba-484b-bd62-eb26318d330b.

be issued [a new suit] for any breach."[405] On the other hand, "If the proceedings have been issued," that is, litigation has begun, "various forms of court order can be sought to give effect to the agreement."[406] These various forms are ways English courts convert settlement agreements into consent orders.[407] At least one of them, the Tomlin Order, permits what is common in the U.S.—settling parties jointly filing with the court a stipulation to dismiss the case with prejudice, pursuant to a separate settlement agreement that remains confidential unless there is later litigation alleging its breach.[408]

In contrast to England and nearly all of the U.S., most jurisdictions around the world have civil law, rather than common law, systems. Some civil law jurisdictions are generally similar to common law jurisdictions in treating settlement agreements basically like other contracts. For example, France's Civil Code states that "a settlement is a contract by which the parties resolve an existing dispute or prevent a dispute from arising."[409] "The settlement prevents the parties from instituting or continuing legal proceedings with the same subject matter."[410] Similarly, the German Civil Code defines a settlement as "a contract by which a dispute or uncertainty of the parties with regard to a legal relationship is removed by way of mutual concession."[411]

---

405 Shahla F. Ali, Court Mediation Reform 76 (2018).

406 Id.

407 Id. See also Philip Chong & Elizabeth Tout, United Kingdom in John Fellas, Settlement and compromise of proceedings—Kinds of settlement and effect on litigation, Transnational Litigation § 29:87 (2024); Watson v. Sadiq [2013] EWCA Civ 822 (affirming refusal to set aside consent order for duress).

408 Zenith Logistics Services (UK) Ltd and others v. Coury [2020] EWHC 774 (QB) (holding that the court has no jurisdiction to request to see a private, confidential settlement agreement identified in the schedule to a Tomlin Order, as it does not form part of the court's order "as such"); id. (stating that the principle of open justice is not derogated by extending confidentiality to the settlement agreement); ABC Ltd v. Y [2010] EWHC 3176 (Ch) (establishing that the recitals to a Tomlin Order should record that the agreed terms are confidential and are not to be filed at court, and holding that a non-party who obtained a copy of the Order was not entitled to a copy of the Schedule containing the confidential terms, since the Order itself stated the Schedule was not filed at court.).

409 Code civil [Civil Code] art. 2044. ("La transaction est un contrat par lequel les parties, par des concessions réciproques, terminent une contestation née, ou préviennent une contestation à naître.")["A settlement is a contract by which the parties, by mutual concessions, terminate a dispute that has arisen, or prevent a dispute from arising."]. (Fr.).

410 Id art. 2052. ("La transaction fait obstacle à l'introduction ou à la poursuite entre les parties d'une action en justice ayant le même objet.")["The settlement prevents the parties from instituting or continuing legal proceedings with the same subject matter."]. (Fr.).

411 Bürgerliches Gesetzbuch [BGB] [Civil Code] § 779(1). ("Ein Vertrag, durch den der Streit oder die Ungewissheit der Parteien über ein Rechtsverhältnis im Wege gegenseitigen Nachgebens beseitigt wird (Vergleich), ist unwirksam, wenn der nach dem Inhalt des Vertrags als feststehend zugrunde gelegte Sachverhalt der

Much as courts in common law jurisdictions often enter judgment on settlements or otherwise convert them into court orders, litigating parties in many civil law jurisdictions can, with court approval,[412] make "court settlements." This process, typically governed by the nation's Code of Civil Procedure, makes the agreement an "enforceable title."[413] However, some civil law systems may not have an analog to what is standard in the U.S.—settling parties jointly filing with the court a stipulation to dismiss the case with prejudice, pursuant to a separate settlement agreement that remains confidential unless there is later litigation alleging its breach (§ 1.43(d)).

*(2) Cross-Border Enforcement*

As in the U.S. and other nations discussed above, the laws of most nations treat settlement agreements as contracts, so enforcing them against the breaching party's property (assets) in most nations requires winning a suit for breach of the settlement agreement in a court of the nation where enforcement is sought. This, as suggested above, tends at best to be slow and expensive, and may depending on the nation's courts also be uncertain. If the settlement agreement has already been converted into a consent judgment, "enforceable title," or other court order, that likely helps enforcement in the nation of that court, but may not help with enforcement elsewhere because, traditionally, "[a]bsent special obligations," courts of one nation "have no obligation to recognize a 'foreign judgment' " from another

Wirklichkeit nicht entspricht und der Streit oder die Ungewissheit bei Kenntnis der Sachlage nicht entstanden sein würde.")["A contract by which a dispute or uncertainty of the parties with regard to a legal relationship is removed by way of mutual concession (settlement) is ineffective if the facts and circumstances on which the contract, by its contents, is premised do not correspond to reality and the dispute or uncertainty would not have occurred if the factual situation had been known."]. (Ger.).

[412] In several civil jurisdictions recording the settlement with a notary may substitute for court approval by creating a notarial deed. The German Code of Civil Procedure permits immediate enforcement not only of a settlement agreement "to resolve the legal dispute either in its full scope or as regards a part of the subject matter of the litigation, before a German court," but also "Based on records or documents that have been recorded . . . by a German notary within the bounds of his official authority, provided that the record or document has been recorded regarding a claim that can be provided for by a settlement." German Code of Civil Procedure § 794(1) 1, 5.

[413] Philipp Anzenberger, The European Dimension of Court Settlements: Open Issues and Regulatory Needs, 111 IUS Gentium 333 (2023) ("Court settlements are one of the core instruments for amicable dispute resolution before court in many European countries"); id. at 340–41 ("in every Member State is the necessity of some sort of involvement of a court when concluding the court settlement. Again, there are various possibilities on how a court can be involved (for example, already before an action was brought in or during proceedings; in the presence of the parties or by a mere written contract submitted to the court; or regarding the mediatory role of the court)"); id. at. 344 ("Probably the most important (procedural) function of a court settlement in practice is its role as an enforcement title.")

nation's courts.[414] This may change—that is, enforcement of foreign courts' judgments may become more reliable—if many nations adopt the 2019 Convention on the Recognition and Enforcement of Foreign Judgments in Civil or Commercial Matters, which obliges contracting states to recognize and enforce civil and commercial judgments rendered in another contracting state (Judgments Convention).[415] However, at present only 32 countries are parties to the Judgments Convention.[416]

Arbitration awards have long been, and remain, ahead of court judgments in cross border enforcement because of widespread adoption and enforcement of the United Nations Convention on the Recognition and Enforcement of Foreign Arbitral Awards (New York Convention), which currently has 172 State parties.[417] For decades, enforcement of a foreign arbitral award has in many countries been simpler and more assured than enforcement of a foreign judgment.[418] So, parties seeking to make their settlement agreement enforceable across borders might be tempted to find an arbitrator willing to convert their settlement into an arbitration award.[419] This

---

414 Bobette Wolski, Enforcing Mediated Settlement Agreements (MSAs): Critical Questions and Directions for Future Research, 7 Contemp. Asia Arb. J. 87, 95 (May 2014).

415 https://www.hcch.net/en/instruments/conventions/full-text/?cid=137.

416 https://www.hcch.net/en/instruments/conventions/status-table/?cid=137.

417 https://www.newyorkconvention.org/contracting-states.

418 Yuliya Zeynalova, The Law on Recognition and Enforcement of Foreign Judgments: Is It Broken and How Do We Fix It?, 31 Berkeley J. Int'l L. 150, 151 (2013) ("Unlike foreign arbitral awards, which are governed by the New York Convention, no treaty outlines the circumstances under which U.S. courts may recognize foreign awards and vice versa. Transnational litigants are therefore more likely to encounter difficulties enforcing their foreign court awards than parties seeking to enforce their foreign arbitral awards."); Theodore J. Folkman, Recognition and Enforcement of Foreign Arbitral Awards, Massachusetts Continuing Legal Education, Inc. (2d ed. 2016) ("[T]he absence of an international convention on the recognition and enforcement of foreign judgments makes recognition and enforcement somewhat complex. [In contrast, t]he New York Convention, the convention governing recognition and enforcement of foreign arbitral awards, greatly simplifies matters when the foreign decision is an award rather than a judgment.").

419 Restatement (Third) U.S. Law of Int'l Comm. Arb. § 1.1 Reporters' Notes a.(iii) (many nations' laws "contemplate that the parties to an arbitration, if reaching a settlement during the arbitration, may request the [arbitral] tribunal to issue an award on agreed terms that incorporates the settlement. The device is intended to allow the parties to add finality to their agreed resolution by conferring upon it the res judicata effects of an arbitral award.") However, in many jurisdictions, a settlement agreement can only be converted to, and enforced as, a consent arbitral award if the arbitration started with a real dispute before that dispute was settled during arbitration. Id. ("Courts in principle will enforce awards on agreed terms, as arbitral awards, but will refrain from doing so when the instrument presented for enforcement cannot be regarded as a legitimate award on agreed terms.")(citing Castro v. Tri Marine Fish Co., 921 F.3d 766, 771 (9th Cir. 2019), in which the Ninth Circuit refused to treat the putative arbitration award as a New York Convention award because, among other things, "There was no dispute to arbitrate, as the parties had fully settled their claims before approaching an arbitrator"). See also Yaraslau Kryvoi & Dmitry

subterfuge (of "rigging" an arbitration award) should not be necessary if the settlement agreement is the product of mediation and the relevant nations have adopted the 2018 Convention on International Settlement Agreements Resulting from Mediation (Singapore Convention),[420] which is discussed in Section 2.16(c).

## § 1.41 Agency Law

Settlements often implicate the law of agency because a lawyer negotiating on behalf of a client is the client's agent. Without a grant of authority from the client, a lawyer cannot settle a claim.[421] As the Restatement of the Law Governing Lawyers explains,

> When a lawyer purports to enter a settlement binding on the client but lacks authority to do so, the burden of inconvenience resulting if the client repudiates the settlement is properly left with the opposing party, who should know that settlements are normally subject to approval by the client and who has no manifested contrary indication from the client. The opposing party can protect itself by obtaining clarification of the lawyer's authority. Refusing to uphold a settlement reached without the client's authority means that the case remains open, while upholding such a settlement deprives the client of the right to have the claim resolved on other terms.[422]

Suppose Plaintiff's lawyer and Defendant's lawyer agree on a settlement. If Plaintiff disapproves of the settlement, she will not be

---

Davydenko, Consent Awards in International Arbitration: From Settlement to Enforcement, 40 Brook. J. Int'l L. 827, 867–68 (2015) ("in most cases consent awards will be enforced as any other arbitral award, but it is important for the parties to demonstrate that not only the underlying settlement agreement was lawful, but also that the dispute was unresolved when the tribunal asserted its jurisdiction.")

[420] U.N. Convention on International Settlement Agreements Resulting from Mediation, Dec. 20, 2018 (adopted), Aug. 7, 2019 (signed), Sept. 12, 2020 (effective), 3369 U.N.T.S. 154, 2019 [hereinafter Singapore Convention] https://uncitral.un.org/sites/uncitral.un.org/files/media-documents/EN/Texts/UNCITRAL/Arbitration/mediation_convention_v1900316_eng.pdf.

[421] 7 Am. Jur. 2d Attorneys at Law § 164 (2024) ("An attorney who represents a client in litigation has no authority to settle a claim of the client absent the client's express authorization or special authorization to do so.") (citing cases); Grace M. Giesel, Enforcement of Settlement Contracts: The Problem of the Attorney Agent, 12 Geo. J. Legal Ethics 543, 556–57 (1999) ("Because a settlement agreement disposing of litigation or possible litigation is a contract, agency principles apply to delineate the circumstances under which an attorney, as agent, may bind a client, as a disclosed principal, to a settlement agreement with a third party. A disclosed principal is a party to a valid contract with a third party and is responsible for any breach if the agent entering into the contract on behalf of the principal had actual or apparent authority to enter into the contract on behalf of the principal.")

[422] Restatement (Third) of the Law Governing Lawyers § 27 cmt. d (2000).

bound by it unless she gave her lawyer authority to bind her.[423] That authority can be *actual* or, in some but not all states, *apparent*.[424] Plaintiff's lawyer would have actual authority if Plaintiff had told her lawyer, for instance, "I will go along with whatever deal you can get," or "I authorize you to settle anywhere over $300,000."

Plaintiff's lawyer would have apparent authority if Plaintiff had led Defendant or Defendant's lawyer reasonably to believe that Plaintiff had given her lawyer authority to bind her to a settlement. While a few courts indicate that a client generally "clothes" her lawyer with apparent authority to settle a case merely by holding out that lawyer as the counsel representing her in the case,[425] most

---

[423] See, e.g., Ocasio v. Six Flags Great Escape, L.P., 2022 WL 4181568, at *6 (N.D.N.Y. Sept. 13, 2022) (not enforcing a purported settlement agreement where "Plaintiff never agreed to the terms set forth by counsel in their phone call, and, upon learning of her counsel's representations to Defendant's counsel that she had accepted the settlement offer, Plaintiff 'made prompt objections' by seeking new counsel and challenging the agreement."); Akers v. Minn. Life Ins. Co., 35 F. Supp. 3d 772, 785 (S.D. W.Va. 2014) (client not bound); Fennell v. TLB Kent Co., 865 F.2d 498, 502 (2d Cir. 1989) (Plaintiff "Fennell made no manifestations to defendants' counsel that Mason and his associates were authorized to settle the case. Fennell's attorneys accordingly had no apparent authority to settle the case for $10,000 without Fennell's consent. The district court's findings that Mason and his associates represented Fennell, and that they were authorized to appear at conferences for him, do not prove otherwise. A client does not create apparent authority for his attorney to settle a case merely by retaining the attorney"); Sharick v. Southeastern Univ. of the Health Scis., Inc., 891 So.2d 562, 565 (Fla. Dist. Ct. App. 2004) (no authority).

[424] Compare Bowers v. BBH SBMC, LLC, 393 So. 3d 20, 31 (Ala. 2023) ("Under Alabama law, a settlement agreement negotiated by an attorney binds the client only when the attorney acts with 'express, special authority' from the client or with apparent authority."); United States v. Int'l Brotherhood of Teamsters, 986 F.2d 15 (2d Cir. 1993) (both actual and apparent authority), with Smith v. King, 953 N.W.2d 258, 280 (Neb. Ct. App. 2020) (" '[A]lthough lawyers retain apparent authority to make procedural and tactical decisions through the existence of the attorney-client relationship, a lawyer cannot settle a client's claim without express authority from the client.' ") (quoting Luethke v. Suhr, 650 N.W.2d 220 (Neb. 2002)); Reutzel v. Douglas, 870 A.2d 787, 789–90 (Pa. 2005) ("The law in this jurisdiction is clear and well-settled that an attorney must have express authority in order to bind a client to a settlement agreement"); Vangjeli v. Banks, 668 F. Supp. 3d 400, 406 (E.D. Pa. 2023) (" 'a settlement is not binding in Pennsylvania if the attorney only has implied actual authority or apparent authority.")

[425] Groves v. Gibbs, 888 S.E.2d 305, 308 n.4 (Ga. Ct. App. 2023) ("It is well settled that, unless the opposing party has knowledge otherwise, an attorney of record has apparent authority to settle a case on the client's behalf, and the client will be bound by the settlement agreement. In such cases, the client's remedy, if any, is against the attorney."); Speed v. Muhanna, 619 S.E.2d 324, 328 (Ga. Ct. App. 2005) (Georgia "Uniform Superior Court Rule 4.12 provides that '[a]ttorneys of record have apparent authority to enter into agreements on behalf of their clients in civil actions"; "The client's remedy, where there have been restrictions [on the attorney's authority] not communicated to the opposing party, is against the attorney who overstepped the bounds of his agency, not against the third party.") See also Capital Dredge and Dock Corp. v. City of Detroit, 800 F.2d 525, 530 (6th Cir. 1986) ("Generally, when a client hires an attorney and holds him out as counsel representing him in a matter, the client clothes the attorney with apparent authority to settle claims connected with the matter."); Turner v. Turner, 2022 WL 413614, at *2 (Mich. Ct. App. Feb. 10, 2022) ("[W]hen a client hires an attorney and holds him out as a counsel representing him

courts do not go so far as to adopt that blanket rule.[426] Instead, most courts adopt a presumption. They "presume that an attorney-of-record who enters into a settlement agreement, purportedly on behalf of a client, had authority to do so."[427] So, the burden of proof is on the party disputing the lawyer's authority to settle.[428] Some cases distinguish settlement agreements made in open court from those made away from the courthouse, with the lawyer's authority to settle more readily found with respect to in-court settlements.[429]

---

in a matter, the client clothes the attorney with apparent authority to settle claims connected with the matter.").

[426] King v. Driscoll, 307 A.3d 134, 138 (Pa. Super. Ct. 2023) ("[T]he ordinary employment of an attorney to represent a client with respect to litigation does not confer upon the attorney the implied or apparent authority to bind the client to a settlement or compromise . . . ."); Fennell v. TLB Kent Co., 865 F.2d 498, 502 (2d Cir. 1989) ("client does not create apparent authority for his attorney to settle a case merely by retaining the attorney."); Restatement (Third) of the Law Governing Lawyers § 27 cmt. d (2000) ("Merely retaining a lawyer does not create apparent authority in the lawyer to [settle a claim].").

[427] Villar v. City of New York, 546 F. Supp. 3d 280, 286 (S.D.N.Y. 2021) (quoting Pereira v. Sonia Holdings (In re Artha Mgmt.), 91 F.3d 326, 329 (2d Cir. 1996)); Makins v. District of Columbia, 861 A.2d 590, 594 (D.C. 2004) (client's actions in sending her attorney to court-ordered settlement conference in employment discrimination action and permitting the attorney to negotiate on client's behalf were insufficient to permit a reasonable belief by the opposing party that attorney had been delegated authority to conclude the settlement).

[428] See, e.g., Hillair Cap. Invs., LP v. Smith Sys. Transp., Inc., 640 F. App'x 49, 52 (2d Cir. 2016) ("To overcome the general presumption that an attorney-of-record has authority to settle, 'any party challenging an attorney's authority . . . bears the burden of proving by *affirmative evidence* that the attorney lacked authority.' "); Bell, LLC v. K&K, Inc., 584 S.W.3d 823, 829 (Mo. Ct. App. 2019) ("Under Missouri law, express authority to settle is presumed where the [party's] attorney of record asserts such authority. . . . The presumption may be overcome by the party disputing the attorney's authority, although that party bears a substantial burden of proof.") (internal quotation marks and citations omitted).

[429] See, e.g., Wilcoxon v. Fletcher, No. 366372, 2024 WL 3738031, at *1 (Mich. Ct. App. Aug. 8, 2024) ("settlement agreement 'is not binding unless it was made in open court, or unless evidence of the agreement is in writing, subscribed by the party against whom the agreement is offered or by that party's attorney' ") (quoting Mich. Ct. R. 2.507(G)); Smith v. King, 953 N.W.2d 258, 278 (Neb. Ct. App. 2020) ("a settlement agreement made in open court on the record, agreed to by all of the parties to the litigation and approved by the court, is enforceable."); S.L. v. J.L.C., 282 So. 3d 26, 34 (Ala. Civ. App. 2019) ("When a client remains silent while her attorney recites a settlement agreement into the record in open court, the court may infer that the lawyer had the client's authority to settle the case."). See also Koval v. Simon Telelect, Inc., 693 N.E.2d 1299, 1307 (Ind. 1998) ("the rule that an attorney has the inherent power to bind the client to an in court judgment applies to proceedings governed by the ADR rules in which the parties are ordered, required by the rule, or agree to appear through authorized representatives. These proceedings are 'in court' for purposes of an attorney's inherent power, irrespective of whether they actually occur inside a courtroom.")

Even if a lawyer lacks actual or apparent authority to settle, the client will be bound by the settlement if the client subsequently ratifies it.[430]

## § 1.42 Multiple Parties: Indemnity, Contribution, and Mary Carter Agreements

A defendant making a settlement payment to the plaintiff may have a right to reimbursement from a third party. Such a right can be created by a contract, such as by a contract clause obligating Third Party to "indemnify" or "hold harmless" Defendant for liability Defendant incurs to Plaintiff as a result of Defendant's performance of its contract with Third Party.[431] Another common example arises in insurance. Insurance companies paying their policyholders' claims generally acquire (are subrogated to) the policyholder's rights against whomever injured the policyholder.[432] A right to indemnity can also

[430] See, e.g., Webb v. First Nat'l Bank of Hinsdale, 711 P.2d 1352, 1355–56 (Mont. 1985) ("When his attorney wrote him a letter advising him of the result of the negotiations, appellant accepted the offer and acknowledged the discount of the amount he owed the Bank. This shows his knowledge at the time of the settlement. Appellant acquiesced for nearly two years in the benefits of the bargain and with specific knowledge of its terms. His conduct amounts to a ratification of the settlement and dismissal."); W. Bradley Elec., Inc. v. Mitchell Eng'g, 318 Cal. Rptr. 3d 747, 759 (Cal. Ct. App. 2024) ("It is well settled that a client may ratify the unauthorized actions of his attorney."); id. (holding that "although [attorney] did not obtain the requisite express authority for the settlement and dismissal, [client's] failure to lodge an objection and promptly take steps to rectify the matter constitutes a ratification that precludes relief.").

[431] See, e.g., Steele Foundations, Inc. v. Clark Const. Grp., 937 A.2d 148, 149 (D.C. 2007) (affirming trial court's ruling that "under a provision of the indemnification clause, [subcontractor] was required to indemnify [contractor] for the amount of the settlement it reached with the injured worker and for the attorneys' fees incurred in responding to the worker's claim."); MSC Mediterranean Shipping Co. S.A. v. Airlift Marine Servs. PVT Ltd., 579 F.Supp.3d 484, 488 (S.D.N.Y. 2022), aff'd sub nom. MSC Mediterranean Shipping Co. S.A. v. Airlift (U.S.A.), Inc., No. 22-406, 2023 WL 4485387 (2d Cir. July 12, 2023) (finding that carrier's agreement with merchant required merchant to reimburse carrier for settlement paid to injured worker. "Brian Diver was seriously injured at work when a bundle of large granite slabs crushed him as he unloaded a shipping container. Diver filed suit . . . against several entities involved in the transportation of that cargo, including Plaintiff MSC . . . the carrier that transported the container across the Atlantic Ocean. MSC later settled with Diver, and now seeks indemnification from the company that arranged for its trans-Atlantic carriage, . . . 'Airlift USA'. Following a bench trial on written submission, the Court finds that MSC's bill of lading with Airlift USA requires indemnification under these circumstances.").

[432] Robert E. Keeton, Alan I. Widiss & James M. Fischer, Insurance Law (2d ed 2017).

> Subrogation, which developed as an equitable doctrine, facilitates an adjustment of rights to avoid unjust enrichment in many types of situations by substituting one person or entity (A) in place of another (B) in regard to some claim or right that (B) has against a third party (C). Subrogation applies in the insurance context when an insurer (A) indemnifies an insured (B) who is entitled to recover compensation for that loss from another source (C), usually, but not always, the tortfeasor who is primarily responsible for causing the loss. In some situations the insurer may be subrogated to the insured's rights. This means the insurer is

be created by non-contract law. For instance, an employer who is vicariously liable for its employee's tort has a right to indemnity from the employee.[433]

Law governing settlement acquires another layer of complexity in multi-party disputes. An example is contribution among joint tortfeasors. In most jurisdictions, joint tortfeasors are jointly and severally liable to the plaintiff, but they have, after paying a judgment, a right to contribution from each other in proportion to degree of fault.[434] Contribution becomes more complicated when one defendant settles before judgment. Cases and statutes are divided on whether non-settling defendants have a right to contribution from the settling defendant.[435] A settlement may include "an agreement whereby the plaintiff indemnifies the settling defendant from any claims of contribution made by the nonsettling parties."[436]

---

> "substituted" for the insured in regard to either all or some portion of the rights that the insured has to receive compensation from another source. An insurer asserting a subrogation right is usually viewed as "standing in the shoes" of the insured so that the insurer's rights are equal to, but no greater than, those of the insured.

Id. § 3.10.

433 Dan B. Dobbs, Paul T. Hayden & Ellen M. Bublick, Hornbook on Torts § 31.1 (2d ed. 2016) (2024 online update).

434 Id. § 35.1.

435 Id. § 35.2 ("Early statutes authorized contribution only when one tortfeasor satisfied a judgment for the plaintiff; the same tortfeasor's settlement with the plaintiff would not support a contribution claim against the other tortfeasors. These statutes have in effect been broadened by judicial decisions creating a contribution right even in cases of settlement, somewhat misleadingly called 'equitable indemnity.' Other statutes specifically authorize contribution in favor of a tortfeasor who satisfies the plaintiff's claim, whether by paying a judgment or effecting a settlement that releases the other tortfeasors."); Restatement (Third) of Torts: Apportionment of Liability § 23(a) (2000) ("When two or more persons are or may be liable for the same harm and one of them discharges the liability of another by settlement or discharge of judgment, the person discharging the liability is entitled to recover contribution from the other, unless the other previously had a valid settlement and release from the plaintiff"); Russell Korobkin, Negotiation Theory and Strategy 417–20 (4th ed. 2024).

436 76 C.J.S. Release § 66 (2024) ("Under the law of some states, a 'Pierringer' release has the effect of releasing the settling defendant from the lawsuit and discharges a part of the cause of action equal to the part attributable to the settling joint tortfeasor's causal negligence, reserves the balance of the whole cause of action against the nonsettling joint tortfeasors, and contains an agreement whereby the plaintiff indemnifies the settling defendant from any claims of contribution made by the nonsettling parties and agrees to satisfy any judgment obtained from the nonsettling tortfeasors to the extent the settling tortfeasor has been released. The elements of a Pierringer release are (1) complete release of the settling defendant by the plaintiff, (2) the plaintiff's express reservation for claims against any remaining and nonsettling defendants, and (3) the plaintiff's agreement to indemnify the settling defendant against claims for contribution or indemnification"). See also R. Lawrence Dessem, Pretrial Litigation: Law, Policy and Practice 549 (2d ed. 2001) (A settlement "may include an agreement by the plaintiff to indemnify the settling defendant if contribution is sought by other potential defendants who are not a party to the present settlement.").

Sometimes one defendant will settle pursuant to an agreement with the plaintiff that makes the amount of the settling defendant's payment turn on the amount the plaintiff wins against the nonsettling defendants. Yet, "the settling defendant remains in the action as if there was no settlement."[437] These so-called "Mary Carter" agreements are often unenforceable or enforceable only if promptly disclosed to the nonsettling defendants.[438] If disclosed to the nonsettling defendant, the agreement is often referred to as a Pierringer settlement.[439]

The Mary Carter agreement is an extreme example of the coalition-building that occurs during many multiple-party litigations.[440] Plaintiffs suing multiple defendants can "divide and conquer" them in many ways. The plaintiff can release a particular defendant from litigation in exchange for:

---

437 Michael Downey, Sinister Secret Settlements, Litigation, Summer/Fall 2012, at 64.

438 See 57B Am. Jur. 2d Negligence § 979 (2024) ("Some courts, including the Florida Supreme Court, have held that a *Mary Carter* agreement, under which a settling defendant gets a financial interest in the outcome of the case and is allowed to continue as a participant in the trial, is void and unenforceable. Other courts have held that *Mary Carter* agreements are not invalid per se.") (internal citations omitted); Patriot Contracting, LLC v. Shelter Prods., Inc., 650 S.W.3d 627, 645 (Tex. App. 2021) ("A Mary Carter agreement exists when a plaintiff settles with one defendant and goes to trial against the remaining defendant, and the settling defendant, who remains a party, guarantees the plaintiff a minimum payment, which may be offset in whole or in part by an excess judgment recovered at trial."); id. ("That type of settlement 'creates a tremendous incentive for the settling defendant to ensure that the plaintiff succeeds in obtaining a sizable recovery' and 'motivates the defendant to assist greatly in the plaintiff's presentation of the case.' Mary Carter agreements are against public policy, and thus invalid, because they 'skew the trial process, mislead the jury, promote unethical collusion among nominal adversaries, and create the likelihood that a less culpable defendant will be hit with the full judgment.' ") (internal citations omitted); 18 Am. Jur. 2d Contribution § 57 (2024) ("Some jurisdictions prohibit Mary Carter agreements. Others permit such agreements but place restrictions, such as disclosure requirements, on their use.") (internal citations omitted); Hodesh v. Korelitz, 914 N.E.2d 186, 189 (Ohio 2009) ("a Mary Carter agreement [is] "a contract between a plaintiff and one defendant allying them against another defendant at trial."); id. ("Mary Carter agreements are per se invalid in some states."); Collings v. City First Mortg. Servs., LLC, 317 P.3d 1047, 1054 (Wash. Ct. App 2013) ("Courts have adopted different approaches to Mary Carter agreements. Some jurisdictions have banned such agreements as a matter of policy. Others have allowed Mary Carter agreements but have required that they be disclosed."); id. ("Some of these courts have required that such agreements must be produced for examination before trial if there is a discovery request.").

439 Roger S. Haydock, Fundamentals of Litigation Practice Ch. 35 Introduction (2025 ed.) ("a Pierringer release and is disclosed to the court and all parties involved. Another type of document is known as a Mary Carter agreement and its existence is only known to the contracting parties.") This type of agreement derives its name from the Wisconsin case, Pierringer v. Hoger et al, 124 NW 2d 106 (Wisc. 1963).

440 On multiple-party negotiations generally, see Russell Korobkin, Negotiation Theory and Strategy ch. 12 (4th ed. 2024); Robert H. Mnookin, Strategic Barriers to Dispute Resolution: A Comparison of Bilateral and Multilateral Negotiations, 8 Harv. Negot. L. Rev. 1 (2003).

- money to finance further litigation against the other defendants,
- information that will strengthen the plaintiff's case against the other defendants, and
- even the testimony of the settling defendant.

Different issues arise when multiple plaintiffs have sued, or might sue, a single defendant and the defendant settles with only some of the plaintiffs. For instance, the early-settling plaintiffs' settlement agreement with the defendant may have a "most favored nations clause." This clause provides that if later-settling plaintiffs negotiate a higher settlement amount than the early-settling plaintiffs, the early-settling plaintiffs' settlement amount will be adjusted up to that higher amount.[441]

[441] See Judith Resnik, Procedure as Contract, 80 Notre Dame L. Rev. 593, 651–52 (2005) ("a settlement agreement can include a provision (a 'most favored nations clause') that, if later settling litigants do better, the originally-settling individual or group may have their awards adjusted upwards. Thus, these clauses can enable a series of settlements with similar terms applied to comparable litigants. Some courts frown on unconditional most favored nations clauses; judges debate whether the clauses facilitate or create disincentives for subsequent settlements because they potentially require additional payments to earlier settlers"); Rice v. N.Y. State Workers' Comp. Bd., 140 N.Y.S.3d 857, 857–58 (App. Div. 2021) (settlement agreements "contained a Most Favored Nation (MFN) clause that provided: '[defendant] shall not enter into any Agreement with other former Trust members . . . which contains more favorable terms than this Agreement unless [defendant] shall agree to extend the same terms to the Member."); In re Nat'l Prescription Opiate Litig., 622 F. Supp. 3d 584, 635 n.89 (N.D. Ohio 2022) ("The Florida Settlement contains a 'most favored nation' provision, so that if a 'Pharmacy enters a global settlement resolving substantially all claims against it brought by states, counties, and/or municipalities nationwide that contains additional injunctive relief provisions, the State of Florida shall have the right to obtain the benefit of those provisions under the terms set forth in any such global settlement.' "); Ficel Transp., Inc. v. New York, 177 N.Y.S.3d 356, 358 (App. Div. 2022) ("the agreements each contained a paragraph providing that the Board would 'not enter into any [a]greement with other former [t]rust members or their representative counsel which contains more favorable terms than this [a]greement unless the Board shall agree to extend the same terms to the [m]ember.' The parties call this the 'most favored nations' clause."); Palmore v. Monsanto Co., No. 2:13-CV-00777-SGC, 2015 WL 7770213, at *1 (N.D. Ala. Sept. 30, 2015), report and recommendation adopted, No. 2:13-CV-777-KOB, 2015 WL 7755491 (N.D. Ala. Dec. 2, 2015), aff'd, 671 F. App'x 736 (11th Cir. 2016) ("The *Owens* settlement agreement contained a 'most favored nation' clause, providing the *Owens* plaintiffs would receive no less per capita than the amount received by any other plaintiff in a similar lawsuit."); Ted A. Donner, Attorney's Practice Guide to Negotiations § 13:12 (2014) ("Under a 'most favored nation' clause in a settlement agreement, the plaintiffs agree not to settle their claims against other defendants absent certain conditions without offering similar terms to the settling defendant.").

## § 1.43 Confidentiality and Settlement Negotiation

### *(a) Generally*

Settlement negotiation is a means of discovery in litigation. So, lawyers are very reluctant to reveal, or approve their client revealing, anything in settlement negotiations that could come back to haunt them if negotiations fail, and litigation (or arbitration) continues. On the other hand, the *problem-solving* approach to negotiation requires honestly disclosing lots of information to the other side (§§ 1.22–1.26). It does so because *positive-sum* negotiation is inhibited by secrecy about a party's interests and priorities. In some cases, mutually beneficial settlement options emerge only when each side reveals sensitive information to the other. So, a problem-solving negotiator may be willing to reveal sensitive information to her counterpart.

However, even if a lawyer involved in settlement negotiation is willing to reveal sensitive information to her counterpart, she may not want that information revealed to anyone else. Such information, if it becomes public, might cause her client embarrassment or financial loss. So, settlement negotiation, especially the problem-solving sort, benefits from tools to reduce the chance that what is revealed to the other side in negotiation will "leave the room" and be shared more widely. These tools are discussed next and, with respect to mediation, in Section 2.28.

### *(b) Rules of Evidence*

Suppose settlement negotiations fail to produce a settlement, and the parties go to trial. One side may seek to introduce as evidence what the other side said during settlement negotiations. Such statements are not likely to be admitted into evidence. Federal Rule of Evidence 408 says "conduct or statements made in compromise negotiations" are not admissible "to prove liability or invalidity of the claim or its amount." While Rule 408 likely applies only to negotiations to settle civil claims,[442] plea bargaining is covered by a somewhat similar rule. Federal Rule of Evidence 410 says "In a civil or criminal case, evidence of the following is not admissible against the defendant who made the plea or participated in the plea discussions: . . . a statement made during plea discussions with an

---

[442] Sarah R. Cole, Craig A. McEwen, Nancy H. Rogers, James R. Coben & Peter N. Thompson, Mediation: Law, Policy, & Practice § 8:7 (2024) ("evidence of attempts to avoid criminal prosecution by negotiating with the victim would not be excluded from evidence by Rule 408 or similar rules").

attorney for the prosecuting authority if the discussions did not result in a guilty plea or they resulted in a later-withdrawn guilty plea."[443]

The full text of Rule 408 is:

> (a) Prohibited Uses. Evidence of the following is not admissible—on behalf of any party—either to prove or disprove the validity or amount of a disputed claim or to impeach by a prior inconsistent statement or a contradiction:
>
> > (1) furnishing, promising, or offering—or accepting, promising to accept, or offering to accept—a valuable consideration in compromising or attempting to compromise the claim; and
> >
> > (2) conduct or a statement made during compromise negotiations about the claim—except when offered in a criminal case and when the negotiations related to a claim by a public office in the exercise of its regulatory, investigative, or enforcement authority.
>
> (b) Exceptions. The court may admit this evidence for another purpose, such as proving a witness's bias or prejudice, negating a contention of undue delay, or proving an effort to obstruct a criminal investigation or prosecution.[444]

Most states have adopted Rule 408 or something similar.[445] The policy behind this rule is to encourage settlement.

Note, however, that Rule 408 does not invariably exclude from evidence all statements made in settlement negotiation. It may not exclude statements relating to a dispute not yet on the verge of litigation.[446] And even statements related to disputes in litigation are

---

[443] Fed. R. Evid. 410(a)(4).

[444] Fed. R. Evid. 408.

[445] David P. Leonard, The New Wigmore Treatise on Evidence § 3.6 (3d ed. 2019) ("Federal Rule 408 has been extremely influential among the states, a large number of which adopted its pre-2006 language verbatim"); id. (all states "maintain the basic rule excluding evidence of compromises and compromise offers, though a number appear to admit independent statements of fact made during the course of compromise discussions.")

[446] Josephs v. Pac.Bell, 2006 WL 903224 (9th Cir. 2006) ("Because the purpose of Rule 408 is to encourage the compromise and settlement of existing disputes," district did not err in admitting statements made prior to filing of discrimination claim); Pierce v. F.R.Tripler & Co., 955 F.2d 820, 827 (2d Cir. 1992) (where a party threatens litigation and has initiated the first administrative steps in litigation, "any offer made between attorneys will be presumed to be an offer within the scope of Rule 408."); Affiliated Mfrs., Inc. v. Aluminum Co. of America, 56 F.3d 521, 527 (3d Cir. 1995) (Rule 408 "applies where an actual dispute or a difference of opinion exists, rather than when discussions crystallize to the point of threatened litigation"); Weems v. Tyson Foods, Inc., 665 F.3d 958, 965 (8th Cir. 2011) ("We agree with our sister circuits in recognizing

admissible if offered for purposes other than "proving liability for or invalidity of the claim or its amount." Such purposes include proving bias or prejudice, undue delay, or obstruction of justice.[447] Also, Rule 408, like any evidence rule, only applies to courts.[448] It may not apply to administrative hearings,[449] or arbitration.[450]

---

a dispute need not "crystallize to the point of threatened litigation" for the 408 exclusion rule to apply. A dispute exists for Rule 408 purposes so long as there is 'an actual dispute or difference of opinion' regarding a party's liability for or the amount of the claim"); State ex rel. Franklin v. Tatterson, 821 S.E.2d 330, 338 (W. Va. 2018) ("While litigation need not have actually commenced in order for Rule 408 to apply, under Rule 408(a) there must be a prior dispute before excluding evidence of an offer to compromise," Rule 408 "does not apply to settlement offers made before the plaintiff has asserted a claim or threatened to assert a claim against the defendant.")

[447] Courts are split on whether Rule 408 allows admission of statements made in settlement negotiation for the purpose of impeaching (by prior inconsistent statements) testimony at trial. Compare, e.g., EEOC v. Gear Petroleum, Inc., 948 F.2d 1542, 1545–46 (10th Cir. 1991) (not admissible), with Hernandez v. State, 52 P.3d 765, 767 (Ariz. 2002) ("Most federal circuit courts agree that Rule 408 does not bar evidence from compromise negotiations if the evidence will be used for impeachment purposes.") id. at 769 ("public policy dictates that evidence obtained in the course of compromise negotiations should be available for impeachment purposes"); Cochenour v. Cameron Sav. & Loan, F.A., 160 F.3d 1187, 1190 (8th Cir. 1998) (admissible).

[448] See Fed. R. Evid. 1101 (applicability of Rules).

[449] Compare Fed. Trade Comm'n v. Cement Inst., 333 U.S. 683, 705–06 (1948) ("[A]dministrative agencies . . . have never been restricted by the rigid rules of evidence."); Johnson v. Boston Pub. Schools, 906 F.3d 182, 192–93 (1st Cir. 2018) (rejecting plaintiff's argument that Federal Rule of Evidence 408 should extend "to settlement discussions before the [administrative] hearing officer. Absent an express requirement, however, administrative hearings are not bound by the Federal Rules of Evidence."); Fed. R. Evid. 101, 1101 (listing covered proceedings), with Cnty. of Cook v. Ill. Lab. Rels. Bd., 976 N.E.2d 493, 501–02, 505 (Ill. App. Ct. 2012) (reversing administrative board's ruling because it relied on "admission of evidence which ignored established rules of evidence when dealing with the admissibility of a comment reportedly made during a settlement conference." The board admitted testimony "that recounted the settlement conference statements." This was contrary to the administrative board's own rules, which provided that "the Administrative Law Judge will, insofar as practicable, apply the rules of evidence applicable in Illinois Courts."); Jutkowitz v. Dep't of Health Servs., 596 A.2d 374, 381 (Conn. 1991) (stating that "[a]llowing evidence of settlement negotiations to be admitted at administrative hearings is inconsistent with both fundamental principles of justice and with the public policy of encouraging settlements. We conclude, therefore, that evidence of attempts at settlement is generally not admissible at adjudicative hearings by agencies," but ultimately concluding that defense counsel's mere mention at administrative hearing that the department had made a settlement offer was not prejudicial).

[450] Stephen J. Ware & Ariana R. Levinson, Principles of Arbitration Law § 34(c) (2d ed. 2023) ("Evidentiary rules, like other aspects of arbitration, are primarily determined by the arbitration agreement. Many agreements incorporate the rules of an arbitration organization such as the American Arbitration Association. The AAA's Commercial Arbitration Rules allow the parties to offer into evidence whatever is relevant and material.")

### *(c) Confidentiality Agreements (Including Protective Orders) About Settlement Negotiation and Discovery*

Rule 408 and similar state statutes protect settlement offers and statements from being introduced as evidence but not from pre-trial discovery. Of course, the party to whom information is revealed in settlement negotiations will not need to discover it. But that party may receive discovery requests from other parties to that case or from parties to other cases. Such discovery requests are likely to be granted by courts applying civil procedure rules generally allowing discovery of, not just admissible evidence, but anything reasonably calculated to lead to the discovery of admissible evidence.[451] However, "several courts have held that the same public policy concerns that support [Rule 408] also support protection from discovery into confidential settlement negotiations."[452]

Moreover, litigating parties seeking confidentiality may jointly seek a court order (called a "protective order" or "PO") requiring the confidentiality of information exchanged in discovery and settlement negotiations.[453] It has long been true that "parties will frequently agree to, and courts will regularly issue, umbrella protective

---

[451] Fed. R. Civ. P. 26(b) ("Unless otherwise limited by court order, the scope of discovery is as follows: Parties may obtain discovery regarding any nonprivileged matter that is relevant to any party's claim or defense and proportional to the needs of the case, considering the importance of the issues at stake in the action, the amount in controversy, the parties' relative access to relevant information, the parties' resources, the importance of the discovery in resolving the issues, and whether the burden or expense of the proposed discovery outweighs its likely benefit. Information within this scope of discovery need not be admissible in evidence to be discoverable.")

[452] In re RDM Sports Group, Inc., 277 B.R. 415, 433 (Bankr. N.D. Ga. 2002) (citing cases). But see Leading Mfg. Sols., LP v. Hitco, Ltd., No. 15CV1852-LAB (PCS), 2017 WL 1336939, at *3 (S.D. Cal. Mar. 24, 2017) ("communications during settlement negotiations are discoverable").

[453] The authority for such orders comes from Federal Rule of Civil Procedure 26(c) and its state counterparts, as well as from a court's inherent authority over litigation before it.

> Rule 26(c) empowers the court to make a wide variety of orders for the protection of parties and witnesses in the discovery process. Whether use of protective orders is expanding is uncertain. At least one district judge believes protective order practice has increased: "Protective orders are, obviously, an ever-expanding feature of modern litigation. They have multiplied to the extent that the Court, itself, has incorporated a model order into its Local Rules. Protective orders recognize that parties engaged in litigation do not sacrifice all aspects of privacy or their proprietary information simply because of a lawsuit. But there remains a concomitant principle favoring full, fair, and open disclosure of the important matters occurring the public's courts."

8 Charles A. Wright et al., Federal Practice and Procedure § 2035 (3d ed. 2024) (quoting In re Mirapex Prods. Liab. Litig., 246 F.R.D. 668, 672–73 (D. Minn. 2007)).

orders,"[454] presumptively covering all material the disclosing party deems confidential.[455] A recent study:

- shows that about 45 percent of protective orders are the product of the parties' joint motion,
- estimates that "judges grant 95 to 97 percent of all joint requests for POs," and
- finds "that over half of the judges who considered at least twenty-five stipulated POs in our dataset never denied a single such request."[456]

A party who breaches a protective order is in contempt of court.[457] However, a protective order is sometimes overcome by a

---

[454] Laurie Kratky Dore, Secrecy by Consent: The Use and Limits of Confidentiality in the Pursuit of Settlement, 74 Notre Dame L. Rev. 283, 332 (1999).

[455] Dustin B. Benham, Foundational and Contemporary Court Confidentiality, 86 Mo. L. Rev. 211, 220–21 (2021) ("In jurisdictions across the country, courts have standing (or 'suggested') protective orders. The orders often include provisions that allow the parties themselves to designate discovery material as 'confidential.' In some cases, using these 'umbrella' provisions, parties designate entire document productions, entire deposition transcripts, or engage in other blanket designation practices. Umbrella confidentiality designations preclude disclosure absent a party challenge").

[456] Nora Freeman Engstrom et al., Secrecy by Stipulation, 74 Duke L.J. 99, 106 (2024).

[457] Lyn-Lea Travel Corp. v. Am. Airlines, Inc., 283 F.3d 282, 291 (5th Cir. 2002) (affirming civil contempt sanctions where a party and its counsel violated multiple protective orders by disclosing confidential discovery material; "The court's protective orders prohibited the use of the confidential documents for any purpose outside of the litigation, thereby prohibiting revelation of the documents' contents as much as their existence. Sedgwick's and Garner's admissions constitute clear and convincing evidence that Lyn-Lea and Gardner violated the court's protective orders. The district court did not abuse its discretion by entry of the contempt order."); Reis v. Iowa Dist. Court for Polk Cnty., 787 N.W.2d 61, 75 (Iowa 2010) (affirming contempt finding against attorney who violated a protective order by using confidential litigation documents for purposes outside the case; "[T]he district court's determination that Stowers be held in contempt of court violation of the protective order is supported by substantial evidence."); Eagle Comtronics, Inc. v. Arrow Commc'n Lab'ys, Inc., 305 F.3d 1303, 1314 (Fed. Cir. 2002) (reversing the district court and holding that Eagle's "undisputed conduct, plus the language of the unambiguous protective order, amount to the clear and convincing evidence needed to demonstrate that Eagle was in civil contempt of court. Under the circumstances of this case, the district court's failure to find a violation of the protective order was most certainly an abuse of discretion."); Grove Fresh Distrib., Inc. v. John Labatt Ltd., 888 F. Supp. 1427, 1445 (1995) aff'd, 134 F.3d 374 (7th Cir. 1998) (holding an attorney in contempt for violating a protection order because"[g]iven the purpose for the orders, the context in which they were issued, and the balancing of the respective interests, the orders are valid: there was good cause to find good cause. However, even assuming that the orders were invalid, Mr. Messina may still be punished for violating them."); Flash v. Holtsclaw, 789 N.E.2d 955, 959 (Ind. Ct. App. 2003) ("There is sufficient evidence to support the trial court's determination that Flash knowingly violated an order of court that he refrain from contacting Holtsclaw and from harassing her. . . [a]s such, the trial court was within its discretion in finding Flash in contempt of court."); Brown v. Colegio de Abogados de Puerto Rico, 765 F. Supp. 2d 133, 138 (D.P.R. 2011) (holding defendant in civil contempt because he violated a protective order that "prohibited Defendant

subpoena in another case if the party seeking the discovery can demonstrate a substantial need or that the protective order was improvidently granted in the first action.[458]

To retain confidentiality if the material is filed with the court or introduced into evidence, umbrella protective orders typically require that designated information be filed under seal.[459] Motions to seal are not as readily granted as motions for protective orders because of the strong constitutional and common law presumption that judicial records be accessible to the public.[460]

---

from engaging in any direct or indirect contact or communication with the class members relating to this case, without leave of Court, until the opt out procedures were completed.)

[458] For courts' diverging views on the standard for breaking the seal, see as 8 Charles A. Wright et al., Federal Practice and Procedure § 2044.1 (3d ed. 2024), See also Carrizosa v. Chiquita Brands Int'l, Inc. (In re Chiquita Brands Int'l, Inc. Alien Tort Statute & S'holder Derivative Litig.), 965 F.3d 1238, 1250 (11th Cir. 2020) (affirming district court's modification of a stipulated protective order in response to subpoenas issued in related civil proceedings, holding that the district court reasonably interpreted its own order and acted within its discretion in concluding plaintiffs failed to show good cause to maintain confidentiality); FTC v. Abbvie Prods. LLC, 713 F.3d 54, 58 (11th Cir. 2013) (affirming district court's decision to modify a protective order to permit disclosure of sealed materials sought by subpoena in another case, reasoning that the passage of time reduced the risk of competitive harm and that the public interest in access outweighed any remaining confidentiality concerns); In re Avandia Mktg., Sales Practices & Prods. Liab. Litig., 924 F.3d 662, 678 (3d Cir. 2019) (vacating district court's order maintaining confidentiality of documents subject to a protective order where the materials were sought under subpoena in separate litigation, holding that the lower court applied the wrong legal standard by failing to require a showing of serious injury to justify continued sealing); Gambale v. Deutsche Bank AG, 377 F.3d 133, 141 (2d Cir. 2004) (quoting *Poliquin v. Garden Way, Inc.*, 989 F.2d 527, 535 (1st Cir.1993) (" 'A protective order, like any ongoing injunction, is always subject to the inherent power of the district court to relax or terminate the order, even after judgment. This retained power in the court to alter its own ongoing directives provides a safety valve for public interest concerns, changed circumstances or any other basis that may reasonably be offered for later adjustment.'. . . As we have held and as the Bank concedes, a district court can modify a protective order when a third party requests judicial documents after the parties have filed a stipulation of dismissal pursuant to settlement.).

[459] Laurie Kratky Dore, Secrecy by Consent: The Use and Limits of Confidentiality in the Pursuit of Settlement, 74 Notre Dame L. Rev. 283, 335 (1999). See also Dustin B. Benham, Foundational and Contemporary Court Confidentiality, 86 Mo. L. Rev. 211, 224 (2021) ("Protective orders often make sealed filings the default. The orders, supported by good cause alone, cannot keep discovery confidential once filed. So, they sometimes require filing all protected information under seal or forbid filing protected material without first seeking a sealing order for the material. Though courts could technically reject the sealing request, it will likely be unopposed and routinely granted"); id. at 252 ("Umbrella protective orders are ubiquitous in complex litigation. The orders effectively delegate the court's Rule 26(c) power to the parties by allowing them to designate, without further court intervention, which materials are confidential and subject to the order").

[460] Fair Lab'y Pracs. Assocs. v. Riedel, 666 F. App'x 209, 211–12 (3d Cir. 2016) ("A strong presumption in favor of public accessibility attaches to judicial records (here the filed settlement agreement). The presumption of public access is a common law doctrine that predates the Constitution. It is designed to promote public confidence in the judicial system. The presumption is not absolute, however, and a party may show

### *(d) Confidentiality Agreements (NDAs) in Settlement Agreements*

All parties to a settlement agreement may want to keep its terms confidential. Or one party—typically the defendant—may value and prioritize confidentiality while the other party is relatively indifferent to it.[461] Suppose, for example, Defendant is willing to make a settlement amount up to $50,000 higher if the settlement agreement includes confidentiality and, while Plaintiff would prefer no requirement of confidentiality, Plaintiff would be willing to promise confidentiality in exchange for an extra $10,000 added to the settlement amount. Under these circumstances, each party benefits if the settlement amount is raised by more than $10,000 and less than $50,000 in order to include confidentiality. This is an example of positive sum "logrolling" discussed in § 1.10(c).

> Because defendants are often incentivized to keep litigation information from the public, the plaintiff who obtains such information holds something of value to sell back to the defendant at settlement. Indeed, parties to a settlement often exchange money for a promise of silence from the plaintiff. But the value in this type of bargain can only be realized if the underlying information is not generally known. For if the information were widely known, a defendant would never pay to keep it secret. Thus, plaintiffs have an incentive to develop the maximum amount of damaging information, keep it secret in the interim, and then sell that secrecy back to defendants for money.[462]

Many settlement agreements have clauses obligating the parties, and sometimes also the lawyers,[463] to keep the settlement's

---

that the interest in secrecy outweighs public access. To do so, the party carries the burden to demonstrate that disclosure will work a clearly defined and serious injury. Broad allegations of harm, bereft of specific examples or articulated reasoning, are insufficient.") (internal quotations omitted).

461 Scott A. Moss, Illuminating Secrecy: A New Economic Analysis of Confidential Settlements, 105 Mich. L. Rev. 867, 878–79 (2007). See also Richard A. Posner, Economic Analysis of Law 783 (9th ed. 2014) (keeping settlement "terms secret . . . becomes an inducement to defendants to settle large cases rather than try them; they avoid a public judgment that would encourage further suits by persons situated similarly to the victorious plaintiff. Ordinarily the plaintiff will be happy to agree to such a confidentiality provision because it will enable a quicker and larger settlement.")

462 Dustin B. Benham, Foundational and Contemporary Court Confidentiality, 86 Mo. L. Rev. 211, 215–16 (2021).

463 Blanca Fromm, Comment, Bringing Settlement Out of the Shadows: Information About Settlement in an Age of Confidentiality, 48 UCLA L. Rev. 663, 676 (2001).

terms confidential.[464] Such non-disclosure agreements (NDAs) are sometimes called "secret settlements"[465] or "hush contracts."[466] NDAs can also be found in a variety of non-settlement transactions including employment, the sale of a business, and the licensing of technology. For example, "Donald Trump and the Trump Organization have extensively used NDAs and non-disparagement clauses in employment, commercial, and personal contracts."[467]

If parties settling their litigation agree to include a confidentiality agreement, they typically execute two documents, the settlement agreement, including the NDA, and a court order dismissing the litigation ("stipulation of dismissal"), with only the latter document filed in court and thus a public record (§ 1.40(b)(2)).[468] Keeping the settlement agreement confidential leaves its provisions, including the NDA, enforceable only with a new suit for breach of contract. Such suits occur and may result in

---

[464] Laurie Kratky Dore, Secrecy by Consent: The Use and Limits of Confidentiality in the Pursuit of Settlement, 74 Notre Dame L. Rev. 283, 384–86 (1999).

[465] Gilat Juli Bachar, The Psychology of Secret Settlements, 73 Hastings L.J. 1 (2022).

[466] See, e.g., David A. Hoffman & Erik Lampmann, Hushing Contracts, 97 Wash. U.L. Rev. 165, 167 (2019) (considering "the emerging political and legal movement surrounding hush contracts—which we define as nondisclosure agreements covering sexual misconduct" and stating, "Public disclosures of contractual secrets are giving breach a good name.")

[467] Mark Fenster, How Reputational Nondisclosure Agreements Fail (or, in Praise of Breach), 107 Marq. L. Rev. 325, 353 (2023).

[468] R. Lawrence Dessem, Pretrial Litigation: Law, Policy and Practice 548 (2d ed. 1996); Judith Resnik, The Privatization of Process: Requiem for and Celebration of the Federal Rules of Civil Procedure at 75, 162 U. Pa. L. Rev. 1793, 1818 (2014) ("stipulations of dismissal need not include underlying agreements"); Dustin B. Benham, Foundational and Contemporary Court Confidentiality, 86 Mo. L. Rev. 211, 229 (2021) ("In some cases, the actual settlement agreement is not filed with the court. In most circumstances, courts dismiss cases upon the agreed request of the parties. The agreement is not filed and only put before the court in the event of a breach as part of a contract action"). See, e.g., Pansy v. Borough of Stroudsburg, 23 F.3d 772 (3d Cir. 1994) (settlement agreement not a public record because it was not filed with court).

monetary,[469] injunctive,[470] and other remedies[471] against the party who breached a confidentiality promise. But pursuing any of these remedies in court may destroy the very confidentiality the NDA was meant to preserve. So, a party seeking to enforce confidentiality may ask a court to seal court filings. For instance, in *Redacted v. Redacted,* the plaintiff brought a breach of contract claim against the defendant for allegedly violating the confidentiality provision of their twenty-year-old settlement agreement.[472] The court

> found that Plaintiff had shown a substantial likelihood that the public filing of the [defendant's] draft complaint would

---

[469] For example, in Sosa v. Jaba Pro Stone Corp., No. 20-61699-CIV, 2021 WL 8939501 (S.D. Fla. July 15, 2021), a Fair Labor Standards Act plaintiff was "entitled to recover a total of $40,000," under a settlement agreement providing

> Plaintiff expressly agrees that the existence of the lawsuit, the existence of the settlement, and the terms of this settlement (including but not limited to the amount of consideration paid hereunder) will not be discussed either directly or indirectly with any party, present or future employees of the Defendant or any other persons. . . . As to the terms of this agreement, Plaintiff may only state that the dispute has been resolved. In the event of any breach of these confidentiality terms, a party may seek both legal and equitable relief, without the requirement of any bond.

Id. at *2–3. Plaintiff breached this provision, and the court found "that, as a result of Plaintiffs breach, Plaintiff should forfeit $10,000," so "Defendants' obligation to pay under the settlement agreement shall cease once Defendants have paid $30,000 total to Plaintiff." Id. See also Ford Motor Credit Co. v. Lyons, 198 F. Supp. 2d 1070 (D. Minn. 2002) (attorneys breached confidentiality provision of settlement agreement by filing agreement with court without requesting that it be sealed; remedy for breach is liquidated damages.); Healix Infusion Therapy, Inc. v. Bellos, No.11-02-00346-CV, 2003 WL 22411873 (Tex. App. 2003) (enforcing confidentiality provision with remedy of liquidated damages).

[470] For example, Fox News host Bill "O'Reilly persuaded a New York state court to enforce the [ ] NDA and enjoin [his accuser] from appearing on the popular daytime television talk-show, The View, to discuss her experiences with him." Mark Fenster, How Reputational Nondisclosure Agreements Fail (or, in Praise of Breach), 107 Marq. L. Rev. 325, 329 (2023) (citing Diana Falzone, O'Reilly Silences Accuser Again, Blocks 'View' Appearance, Daily Beast (July 21, 2021, 4:55 PM), https://www.thedailybeast.com/bill-oreilly-gets-restraining-order-against-andrea-mackris-appearance-on-the-view [https://perma.cc/64P7-R4Z5]). In Youngblood-W. v. Aflac Inc., 796 F. App'x 985 (11th Cir. 2019), "Youngblood-West and her husband received $75,000 to release existing and future claims 'against each and all of the parties,'" and "received an additional $50,000 for their agreement not to disclose 'the fact or existence of this release agreement, any of [its] terms' and 'any such matters or any medical or legal services pertaining to any of the parties released. . . .'" Id. at 988. One of the defendants then filed "a complaint that Youngblood-West had breached her nondisclosure agreements," and the district court found that breach and "entered a permanent injunction that enforced those agreements." Id. at 989–90. The Eleventh Circuit affirmed, finding the NDAs enforceable under Georgia law. Id. at 992. See also TES Franchising, LLC v. Feldman, No.CV05401319S, 2006 WL 391458 (Conn. Super. Ct. Feb. 2, 2006) (enforcing confidentiality provision with remedy of temporary injunction).

[471] Thomas v. HUD, 124 F.3d 1439 (Fed. Cir. 1997) (material breach of settlement agreement's confidentiality provision by employer discharged duties agreement had imposed on employee).

[472] [redacted] v. [redacted], 326 F. Supp. 3d 1349, 1351 (M.D. Ga. 2018).

> violate the confidentiality provisions of the settlement agreements, that Plaintiff would suffer irreparable injury by the public disclosure of such confidential information, and that the public interest would not be harmed by granting temporary injunctive relief. Noting the presumption in favor of public access to court proceedings and related documents, the Court then balanced the public's interest in disclosure against the legitimate interests of the parties, including the potential loss of part of the parties' bargained-for privacy. The Court found that requiring Plaintiff to file the draft complaint and related matters under seal and sealing the present action was appropriate because the parties agreed that such matters should remain confidential and because the harm to the public's interest in disclosure was reduced in light of the temporary nature of the access restriction.
>
> The Court entered temporary injunctive relief as follows: (1) restricting access to any documents filed in the present action to the parties to this action, their counsel, and court personnel; (2) requiring Defendant to file any matters related to the draft complaint, including the complaint itself, under seal; and (3) prohibiting Defendant and anyone acting on her behalf from publicly disclosing or discussing the subject matter of the draft complaint and any other documents required to be sealed or restricted by the Court's order.[473]

Another way parties try to keep confidential the enforcement of confidentiality provisions is for an NDA to add an arbitration agreement to increase the possibility of enforcement in ordinarily-confidential arbitration rather than ordinarily-public litigation. But if the party against whom arbitration is sought responds with a declaratory judgment action in court—as Stephanie Clifford did regarding Donald Trump[474]—confidentiality may be destroyed.

---

[473] Id. at 1352–53.

[474] See Complaint for Declaratory Relief at 5, Clifford v. Trump, No. BC696568 (Cal. Super. Ct. Mar. 6, 2018), http://www.documentcloud.org/documents/4403880-Stormy-Daniels-complaint.html; Mark Fenster, How Reputational Nondisclosure Agreements Fail (or, in Praise of Breach), 107 Marq. L. Rev. 325, 354–56 (2023) ("Trump's use of NDAs became widely known during his presidency when news leaked of his earlier sexual liaison with the adult film star Stormy Daniels (whose given name was Stephanie Clifford). Just before the 2016 election, his legal 'fixer,' Michael Cohen, had negotiated, drafted, and executed an agreement with Daniels to prevent her from discussing her relationship with Trump from several years prior. The agreement included a meta-confidentiality clause to keep the agreement secret as well as a liquidated damages clause that would have imposed an award of $1 million per breach. But it failed spectacularly when the agreement and Trump's dalliance with Daniels became public and, soon thereafter, when Daniels openly breached on 60 Minutes.

Similarly, if the party against whom an arbitration award is rendered refuses to comply with it, the prevailing party may have no alternative but to seek court confirmation and enforcement of the arbitral award which is likely to end its confidentiality.

Alternatively, parties settling litigation may ask the court to enter their settlement, including its NDA, as a judgment, which can add to its enforceability by making a violation contempt of court.[475] But converting a settlement into a judgment typically makes it a court record, presumptively open to the public,[476] so parties sometimes request and receive court orders sealing their filed settlements.[477] Even a settlement sealed by the court may be opened in favor of a party seeking discovery in another case, however.[478]

---

After Cohen sought to enforce the contract in arbitration, Daniels filed suit in state court seeking declaratory relief.")

[475] Baella-Silva v. Hulsey, No.05–1214, 454 F.3d 5 (1st Cir. 2006) (affirming liquidated damages plus additional sanction as remedy for breach of confidentiality provision in settlement judgment); Grove Fresh Distribs., Inc. v. John Labatt Ltd., 888 F. Supp. 1427 (N.D. Ill. 1995); PCI Energy Servs., Inc. v. Wachs Technical Serv., Inc., 470 S.E.2d 565 (N.C. Ct. App. 1996) (press release in violation of consent judgment's confidentiality provision constituted contempt). The *PCI Energy* court distinguished between consent judgments which are "merely a recital of the parties' agreement and not an adjudication of rights," and those which go beyond a "rubber stamp" and "actually involve[ ] the court's determination and adjudication of the parties' rights." Id. at 566–67. Only the latter are enforceable through the contempt powers of the court. Id.

[476] See Compare FTC v. Standard Financial Management Corp. 830 F.2d 404 (1st Cir. 1987) (public access to settlement); Bank of America Nat. Trust & Sav. Ass'n v. Hotel Rittenhouse Associates, 800 F.2d 339 (3rd Cir. 1986) (same), with Minneapolis Star & Tribune Co. v. Schumacher, 392 N.W.2d 197 (Minn. 1986) (keeping settlement private).

[477] Nora Freeman Engstrom et al, Secrecy by Stipulation, 74 Duke L.J. 99, 106 (2024). Robert Timothy Reagan et al., Sealed Settlement Agreements In Federal District Court 3–5 (2004), https://www.uscourts.gov/sites/default/files/sealset3_1.pdf [https://perma.cc/K8TS-NDXB] (Study which examined 288,846 civil cases and found 1,270 cases with sealed settlement agreements (0.44%), or one in approximately 227 cases).

[478] EEOC v. Astra, 94 F.3d 738, 741–42 (1st Cir. 1996) (holding unenforceable as against public policy settlement agreements defendant Astra required its employees to sign prohibiting them from discussing the incidents that gave rise to their claims, including discussing the matters with the EEOC during the course of an ongoing investigation); it at 744 (ban on communications with the EEOC undermined the EEOC's important enforcement role in remedying discrimination); Bank of America Nat'l Trust & Sav. Ass'n v. Hotel Rittenhouse Assocs., 800 F.2d 339 (3d Cir. 1986); Janus Films, Inc. v. Miller, 801 F.2d 578 (2d Cir. 1986); Solaia Tech. LLC v. Arvinmeritor, Inc., 2004 WL 549449 (N.D. Ill. 2004) (granting the party's motion to unseal a confidential settlement agreement); Cleveland Constr. Inc. v. Whitehouse Hotel Ltd., 2004 WL 385052 (E.D. La. 2004) (unsuccessful motion to quash a subpoena duces tecum); Anderson v. Home Ins. Co., 924 P.2d 1123 (Colo. Ct. App. 1996) (vacating a limited access order to allow for discovery of a confidential settlement agreement). But see Hasbrouck v. Bankamerica Housing Servs., 187 F.R.D. 453 (N.D.N.Y. 1999) (granting a protective order to prevent a third party from discovering a private settlement agreement).

Public policy generally voids agreements to withhold evidence from judicial proceedings.[479]

Confidentiality agreements in settlements have long been criticized for hiding dangers, such as discrimination,[480] "hazardous products and environmental dangers."[481] Consequently, several states enacted "Sunshine in Litigation" statutes, "which generally required judges to consider public health and safety concerns before sealing court records."[482] As the Catholic Church's sexual abuse scandal grew,

> dozens of people who had settled claims under confidentiality agreements came forward in the media with details of their abuse and the payment they received. It was generally acknowledged that although the secrecy clauses might be legally enforceable (unless declared void as violative of public policy), any attempt to silence abuse victims would be a public relations disaster.[483]

---

[479] See State *ex rel.* Balderas v. ITT Educ. Servs., Inc., 421 P.3d 849, 855 (N.M. Ct. App. 2018) (holding that ITT could not use its confidentiality agreements with students to shield itself from the State's subpoenas in litigation the state brought against ITT, because enforcing the confidentiality clauses in that context would be contrary to public policy); id. ("under the circumstances of this case, it would be contrary to public policy to allow ITT to use the confidentiality clause with its students to shield itself from the State's investigation and litigation authorized under the [Unfair Practices Act]"); [redacted] v. [redacted], 326 F. Supp. 3d 1349, 1355 (M.D. Ga. 2018) (stating that courts have found that confidentiality agreements "implicitly allow for" parties to disclose information to "testify or otherwise comply with a subpoena, court order, or applicable law." (citing Barger v. Garden Way, Inc., 499 S.E.2d 737, 741 (Ga. Ct. App. 1998)).

[480] Minna J. Kotkin, Invisible Settlements, Invisible Discrimination, 84 N.C. L. Rev. 927 (2006).

[481] Id. at 946; Pansy v. Borough of Stroudsburg, 23 F.3d 772, 785–86 (3d Cir. 1994) (complaining that "[b]ecause defendants request orders of confidentiality as a condition of settlement, courts are willing to grant these requests in an effort to facilitate settlement without sufficiently inquiring into the potential public interest in obtaining information concerning the settlement agreement."); Richard A. Zitrin, The Case Against Secret Settlements (Or, What You Don't Know Can Hurt You), 2 J. Inst. Stud. Legal Ethics 115, 119 (1999) (arguing against secret settlements in a variety of tort-related cases, including defective products); Joseph F. Anderson Jr., Hidden from the Public by Order of the Court: The Case Against Government-Enforced Secrecy, 55 S.C. L. Rev. 711 (2004).

[482] Minna J. Kotkin, Invisible Settlements, Invisible Discrimination, 84 N.C. L. Rev. 927, 946 (2006). See also Fla. Stat. Ann. § 69.081 ("[a]ny portion of an agreement or contract which has the purpose or effect of concealing" either a "public hazard" or a government settlement "is void, contrary to public policy, and may not be enforced."); Wash. Rev. Code Ann. § 4.24.611; La. Stat. Ann. § 44:31; Christopher R. Drahozal & Laura J. Hines, Secret Settlement Restrictions and Unintended Consequences, 54 U. Kan. L. Rev. 1457, 1477 (2006) (discussing Florida's act and a federal court's "local rule precluding courts from approving sealed settlements").

[483] Minna J. Kotkin, Invisible Settlements, Invisible Discrimination, 84 N.C. L. Rev. 927, 960–61 (2006).

The #MeToo movement contributed to a similar dynamic respecting sexual harassment, especially in the workplace.[484] This movement led California to enact legislation prohibiting confidentiality agreements in a sexual harassment or workplace discrimination cases,[485] and other states to take various legislative steps in that direction.[486] In late 2022, President Biden signed the Speak Out Act, which says "with respect to a sexual assault dispute or sexual harassment dispute, no nondisclosure clause or nondisparagement clause agreed to before the dispute arises shall be judicially enforceable in instances in which the conduct is alleged to have violated Federal, Tribal, or State law."[487] As the Act applies only to agreements entered "before the dispute arises," it presumably does not apply to settlement agreements resolving claims already raised.[488]

# G. PLEA BARGAINING

## § 1.44 Plea Bargaining

### *(a) Plea Agreements*

Much as a civil settlement is the sale of a claim by Plaintiff to Defendant, we might—perhaps more controversially—think similarly of a plea bargain as the prosecuting government's "sale" of a charge, with the "price" to be paid by the defendant often expressed

---

484 Gilat Juli Bachar, The Psychology of Secret Settlements, 73 Hastings L.J. 1, 44 (2022) ("NDAs are also known for their role in the current wave of revelations surfacing years of sexual harassment in a variety of industries. The #MeToo movement exposed the dark side of these agreements: their potential use as a tool to silence victims of sexual wrongdoing who raise their voice against their wrongdoers").

485 Cal. Civ. Proc. Code § 1001 (2023) ("a provision within a settlement agreement that prevents or restricts the disclosure of factual information related to a claim filed in a civil action or a complaint filed in an administrative action, regarding any of the following, is prohibited . . .").

486 Blair Druhan Bullock & Joni Hersch, The Impact of Banning Confidential Settlements on Discrimination Dispute Resolution, 77 Vand. L. Rev. 51, 72 tbl.1 (2024) (citing statutes); Dustin B. Benham, Foundational and Contemporary Court Confidentiality, 86 Mo. L. Rev. 211, 232 (2021) ("In the wake of several high-profile sex assault scandals, and in response to the #MeToo movement, several states have moved to limit confidentiality agreements and orders") (citing statutes).

487 42 U.S.C. § 19403(a). See also Speak Out Act, H.R. 8227, 117th Cong. (2022).

488 See Steward Partners Glob. Advisory, LLC v. Tucker, No. 23-CV-6532 (JGLC), 2024 WL 4202697, at *5 (S.D.N.Y. Sept. 16, 2024) ("The statute only bars the enforcement of nondisparagement clauses agreed to *before a sexual harassment or assault dispute arises*. Here, the Complaint, and documents incorporated therein, do not indicate whether the parties entered into the Separation and Redemption Agreements before the former employee's alleged sexual harassment dispute arose. For that reason, the Court cannot dismiss Plaintiffs' claims to enforce the Tucker's nondisparagement agreement under the Speak Out Act." (emphasis in original) (internal citation and footnote omitted)).

in months of incarceration rather than in dollars.[489] And, in many ways, law in the U.S. treats similarly both sorts of "sales," civil claims and criminal charges.[490] Much as civil plaintiffs often trade away several claims for one settlement payment from defendant, "plea deals [often] trade away numerous indicted charges in exchange for the defendant's guilty plea to an agreed charge."[491] "The fundamental dynamics of settlement" in the criminal and civil contexts are similar in that both involve "parties bargaining toward mutual promises because they each believe they will be better off with an agreement than without one."[492]

On the other hand, in some important ways, plea agreements are less enforceable than civil settlement agreements. Most civil settlements do not require court approval to be legally binding (§ 1.40(c)(4)). In contrast, plea bargains do require court approval to be legally binding because a government's punishment, including "physical incarceration of a defendant," "cannot be a valid term in a private contract, at least not one that the parties can lawfully perform and enforce without the involvement of a court."[493] Consequently,

> A prosecutor can promise to recommend a given sentence (or sentencing range), but she cannot guarantee that the defendant will actually receive that sentence. The judge alone decides the defendant's sentence, save for cases in which a legislatively mandated sentence exists. The most that can be done is to condition the defendant's plea on the receipt of a particular sentence (meaning that if the judge rejects the prosecutor's recommendation the plea is rescinded), and this practice is discouraged or prohibited in many jurisdictions. . . . [T]he agreement is curiously one-sided: the defendant's plea is ordinarily binding, while the prosecutor's words constitute mere advice that the court can accept or ignore as it wishes.[494]

---

489 Frank H. Easterbrook, Criminal Procedure as a Market System, 12 J. Legal Stud. 289, 308 (1983) ("Plea bargaining establishes the price for most crimes.")

490 Robert E. Scott & William J. Stuntz, Plea Bargaining as Contract, 101 Yale L.J. 1909 (1992). On enforcement of plea bargains, see G. Nicholas Herman & Jean M. Cary, Legal Counseling and Negotiation: A Practical Approach § 19.11 (2d ed. 2009).

491 United States v. Stevenson, 425 F. Supp. 3d 647, 652 (S.D. W.Va. 2018). See also Cynthia Alkon & Andrea Kupfer Schneider, Negotiating Crime: Plea Bargaining, Problem Solving, and Dispute Resolution in the Criminal Context 25 (2019) ("Plea negotiations often include both sentence and charge bargaining.")

492 Richard Lorren Jolly & J.J. Prescott, Beyond Plea Bargaining: A Theory of Criminal Settlement, 62 B.C. L. Rev. 1047, 1049 (2021).

493 Id. at 1050.

494 Robert E. Scott & William J. Stuntz, Plea Bargaining as Contract, 101 Yale L.J. 1909, 1953–54 (1992).

The Federal Rules of Criminal Procedure say that "If the court rejects a plea agreement," the court must "give the defendant an opportunity to withdraw the plea."[495] While judges in many states can reject plea agreements,[496] few do.[497] In sum, "sentencing judges tend to validate and encourage bargains through a 'plea discount' (or a trial penalty): They impose lighter sentences on those who waive their right to trial."[498]

### *(b) Why Do Most Criminal Cases in the U.S. Settle?*

Criminal cases in the U.S. usually end in a settlement (plea bargain) rather than proceeding to a trial's verdict or other conclusive ruling by the court.[499] Why do prosecuting governments and criminal defendants typically settle, rather than pursue litigation to completion? As Section 1.4 notes, agreements occur because, at the time parties make them, each party thinks that making the agreement is better than that party's alternatives. In the context of criminal litigation, that means plea deals occur when each party (the

---

[495] Fed. R. Crim. P. 11(c)(5)(B). See also Cal. Penal Code § 1192.4 ("If the defendant's plea of guilty . . . is not accepted by the prosecuting attorney and approved by the court, the plea shall be deemed withdrawn and the defendant may then enter such plea or pleas as would otherwise have been available."); N.Y. Crim. Proc. Law § 220.60 ("At any time before the imposition of sentence, the court in its discretion may permit a defendant who has entered a plea of guilty to the entire indictment or to part of the indictment. . . to withdraw such plea, and in such event the entire indictment, as it existed at the time of such plea, is restored.").

[496] Dylan R. McDonough, In the Shadow of the Bench: Judicial Discretion to Reject Plea Agreements, 57 Colum. J.L. & Soc. Probs. 633, 660 (2024) ("The most common consideration trial courts cite when rejecting a plea agreement is the sentence contemplated by the agreement. Trial courts frequently reject plea agreements as too lenient. This applies equally in cases of charge bargains as in cases of sentence bargains.")

[497] A study of Michigan and Texas "found around extremely low rejection rates in both states—around 1%." Jenia I. Turner, Virtual Guilty Pleas, 24 U. Pa. J. Const. L. 211, 230 (2022).

[498] Ronald Wright & Marc Miller, The Screening/Bargaining Tradeoff, 55 Stan. L. Rev. 29, 39–40 (2002).

[499] Missouri v. Frye, 566 U.S. 134, 143 (2012) ("Ninety-seven percent of federal convictions and ninety-four percent of state convictions are the result of guilty pleas"). John Gramlich, Only 2% of Federal Criminal Defendants Went to Trial in 2018, and Most Who Did Were Found Guilty, PEW RSCH. CTR. (June 11, 2019), https://www.pewresearch.org/fact-tank/2019/06/11/only-2-of-federal-criminal-defendants-go-to-trial-and-most-who-do-are-found-guilty [https://perma.cc/BG92-MVK9] (noting that in 2018, ninety percent of federal criminal defendants pleaded guilty, eight percent were dismissed, and of the approximately two percent of defendants that did proceed to trial, eighty-three percent were convicted); 9 Nicole L. Mott, et al., Caseload Highlights: Examining the Work of State Courts, 1 (May 2003) https://www.courtstatistics.org/__data/assets/pdf_file/0022/30559/A-Profile-of-Hung-Juries.pdf. (study of state felony dispositions in 30 counties found "Approximately 70 percent of the 1.2 million cases examined ended in a guilty plea, about 24 percent were dismissed or disposed as an 'other' disposition (e.g., diversion to an alternative court program such as a drug court or transfers to a federal court), and less than 3 percent were resolved by jury trial.")

government, as represented by the prosecutor, and the defendant) believes it is better off with the deal than litigating further.

As the Supreme Court has put it, "For a defendant who sees slight possibility of acquittal, the advantages of pleading guilty and limiting the probable penalty are obvious."[500] The prosecuting government also benefits because, "with the avoidance of trial, scarce judicial and prosecutorial resources are conserved for those cases in which there is a substantial issue of the defendant's guilt or in which there is substantial doubt that the State can sustain its burden of proof."[501] In sum, the Court said in 1970,

> It is this mutuality of advantage that perhaps explains the fact that at present well over three-fourths of the criminal convictions in this country rest on pleas of guilty, a great many of them no doubt motivated at least in part by the hope or assurance of a lesser penalty than might be imposed if there were a guilty verdict after a trial to judge or jury.[502]

Since then, the portion of convictions in the U.S. resting on pleas has grown even higher, exceeding ninety percent.[503] While the U.S. has long been thought the leader in plea bargaining, over the last few decades most jurisdictions worldwide have adopted something broadly similar.[504]

To reiterate, criminal cases settle (plead out) only when each party believes it is made better off by the plea deal than by litigating further. In other words, litigating further is the only, and therefore best, alternative to a negotiated agreement (BATNA, § 1.5) of a party engaged in plea negotiation. Accordingly, formulating a party's *bottom line* (§ 1.6) in plea negotiation requires determining the expected result (§ 1.7) of further litigation (valuing a case §§ 1.35–1.38), and then valuing the differences between what the party would get from that expected result of litigation with what the party can get in a plea deal. This is an example of Section 1.6's observation that your *bottom line* in negotiation "should be tied to" your BATNA

[500] Brady v. United States, 397 U.S. 742, 752 (1970).

[501] Id.

[502] Id.

[503] Missouri v. Frye, 566 U.S. 134, 143 (2012) ("Ninety-seven percent of federal convictions and ninety-four percent of state convictions are the result of guilty pleas").

[504] Gabriele Paolini, Elena Kantorowicz-Reznichenko and Stefan Voigt, Plea Bargaining Procedures Worldwide: Drivers of Introduction and Use, 22 J. of Empirical Legal Studies 27, 42 (2024) ("Over the last few decades, the adoption of plea-bargaining procedures has been described as one of the most important trends in criminal procedure worldwide"); id. ("we survey 174 jurisdictions worldwide, finding that 101 of them formalized plea bargaining, and coding several aspects characterizing the legal design of each procedure of this kind. The resulting dataset is, to the best of our knowledge, the most complete and comprehensive one regarding the legal design of plea bargaining").

because agreeing in a negotiation to something worse than your best alternative to it would be "the most basic negotiating mistake—agreeing to a deal when [you] would have been better off walking away from the [negotiating] table with no agreement."[505]

The following two subsections discuss how parties to criminal cases value them, starting with the defendant and then turning to the prosecuting government.

### *(c) Defendant's Valuation of a Criminal Case*

Many of the factors that influence how parties and their lawyers value civil cases (§§ 1.35–1.38) operate similarly in criminal cases.[506] From the defendant's standpoint, a criminal case in which the defendant "pays" with prison time is analogous to a civil case in which the defendant pays with money insofar as both sorts of defendants prefer paying less to paying more.[507] So, if a prosecutor offers a defendant a plea deal, the defendant may try with the help of counsel to foresee the results of further litigation to decide whether to take the offer or "roll the dice" on a trial, much as a civil defendant considering a plaintiff's proposed terms of settlement may try to foresee the results of further litigation to decide whether to take the settlement deal or continue litigating.

Another factor applicable to both civil settlement negotiation and plea bargaining is *risk aversion*, which is the willingness to pay for increased certainty (§ 1.37). Compared with the uncertainties of further litigation, a plea deal increases certainty. So, a risk averse defendant prefers a deal with a certain sentence, say three months in jail, to an uncertain trial with an expected outcome (§ 1.7) of three months in jail, but with possibilities ranging from acquittal to a year in jail. A criminal defendant may exhibit a high degree of risk aversion because, as Section 1.37(b) explains, a one-time litigant is likely to be more risk-averse than a repeat litigant. And this may be especially true in the context of criminal cases where the defendant's freedom is likely to rest on this one case, while the prosecuting government brings many cases.[508] On the other hand, Section 1.37(a)

---

505 Russell Korobkin, A Positive Theory of Legal Negotiation, 88 Geo. L.J. 1789, 1797 (2000).

506 See also Rebecca Hollander-Blumoff, Note, Getting to "Guilty": Plea Bargaining as Negotiation, 2 Harv. Neg. L. Rev. 115 (1997).

507 William J. Stuntz, Plea Bargaining and Criminal Law's Disappearing Shadow, 117 Harv. L. Rev. 2548, 2554 (2004) ("A civil plaintiff has the incentive to take every dollar he can, just as the defendant wishes to pay as little as possible. In criminal cases, one of the two parties is like that: the defendant almost always prefers freedom to incarceration and less incarceration to more.")

508 Russell M. Gold, Carissa Byrne Hessick & F. Andrew Hessick, Civilizing Criminal Settlements, 97 B.U. L. Rev. 1607, 1623–24 (2017) ("Prosecutors' leverage in plea bargaining is compounded by the fact that prosecutors have much less at stake

notes psychological research showing that "people tend to make risk-averse decisions when choosing among options that appear to be gains and risk-seeking decisions when choosing among options that appear to be losses." So, the criminal defendant considering a plea deal with three months in jail may choose to roll the dice on a slim hope for acquittal.

The criminal defendant tempted to roll the dice on a trial will not typically be constrained by a large cost that burdens most civil defendants who go to trial—the legal fees of trying a case. Trials, including their preparation, consume lots of lawyer hours, so a lawyer billing the client by the hour will charge the client a lot for trying a case. Lawyers who bill by the hour are sometimes thought to resist settlement early in litigation (§ 1.36(b)(1)). While some criminal defendants pay their lawyers by the hour, many criminal defendants lack the money to do that, so, the state provides them with a "free" lawyer. However, the state does not pay the defendant's lawyer by the hour, but instead with a fixed fee, regardless of how much time it takes the lawyer. This gives the lawyer an incentive to settle and the client an incentive to shun settlement (§ 1.36(b)(3)).

Public defenders are generally "paid fixed salaries to represent large numbers of indigent clients."[509] In jurisdictions without public defenders, or to supplement them, "[p]rivate attorneys are appointed by the court to represent indigent persons accused of crimes," and "[i]n about half of the states, they are subject to fee caps that dictate the maximum amount an attorney can earn on a given case, which incentivizes attorneys to do less work on a case once they reach the maximum threshold."[510]

> For many private defense attorneys, a guilty plea is a quick buck. These attorneys collect their fees in advance,

---

than defendants. . . . For defendants, . . . a loss can be devastating. In addition to direct punishment such as imprisonment, criminal convictions often carry significant collateral consequences. Risk averse defendants who wish to minimize harsh penalties or collateral consequences may be eager to plead guilty to a lesser offense or for a reduced sentence.")

[509] Stephanos Bibas, Plea Bargaining Outside the Shadow of Trial, 117 Harv. L. Rev. 2463, 2476 (2004).

[510] Bryan Furst, A Fair Fight: Achieving Indigent Defense Resource Parity, Brennan Center For Justice 5–6 (Sept. 9, 2019), https://www.brennancenter.org/our-work/research-reports/fair-fight. See also Tina Peng, I'm a Public Defender. It's Impossible For Me to Do a Good Job Representing My Clients, WASH. POST (Sept. 3, 2015), https://www.washingtonpost.com/opinions/our-public-defender-system-isnt-just-broken--its-unconstitutional/2015/09/03/aadf2b6c-519b-11e5-9812-92d5948a40f8_story.html ("Many counties also pay attorneys who accept public defense contracts a flat fee, regardless of the number or seriousness of the cases each lawyer handles."); Maybell Romero, Lowball Rural Defense, 99 Wash. U. L. Rev. 1081, 1090–91 (2021) (surveying six ways to pay private lawyers for indigent defense in criminal cases).

> and once they have obtained their fees, their interests lie in disposing of their cases rapidly. This financial conflict of interest influences even well paid, conscientious lawyers, and the bar includes some lawyers who are not well paid and conscientious. These lawyers handle a high volume of cases for small fees and rarely take a case to trial.[511]

The prevalence of fixed fees in criminal defense leads to a pervasive divergence between the lawyer's and client's interests. The lawyer makes more money (or works less time) "by pushing clients to plead,"[512] while clients do not bear the cost of the valuable resource (a lawyer's time) consumed by choosing to reject a plea offer and go to trial. Yet the vast majority of criminal cases plead out because the defendant gets from the prosecution a deal so much more lenient than the expected result of trial, as discussed next.

### *(d) Prosecution's Valuation of a Criminal Case*

#### *(1) Political Decisionmakers Pursuing Convictions on the Cheap*

The previous subsection notes that, from the defendant's standpoint, a criminal case in which the defendant "pays" with prison time is analogous to a civil case in which the defendant pays with money insofar as both sorts of defendants prefer paying less to paying more.[513] But while high payments by civil defendants enrich plaintiffs (and typically their lawyers) more than low payments by

---

[511] Albert W. Alschuler, A Nearly Perfect System for Convicting the Innocent, 79 Alb. L. Rev. 919, 938 (2016).

[512] Stephanos Bibas, Plea Bargaining Outside the Shadow of Trial, 117 Harv. L. Rev. 2463, 2477 (2004). Accord Richard Birke, Reconciling Loss Aversion and Guilty Pleas, 1999 Utah L. Rev. 205, 242 ("defense attorneys have a positive incentive to please the judges and to plead out cases, disincentives for failure to conform, and financial incentives that favor settlement over trial.")

Some suggest that prosecutors' interests also tend toward plea bargains. Stephen J. Schulhofer, Plea Bargaining as Disaster, 101 Yale L.J. 1979, 1988 (1992) ("the prosecutor's position as an agent means that guilty plea settlements negotiated case by case tend to diverge from those that would most efficiently serve the public interest in optimal deterrence. This divergence usually takes the form of unduly lenient sentence offers."); Stephanos Bibas, Plea Bargaining Outside the Shadow of Trial, 117 Harv. L. Rev. 2463, 2546 (2004) ("prosecutors do not simply maximize sentences as a contingency-fee plaintiff's lawyer might maximize damages. Rather, they induce pleas with deep discounts off inflated post-trial sentences. They can maximize their win-loss rates, leisure time, and volume of cases brought, while still remaining tough enough to satisfy their and the public's sense of justice.") (citing William J. Stuntz, Plea Bargaining and Criminal Law's Disappearing Shadow, 117 Harv. L. Rev. 2548, 2554 (2004)).

[513] William J. Stuntz, Plea Bargaining and Criminal Law's Disappearing Shadow, 117 Harv. L. Rev. 2548, 2554 (2004) ("A civil plaintiff has the incentive to take every dollar he can, just as the defendant wishes to pay as little as possible. In criminal cases, one of the two parties is like that: the defendant almost always prefers freedom to incarceration and less incarceration to more.")

civil defendants do, high "payments" by criminal defendants often come in the form of more time incarcerated or otherwise under government supervision, which does not enrich the prosecuting government and typically burdens its or another government's budget more than would a lower "payment" (less prison or jail time) by the criminal defendant. In short, administering the criminal justice system is costly for government and the "finite nature of" government's "criminal justice resources ultimately constrains the prosecutor's bargaining position."[514]

> In the criminal justice marketplace, the supply and demand of "system" resources necessarily influence the going rate for settling criminal cases. Prosecutors are more willing to offer defendants deep sentencing discounts when case congestion causes the costs of not settling to be especially high for the state—and, particularly and more realistically, for their own offices' budgets.[515]

Because prosecutors' offices are typically "stretched for dollars," they routinely have more strong cases (likely convictions) to pursue than personnel available to pursue them.[516] In contrast, imagine if the number of strong civil plaintiffs' cases (recovering money to pay the plaintiffs' lawyers) exceeded the personnel available to pursue them. Those strong available cases would be profitable opportunities attracting new lawyers into plaintiffs' work until the supply of plaintiffs' lawyers grew to satisfy the willingness to pay for their services. But that sort of financial incentive to add enough lawyers to bring all the strong cases is largely absent from the criminal prosecution context,[517] and thus does not drive up the number of prosecutors. Instead, the number of prosecutors is determined by political decisions about the levels of government revenue and how government funds should be allocated among prosecutors' offices and

---

[514] Richard Lorren Jolly & J.J. Prescott, Beyond Plea Bargaining: A Theory of Criminal Settlement, 62 B.C. L. Rev. 1047, 1061–62 (2021) ("For the state, administering the criminal justice system is resource intensive. The costs of investigating and prosecuting crimes, securing defendants' rights, maintaining often overcrowded courts and jails, and ultimately enforcing sentences all fall solely on the state.")

[515] Id.

[516] William J. Stuntz, Plea Bargaining and Criminal Law's Disappearing Shadow, 117 Harv. L. Rev. 2548, 2555 (2004). See also Jed Rakoff, Why Innocent People Plead Guilty, New York Review Of Books (Nov. 20, 2014), https://www.nybooks.com/articles/2014/11/20/why-innocent-people-plead-guilty/ [http://perma.cc/RC53-8RPP] (describing prosecutors as "often overworked and understaffed").

[517] As Andrea Kupfer Schneider observes, while "[c]ivil litigators" "work to maximize financial returns," "[p]rosecutors have an incentive to maximize their conviction rate and, therefore, are more likely to only go to trial with sure winners. . . . Doubtful or hard cases can be avoided by a prosecutor who does not press charges." Andrea Kupfer Schneider, Cooperating or Caving in: Are Defense Attorneys Shrewd or Exploited in Plea Bargaining Negotiations?, 91 Marq. L. Rev. 145, 158 (2007).

other government agencies. Those decisions are made by elected officials and their appointees, so in some sense they are ultimately made by the voters who elect those officials.

If these political decisionmakers wanted a trial for every strong (likely conviction) criminal case, they would have to divert vast amounts of money from other purposes to hiring many more prosecutors, judges, and others in the criminal judicial system. But if these political decisionmakers want convictions on the cheap,[518] they can instead empower prosecutors in plea bargaining by enacting many broad and overlapping criminal statutes with severe mandatory sentences.[519] Because a defendant convicted after trial pays dearly enough that pleading guilty to a lesser charge with a lesser sentence is the lesser evil from the defendant's perspective,[520] prosecutors can secure lots of convictions simply by offering lesser sentences than conviction after trial would yield. As influential scholars put it, "where the legislature drafts broad criminal statutes and then attaches mandatory sentences to those statutes, prosecutors have an unchecked opportunity to overcharge and generate easy pleas."[521]

---

518 Russell M. Gold, Prosecutors and Their Legislatures, Legislatures and Their Prosecutors, in The Oxford Handbook of Prosecutors and Prosecution 330 (Wright & Levine eds. 2021) ("The public wants not only prosecutions but convictions; some evidence of this desire comes from the frequency with which conviction statistics arise in prosecutor campaign discourse"); id. (legislatures can reduce risk that prosecutors "may prosecute too little" "by making prosecutions as cheap as possible. Making prosecution more efficient serves legislators' goals in potentially two different ways: it allows prosecutors to bring more cases with the same resources—what some call net-widening—or save money for the public fisc. Legislators are thus well served when prosecutors possess maximum plea leverage, and they can provide such leverage through broad and deep criminal codes as well as harsh sentence ranges").

519 Andrew Manuel Crespo, The Hidden Law of Plea Bargaining, 118 Colum. L. Rev. 1303, 1304–05 (2018) ("Substantive criminal law, after all, now penalizes so much conduct, so severely, and so many times over that it serves simply to delegate power to prosecutors, transforming them into administrators of an unwritten criminal law that consists only of their own discretionary decisions to charge certain offenses or to offer certain deals")(internal quotations omitted); Russell M. Gold, Carissa Byrne Hessick & F. Andrew Hessick, Civilizing Criminal Settlements, 97 B.U. L. Rev. 1607, 1619 (2017) ("criminal codes often include multiple, overlapping statutes criminalizing similar conduct. The penalties associated with these overlapping crimes often differ, with some including mandatory minimum sentences and higher potential maximum sentences. These overlapping laws expand prosecutors' charging discretion."); id. ("Stacked charges also increase the risk that a defendant will be convicted. Every time a prosecutor takes a case to trial, she runs the risk of losing. To the extent that overlapping statutes contain slightly different elements, the prosecutor can reduce the risk that the defendant will be acquitted by bringing more charges.")

520 Examples can be found in Carissa Byrne Hessick, Punishment Without Trial ch. 3 (2021).

521 Robert E. Scott & William J. Stuntz, Plea Bargaining as Contract, 101 Yale L.J. 1909, 1965 (1992). As noted above, "plea deals [often] trade away numerous indicted charges in exchange for the defendant's guilty plea to an agreed charge." United States v. Stevenson, 425 F. Supp. 3d 647, 652 (S.D. W.Va. 2018).

### (2) *The Plea Discount or Trial Penalty*

The prevalence of this perspective has led scholars to "study sentencing severity and the differential between outcomes after trial and after a guilty plea—the gap known as a 'trial penalty' or 'plea discount.' "[522]

> Quoting Professor Bibas, the Supreme Court noted in Lafler v. Cooper, "The expected posttrial sentence is imposed in only a few percent of cases. It is like the sticker price for cars: only an ignorant, ill-advised consumer would view the full price as the norm and anything less a bargain."[[523]] Quoting Professor Barkow, the Court added in Missouri v. Frye, "[Defendants] who do take their case to trial and lose receive longer sentences than even Congress or the prosecutor might think appropriate, because the longer sentences exist on the books largely for bargaining purposes.[[524]]"[525]

This phenomenon of longer sentences "on the books largely for bargaining purposes," so convictions after trial yield longer sentences than even "the prosecutor might think appropriate," is key in distinguishing plea bargaining from civil settlement negotiation.

> Prosecutors are not like civil plaintiffs. . . . extra months in prison are not like marginal dollars in civil cases. Once the defendant's sentence has reached the level the prosecutor prefers—or, if you like, the level that the local voters who elect her boss demand—adding more time offers no benefit to the prosecutor. Indeed, prosecutors may actually value "extra" prison time negatively.[526]

---

[522] Ronald F. Wright et al., The Shadow Bargainers, 42 Cardozo L. Rev. 1295, 1302 (2021).

[523] Lafler v. Cooper, 566 U.S. 156, 168 (2012) (quoting Stephanos Bibas, Regulating the Plea-Bargaining Market: From Caveat Emptor to Consumer Protection, 99 Calif. L. Rev. 1117, 1138 (2011)).

[524] Missouri v. Frye, 566 U.S. 134, 144 (2012) (quoting Rachel E. Barkow, Separation of Powers and the Criminal Law, 58 Stan. L. Rev. 989, 1034 (2006)).

[525] Albert W. Alschuler, A Nearly Perfect System for Convicting the Innocent, 79 Alb. L. Rev. 919, 925 (2016). See also Russell M. Gold, Carissa Byrne Hessick & F. Andrew Hessick, Civilizing Criminal Settlements, 97 B.U. L. Rev. 1607, 1609 (2017) ("the sentences prescribed for defendants who are convicted after trial are extremely high. These high penalties are, in some instances, legislatively designed to impose the appropriate punishment only when discounted for guilty pleas.")

[526] William J. Stuntz, Plea Bargaining and Criminal Law's Disappearing Shadow, 117 Harv. L. Rev. 2548, 2553 (2004). A prosecutor valuing a case may consider factors such as:

> (1) "the severity of the crime, the strength of the evidence, . . . the defendant's record and need for punishment," (2) sentences recently given to similarly-situated defendants, (3) "the need to deter, incapacitate, rehabilitate, reform,

In many, perhaps most, criminal cases the expected result of litigation is a "virtually certain"[527] conviction with a more severe sentence (such more prison time) than the prosecutor prefers.[528] By contrast, the expected result of civil litigation is rarely, if ever, a higher award of damages than the plaintiff prefers. The expected result of civil litigation is nearly always a compromise between what the plaintiff prefers and what the defendant prefers. Consequently, a plaintiff must compromise with the defendant to negotiate a settlement between their preferred outcomes.

In contrast, a prosecutor is in the powerful position of desiring a result that is a compromise between what the defendant prefers and what is likely to happen if the parties pursue litigation to the end. If they pursue litigation to the end, the likely result is a conviction at which time the prosecutor may recommend a sentence more severe than the prosecutor prefers, in part to deter other defendants from rejecting plea deals. So, at the time of plea bargaining before trial, the prosecutor can offer her desired result to the defendant, take-it-or-leave-it, and the defendant will generally take it because the alternative, the expected result of litigation, is worse for the

---

> and inflict retribution," (4) mercy to deserving defendants, (5) the value of "driv[ing] hard bargains on particular crimes to send messages, teach lessons, and deter especially harmful or prevalent crimes."

Stephanos Bibas, Plea Bargaining Outside the Shadow of Trial, 117 Harv. L. Rev. 2463, 2470 (2004). Whether all these factors have analogs for the typical civil plaintiff is doubtful.

[527] Robert E. Scott & William J. Stuntz, Plea Bargaining as Contract, 101 Yale L.J. 1909, 1935 & n.99 (1992) (citing Milton Heumann, Plea Bargaining 58, 60–61 (1978) (noting that new defense attorneys quickly learn that most of their clients are not only guilty but lack any plausible defense)). See also Rodney J. Uphoff, The Criminal Defense Lawyer as Effective Negotiator: A Systematic Approach, 2 Clinical L.Rev. 73 (1995).

> Defense lawyers all too often find themselves representing an unsympathetic defendant with a lengthy criminal record in a case without any apparent defense. The zealous advocate with a case in which the defendant has little or no leverage confronts a daunting challenge. Many defense lawyers have endured the unpleasant task of going to negotiate on behalf of an unemployed recidivist who simply wants to plead guilty and "bargaining" with a particularly hard-headed prosecutor who is perfectly aware that the state's case is virtually unassailable. In such a case, defense counsel may feel more like a beggar than a bargainer, left with little more than the unenviable chore of imploring a mean-spirited prosecutor to be fair or reasonable.

Id. at 94.

[528] William J. Stuntz, Plea Bargaining and Criminal Law's Disappearing Shadow, 117 Harv. L. Rev. 2548, 2553–54 (2004) ("First, prosecutors do not try to maximize total prison time. Second, due to docket pressure, prosecutors lack the time to pursue even some winnable cases. And third, the legally authorized sentence is harsher than the sentence prosecutors want to impose. While these conditions do not all hold true for all criminal cases, each one does hold true for a large fraction of criminal cases, and there are many cases in which all three conditions are satisfied.")

defendant.[529] As one federal judge put it, in plea bargaining "the prosecutor has all the power,"[530] so the resulting deal is "like a 'contract of adhesion' in which one party can effectively force its will on the other party."[531]

This troubles people who believe that "it's hard[ ] to justify increasing the" sentence because a defendant exercises his constitutional right a jury trial.[532] "A large majority of criminal law scholars appear to agree that prosecutors shouldn't seek higher punishments than a defendant should otherwise receive simply for exercising the right to trial."[533] In contrast, as noted earlier in this subsection, legislatures have given prosecutors the tools to do this and prosecutors' incentives, with more strong cases than personnel available to pursue them, are often to use these tools. All of which results in more convictions per dollar of government spending than would occur if prosecutors lacked or did not use these tools.

In other words, the typical plea bargain involves *logrolling* (§ 1.10(c)), the form of positive sum negotiation in which negotiators trade away their lower priorities to receive their higher priorities. The defendant's high priority is minimizing the sentence, while the typical prosecutor's high priority is a moderate sentence obtained quickly and cheaply. "This asymmetry allows prosecutors to trade

---

529 A defendant can break out of this bind if he can provide something the prosecutor seeks, such as testimony against another defendant or cooperation with a government investigation. Then there may be more give-and-take in the plea negotiation as the defendant forces the prosecutor to choose between her desired sentence for the defendant and her desire for the defendant's testimony or other cooperation.

530 Jed Rakoff, Why Innocent People Plead Guilty, New York Review Of Books (Nov. 20, 2014), https://www.nybooks.com/articles/2014/11/20/why-innocent-people-plead-guilty/ [http://perma.cc/RC53-8RPP]. See also Robert Elias, The Law of Personhood: A Review of Markus Dirk Dubber's Victims in the War on Crime: The Use and Abuse of Victim's Rights, 52 Buff. L. Rev. 225, 240–41 (2004) ("Plea-bargaining reflects the fundamental inequality of power between the defendant and the state. While it promotes efficiency, it rarely produces any bargain and typically amounts to an unconditional surrender."); Donald G. Gifford, A Context-Based Theory of Strategy Selection in Legal Negotiation, 46 Ohio St. L.J. 41, 76 (1985) ("In most cases, the prosecutor possesses much greater power in plea bargaining than does the defense attorney.")

531 Jed Rakoff, Why Innocent People Plead Guilty, New York Review Of Books (Nov. 20, 2014), https://www.nybooks.com/articles/2014/11/20/why-innocent-people-plead-guilty/ [http://perma.cc/RC53-8RPP]. "On the other hand, . . . in a typical white-collar fraud investigation, defense counsel do not look like shoppers at a 'take-it-or-leave-it' department store. They will often spend hour after hour in the prosecutor's office, making presentations and arguments, eventually perhaps making and receiving proposals and counter-proposals for the disposition of the case, looking, in short, very much like negotiators." Gerard E. Lynch, Our Administrative System of Criminal Justice, 66 Fordham L.Rev.2117, 2130 (1998).

532 Ben Grunwald, Distinguishing Plea Discounts and Trial Penalties, 37 Ga. St. U. L. Rev. 261, 281 (2021).

533 Id.

away 'extra' years of incarceration that the defendant desperately wants to avoid but that the prosecutor doesn't particularly value."[534] So, "[f]or all involved, the best pleas are quick pleas. And quick pleas are most efficiently reached at low market prices, because—although prosecutors may abandon sentence maximization—defendants always remain sentence minimizers."[535]

---

[534] Andrew Manuel Crespo, The Hidden Law of Plea Bargaining, 118 Colum. L. Rev. 1303, 1311–13 (2018).

[535] Josh Bowers, Punishing the Innocent, 156 U. Pa. L. Rev.1117, 1122–23 (2008).

# Chapter 2

# MEDIATION AND OTHER PROCESSES IN AID OF NEGOTIATION

*Table of Sections*

---

# A. OVERVIEW

## § 2.1 Mediation's Popularity

Mediation is popular in the United States, having grown tremendously over the last half-century. Starting in the 1970s, an ADR Movement emerged,[1] consisting of lawyers, judges, academics, psychologists, marriage counselors, social workers, and others. The ADR Movement coalesced around mediation as its preferred dispute-resolution process,[2] and over several decades succeeded in spreading enthusiasm for mediation among courts and legislatures seeking ways to relieve court congestion, delay, and expense.[3] Federal and

---

1 See, e.g., Sarah R. Cole, Craig A. McEwen, Nancy H. Rogers, James R. Coben & Peter N. Thompson, Mediation: Law, Policy, & Practice § 4:2 (2024); Jeffrey W. Stempel, Reflections on Judicial ADR and the Multi-Door Courthouse at Twenty: Fait Accompli, Failed Overture, or Fledgling Adulthood? 11 Ohio St. J. on Disp. Resol. 297, 309–61 (1996).

2 James J. Alfini, Sharon B. Press, Jean R. Sternlight & Joseph B. Stulberg, Mediation Theory and Practice 2 (2001) ("Mediation became the 'darling child' of [the ADR] movement in large measure because it reserves to the parties the ultimate authority to 'settle' the matter.")

3 See Sarah R. Cole, Craig A. McEwen, Nancy H. Rogers, James R. Coben & Peter N. Thompson, Mediation: Law, Policy, & Practice § 4:3 (2024) (courts attracted to mediation as a way to clear dockets). See also Dorothy J. Della Noce, Mediation Theory and Policy: The Legacy of the Pound Conference, 17 Ohio St. J. on Disp. Resol. 545, 545 (2002) ("The [1976] Pound Conference marked an important moment in the history of mediation: the beginning of a concerted effort to stimulate court-connected mediation programs in the United States by framing the contemporary mediation movement—projects then underway in various countries, communities, agencies and courthouses—as a potential remedy for the perceived popular dissatisfaction with the administration of justice."); Jeffrey W. Stempel, Reflections on Judicial ADR and the Multi-Door Courthouse at Twenty: Fait Accompli, Failed Overture, or Fledgling Adulthood? 11 Ohio St. J. on Disp. Resol. 297, 316 (1996) ("the thrust of the Pound

state administrative agencies joined the mediation bandwagon.[4] Litigators and frequent litigants adapted with varying degrees of enthusiasm.

Mediation's growth enables many people to make a full-time job out of serving as a mediator. Some full-time mediators are employed by courts, other government agencies, or non-profit organizations. Other full-time mediators, often lawyers or former judges, offer their mediator services as independent contractors, often on the roster of an ADR organization. Some successful mediators are paid quite handsomely,[5] with reliable sources quoting $12,000–$18,000 per day for highly regarded mediators of complex civil cases.

While some lawyers become mediators, far more lawyers represent clients in mediation. From family law to personal injury to commercial contract disputes, representing clients in mediation is a routine part of practicing law in the U.S., and has been since the 1990s.[6]

## § 2.2 Mediation Defined

Mediation is facilitated negotiation. A mediator is simply someone who helps the negotiators negotiate.[7] While negotiation involves only the parties and their agents, such as their lawyers, mediation adds the mediator, who is not an agent of either party. The mediator is neutral.

Because mediation is "negotiation plus," one's understanding of mediation typically builds on one's understanding of negotiation. So, Chapter 1, which discusses negotiation, precedes this chapter.

Mediation should be distinguished from *adjudication*, although the line between them can get fuzzy. Adjudication is the process by which somebody (the adjudicator) decides the result of a dispute

---

Conference, even from speakers generally regarded as liberals, was that courts were becoming clogged").

[4] Sarah R. Cole, Craig A. McEwen, Nancy H. Rogers, James R. Coben & Peter N. Thompson, Mediation: Law, Policy, & Practice § 4:3 (2024).

[5] See, e.g., John S. Kiernan & William H. Taft V, Benefits of mediation, 4B N.Y. Prac., Com. Litig. In New York State Courts § 68:5 (5th ed. Oct. 2021) ("if the parties retain as their mediator a private attorney from a law firm or a major ADR organization, the hourly rate for such a mediator may be the attorney's customary billable rate or higher (some lawyers charge a premium over regular rates because their mediation work is unleveraged; one highly sought-after mediator routinely charges $50,000 per day during mediations).")

[6] See Richard C. Reuben, The Lawyer Turns Peacemaker, A.B.A. J., Aug. 1996, at 54, 55.

[7] Sarah R. Cole, Craig A. McEwen, Nancy H. Rogers, James R. Coben & Peter N. Thompson, Mediation: Law, Policy, & Practice § 1:1 (2024) ("Mediators are 'third parties,' not otherwise involved in a controversy, who assist disputing parties in their negotiations.")

(§ 1.2(a)). Adjudication typically is legally binding. *Litigation* is adjudication in a court or other government forum, and it is legally binding. So, typically, is *arbitration*, which is adjudication in a private, i.e., non-government, forum (§ 1.2(a)). What makes litigation and arbitration *binding* is the fact that the adjudicator's decision in these processes is backed by the force of government. The adjudicators' decisions in litigation and arbitration are enforced, ultimately, by sheriffs and marshals with guns and badges. Parties who fail to comply with these adjudicators' decisions may find their property forcibly taken from them or even find themselves jailed. In contrast, *non-binding adjudication* (discussed in §§ 2.31–2.34) lacks such enforcement. The parties to non-binding adjudication get a decision from the adjudicator, but a party's failure to comply with that decision does not subject that party to governmental enforcement. A party is free to disregard the non-binding adjudicator's decision and to pursue binding adjudication to its conclusion.

Mediation is certainly not binding adjudication.[8] Even if a mediator says how a dispute should be resolved, each party is free to disregard the mediator's statement and pursue litigation or arbitration to its conclusion. While litigation and arbitration are the two processes capable of producing legally-binding results without a post-dispute agreement by the parties,[9] mediation is like negotiation in that it can produce a legally-binding result only with each party's post-dispute consent to that result—a settlement agreement. In other words, mediation is a process that does not by itself resolve disputes but rather is a "process in aid of negotiation"—a process that helps the parties negotiate a resolution to the dispute. In stark contrast, binding adjudication (litigation and arbitration) resolves disputes wholly apart from any negotiation between the parties. So, a sharp line distinguishes mediation from binding adjudication.

---

[8] Sarah R. Cole, Craig A. McEwen, Nancy H. Rogers, James R. Coben & Peter N. Thompson, Mediation: Law, Policy, & Practice § 1:1 (2024) ("the mediator does not issue a decision that the parties must obey"). See, e.g., Wasinger v. Roman Cath. Diocese of Salina, 407 P.3d 665, 667 (Kan. App. 2017) (parties' contract contained a "clause requiring the parties to submit to 'binding mediation,' " and so-called "mediator issued a final decision," but Court of Appeals refused to enforce it because under Kansas law "Mediation cannot be considered binding since [Kansas Statute] 5–502(f) defines it as the act of an independent third party entering the dispute and trying to facilitate an agreement.' "); id. at 670 ("Kansas law does not recognize binding mediation and we must adhere to that principle").

[9] A party has the right to pursue litigation rather than arbitration unless that party has formed an arbitration agreement, in which case it has the right to pursue arbitration rather than litigation. Predispute arbitration agreements are common and typically enforceable. See Stephen J. Ware & Ariana Levinson, Principles of Arbitration § 3 (2d ed. 2023).

The line between mediation and non-binding adjudication is fuzzier, but a line, nevertheless. A mediator who says how the dispute should be resolved—that is, gives the parties a specific, concrete "decision"—has crossed the line from mediation to (non-binding) adjudication. Professionals calling themselves "mediators" rarely cross this line by making pronouncements specifying precisely how the dispute should be resolved, unless the parties jointly request a mediator's proposed settlement terms. However, many mediators often evaluate (§ 2.13). *Evaluation* is less precise than adjudication. Evaluation is an assessment of the merits of a case that does not go so far as to decree a specific, concrete result. For example, an adjudicator tells the parties that "Defendant is liable to Plaintiff in the amount of $250,000." In contrast, an evaluator might say "Plaintiff has a very strong argument that Defendant breached the contract, and damages appear to be in the low six figures," or "I've seen verdicts in similar cases range around two or three hundred thousand dollars." Other examples of evaluation include "Defendant's contributory negligence argument is unlikely to persuade a jury," or "Plaintiff seems to have shown strong evidence of price-fixing." While some mediators are more evaluative than others, it is the rare mediator who never evaluates at all (§ 2.13(b)(2)). Evaluative mediation is still mediation and does not cross the line into (non-binding) adjudication.

Moreover, while non-binding adjudication "tend[s] to follow the traditional order of trials," with a structured focus on evidence and argument, mediation tends to be more flexible, intuitive, and improvisational. "Often the mediator arranges meetings among disputing factions, listens, empathizes, encourages emotional outbursts when constructive, presses the parties to face facts, urges them to listen, and commends their efforts to accommodate."[10]

## § 2.3 Dispute Mediation and Transactional Mediation

Section 1.1 says that because much of the work lawyers do is either on a transaction or a dispute, lawyers negotiating for their clients are often engaged in transactional negotiation or dispute negotiation. Similarly, mediation can be divided into two types: *transactional* and *dispute*. Transactional mediation is when a mediator helps parties form a deal, such as the sale of a business or a collective bargaining agreement between a labor union and an employer (§ 2.18).[11] Transactional mediation is less common in the

---

10 Sarah R. Cole, Craig A. McEwen, Nancy H. Rogers, James R. Coben & Peter N. Thompson, Mediation: Law, Policy, & Practice § 1:1 (2024) ("the mediator does not issue a decision that the parties must obey").

11 Gerawan Farming, Inc. v. Agric. Lab. Rels. Bd., 3 Cal. 5th 1118, 1130, 405 P.3d 1087, 1089 (2017) (under California's Agricultural Labor Relations Act, "In certain

U.S. than dispute mediation and is only rarely mentioned in this chapter, which focuses on the mediation of *disputes*.

Section 1.2 points out that most dispute negotiation occurs without the involvement of lawyers. For example, disputes among family members or roommates about who will do various household chores are nearly always resolved without lawyers. Parties to such disputes do not often hire lawyers to help them win, or negotiate a resolution of, the dispute. Disputing parties tend to hire lawyers to help them only with disputes already in, or likely to go to, litigation or another form of legally binding adjudication, arbitration. Negotiation of these disputes is commonly called *settlement negotiation* (§§ 1.34–1.43). In other words, settlement negotiation is the negotiation of disputes that are already in binding adjudication (litigation or arbitration) or are likely to go there if negotiation does not result in agreement. *Plea bargaining* (§ 1.44) is the settlement negotiation of criminal cases.

Similarly, *settlement mediation* is the mediation of a narrow class of disputes likely to involve lawyers: disputes that are in binding adjudication or likely to go to binding adjudication if mediation fails to reach a settlement.

The reasoning of this chapter generally applies to both settlement mediation of disputes headed to litigation and settlement mediation of disputes headed to arbitration. To avoid wordiness though, the rest of this chapter is written entirely in terms of disputes headed to litigation.

## § 2.4 Mandatory Mediation and Voluntary Mediation

Settlement mediation can be divided into two categories: mandatory and voluntary. Some settlement mediation occurs because a court or other government agency mandates it (§ 2.30(a)). Such mandatory mediation raises several legal and policy issues not raised by voluntary mediation, which occurs only because the parties agree to it. While such agreements are typically formed after a dispute arises, some parties' pre-dispute contracts say that if a dispute arises, the parties promise to mediate before either party pursues binding adjudication. Such agreements are typically enforceable (§ 2.29).

---

cases in which an employer and a labor union have failed to reach a first contract, either party may invoke MMC [mandatory mediation and conciliation], which involves a mediation process before a neutral mediator. If the parties do not reach an agreement on all terms through mediation, the mediator resolves the disputed terms and submits a proposed contract to the [California Agricultural Labor Relations] Board, which can then impose that contract on the parties."); Scott R. Peppet, Contract Formation in Imperfect Markets: Should We Use Mediators in Deals?, 19 Ohio St. J. on Disp. Resol. 283, 339–44 (2004).

## B. GOALS OF DISPUTE MEDIATION

### § 2.5 Generally

Understanding the *goals* of mediation is helpful to understanding the *process* of mediation. Accordingly, the goals of dispute mediation are discussed in the next few Sections (§§ 2.6–2.8), while the process of mediation is discussed thereafter (§§ 2.10–2.16).

Of course, mediation itself has no goals. The goals belong to those who participate in mediation: mediators, parties, lawyers, and others. The goals of the participants in each mediation shape that particular mediation. The major goals of *settlement mediation* (§ 2.3) can be placed on a continuum from the least ambitious to the most ambitious.

| Settle case | Positive sum | Moral growth |
|---|---|---|
| Least ambitious | | Most ambitious |

The least ambitious goal of settlement mediation is to resolve the dispute, that is, to settle the case or potential case. A settlement agreement, like any agreement, creates value in the sense that it gives each side something it values more than whatever alternatives it had (§ 1.4), including its Best Alternative to a Negotiated Agreement (BATNA, § 1.5), which in settlement negotiation or mediation is further litigation (§ 1.35(a)).

Going beyond just a settlement agreement, *positive-sum* (§ 1.10) agreements are better for each party (in that party's assessment at the time) than other possible agreements between them. So, reaching a positive-sum deal, through *problem-solving* negotiation, is a more ambitious goal than just settling the dispute by reaching a deal.

The third and most ambitious goal of dispute mediation is the moral growth of the parties. By "moral growth," advocates mean improving parties' abilities to prevent and resolve future disputes.

These three are not the only possible mediation goals, but they seem to be the most common.[12] The participants in a mediation may have different and even conflicting goals. For example, the lawyers

---

[12] Compare Carrie Menkel-Meadow et al., Dispute Resolution: Beyond the Adversarial Model 269–71 (2005) (listing advantages of mediation as: "settlement: avoiding the expense, delay, and risk of adjudication," "participation and self-determination: giving parties voice and choice," "better outcomes: generating creative problem solving," and "relationship, community, and harmony: building bridges between people.")

may be focused on settling a case, while the parties are focused on problem-solving, and the mediator seeks to engender moral growth.

One might initially think mediation participants should pursue all three goals because even if they do not achieve all of them, there is no harm in trying. But tradeoffs abound. It is likely to cost more time and money, at least in the short run, to try to help the parties improve their dispute-prevention and resolution skills (moral growth) than to try to settle a case. It also costs time and money to search for positive-sum opportunities that may or may not exist (§ 1.10(e)). By consuming time and money, the pursuit of more ambitious goals may make settlement less likely than if the participants single-mindedly focus on settlement as the only goal.

On the other hand, some cases can settle only after positive-sum negotiation creates a *settlement zone* that would not otherwise exist (§§ 1.10(f), 1.39). And other cases can settle only after one or more of the parties themselves has reconsidered its interests and priorities in some important way we consider moral growth. So, pursuing goals more ambitious than merely settling may be the only way to achieve the less ambitious goal of settling.

## § 2.6 Settle Cases

Most participants in settlement mediation seek settlement, but not all do. For example, a litigant who wants something that a court, but not a settlement, can provide, like a favorable precedent for future cases (§§ 1.35(a), 1.39(b)), may be participating in mediation only because the court has ordered it (§ 2.30). Leaving these exceptions aside, participants in settlement mediations tend to share the goal of settling, although the disputing parties obviously tend to differ with each other about the terms of settlement they seek.

In many cases, at least one possible set of settlement terms seems better to each party than litigating further, its BATNA (§ 1.5). In other words, at least one possible set of settlement terms seems better to each party than the value that party has placed on the case (§ 1.35), so the parties' bottom lines create a *settlement zone* (§ 1.39). While it is in the interests of all parties for cases with a settlement zone to settle within that zone, such cases do not always settle. This failure of negotiation to reach a settlement is often due to a few common, well-understood causes (§ 1.11). These common obstacles to settlement can be overcome by mediation (§§ 2.11–2.13).

Consequently, many parties and lawyers seek a *settlement-oriented* mediator who is known for successfully bringing disputing parties to agreement (§§ 2.13, 2.24). And many courts encourage, or even require, cases to go to mediation because they want mediation to make cases settle and thus disappear from the court's docket.[13] The endorsement of mediation to reduce court congestion, delay, and expense is even found in legislation and court rules.[14]

## § 2.7 Positive-Sum or Problem-Solving

While settlement is the least ambitious mediation goal, a more ambitious mediation goal is to reach a settlement that exploits opportunities for *positive-sum* negotiation. Positive-sum negotiation finds those possible settlements that are better *for both parties* than other possible settlements (§ 1.10(a)). While any agreement creates value in the sense that it gives each side something it values more than whatever alternatives it had (§ 1.4), many possible agreements may do that, and *problem-solvers* try to find the agreement that does it as much as possible (§ 1.22).

Negotiators, whether negotiating or mediating, do not have complete control over whether their negotiation is zero-sum or positive-sum. Negotiators trying to find a positive-sum opportunity may fail because no such opportunity exists. The parties' interests may be so diametrically opposed that they have no coinciding interests (§ 1.10(d)). And the parties may prioritize issues so similarly that it is not possible to trade concessions on low priority issues for gains on higher priority issues (*logrolling*, § 1.10(c)). In short, the situation may be zero-sum, thus precluding positive-sum negotiation.

---

[13] Sarah R. Cole, Craig A. McEwen, Nancy H. Rogers, James R. Coben & Peter N. Thompson, Mediation: Law, Policy, & Practice § 9:2 (2024) ("Courts favor mediation on efficiency grounds and are willing to exercise the power to order mediation and to compel the attendance of necessary parties."); Donald L. Swanson, Mandated Mediation: An Effective Dispute-Resolution Tool, 40 Am. Bankr. Inst. J. 16, 16 (September 2021) ("[J]udicial opposition to mandated mediation tends to last only as long as caseloads remain manageable. Once caseloads become heavy and overwhelming, judges look for solutions—and mandated mediation is one that is commonly adopted."); Roger L. Carter, Oh, Ye of Little (Good) Faith: Questions, Concerns and Commentary on Efforts to Regulate Participant Conduct in Mediations, 2002 J. Disp. Resol. 367, 395 ("Judges and court personnel have embraced mediation, in no small part, because they believe that it clears dockets."); Forrest S. Mosten, Institutionalization of Mediation, 42 Fam. Ct. Rev. 292, 298 (2004) ("An overriding problem of court mediation is the coercive pressure on the mediators to clear dockets by settling cases. Rather than being selected for the benefits of citizen empowerment and satisfaction of result, many court programs are encouraged and supported by the judiciary to relieve them of staggering caseloads.")

[14] Ark. Code Ann. § 9–31–405 ("The Arkansas Youth Mediation Program's goals are to: (1) Reduce economic, psychological, and social costs to individuals and public and private institutions arising from disputes involving youth; (2) Reduce court dockets and delays; . . .[and] reducing unnecessary adversarial behavior and expense in litigation throughout Arkansas."); N.J. Ct. R. 1:40–1 ("Complementary Dispute Resolution Programs (CDR) provided for by these rules are available in the Superior Court and Municipal Courts and constitute an integral part of the judicial process, intended to enhance its quality and efficacy.").

On the other hand, the parties' interests may present opportunities for positive-sum negotiation that go unexploited because the negotiators do not find them. In such a case, a zero-sum negotiation occurs in a positive-sum situation. To put it another way, positive-sum situations can yield either positive-sum or zero-sum negotiations, while zero-sum situations can yield only zero-sum negotiations. Having a zero-sum negotiation in a positive-sum situation is not necessarily a failure. The value created by exploiting a positive-sum opportunity may be lower than the value of the time and effort required to find it (§ 1.10(e)).

While having a zero-sum negotiation in a positive-sum situation is not necessarily a failure, it often is. Often the negotiators could, with little time and effort, exploit a valuable positive-sum opportunity, but they fail to do so. This is because positive-sum negotiation is unlikely to occur unless both negotiators use the *problem-solving* approach to negotiation, which requires each side to honestly disclose its interests and priorities (§§ 1.22–1.26). And while both parties benefit if both use the problem-solving approach, each party's individual incentive may be to use the *adversarial/competitive* approach to which the problem-solving approach is vulnerable (§ 1.26). So, there is a divergence between what is good for the parties in total (both using the problem-solving approach) and each negotiator's individual incentive to use the adversarial/competitive approach to exploit the problem-solving counterpart.

Mediation is well-suited to narrowing this divergence (§ 2.12) between the parties' joint interest and their individual incentives. Mediation reduces the problem-solving negotiator's risk of being exploited by the other side's adversarial/competitive approach. Mediation thus increases the likelihood both sides will use the problem-solving approach. Mediators who successfully encourage negotiators to problem-solve can be called *problem-solving* mediators. Just as problem-solving negotiators orient toward finding positive-sum opportunities, so do problem-solving mediators. Mediation with a problem-solving mediator seems well-suited to finding those settlement terms that are better for both parties than other settlement terms.

## § 2.8 Moral Growth

Some mediators seek not only to resolve disputes and to facilitate positive-sum negotiation, but also to help people improve, particularly to improve their abilities to prevent and resolve disputes. This sort of "moral growth" may be particularly relevant in family and other ongoing-relationship disputes, for example a divorce in which the separating parents will be jointly navigating co-parenting challenges for years to come.

Mediation aimed at fostering such moral growth is often called *transformative mediation*. Its advocates contend that mediation has "a unique potential for transforming people—engendering moral growth."[15] Mediation can help empower the parties and evoke in each party an appreciation for the problems of others.[16] If this occurs, one or more of the parties may reconsider its *interests and priorities* (§ 1.23) in a way that moves that party toward the other party's interests, and therefore positions, thus fostering settlement. Even where transformative mediation produces no settlement of the dispute at hand,[17] it may have succeeded in producing parties better able later to resolve this dispute on their own. And it may have succeeded in improving the parties' abilities to resolve future disputes they have with each other and with others.

Transforming people to engender moral growth is the most ambitious of the three major mediation goals.[18] This goal rests on a very different view of conflict than underlies the problem-solving and settlement-oriented approaches to mediation. Those two approaches to mediation are "based upon an essentially psychological/economic view of human conflict."[19] They reflect "an individualist ideology, in which human beings are [allegedly] assumed to be autonomous, self-contained, atomistic individuals, each motivated by the pursuit of satisfaction of his or her own separate self-interests."[20] By contrast, transformative mediation "takes an essentially social/communicative view of human conflict" rooted "in the postmodern and social

---

15 Robert A. Baruch Bush & Joseph P. Folger, The Promise of Mediation: Responding to Conflict Through Empowerment and Recognition 2–12 (1994).

16 Lon Fuller, Mediation—Its Forms and Functions, 44 S. Cal. L. Rev. 305, 325 (1971) (mediation's core is its "capacity to reorient the parties toward each other, not by imposing rules on them, but by helping them to achieve a new and shared perception of their relationship, a perception that will direct their attention toward each other.")

17 Robert A. Baruch Bush & Joseph P. Folger, The Promise of Mediation: Responding to Conflict Through Empowerment and Recognition 200–01 (1994). See also Deborah M. Kolb & Kenneth Kressel, The Realities of Making Talk Work in When Talk Works: Profiles of Mediators 466–68 (Deborah M. Kolb et al. eds. 1994).

18 Robert A. Baruch Bush & Joseph P. Folger, The Promise of Mediation: Responding to Conflict Through Empowerment and Recognition 200–01 (1994). See also Deborah M. Kolb & Kenneth Kressel, The Realities of Making Talk Work in When Talk Works: Profiles of Mediators 466–68 (Deborah M. Kolb et al. eds. 1994).

19 Dorothy J. Della Noce, Robert A. Baruch Bush & Joseph P. Folger, Clarifying the Theoretical Underpinnings of Mediation: Implications for Practice and Policy, 3 Pepp. Disp. Resol. L.J. 39, 48 (2002) (describing problem-solving mediation).

20 Id. at 49 (describing problem-solving mediation).

constructionist literature of the social sciences, particularly in the discipline of communication science."[21]

While transformative mediation may be a postmodern alternative to more individualistic approaches to mediation, its focus on moral growth is also found in a very old form of mediation, that performed by members of the clergy.[22] Perhaps traditional practices dating back to the pre-modern era and post-modern approaches to conflict share traits in opposition to modernity's individualistic "psychological/economic" perspective underlying the problem-solving and settlement-oriented approaches to mediation.

# C. THE MEDIATION PROCESS

## § 2.9 Goals Shape Process

The three major goals of mediation participants—the mediator, parties, lawyers, and others—are to settle cases, exploit positive-sum opportunities, and engender moral growth (§§ 2.5–2.8). Each participant may have some or all these goals. In some cases, all participants have similar goals, while in other cases, they do not. For example, the lawyers may be focused on settling a case, while the parties are focused on positive-sum opportunities, and the mediator seeks to engender moral growth. Whatever goals the participants have shape that particular mediation, so any description of the mediation process necessarily makes generalizations that do not always hold true. Nevertheless, some features are common to most *settlement mediations* (§ 2.3) in the U.S., and these features are surveyed in Section 2.10. Then, Sections 2.11–2.16 discuss important benefits of, and issues regarding, the mediation process.

---

21 Id. at 50, 65 n.49.

22 Members of the clergy have long served as mediators and religion continues to have a central role in many mediations. See, e.g., Associated Hat Mfrs. v. Baird-Unteidt Co., 91 A. 373, 379 (Conn. 1914) (discussing a labor strike in which "two of the clergy, acting as self-appointed mediators, brought about an agreement"); R. Seth Shippee, Peacemaking, Applying Faith to Dispute Resolution, 10 Disp. Resol. Mag. 3, Spring 2004, at 3 ("Since the Middle Ages, Christian clergymen have been called upon to act as mediators in disputes ranging from minor family squabbles to international diplomatic clashes between nations on the brink of war"); Isaac Altman, Religious Mediation as A Tool to Resolve Disputes Between Religious Universities and Their LGBT Students, 23 Cardozo J. Conflict Resol. 433, 466 (2022) ("Religious mediation, in which coreligionist parties use a religious authority from their shared religion as a mediator, has a number of benefits, especially in disputes over particular interpretations of how religious values would dictate a response to a given situation."); F. Matthews-Giba, Religious Dimensions of Mediation, 27 Fordham Urb. L.J. 1695 (2000); Margaret Graham Tebo, Dispute Resolution Clauses Keep the Faith: Many Clients Asking for Mediation Under Christian Principles, A.B.A. J. Report, May 30, 2003 (discussing Institute for Christian Conciliation).

## § 2.10 The Mediation Process Generally

### *(a) Participants*

Mediation requires at least three people: a mediator and two negotiators. In *settlement mediation* (§ 2.3), whether the main negotiators are lawyers or clients varies. Parties, lawyers, and mediators are not the only possible participants in mediation. Anyone can participate with the permission of the parties and mediator. Depending on the sort of dispute, those participants might include anyone from family members or religious leaders to accountants or scientific experts.

### *(b) Starting to Mediate*

Before the first mediation session, the parties or their lawyers may have provided the mediator with information about the dispute, which may influence how the mediator conducts the following steps. Such pre-session communications have long been standard in commercial and other civil cases,[23] but may still be the exception in family mediation where fewer resources to produce them tends to be available.[24]

If mediation begins, as it often does, with both parties, their lawyers, and the mediator in the same room, the mediator typically welcomes everyone and then explains the mediation process.[25] While this explanation may be friendly and conversational, the mediator has probably given it careful thought because she knows it can "establish the tone and tenor of the entire mediation session."[26] From

---

[23] As long ago as 2010, an experienced mediator noted that ten or 15 years earlier (the 1990s), "it was quite common for commercial mediators, immediately following her or his engagement, to simply set the date, time, and location for the face-to-face mediation and take no further action until the mediation was convened." But by 2010, "in the increasingly sophisticated world of commercial mediation, the failure of the mediator to schedule a meeting with legal counsel and/or the parties by telephone or in person in advance of the face-to-face mediation is more the exception than the rule." Larry R. Rute, The Evolution of Commercial Mediation in the Midwest: Best Practices, Confidentiality and Good Faith, J. Kan. B. Ass'n, January 2010, at 24, 25.

[24] Roselle L. Wissler, Art Hinshaw, What Happens Before the First Mediation Session? An Empirical Study of Pre-Session Communications, 23 Cardozo J. Conflict Resol. 143, 178 (2022) ("The present study shows that a sizeable number of mediators do not have communications with the mediation participants or do not have access to case documents before the first formal mediation session, especially in family cases. Pre-session communications were not held in roughly one-third of civil cases and two-thirds of family cases").

[25] Roselle L. Wissler, Art Hinshaw, The Initial Mediation Session: An Empirical Examination, 27 Harv. Negot. L. Rev. 1, 3 (2021) ("The mediator's opening remarks typically include an explanation of the mediation process and its confidentiality, the mediator's impartiality and role, the parties' roles, and the ground rules for the mediation.")

[26] See, e.g., Kimberlee K. Kovach, Mediation: Principles and Practice 158–59 (3d ed. 2004).

the outset, "mediators want to establish their integrity, competence, and concern for the parties."[27] The mediator's introduction often addresses ground rules for communication and the extent to which the mediator and other participants have duties to keep what is said in mediation confidential.[28]

After the mediator's introduction, he may ask each party to take turns explaining the dispute, while the other participants listen quietly. These *opening statements* may be made by the lawyers, rather than the parties. In some cases, the mediator will prefer that they be made by the parties, while in others the mediator will prefer that they be made by the lawyers. In *settlement mediation* (§ 2.3), whether the main negotiators are lawyers or clients varies. Mediation of family, community, and small claims disputes often prioritizes involvement of the parties, so if the mediation includes all the participants around a table, the parties often sit closest to the mediator and do most of the talking, while their lawyers, if present at all, sit farther from the mediator and say less.[29] In contrast, "much commercial and civil mediation" "tends to be dominated by attorneys who often sit closest to the mediator and take the lead in presenting their arguments."[30]

After opening statements, mediators often ask those present to plan an agenda, that is, to discuss what they should discuss. Reaching agreement on an agenda can provide encouragement to the participants ("Hey, look, we can agree on something!") and thus generate momentum toward agreement on substantive issues. For similar momentum-building reasons, mediators often like to put relatively easy issues early on the agenda. If the participants spend a little time reaching agreement on some issues, they may become increasingly confident in the mediator and increasingly invested in the mediation process, which hopefully strengthens their commitments to reaching a deal that will resolve the whole dispute. People tend not to want their initial accomplishments to go to waste, which might be the result of a later impasse requiring the dispute to be resolved in *adjudication* (litigation or arbitration, (§ 1.2(a)), rather than mediation.

Seeking agreement on an agenda for the mediation may reveal that fully resolving the dispute requires the parties, lawyers, or the mediator to gather additional information or even to bring in

---

[27] Sarah R. Cole, Craig A. McEwen, Nancy H. Rogers, James R. Coben & Peter N. Thompson, Mediation: Law, Policy, & Practice § 3:2 (2024).

[28] Confidentiality in mediation is discussed in § 2.28.

[29] Sarah R. Cole, Craig A. McEwen, Nancy H. Rogers, James R. Coben & Peter N. Thompson, Mediation: Law, Policy, & Practice § 3:2 (2024).

[30] Id.

additional participants. So, the mediation may need to pause and resume another day. While some mediations reach a settlement agreement in one session of just a few hours, others finally reach a settlement only after multiple sessions spread over weeks or months.

### (c) Joint Sessions, Private Caucuses, and Shuttle Diplomacy

In mediation, a *joint* or *open session* is when both sides of a dispute and the mediator are present. During joint sessions, the mediator typically keeps order and facilitates communication in a variety of ways discussed in Section 2.10(d). In contrast, a private session or *caucus* is when the mediator is meeting with only one side of a dispute. Both joint and private sessions increasingly moved to Zoom and other online platforms during the COVID-19 pandemic,[31] and many lawyers are now comfortably used to that.

Some mediations consist entirely of private caucuses. Others consist almost entirely of private caucuses, with joint sessions only at the beginning and, hopefully, the end when a settlement agreement is signed. These caucus-driven mediations tend to be lawyer-dominated mediations and thus more common in business, commercial, and other civil cases, such as personal injury, than in family, community, or small claims cases. "The move to caucus-driven mediation reflects to some extent the preferences of attorneys who are not anxious to have their clients sharing information with the other party."[32] In these lawyer-dominated mediations, the mediator conducts *shuttle diplomacy* by traveling back and forth between private caucuses with each side.

Shuttle diplomacy can prevent the parties from angering each other. "For instance, if Party A says, 'I think B is a filthy liar and I can't believe a word he says,' the mediator can explain that to B as follows: 'A has some doubts about whether she can rely upon your promises.' "[33] Shuttle diplomacy also allows the mediator to carry one party's settlement offer to the other party. This reduces the problem of *reactive devaluation* in which one party rejects proposals from the other party "out of 'spite,' " because humans "prefer not to agree with

[31] Norman Feit, Plenary Sessions in A Paradigm of Presumptive and Virtual Mediation, 40 Alternatives to High Cost Litig. 107 (2022) ("The advent of Zoom mediations necessitated by the pandemic has facilitated that model in virtual form, congregating the participants through a Zoom general session followed by the mediator shuttling between breakout rooms."); Henriquez v. Georgia Dep't of Revenue, 2020 WL 10147132, at *7 (N.D. Ga. Dec. 9, 2020) ("During the COVID-19 pandemic, most mediations are conducted via Zoom and can be quite cost-effective.")

[32] Sarah R. Cole, Craig A. McEwen, Nancy H. Rogers, James R. Coben & Peter N. Thompson, Mediation: Law, Policy, & Practice § 3:2 (2024).

[33] Leonard L. Riskin et al., Dispute Resolution and Lawyers 347 (3d ed. 2005).

a distrusted or disliked adversary."[34] Also, the mediator carrying one party's settlement offer into the other party's private caucus avoids hard feelings when the mediator, not the offeror, hears an initial reaction to the offer like: "That offer is fucking insulting! We're going to trial unless they get realistic." The mediator can give a softer translation of that message back to the offeror, perhaps with a counteroffer.

The mediator is not the only one who can call for a private caucus. Parties and lawyers often ask for them. Before breaking into caucus, the mediator may re-visit the issue of whether and to what extent what is said during mediation will remain confidential.[35]

### *(d) Facilitating Communication*

#### *(1) Overview*

Much of what mediators do involves facilitating communication between the parties.[36] If that seems easy, recall that many disputes get to mediation only after negotiation has failed and litigation has bogged down into a costly, nasty war of attrition draining each party of its wealth and sanity. The parties may hate each other and view each other as enemies to be destroyed. In this environment, facilitating communication can be a major accomplishment. "Negotiation experts advise negotiating parties to separate the 'people from the problem,' but . . . parties may resist constructive negotiation efforts because of anger and distrust that arise either from the underlying grievance—e.g., a medical error by a physician—or from the way that they perceive the grievance was handled—e.g., denial and refusal to apologize."[37]

#### *(2) Direct Communication*

In joint sessions, mediators often try to facilitate *direct* communication between the parties. For example, rather than describe the dispute, the mediator can ask each party to describe the dispute as he sees it. This tactic tends to foster communication for a variety of reasons.

---

[34] Sarah R. Cole, Craig A. McEwen, Nancy H. Rogers, James R. Coben & Peter N. Thompson, Mediation: Law, Policy, & Practice § 3:13 (2024).

[35] Confidentiality in mediation is discussed in § 2.28.

[36] Leonard L. Riskin, Understanding Mediator Orientations, Strategies, and Techniques: A Grid for the Perplexed, 1 Harv. Neg. L. Rev. 7, 24 (1996) (facilitative mediators seek primarily "to enhance communication between the parties in order to help them decide what to do.").

[37] Sarah R. Cole, Craig A. McEwen, Nancy H. Rogers, James R. Coben & Peter N. Thompson, Mediation: Law, Policy, & Practice § 3:8 (2024).

First, it is the parties communicating directly with each other, rather than through their lawyers or through the mediator.[38] This may, for example, be the first time Plaintiff hears Defendant tell Defendant's side of the story, as opposed to hearing Defendant's lawyer tell Defendant's side of the story.[39] Also, parties communicating directly with each other allows the mediator to hear the parties' views of the dispute, as distinct from the lawyers' views, which may enable the mediator to be more helpful later in the mediation. One or both of the parties may characterize the issues differently from the way the lawyers, or the court, or the mediator would have characterized them. Perhaps one of the parties sees an issue others do not see, so that issue will have to be resolved before that party will agree to a settlement. Or if the parties do not see an issue that other participants do see, perhaps it is not an issue at all, or at least not one that needs to be addressed to reach a settlement.

When asked by the mediator to describe the dispute as he sees it, a party may not respond with a thorough, well-organized answer. This might occur because of the party's weak communication skills, nervousness about mediation, or embarrassment about some part of the dispute. Or it might be due to an instruction from his lawyer to say as little as possible (§ 2.25). Probably, the mediator will want to know which of these factors is present. Also, the mediator will still want to hear the party describe the dispute as he sees it. So, the mediator may ask the party broad, open-ended questions. "Why?" questions are a common example: "Why do you pick $300,000 as your settlement offer?" or "Why are you concerned about pollution in the lake?" Sometimes more indirect questions, such as "what are your hobbies?", elicit more telling information (§ 1.23). After asking questions, the mediator listens carefully. She is alert to any non-verbal signals the party may, intentionally or not, be conveying. Facial expressions and body language can be significant.[40]

While gathering information from the parties, the mediator often summarizes what each party has said or encourages a party's

---

38 For the benefits of parties communicating directly with each other, see Leonard L. Riskin, The Represented Client in a Settlement Conference: The Lessons of G. Heileman Brewing Co. v. Joseph Oat Corp., 69 Wash. U.L.Q. 1059 (1991).

39 Sarah R. Cole, Craig A. McEwen, Nancy H. Rogers, James R. Coben & Peter N. Thompson, Mediation: Law, Policy, & Practice § 3:12 (2024) ("Mediation provides the chance for parties to participate directly in negotiation—to speak and be heard and to be treated respectfully and attentively both by a trusted and impartial mediator and by the other party. Mediators enforce norms of respectful conduct and manage the process in ways that contribute to almost universally high perceptions of trust and fairness among participants. Thus, . . . mediation has the potential to enhance considerably the experience of procedural justice").

40 See Edward Brunet, Charles B. Craver & Ellen Deason, Alternative Dispute Resolution: The Advocate's Perspective 46–60 (5th ed. 2016); Donald G. Gifford & Robert J. Rhee, Legal Negotiation: Theory and Practice 137–43 (3d ed. 2017).

communication with affirmations like "I see" and "I understand." These *active listening* tactics (§ 1.23(b)) are designed to build the party's confidence in the mediator by showing him that the mediator listened to him and understands his perspective.[41]

The mediator may ask each party to summarize the views of the other side. Such summaries reveal the extent to which each party has listened to and understood the other side. Also, summarizing the views of the other side tends to promote a little grudging respect for the interests and arguments on the other side, thus bringing the parties a bit closer to each other and to settlement.

The mediator may also try to facilitate communication with environmental factors. A classic example is to arrange the seating so the parties are not sitting directly across from each other at a rectangular table but rather sitting next to each other at a round table, which is a less adversarial posture. The mediator may also seek to ensure that everyone is comfortable in terms of temperature, food, drink, etc. In fact, food often plays a predictable role in the "typical daylong mediation" lawyers experience.[42] "High volume mediation offices frequently have kitchens containing cookies, candies, and other snacks available for negotiators whenever they would like," and "mediators commonly provide lunch at the mediator's office. During the lunch break, the mediator often eats with negotiators in order to 'break bread' and get closer to them on a personal level."[43]

More substantively, mediators also typically facilitate communication by clarifying issues and keeping joint sessions organized. Organized does not, however, mean keeping order the way a judge with a gavel keeps order in a courtroom, by insisting that everyone communicate in a controlled, highly structured manner. More likely, the mediator sees value in spontaneity and informality. The mediator may even see value in angry or emotional outbursts[44] if the mediator believes the problem cannot be solved until the parties "get some things off their chest" by venting their feelings. So, "Mediators establish rules of conduct and exchange that can both permit and control emotional outbursts."[45] "Parties often believe that they have been treated disrespectfully by the other side," so "mediators may encourage parties to explain the context and reasons

---

[41] The mediator typically accepts each party's characterization of the dispute. If the parties reject each other's characterization of the dispute, the mediator tries not to adopt either characterization, but instead to be even-handed.

[42] Baumeister, Simpson, Ware and Weber, The Glucose Model of Mediation, 15 Pepp. Disp. Resol. L.J. 377, 400–02 (2015).

[43] Id.

[44] Kimberlee K. Kovach, Mediation: Principles and Practice 164 (3d ed. 2004).

[45] Sarah R. Cole, Craig A. McEwen, Nancy H. Rogers, James R. Coben & Peter N. Thompson, Mediation: Law, Policy, & Practice § 3:8 (2024).

for their actions to one another and offer apologies where appropriate."[46] Mediators can help parties "maintain a sense of dignity and respect even in the context of acknowledging error, taking responsibility and accepting compromise."[47]

In sum, mediation allows parties room for the personal and the emotional, as well as the abstract and the rational.[48]

*(3) Indirect Communication*

In addition to facilitating direct communication between the parties, many mediators facilitate indirect communication between the parties. A very important way of facilitating indirect communication is to obtain each party's confidential information in private caucus and then combine all that information to identify settlement zones and positive-sum opportunities (§§ 2.11–2.12). The mediator can then communicate these settlement zones and positive-sum opportunities to each party in a way that gives only an imprecise or "noisy" translation of the other party's confidential information. Delicate use of this important tactic is a mark of a mediator who excels at her craft.

***(e) Settlement Offers***

Mediators may play a variety of roles in the formulation and communication of settlement offers (§§ 2.11–2.16). As noted above, the mediator carrying one party's settlement offer into the other party's private caucus avoids hard feelings when the mediator, not the offeror, hears a very negative initial reaction to the offer (§ 2.10(c)). The mediator may *evaluate* a settlement offer (§ 2.13). For example, the mediator may say to the offeree, "That offer is probably about as good a result as you're going to get from a court." Or the mediator may say, "That sounds like a proposal that will go a long way toward achieving both parties' goals." If an offeree rejects an offer, the mediator may seek to improve upon it, to find a variation of it that is acceptable to both parties. The mediator may go so far as to make her own proposals for terms of settlement. Many mediators, however, prefer that proposals come from the parties to increase the parties' sense of control over the settlement process and to allow the mediator to remain more objective.[49]

---

[46] Id.

[47] Id.

[48] See, e.g., Leonard L. Riskin, Mediation and Lawyers, 43 Ohio St. L.J. 29, 43–48 (1982).

[49] Leonard L. Riskin et al., Dispute Resolution and Lawyers 345 (3d ed. 2005).

### *(f) Agreements*

Mediation may involve several agreements, typically written and signed, even if mediation does not produce an agreement to settle the dispute.[50] Before a dispute arises, the parties may have agreed that, in the event of a dispute, the parties will try to resolve it in mediation (§ 2.29). In the absence of such a *pre-dispute* agreement to mediate, the parties may form a *post-dispute* agreement to mediate. And even if a court or other government agency orders the parties to mediate (§ 2.30), the parties may still form an agreement specifying who the mediator will be (§ 2.27(c)(1)).

The mediator may have an agreement with the parties regarding how, when, and where the mediation will be conducted, and the extent to which what is said during mediation shall remain confidential (§ 2.28(b)). Also, the mediator may have an agreement with the parties regarding the mediator's compensation. While some mediators are paid by the parties,[51] other mediators are paid by a court, another government agency, or a non-profit organization. (§ 2.27(c)(1)). Some mediators perform their services without charge.

The following is a sample post-dispute agreement to mediate.[52]

**MEDIATION AGREEMENT**

This is an agreement between [*name 1*] and [*name 2*] (Parties) and [*name 3*], (Mediator) to mediate an issue Parties wish to resolve. The Mediator and Parties agree as follows:

**ISSUE IDENTIFICATION AND RESPONSIBILITY FOR RESOLUTION**

1.

The issue Parties want to resolve is [*describe*]. Parties and Mediator understand that Parties, not Mediator, determine the issues.

2.

Parties come to this mediation with the authority to settle the issue between them.

---

50 Mediated settlement agreements are discussed in § 2.16.

51 While most mediators charge by the hour or day, other arrangements are possible. For an argument that mediators and parties should be free to make the mediator's compensation contingent on the outcome of the mediation, see Scott R. Peppet, Contractarian Economics and Mediation Ethics: The Case for Customizing Neutrality Through Contingent Fee Mediation, 82 Tex. L. Rev. 227 (2003).

52 Jay E. Grenig, 2 Alternative Dispute Resolution, App. R Form 6 (4th ed. 2022).

3.

Parties agree to participate in and demonstrate good faith to resolve the issue.

4.

Mediation is not therapy for individuals, but a process to resolve disagreements. Mediator is present to help the parties themselves reach a constructive and fair agreement. Mediator does not and will not impose a solution upon the parties.

5.

Mediator is a neutral and impartial person in this problem solving process. No party will be given any preference over the other.

**INVOLVEMENT OF LEGAL COUNSEL**

6.

Parties understand that they may have attorneys present during the mediation, and that they may seek legal advice at any point before, during, or after the mediation process.

7.

Mediator is [*not*] an attorney. Mediator will not give legal advice during this mediation.

**THE MEDIATION PROCESS**

8.

Mediator may stop the proceedings at any time and for any reason. Parties may stop the proceedings at any time and for any reason.

9.

Caucuses may be needed at points in the mediation, at the discretion of Mediator or at the request of either Party. Discussions during caucuses are confidential, unless otherwise agreed by the Party in the caucus.

10.

In order to insure the success of the mediation, Parties agree to give information to the mediator, who has the authority to give that information to the other party if it is necessary and relevant to the discussions for resolution and if the Party with the information agrees to its release.

**CONFIDENTIALITY AND ADMISSIBILITY**

11.

Mediation is normally a confidential process. A signed mediated agreement is usually not admissible in judicial proceedings unless the parties agree. All communications, written or oral, are generally not admissible, regardless of who is responsible for the communication. Mediation is a [form] of settlement negotiations, and no one involved in the mediation normally may be compelled to testify about what happened during the mediation process.

12.

Professional ethics, and some laws, direct that confidentiality is not applicable where Mediator suspects another person may be in danger of harm. Confidentiality can also be waived if all participants agree to disclose a particular matter.

**MEDIATOR FEES**

13.

Mediator's fee will be handled in the following manner: [*describe*].

We have read and understand this agreement and agree to use mediation as described above as the problem solving mechanism for this issue.

Dated:__________

[signature, etc.]

Dated:__________

[signature, etc.]

Dated:__________

Mediator

## § 2.11 Identifying Settlement Zones and Overcoming Barriers to Settlement

In many cases, at least one possible set of settlement terms seems better to each party than its BATNA of litigating further. In other words, at least one possible set of settlement terms seems better to each party than the value that party has placed on the case (§ 1.35), so the parties' bottom lines create a *settlement zone* (§ 1.39). Suppose, for example, that Plaintiff values the case at $150,000, and thus is willing to settle for any amount over $150,000, while Defendant values the case at $200,000, and thus is willing to settle for any amount under $200,000. In other words, Plaintiff's *bottom line* (§ 1.6) is $150,000 and Defendant's bottom line is $200,000. This is depicted in Diagram 2-1.

Diagram 2-1

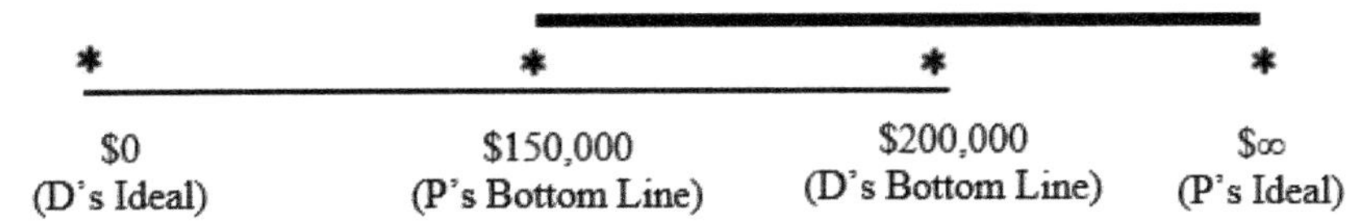


The thin line represents possible settlement terms acceptable to Defendant. The thick line represents possible settlement terms acceptable to Plaintiff. The possible settlements from $150,000 to $200,000 comprise the *settlement zone* (§ 1.39). A settlement cannot occur outside this zone unless a party changes its bottom line (§ 1.32(b)). Any settlement must, by definition, seem to each party better than its bottom line, which is the worst deal a party will accept.

If the parties settle anywhere in the settlement zone, they each believe they have made themselves better off than they would have been had they continued to litigate.[53] Accepting those beliefs, settling at $175,000, for example, benefits both parties when compared to not settling at all. Plaintiff would rather take $175,000 than continue litigating, and Defendant would rather pay $175,000 than continue litigating. Given these preferences, both parties make themselves better off by settling at $175,000, or anywhere else between $150,000 and $200,000.

While settlement of a case with a settlement zone benefits both parties compared to non-settlement, such cases do not always settle. Negotiators may not even realize a settlement zone exists because negotiators ordinarily conceal their bottom lines from each other and often try to make their bottom lines appear tougher than they really are (§§ 1.11, 1.14, 1.15). With each negotiator guessing about the other's bottom line, negotiators rarely are sure that a settlement zone exists and are even less likely to know the precise boundaries of the zone.

Mediation can overcome this problem. The mediator can hold a *private caucus* (§ 2.10(c)) with each party at which the party can privately reveal its bottom line to the mediator who promises to keep

---

[53] Of course, the results of litigation could have turned out better for one party than the settlement. But at the pertinent time, the time at which the offer can be accepted, accepting it is better than the party's *expected value* of litigating further. See § 1.7.

this information secret from the other party.[54] The mediator can then meet with both parties in a joint session and tell them only whether there is a settlement zone.[55] If there is, the parties now know they are each better off settling than they are pursuing adjudication to the end. So, they become more committed to reaching a deal in mediation. If each party trusts the mediator with sensitive confidential information, (the bottom line,) the mediator can combine the information to great effect.

Even if the mediator cannot get each party's honest and direct answer to "What is your bottom line?", mediators can often get a more general feel of each party's bottom line, an approximation, rather than precise terms.[56] So, mediators often use gentler variants of asking each party in private caucus its bottom line and then telling the assembled parties nothing other than whether settlement is possible. These variants usually involve being more indirect and imprecise than bluntly asking a party what its bottom line is. And mediators do not often tell the parties whether they have a settlement zone in blunt yes-or-no terms. Mediators are, again, usually more indirect and imprecise in saying things like "I think we can work out a deal here."

In mediation, as in negotiation, discovering that a settlement zone exists does not ensure a deal (§ 1.39(e)). For example, a settlement of the case depicted in Diagram 2-1 will create $50,000 in value.[57] But who gets how much of that value depends on where the settlement price falls in the zone between $150,000 and $200,000. If the parties settle at $150,001 then Defendant captures virtually all

---

[54] See, e.g., Peter Contuzzi, Should Parties Tell Mediators Their Bottom Line?, Disp. Resol. Mag., Spring 2000, at 30–32. On the party's incentives to be truthful about, or to misrepresent, its bottom line to the mediator, see Jennifer Gerarda Brown & Ian Ayres, Economic Rationales for Mediation, 80 Va. L. Rev. 323, 335 (1994).

[55] An online service can perform this function by allowing each side to communicate its bottom line offer to the online mediator (which can be a computer, rather than a human,) and then the computer-mediator produces a settlement between the two offers if there is a settlement zone, but keeps the offers secret if there is no settlement zone. See Cybersettle, Cybersettle Overview, http://www.cybersettle.com (last visited April 6, 2026) ("double-blind negotiation for the digital age"). See also Robert H. Gertner & Geoffrey P. Miller, Settlement Escrows, 24 J. Legal. Stud. 87 (1995).

[56] See, e.g., Kimberlee K. Kovach, Mediation: Principles and Practice 198 (3d ed. 2004) ("In mediation, particularly in litigation cases, parties are not forthcoming with the 'bottom line.' Often, however, the mediator will learn information which creates an overlap, and part of his role is to find a place within this zone where both or all parties will be satisfied.")

[57] Settlement creates $50,000 in value because settlement transfers from Plaintiff to Defendant an asset (the claim) Plaintiff values at $150,000 and Defendant values at $200,000. Claims, like other assets, have no intrinsic value. Value is subjective so total value increases when assets are sold by those who value them less to those who value them more.

of the value created by settling. Plaintiff is barely made better off by the settlement.

The negotiators may spend much time and money negotiating within the settlement zone. Indeed, each negotiator may be so determined to capture the potential value from a settlement that they never reach a deal.[58] Defendant's lawyer may say to Plaintiff's lawyer "We will not pay more than $150,001. You should agree to it because it is better for your client than continuing litigation." Plaintiff's lawyer may say to Defendant's lawyer "We will not take less than $199,999. You should agree to it because it is better for your client than continuing litigation." These lawyers are playing the game of "chicken" discussed in Section 1.11(c).

Mediators often stop the game of chicken from preventing agreement. With a sense of each party's bottom line, the mediator can guide the parties toward the middle of the settlement range. Again, few mediators will explicitly tell the parties: "You should settle at $175,000 because that's the middle of your settlement zone." But in a more indirect and imprecise way, the mediator can encourage a party who is making an offer toward the middle of the zone and caution a party who refuses to make such an offer that her inflexibility is preventing a deal that will be good for her. In other words, the mediator will preserve the confidentiality of each side's bottom line, while providing an imprecise or "noisy" translation of it for the other party.[59]

In contrast, if no settlement zone exists, the mediator can help the parties create one. One way to do so is for the mediator to *evaluate* the legal merits of the case. As Section 2.13 explains, the evaluation may cause one or both of the parties to move its bottom line toward the other party's position; enough movement creates a settlement zone. Another way the mediator can help the parties try to create a settlement zone is to help them identify *positive-sum* opportunities. As Section 2.12 explains, positive-sum negotiation can create settlement zones that would not otherwise exist. And a third way ("*moral growth*," § 2.8) the mediator can help to create a settlement zone is to persuade one or more of the parties to reconsider its

---

[58] Herein lie the transaction costs of the *bilateral monopoly* that is settlement negotiation. See § 1.3. See also Richard A. Posner, Economic Analysis of Law 779 (9th ed. 2014) ("Settlement negotiations are a classic example of bilateral monopoly. The plaintiff can settle only with the defendant and the defendant only with the plaintiff, and each party is eager to engross as much as possible of the surplus that settlement will generate over litigation. Indeed, the larger the settlement range, the more the parties will stand to gain from hard bargaining and the likelier (it may seem) the parties are to end up litigating because they cannot agree on how to divide the available surplus.")

[59] Jennifer Gerarda Brown & Ian Ayres, Economic Rationales for Mediation, 80 Va. L. Rev. 323, 356–71 (1994).

*interests and priorities* (§ 1.23) in a way that moves that party toward the other party's interests and therefore its positions.

## § 2.12 Positive-Sum

### *(a) Distinguishing Positive-Sum from Zero-Sum Negotiation*

A classic metaphor for distinguishing *zero-sum* (§ 1.9) from *positive-sum* negotiation is the contrast between dividing a pie and expanding it. In zero-sum negotiations, negotiators discuss only how to divide a pie, while in positive-sum negotiations, negotiators find ways to expand the size of the pie. This terminology is fine unless it leads people to forget that any agreement—even if purely zero-sum—creates value in the sense that it gives each side something it values more than whatever alternatives it had (§§ 1.4–1.5). So, we might think of zero-sum negotiation as dividing a pie that neither side gets any of if they fail to agree on how to divide it.

Negotiation theorists distinguish creating value from dividing it.[60] Many negotiation analysts call zero-sum negotiation *distributive* bargaining because it distributes (divides) among the parties value that existed prior to the negotiation. These theorists call positive-sum negotiation *integrative* bargaining because it integrates or combines different topics to add new value created by negotiating. Again, this terminology is fine unless it leads people to forget that any agreement—even if purely distributive—creates value in the sense that it gives each side something it values more than whatever alternatives it had, such as further litigation (§§ 1.4–1.5).

Many negotiations have both a positive-sum part and a zero-sum part. While some negotiations are purely zero-sum, few if any negotiations are purely positive sum because "No matter how much creative problem solving enlarges the pie, it must still be divided; value that has been created must be claimed."[61]

To define positive-sum negotiation more precisely, positive-sum negotiation finds possible agreements that appeal to *both parties* more than other possible agreements between them. In other words, positive-sum negotiation finds agreements that are, in each party's assessment at the time, better *for each party* than other possible agreements between them. While zero-sum deals appeal to each party more than no deal, positive-sum deals appeal to each party more than both no deal and other possible deals.

---

[60] David A. Lax & James K. Sebenius, The Manager as Negotiator: Bargaining for Cooperation and Competitive Gain 33 (1986).

[61] Id. Accord Gerald B. Wetlaufer, The Limits of Integrative Bargaining, 85 Geo. L.J. 369, 373 (1996).

Positive-sum opportunities are exploited by negotiators who use the *problem-solving* approach to negotiation (§§ 1.22–1.25). Problem-solving mediators encourage negotiators to use this approach (§ 2.7).

The key to positive-sum negotiation is considering multiple issues. Positive-sum negotiation almost never occurs if only one issue is considered, especially if that issue is the amount of money Defendant will pay Plaintiff. The interests of the parties are almost certain to be diametrically opposed on the issue of money; Plaintiff wants to receive as much as possible, while Defendant wants to pay as little as possible. In contrast, if issues other than the amount of money are considered, it may be possible to find one on which the parties' interests coincide or to engage in *logrolling*. Coinciding interests and logrolling are discussed in the following two sections.

### *(b) Coinciding Interests*

For an example of an issue on which the parties' interests coincide, consider settlement of a negligence claim for compensatory damages arising from a physical injury Defendant caused while engaged in its ordinary business activities. Both Plaintiff and Defendant may prefer that a settlement payment be made in late December, rather than early in the next month, January. Ordinarily, the *time-value of money* (§ 1.10(b)) causes plaintiffs to want settlement payments they receive to occur sooner and defendants to want the settlement payments they make to occur later. Tax law, however, probably permits Defendant to deduct this payment from its income because tax law generally permits deductions of settlement payments arising out of Defendant's business activities.[62] The time value of money leads taxpayers (here Defendant) to take deductions in the current tax year, rather than waiting until next year.[63] In other words, Defendant's tax benefit of paying in late

---

[62] Generally, payments pursuant to a settlement or judgment (along with attendant legal fees) are deductible if the payments arose out of defendant's business activities, as opposed to personal or family activities. See Deductibility of legal expenses, generally, 5 Mertens Law of Fed. Income Tax'n § 24A:18 (2022) ("If the origin of the claim arises out of the taxpayer's business, the taxpayer may deduct legal expenses paid or incurred in connection with such claim under Section 162. Similarly, if the origin of the claim arises out of an income-producing or investment activity, the taxpayer may deduct legal expenses paid or incurred in connection with such claim under Section 212. If the origin of the claim is for a personal matter unconnected with a business or the production of income, litigation expenses are not deductible.") However, no deduction is generally allowed for fines paid to government, 26 U.S.C. § 162(f), or for settlement payments and legal fees paid in connection with cases of sexual harassment or sexual abuse if such payment is subject to a nondisclosure agreement. 26 U.S.C. § 162(q).

[63] See, e.g., Mark J. Cowan & Joshua Cutler, Cross-Fertilizing the Tax Classroom, 19 Pitt. Tax Rev. 329, 358 (2022) ("Tax planning is often presented as a time value of money exercise: all else being equal, defer income and accelerate deductions where possible"); Karie Davis-Nozemack & Sarah Webber, Paying the IRS Whistleblower: A Critical Analysis of Collected Proceeds, 32 Va. Tax Rev. 77, 122–23

December of this year may exceed the interest it could earn on the money by waiting until early January of next year to pay. If so, Defendant would likely prefer making its payment in late December, rather than early January. Plaintiff also prefers the payment to occur in late December rather than early January because no tax law, or other factor, offsets Plaintiff's desire to start earning interest on the money sooner rather than later.[64] In short, both parties prefer that the payment occur in late December, rather than early January. A settlement providing for payment in early January would make both parties worse off than a settlement providing for payment in late December. Agreeing on payment in late December is a clear example of positive-sum negotiating because the parties' interests coincide on this question of when the payment occurs.

Issues on which parties' interests coincide are rare. They tend not to become issues precisely because the parties' interests coincide, and the negotiators realize that, so they agree to the terms that both parties prefer. On the other hand, tax issues are examples of issues that litigators and their clients may forget or misunderstand,[65] so a mediator can add value by raising them.

### *(c) Logrolling Multiple Issues*

Even in the absence of issues on which the parties' interests coincide (§ 2.12(b)), considering multiple issues can reveal opportunities for both parties to gain. This is because the degree of importance the parties attach to an issue may differ. Suppose Plaintiff cares a lot about Issue A, but not much about Issue B, while Defendant cares a lot about Issue B, but not much about Issue A. The negotiators can create value by having Defendant concede on Issue A in exchange for Plaintiff's concession on Issue B. Each party gives on something she cares about a little to get what she cares about a lot. This sort of trade, often called *logrolling*,[66] is the basis of most

(2012) ("Taxpayers have an incentive to defer income recognition into subsequent years to delay paying tax, and taxpayers have an incentive to accelerate deductions to minimize current taxable income").

[64] Carina Bryant, Proceeds of Lawsuits, 1 Mertens Law of Fed. Income Tax'n § 5:17 (2022) ("Amounts received in settlement of a claim for damages on account of a personal physical injury or physical sickness are excluded from income"). By contrast, recoveries for many other sorts of losses generally are taxable income. Id.

[65] See, e.g., French v. Domnarski, No. CV94 0048532S, 1995 WL 573787, *1 (Conn. Super) (describing a client who settled a claim, relying on an attorney's mistaken advice that alimony and certain mortgage payments would be tax deductible); Jalali v. Root, 1 Cal. Rptr. 3d 689 (Ct. App. 2003) (plaintiff "Jalali claimed that, before she accepted the $2.75 million settlement, [her lawyer] Root told her that her taxes on the settlement would be 'forty percent of your share,' that is, Jalali's share after deducting Root's contingency fee. However, Jalali ended up paying taxes on the whole $2.75 million received, not just her portion after deducting her attorney's fee.")

[66] The name logrolling apparently comes "from a former American custom of neighbors assisting one another in rolling logs into a pile for burning," so "logrolling"

positive-sum negotiation. It works even where the parties disagree on every issue if they prioritize issues differently. For an example of logrolling, see Section 1.10(c).

Logrolling happens only when multiple issues are considered together, rather than each issue considered in isolation. Negotiators often make the mistake of considering one issue, resolving it, and moving on to the next issue without ever returning to reconsider the first issue. This approach, while neat and organized, precludes logrolling, so problem-solving mediators discourage negotiators from using it. Problem-solving mediators encourage negotiators to consider multiple issues simultaneously and to trade concessions on low-priority issues for gains on high-priority issues.

Even where negotiators do consider multiple issues simultaneously and trade concessions, they may make the wrong trades. As just noted, if Plaintiff cares a lot about Issue A and Defendant cares a lot about Issue B, then value is created when Plaintiff concedes on Issue B in exchange for Defendant's concession on Issue A. In contrast, value is not necessarily created, and may even be destroyed, if Plaintiff concedes on Issue B in exchange for Defendant's concession on Issue C, D, or E. And value is certainly destroyed if Plaintiff concedes on Issue A (his high-priority issue) in exchange for Defendant's concession on Issue B (her high-priority issue). Negotiators risk making these "wrong trades"—trades that miss opportunities to create value and may even destroy value—if they have not revealed to each other their side's underlying interests and priorities (§ 1.24). This lack of openness is common because negotiators often have strong incentives not to reveal their interests and priorities. To honestly disclose one's interests and priorities, and reveal information, especially information about bottom lines, makes one vulnerable to an *adversarial/competitive* negotiator (§§ 1.14, 1.26). Mediation, as explained next, is well-suited to solving this problem.

### *(d) Trusted Intermediary Combining Information*

A negotiator who is open about his side's interests and priorities is using the *problem-solving* approach to negotiation (§§ 1.22–1.25), while a negotiator who conceals or misrepresents them is using the *adversarial/competitive* approach (§§ 1.13–1.17). A problem-solving negotiator is often vulnerable to an adversarial/competitive counterpart who will exploit the problem-solver's openness by insisting on a settlement at the problem-solver's *bottom line* (§ 1.26). While the problem-solving negotiator has tactics to avoid this

---

became more widely used to mean "the exchanging of assistance or favors." https://www.merriam-webster.com/dictionary/logrolling.

vulnerability, these tactics are unlikely to work with a counterpart determined to remain adversarial/competitive. So, the problem-solving negotiator must basically give up on problem-solving, especially the disclosure of important information, unless and until the other side reveals its own important information (§ 1.26).

One can summarize this *Negotiator's Dilemma* as follows. Both sides would be better off if they each revealed their interests and priorities, that is, used the problem-solving approach. But in many cases each side's individual incentive is to conceal and misrepresent its interests and priorities, that is, to use the adversarial/competitive approach. As a result of each side following its individual incentives, neither side reveals its interests and priorities. Both sides take the adversarial/competitive approach, thus greatly reducing the likelihood of positive-sum negotiation (§ 1.26). This *Negotiator's Dilemma* is an example of the *Prisoner's Dilemma* (§ 1.20(a)) because each party trying to do what is good for itself ends up harming them both compared to the problem-solving alternative.

Mediation can solve the dilemma by using private caucuses in which the mediator, but neither party, receives full information. If Plaintiff is sure the mediator will keep confidences (§ 2.28), Plaintiff can be open about his interests and priorities to the mediator. Plaintiff can reveal even the most sensitive information, without worrying that Defendant will learn and exploit it. Conversely, if Defendant is sure the mediator will keep confidences, Defendant can be similarly open with the mediator, thus giving mediator the combined information of both parties.

Once the mediator has gathered all this important information, she can identify issues on which the parties' *interests coincide* (§ 2.12(b)), and opportunities for positive-sum *logrolling* (§ 2.12(c)). She can see that Plaintiff's concession on Issue B in exchange for Defendant's concession on Issue A really will make both parties better off because Plaintiff really does care more about Issue A and Defendant really does care more about Issue B. The mediator can also help the parties avoid "wrong trades" (§ 2.12(c)). She can see that Plaintiff's concession on Issue B in exchange for Defendant's concession on Issue C would destroy value because Plaintiff never really cared much about Issue C.

The mediator can identify the possible settlement terms that are better for both parties than other possible settlement terms because she has received extensive disclosures from both sides.[67] This includes disclosures that the parties refuse to make to each other

[67] See, e.g., Scott R. Peppet, Contract Formation in Imperfect Markets: Should We Use Mediators in Deals?, 19 Ohio St. J. on Disp. Resol. 283, 297 (2004).

simply because they do not trust each other the way they trust the mediator.

This function of combining information to create a much more complete picture of the parties' interests and priorities is an important way that mediators add value. When combined with mediators combining information from each party about its bottom line (§ 2.11), many mediations achieve results better for both parties than negotiation would have achieved because the mediator combines each side's otherwise confidential information.

Of course, the mediator is most likely to accomplish this if the parties trust that what they tell the mediator will remain confidential.[68] This is not just a question of whether the mediator will consciously break her promise not to tell one side's secrets to the other side. It is also a question of whether the mediator will inadvertently reveal something. And it is also a question of whether the mediator may reveal confidential information after the mediation is over. Suppose, for example, that the mediator is subpoenaed in another case and asked under oath to reveal what she was told by one party during a private caucus. Confidentiality in mediation is discussed in Section 2.28.

## § 2.13 Evaluation by the Mediator

### *(a) The Appeal of Evaluation*

Mediators can use a wide variety of "evaluative" tactics. An extreme example of mediator evaluation, bordering on (non-binding) *adjudication* (§ 2.3) would be the mediator telling the parties and their lawyers something like: "I have considered the strengths and weaknesses of each party's arguments on the law and on the facts and, predicting how further litigation is likely to go, conclude that the current settlement value of this case is $200,000."[69] Most mediators are rarely, if ever, that evaluative unless the parties jointly ask for it. In contrast, a milder and more typical form of evaluation might be "Plaintiff has a very strong argument that Defendant breached the contract, and damages appear to be in the low six figures," or "I've seen verdicts in similar cases range around two or three hundred thousand dollars." Other examples of mediator evaluation are when the mediator tells the parties and their lawyers

---

68 Kimberlee K. Kovach, Mediation: Principles and Practice at 173–75 (3d ed. 2004) ("It is essential that the mediator be able to establish trust with the parties for a number of reasons. If the parties are to share information, particularly private or personal information, they must trust the mediator.")

69 For an example of similar evaluation by the mediator, see Lavinia Hall, Eric Green: Finding Alternatives to Litigation in Business Disputes, in Deborah M. Kolb & Kenneth Kressel, The Realities of Making Talk Work in When Talk Works: Profiles of Mediators 295–99 (Deborah M. Kolb et al. eds. 1994).

something like: "Defendant's contributory negligence argument is unlikely to persuade a jury" or "Plaintiff seems to have shown strong evidence of price-fixing."

Many parties and lawyers value a mediator who is willing to evaluate a case and is accurate in her evaluations.[70] To improve this accuracy, evaluative mediators need the sort of evidence and argument a court would receive. So, "[e]valuative mediations often are preceded by written submissions by attorneys for both sides, summarizing the facts as they know them and making best case arguments for their client."[71]

The appeal of neutral-evaluation can be understood in light of the fact that a case cannot settle unless there is a *settlement zone* (§ 1.39(a)). Other than the exceptional cases in which a party seeks something from litigation that cannot be provided by settlement, the only cases lacking a settlement zone are those in which Plaintiff expects a more pro-Plaintiff result from litigation than Defendant expects (§ 1.39(c)). If, for example, Plaintiff expects a $250,000 verdict, while Defendant expects a $200,000 verdict, there may be no settlement zone. These cases in which Plaintiff expects a more pro-Plaintiff result than Defendant expects can be called cases of over-optimism. If Plaintiff expects a verdict of $250,000 and Defendant expects a verdict of $200,000, then at least one of the parties is overly optimistic about its likely success at litigation. These cases lacking a settlement zone are cases in which at least one of the parties is in for a disappointment at the end of litigation.

Because parties' over-optimism about their success at litigation can prevent settlement zones, advocates of settlement seek to reduce party over-optimism and thus make the parties' expectations about litigation results converge. Neutral evaluation tends to do that. It reduces the gap between the parties' expectations by giving them information (the neutral's evaluation of the case) that causes the parties' expectations about the results of litigation to converge around the neutral's evaluation. The neutral, because her judgment

---

[70] See, e.g., Sarah R. Cole, Craig A. McEwen, Nancy H. Rogers, James R. Coben & Peter N. Thompson, Mediation: Law, Policy, & Practice (2024).

> The [2008] Report of the Task Force on Mediation Quality of the ABA Section on Dispute Resolution, which relied heavily on the responses of attorneys with private civil practices who have experience in mediation, found strong support for evaluative mediation techniques. Ninety-five percent of attorney respondents favored mediator analysis of strengths and weaknesses of cases, 60% favored predictions about likely court outcomes, 84% approved of recommendations of a specific settlement, and 74% supported application of "some pressure to accept a particular solution." Thus, the market demands of attorneys who use mediation may shape the choice of mediation style.

Id. § 3:3.

[71] Id.

is respected by the parties, persuades the parties to change their expectations.

Suppose, for example, Plaintiff expected a verdict of $800,000, and Defendant expected a verdict of $100,000, before the mediator provided an evaluation suggesting the verdict would most likely be between $300,000 and $400,000. The mediator's evaluation succeeded if it caused Plaintiff now to expect a verdict below $800,000 and Defendant to expect a verdict above $100,000. The evaluation succeeded marvelously if it caused each party now to expect a verdict close to $350,000. The more the evaluation reduces the $700,000 gap between the parties' expectations, the more the evaluation succeeded.

Consequently, successful evaluations come from a neutral whose judgment is respected by the parties as a good predictor of litigation. For example, if the case involves a personal injury arising out of an auto accident and the mediator is a local judge who has presided over the trials of hundreds of similar cases, the parties and lawyers may have great confidence that this neutral can predict quite well the results of litigating this case. The better a predictor of litigation the parties believe the evaluation to be, the better the evaluation is likely to be at reducing the gap in the parties' expectations.

Unsurprisingly, some evidence suggests that mediators who evaluate have higher settlement rates than those who do not.[72]

### *(b) Concerns About Evaluation*

#### *(1) Interests vs. Rights*

Mediators should not evaluate if they believe that mediation should focus on the parties' *interests*, as opposed to the parties' *positions* or *rights*.[73] A party may have no interest in something to which he has a right, for example reinstatement at the job from which he was fired. Conversely, he may have an interest in something to which he has no right, such as the defendant's public apology and admission of wrongdoing.[74] By evaluating, a mediator focuses the mediation on the parties' rights. Litigation *adjudicates* parties' legal rights (§ 1.2), and when a mediator predicts the results of litigation,

---

[72] Roselle L. Wissler, The Effectiveness of Court-Connected Dispute Resolution in Civil Cases, 22 Conflict Resol. Q. 55, 69 (2004) ("All three studies that examined [the] issue found that settlement was more likely if the mediators were more active and disclosed their views about the strengths and weaknesses of the case, case settlement value, or likely court outcome than if they did not.")

[73] See § 1.23(a) (defining and contrasting *interests* and *positions*).

[74] Courts cannot order an apology. See Brent T. White, Say You're Sorry: Court-Ordered Apologies as a Civil Rights Remedy, 91 Cornell L. Rev. 1261, 1262 & n.2 (2006).

she is saying what she thinks the parties' rights are. Even if she does not go so far as to predict specific results of litigation but merely assesses the strength of a particular legal argument, she is giving her views on what she thinks the parties' rights are.

In contrast, a focus on interests, rather than rights, is essential for *positive-sum* negotiation. Positive-sum negotiation requires the identification of issues on which the parties' interests coincide or on which they place a different level of priority (§ 2.12). Identifying such issues cannot be done by discussing the parties' rights, only by discussing their interests. So, by focusing on rights rather than interests, evaluative mediation encourages the parties to treat the situation as *zero-sum*, whether or not it is.

One might hope that a mediator can both (1) explore the parties' interests with an eye toward positive-sum opportunities and (2) evaluate the parties' rights. But this is usually not possible because evaluation generally prevents an exploration of *interests* (§ 1.23). To see why, imagine yourself as the lawyer representing a party in mediation of a case in which the mediator will evaluate the merits of the case. You have a strong incentive to persuade the mediator that the legal merits are strongly on your side, that is, that your client is very much in the right. If you persuade the mediator of this, you can make the mediator your ally against the other side. You can tell the mediator: "Of course we won't settle for anything less than X because we have a right to X and our case is so strong that, if we litigate to conclusion, a court will give us X." If you can persuade the mediator of all this, and if the mediator wants the case to settle, as most do (§ 2.6), then the mediator will try to persuade the other side to agree to a settlement that gives you X. The mediator knows that a settlement will not occur unless you get X because you cannot be talked into a settlement that is worse for you than the expected result of litigation (§ 1.39).

Conversely, the other side has an incentive to persuade the mediator that it is very much in the right and that you are not entitled to X. So, both sides will be arguing their cases to the mediator. Both lawyers will be advocates trying to win over the mediator. In this manner, lawyerly advocacy of legal rights prevents an exploration of the parties' *interests* (§ 1.23). Rather than being open to the mediator about his client's interests and priorities, the lawyer-advocate refuses to make such disclosures. Indeed, he conceals and misleads (§§ 1.13–1.18.). Or, as he would put it, he presents the case in the light most favorable to his client.

Accordingly, the mediator who seeks to explore interests and exploit positive-sum opportunities tries to persuade the lawyers (and the parties) that advocacy is useless in mediation. There is no point in persuading the mediator that your side is in the right because the mediator does not care about that. The mediator will not be influenced by arguments about who breached what legal duties to whom or what remedies a court would likely order because she is not thinking in those rights-oriented terms. She tells the lawyers and parties that if they want their dispute resolved according to arguments about rights, then they should litigate, not mediate. Instead, the mediator will do what a court does not: the mediator will focus on the parties' interests to help them negotiate an agreement that, to the extent possible, satisfies all parties' interests, without regard to who has a right to what.

This sort of mediator, who seeks to focus mediation on interests rather than rights, is a non-evaluative or *facilitative* mediator.[75] Such mediators generally seek to increase the participation of the parties and reduce the participation of lawyers. When it comes to the client's interests and priorities, the client typically knows better than the lawyer (§ 1.30). In part, this is simply because every person knows his own values, preferences, and tastes in a way that others can never know. Moreover, lawyers are accustomed to thinking about rights, rather than interests and priorities. "Lawyers are trained to put people and events into categories that are legally meaningful, to think in terms of rights and duties established by rules, to focus on acts more than persons."[76] So, when the client's participation is overshadowed by the lawyer's participation, mediation typically becomes "a rights-based process."[77]

A lawyer may be so focused on rights that she never thinks of asking her client about his interests and priorities.[78] And even if the

---

75 Mediator approaches are often placed along a continuum with "facilitative" at one end and "evaluative" at the other, so that the more facilitative a mediator is, the less evaluative she is, and vice versa. See Leonard Riskin, Understanding Mediators' Orientations, Strategies, and Techniques: A Grid for the Perplexed, 1 Harv. Neg. L. Rev. 7, 23–25 (1996) (discussing the "facilitative-evaluative continuum"). But evaluation may be exactly what is needed to facilitate agreement. See § 2.13(a). And "[e]valuating and facilitating are not really opposites, any more than playing football and kicking a football are opposites. Besides, most mediators use techniques that fall into both these categories. For those reasons, I proffer a "New Old Grid," which is just like the 'Old Grid' except that it replaces 'evaluative' with 'directive' and 'facilitative' with 'elicitive.' " Leonard L. Riskin, Replacing the Mediator Orientation Grids, Again: Proposing A "New New Grid System", 23 Alternatives to High Cost Litig. 127 (2005).

76 Leonard L. Riskin, Mediation and Lawyers, 43 Ohio St. L.J. 29, 45 (1982). "This view requires a strong development of cognitive capabilities, which is often attended by the under-cultivation of emotional faculties. This combination of capacities joins with the practice of either reducing most nonmaterial values to amounts of money or sweeping them under the carpet." Id.

77 Jacqueline M. Nolan-Haley, Alternative Dispute Resolution in a Nutshell 98–103 (2d ed. 2000) (describing this as a "considerable downside[ ]" to heavy lawyer participation).

78 See § 1.30 (encouraging lawyers to take the time to identify their clients' interests).

lawyer does know her client's interests and priorities, she may be reluctant to disclose them to the mediator (§ 1.26). Lawyers are still mostly trained to be adversarial and, even if the mediator stresses that she will not evaluate, some lawyers cannot break free of the adversarial mindset. They believe that they best represent their client by giving the mediator zealous advocacy of the client's rights, rather than a forthright analysis of the client's interests and priorities. Finally, there is the possibility that the lawyer's interests differ somewhat from the client's interests, and the lawyer is not wholeheartedly pursuing the client's interests (§§ 1.23(b), 1.36). Mediators often try to speak directly with clients to overcome such lawyers. In short, lawyers are often obstacles to the mediator's desire to shift the focus of dispute resolution from rights to interests.

*(2) Is "Evaluative Mediation" an Oxymoron?*

Many scholars of mediation emphasize the distinction between interests-based processes of dispute resolution and rights-based processes, and some of these scholars consider "evaluative mediation" an oxymoron.[79] According to these scholars, a neutral's evaluation of a case may sometimes be desirable, but it should not be called "mediation" because doing so blurs the distinction between an interests-based process (mediation) and a rights-based process (neutral evaluation) which is discussed in a Section 2.35.

While this argument is strong because the distinction between rights and interests is important, this book nevertheless uses the term "evaluative mediation." Evaluation is a matter of degree and once one concedes that some mild evaluation is consistent with being a "mediator," it is difficult, perhaps impossible, to draw the line at the maximum level of evaluation consistent with being engaged in "mediation," rather than "neutral evaluation."

Whether a mediator is evaluative is a matter of degree. A mediator who puts a dollar amount on the settlement value of a case is as evaluative as possible. Such precise and all-encompassing evaluation borders on (non-binding) adjudication (§§ 2.2, 2.33). To a lesser degree, though, even mediators who consider themselves non-evaluative often do some evaluating. For instance, a party who boldly proclaims that he is certain to win a smashing victory in court may elicit a question from the mediator like: "Are you sure judges and juries never make mistakes?" This mediator is gently cautioning the party that there is always some uncertainty when going to trial. This reminder about uncertainty may help moderate the party's

[79] Kimberlee Kovach & Lela P. Love, Evaluative Mediation is an Oxymoron, 14 Alternatives to the High Cost of Litigation 31 (1996); Lela P. Love, The Top Ten Reasons that Mediators Should Not Evaluate: Reflections on the Evaluative-Facilitative Debate, 24 Fla. St. U.L. Rev. 937 (1997).

unrealistic expectations and thus is evaluation by the mediator. The mediator is talking about legal rights, rather than interests, and is doing so in a way calculated to reduce party optimism, that is, to make the parties' expectations about the results of litigation converge, however slightly.

This sort of gentle, elliptical evaluation may be virtually inevitable in mediation. It is the rare mediator who never betrays even a hint of her views about the strengths of the parties' positions. Even mediators who do not think of themselves as evaluative often "aggressively prod one or more parties to reconsider its proposed position" or "challenge party proposals (perhaps in caucus) as unworkable or misleading."[80] The typical mediator cannot help but interject her views about the merits of the case by the questions she chooses to ask or not to ask, the statements she pursues or ignores, her tone of voice, her facial expressions, and so on. Despite the mediator's efforts to be non-evaluative, to focus on interests, she will usually betray at least some hint of her views on the merits. Few people are capable of being purely non-judgmental.

*(3) Mediator's Credibility*

When a mediator evaluates, the mediator risks losing her credibility with at least one of the parties. At least one party is likely to feel that he has "lost" the evaluation. This "loser" and his lawyer may conclude that the mediator "decided against" them because she is biased toward the other side.[81] Or perhaps she is incompetent; she did not listen to or understand them. Either way, it is unlikely the "loser" and his lawyer will participate constructively with the mediator after "losing" the evaluation. If further mediation is to make any progress, it may have to be with a new mediator.

For this reason and others, extensive evaluation by the mediator, if done at all, may be better done toward the end of mediation.[82] If the mediator and parties have made a good faith attempt to resolve the dispute without evaluation and have truly

---

[80] Joseph B. Stulberg, Facilitative Versus Evaluative Mediator Orientations: Piercing the "Grid" Lock, 24 Fla. St. U.L. Rev. 985, 1002–03 (1997).

[81] "It is difficult enough for mediators to maintain the appearance of impartiality when engaging in common mediator practices such as asking probing questions, playing the role of devil's advocate, encouraging objectivity, defusing unrealistic expectations, or stimulating creative or empathetic thinking. When a mediator actually expresses an opinion regarding the merits of an issue or the entire case, the appearance of impartiality is severely challenged." Murray S. Levin, The Propriety of Evaluative Mediation: Concerns About the Nature and Quality of an Evaluative Option, 16 Ohio St. J. on Disp. Resol. 267, 294 (2001).

[82] Marjorie Corman Aaron, Evaluation in Mediation, in Dwight Golann, Mediating Legal Disputes: Effective Strategies for Lawyers and Mediators 267, 283 (1996).

reached impasse, then the choice is between litigation and an evaluation that might stimulate some additional offers of settlement (§ 2.13(a)). So, last-ditch evaluation has much appeal. But if parties have expected this eleventh-hour evaluation since the mediation began, they may throughout the mediation have tried to "win over" the mediator by arguing their rights and being less than candid about their interests (§ 2.13(b)(1)). So once word gets around that an ostensibly non-evaluative mediator will evaluate as a last-ditch attempt toward settlement after everything else has failed, she may have increased the likelihood that everything else will fail, so her facilitative interests-based side is no longer effective.

### (c) *Mediator's Evaluation Given to the Court*

A mediator's evaluation is sometimes given to the court as well as to the parties (§ 2.30(e)). Giving a mediator's evaluation to the court likely increases the evaluation's effectiveness in promoting settlement because the mediator's report is likely to influence the court.[83] The parties' predictions about the results of litigation are especially likely to converge if the mediator's evaluation goes to the court because then the mediator's evaluation is not merely a prediction of how the case will be decided but also likely an influence on how the case is decided.

Conversely, the risks of evaluation are heightened by mediator reports to the court because parties' anticipation of that report encourages them throughout mediation to argue their cases as they would in court, thus making it very likely the mediation will focus on rights, rather than interests. "The concern in such a case is that parties will not be candid in the mediation because they are concerned that the information they provide to the mediator will harm them in a later court proceeding."[84] For these reasons, the Uniform Mediation Act[85] protects mediators from having to "communicate with a court about a mediation except to convey limited information on the status of the process or disclosures excepted from the privilege, and courts may not consider a communication made in violation of the rule."[86]

---

[83] Sarah R. Cole, Craig A. McEwen, Nancy H. Rogers, James R. Coben & Peter N. Thompson, Mediation: Law, Policy, & Practice § 8:40 (2024) ("To increase settlement rates, some statutory schemes permit the mediator to issue a more substantive report or recommendation if no settlement is reached.").

[84] Id.

[85] The Uniform Mediation Act has been adopted by thirteen states and the District of Columbia. https://www.uniformlaws.org/committees/community-home?communitykey=45565a5f-0c57-4bba-bbab-fc7de9a59110.

[86] Ellen E. Deason, Procedural Rules for Complementary Systems of Litigation and Mediation—Worldwide, 80 Notre Dame L. Rev. 553, 571 (2005) (citing Unif. Mediation Act § 7(b), (c)).

## § 2.14 Few or Many Issues

Depending on their goals (§§ 2.5–2.8.), participants in mediation may seek to broaden or narrow the number of issues discussed in mediation. Participants who see mediation primarily as a way of settling cases (§ 2.6) generally want to resolve and thus eliminate issues—like checking tasks off a to-do list.[87] The fewer the remaining issues, the less that needs to be resolved to reach a settlement agreement. For this reason, most settlement-oriented participants try to keep the discussion focused on the essentials and avoid being distracted by extraneous issues which threaten to become new tasks lengthening the to-do list.

On the other hand, sometimes settlement cannot be reached without positive-sum negotiation, which typically consists of *logrolling* (§§ 1.10(c), 2.12(c)). Logrolling is the process in which the parties consider multiple issues simultaneously and make concessions on low-priority issues in exchange for gains on high-priority issues. If settlement cannot be achieved without logrolling, the settlement-oriented participant may be more likely to achieve her goal by broadening the discussion to include additional issues, perhaps even brainstorming "How else might these parties offer something to each other?"

Participants who see mediation as more than just a way to settle cases often see it as a way to achieve positive-sum solutions (§§ 2.7, 2.12(c)), or, especially in family and other ongoing relationship cases, as a way to help the parties improve their abilities to prevent and resolve future disputes ("moral growth," § 2.8). These participants tend more than the settlement-oriented participant to broaden the number of issues discussed in mediation. The more issues considered, the more likely the negotiators and mediator are to identify logrolling opportunities for positive-sum negotiation. And the more issues considered, the more practice parties have developing their dispute resolution skills.

Sometimes the mediator seeks to broaden the number of issues discussed but the parties and lawyers, accustomed to thinking in zero-sum terms, believe only one issue is central—such as "How much money will Defendant pay Plaintiff? or "How much pollution will flow into the lake?" The mediator must then decide how hard to push the parties and lawyers toward considering additional issues without threatening the principles of party self-determination and mediator impartiality, which are discussed next.

---

87 See Leonard L. Riskin, Understanding Mediator Orientations, Strategies, and Techniques: a Grid for the Perplexed, 1 Harv. Neg. L. Rev. 7, 42–43 (1996).

## § 2.15 Party Self-Determination and Mediator Impartiality

Three organizations prominent in ADR—the American Arbitration Association, the American Bar Association's Section on Dispute Resolution, and the Association for Conflict Resolution—approved Model Standards of Conduct for Mediators.[88] The first two Standards state in part:

> "A mediator shall conduct a mediation based on the principle of party self determination. Self-determination is the act of coming to a voluntary, uncoerced decision in which each party makes free and informed choices as to process and outcome."
>
> "A mediator shall decline a mediation if the mediator cannot conduct it in an impartial manner. Impartiality means freedom from favoritism, bias or prejudice."

While these two Standards of self-determination and impartiality receive nearly universal assent, they are so general that they leave room for substantial disagreement.

Consider two views summarized by James Boskey. One view, which can be called the *libertarian* view, is that the parties "are capable of making their own decisions as to what does or does not constitute an appropriate or just result to their negotiations, and it would be presumptuous, to say the least, for the mediator to impose his or her sense of fairness or justice on them."[89] The alternative view, which can be called the *egalitarian* view, "is that one of the primary purposes of mediation, if not the primary purpose, of mediation is to balance the power between the parties to insure that a 'fair' agreement results."[90] Power might be measured in a variety of ways, including: the expected strength of one's case in court, one's financial and psychological resources to pursue that case, one's skill as a negotiator, and so forth.

While the libertarian and egalitarian views are quite opposed to each other, each can claim fidelity to the Standards of self-determination and impartiality. Both views claim to provide self-determination, that is, a voluntary, uncoerced agreement, because

---

[88] Model Standards of Conduct for Mediators (2005), available at https://www.americanbar.org/content/dam/aba/administrative/dispute_resolution/dispute_resolution/model_standards_conduct_april2007.pdf.

[89] James B. Boskey, The Proper Role of the Mediator: Rational Assessment, Not Pressure, 10 Neg. J. 367, 367 (1994).

[90] Id.

each view rests on its own understanding of coercion and partiality.[91] The egalitarian view rests on the premise that the pre-existing inequality between the parties is inherently coercive to the less-powerful party. So, to the extent the mediator can reduce the pre-existing inequality, the mediator increases the voluntariness of any agreement that results. The mediator's failure to reduce the pre-existing inequality would be partiality toward the more powerful party.

In contrast, the libertarian view rests on the premise that the pre-existing inequality is not coercive, while mediator attempts to equalize the parties are coercive and constitute partiality toward the less powerful party. A mediator who pursues her notions about what constitutes a fair result is no longer a mediator, but an advocate or moral judge.[92] Under the libertarian view, so long as the enforceability of the resulting agreement is not jeopardized by duress, unconscionability, or the like, the mediator should not try to stop the parties' relative strengths from being reflected in the terms of settlement.

The libertarian view seems more common in commercial, personal injury, and other cases in which all parties are represented by lawyers.[93] In contrast, the egalitarian view is built into laws requiring mediation before home foreclosure or eviction (§ 2.19), and frequently voiced in family contexts, such as divorce and child custody (§ 2.17), in which parties often lack lawyers, emotions tend to run especially high, and the interests of young children must be protected.[94]

---

[91] Among the many excellent resources exploring the concept of coercion in law and philosophy are Alan Wertheimer, Coercion (1987); XIV Nomos: Coercion (J. Roland Pennock & John W. Chapman eds., 1972).

[92] Joseph B. Stulberg, The Theory and Practice of Mediation: A Reply to Professor Suskind, 6 Vt. L. Rev. 85, 116 (1981). Accord Christopher W. Moore, The Mediation Process: Practical Strategies for Resolving Conflict 17–18, 389–93 (3d ed. 2003).

[93] "[T]he dominant approach in statutes to defining fairness is consent (sometimes informed consent) by parties to settlements without pressures to settle created by special burdens of the mediation process." Sarah R. Cole, Craig A. McEwen, Nancy H. Rogers, James R. Coben & Peter N. Thompson, Mediation: Law, Policy, & Practice § 2:2 (2024). As mediation is usually an alternative to negotiation, "it is not surprising that the consent standard has emerged as dominant and does not impose on mediation substantially greater expectations for fairness than provided by negotiation. This approach is especially appropriate if attorneys are involved in the mediation sessions." Id. The libertarian view seems quite similar to what Cole et al. call the "consent" approach to fairness, but the libertarian view differs from the "informed consent" approach.

[94] See, e.g., Cal. Fam. Code § 3162(b)(3) (mediator "of cases involving custody and visitation concerning children" shall "conduct[ ] negotiations in such a way as to equalize power relationships between the parties.") Family mediation is discussed in § 2.17.

## § 2.16 The Mediated Settlement Agreement

### *(a) Practice, Including the Single-Text Approach*

People participating in mediation voluntarily, and even many people participating only because a court has ordered it (§ 2.30), tend to seek settlement. In some mediations, the parties reach an oral agreement and do not reduce it to writing. But this is rare in *settlement mediation*, that is, mediation of a dispute in, or headed to, litigation or arbitration (§ 2.3). Typically, the parties to settlement mediation will sign a written release or settlement agreement. For examples of such documents, see Section 1.40.

Some mediators participate in, or even lead, writing the settlement agreement. The mediator may even draft a written proposal during mediation and use it as a starting point for the parties to critique. After each critique, the mediator re-writes the proposal to reflect those party suggestions the mediator wishes to incorporate. With this *single-text* approach, the mediator may control the drafting process from start to finish. One advantage of this approach is that, psychologically, parties may be more willing to consider settlement term proposals made by the mediator than those made by their adversaries.[95]

In contrast, other mediators object to the single-text approach on the ground that it raises the role of the mediator above that of the parties and threatens the principles of party self-determination and mediator impartiality discussed in Section 2.15. Heavy mediator involvement in drafting is also likely to make the mediator more *evaluative* (§ 2.13), because it requires the mediator to make more decisions about how the dispute should be resolved. Every decision about whether to use this word or that word in the settlement agreement is a chance for (possibly subconscious) evaluation by the mediator.

Mediators who become involved in drafting settlement agreements may incur legal risks. Non-lawyer mediators who draft settlement agreements may violate prohibitions on the unlicensed practice of law (§ 2.27(c)(3)). And lawyer-mediators who draft settlement agreements may violate their rules of professional

---

[95] This is related to the well-documented psychological phenomenon of "reactive devaluation," § 2.10(c), which is "the tendency of a party to devalue a settlement proposal simply because it originated with the other side. . . . [A] compromise or concession made unilaterally by a party is often valued less highly than one that is initially withheld and subsequently extracted through reciprocal proposals or concessions." G. Nicholas Herman & Jean M. Cary, Legal Counseling and Negotiation: A Practical Approach 146 (2d ed. 2009).

conduct, especially if the parties are not represented by their own lawyers (§ 2.27(c)(2)).

### *(b) Enforceability of Mediated Settlement Agreements*

#### *(1) Ordinary Law Governing Settlements Generally Applies in Mediation*

Section 1.40 explains that general contract law largely governs negotiated settlement agreements. Similarly, general contract law largely governs mediated settlements.[96] So, the law summarized in Section 1.40 presumptively applies here in the mediation context, and the following paragraphs emphasize the differences and issues unique to, or especially common among, mediated settlements.

#### *(2) Preliminary Agreements*

At the end of some mediation sessions, the participants draft and edit a thorough settlement agreement, which the parties then promptly sign before leaving the site of the mediation. In other cases, though, such as on a Friday night after a grueling 12-hour mediation session, the parties sign just a short memo, outline, or "term sheet" of their deal and ask their lawyers to convert it into a more thorough formal contract the following day or week.[97] But sometimes no later document is signed and parties dispute whether the document signed at the end of mediation is a binding settlement or merely an unenforceable "agreement to agree." For instance, in a First Circuit case,

> At the close of the session, the mediator drafted a hand-written document entitled, "Settlement Memorandum of Understanding." It stated in full:
>
> > 1. Fidelity and Guaranty Ins. Co. ("Fidelity") will pay to the Seekonk Water District/Town of Seekonk, Mass., the sum of Fifty Thousand dollars ($50,000.00);

---

[96] Sarah R. Cole, Craig A. McEwen, Nancy H. Rogers, James R. Coben & Peter N. Thompson, Mediation: Law, Policy, & Practice § 7:2 (2024) ("Most disputes involving enforcement of mediated settlement agreements are resolved based on traditional contract principles"); id. § 7:19 (discussing exceptions); James R. Coben & Peter N. Thompson, Disputing Irony: A Systematic Look at Litigation About Mediation, 11 Harv. Negot. L. Rev. 43 (2006) (reviewing case law on mediation and repeatedly identifying application of general contract law principles). See, e.g., Igani v. Summit Physical Therapy, No. 1:18-CV-155, 2019 WL 13299291, at *3 (E.D. Tenn. Dec. 20, 2019) (in the context of a mediated settlement agreement, stating that "The enforceability of a purported settlement agreement is governed by state contract law").

[97] Igani v. Summit Physical Therapy, No. 1:18-CV-155, 2019 WL 13299291, at *3 (E.D. Tenn. Dec. 20, 2019) ("Here, the Mediation Settlement Agreement states that '[t]he parties' agreement will be reduced to a formal writing . . . to be prepared initially by counsel for the Defendant and delivered to counsel for the Plaintiff.' ")

> 2. The parties hereto agree to Release all claims asserted in the action entitled Fidelity & Guaranty Ins. Co. v. Star Equipment Corp., et al., # 1:04-cv-10250-EFH (D.Mass.) except that Star, Charlene Foran & John Foran and Fidelity do not release claims & defenses they have against each other.
>
> 3. This settlement is conditioned upon:
>
> (a) Approval by appropriate municipal authorities; and
>
> (b) Execution of customary releases and settlement agreement.
>
> The document was signed by each of the parties, their counsel, and the mediator. The mediator reported to the court that "significant progress was made towards full settlement of this matter."[98]

Later, releases were drafted but the Forans refused to sign them. Nevertheless, the trial court granted a motion to enforce the "Settlement Memorandum of Understanding" as a settlement agreement. The First Circuit affirmed, writing "the fact that the hand-written agreement contemplated execution of a more formal agreement does not preclude enforcement of the hand-written agreement."[99] Along the same lines, a Kansas case held that a handwritten document the parties drafted at the end of their mediation session was an enforceable settlement agreement, rather than merely their expression of intent to execute such an agreement in the future.[100] Even though

> the handwritten document expressly provides for the subsequent execution of a journal entry of dismissal with prejudice, a general release, a joint and mutual confidentiality agreement, and an agreement not to seek rehire, these are ordinary documents the parties agreed to submit to implement the settlement agreement. That these documents would be executed by the parties in the future was material to the agreement, but the particular language of these standard documents was not material to the contract. In the ordinary course of settling litigation, documents implementing the settlement agreement are

---

98 Fid. & Guar. Ins. Co. v. Star Equip. Corp., 541 F.3d 1, 4 (1st Cir. 2008).

99 Id. at 6.

100 Hill v. Hutchinson Care Ctr., L.L.C., 357 P.3d 313 (Kan. Ct. App. 2015).

> typically and necessarily left for future handling by the parties.[101]

In contrast, other cases have found similar documents signed at the end of mediation not enforceable.[102]

*(3) Oral Settlements and Mediation's Confidentiality*

The sort of litigation just discussed—litigation over whether the document signed at the end of mediation is a binding settlement or merely an unenforceable "agreement to agree" can reduce mediation's confidentiality (§ 2.28) as a "court seeks evidence to ascertain what went on at the mediation to determine" if the parties formed a settlement agreement.[103] This reduction in mediation's confidentiality is even more likely if a court seeks enough evidence to enforce an alleged oral settlement agreement reached in mediation but never reduced to writing. So, several jurisdictions have statutes or court rules providing that mediated settlements are enforceable only if written.[104] For example, a Missouri trial court's order directed parties to mediation pursuant to court rules providing:

> Any settlement reached between the Parties over the matters at issue shall, in order to be binding, be in the form of a written agreement, approved in writing by the attorneys for the Parties, signed by the Parties and witnessed by the Mediator.

And:

> Any communication relating to the subject matter of such dispute made during the alternative dispute resolution

---

[101] Id.

[102] Habu v. Topacio, 12 Wash. App. 2d 1006, 2020 WL 533947, *1 (2020), review denied, 471 P.3d 210 (Wash. 2020) (term sheet signed by parties after two days of mediation was not an agreement as to all material terms); Catamount Slate Products, Inc. v. Sheldon, 845 A.2d 324, 327 (Vt. 2003) (reversing trial court's conclusion that "attorneys' notes taken at the end of the mediation and the unsigned drafts of the Lease and Settlement Agreements sufficiently memorialized the agreement between the parties and thus constituted an enforceable settlement agreement.")

[103] Sarah R. Cole, Craig A. McEwen, Nancy H. Rogers, James R. Coben & Peter N. Thompson, Mediation: Law, Policy, & Practice § 7:2 (2024).

[104] Greenway Mews Realty, L.L.C. v. Liberty Insurance Underwriters, Inc., 118 N.Y.S.3d 104 (App. Div. 2020) (refusing to enforce an oral settlement agreement made during mediation because it was not "sufficiently documented, recorded or memorialized" as required by New York's Civil Practice Law & Rules); Scott v. Tischler, 882 So.2d 461 (Fla. Dist. Ct. App. 2004) (failure to sign a mediated settlement fails to meet requirements of Fla. R. Civ. P. 1.730 and is therefore unenforceable); Barnett v. Sea Land Serv., Inc. 875 F.2d 741 (9th Cir. 1989) (citing Washington District court Local Rule 39.1(d)(3)); Murphy v. Padilla, 49 Cal.Rptr.2d 722 (Ct. App. 1996); Burckhard v. Del Monte Corp., 56 Cal. Rptr.2d 569 (Ct. App. 1996).

> process by a participant or any other person present at the process shall be a confidential communication.[105]

The trial court enforced a settlement signed by defendants and the mediator but not by the plaintiff. The appellate court reversed, noting that the rule requiring "that the parties reduce the essential terms of their agreement to an executed writing" "prevents the sort of 'he said, she said' disputes that have occurred in this case," and "protects the confidentiality of mediation proceedings from inevitable erosion if parties are permitted to attempt to prove up oral agreements reached during mediation."[106]

The requirement of a writing for mediated settlements may be an effect of law creating a *mediation privilege* (§ 2.28(d)) because the privilege precludes testimony necessary to prove that an oral agreement was formed. As the Utah Supreme Court said,

> A rule permitting courts to enforce only written mediation agreements operates in tandem with the rules providing mediation confidentiality. The existence of an executed agreement provides a court with the means to use its power to enforce the terms of a written agreement or to determine whether the terms of the written agreement have been violated without requiring it to delve into the confidential process that led to the creation of the agreement.[107]

In short, the law in several states may be developing what amounts to a Statute of Frauds for mediated settlements,[108] but not for negotiated settlements.[109] In other jurisdictions, by contrast, courts have enforced oral settlements reached in mediation.[110]

---

[105] Williams v. Kansas City Title Loan Co., 314 S.W.3d 868, 870 (Mo. Ct. App. 2010) (quoting Mo. Sup. Ct. Rule 17).

[106] Id. at 873.

[107] Reese v. Tingey Const., 177 P.3d 605, 609 (2008).

[108] As with other Statutes of Frauds, mediated oral agreements are enforceable if they are partially performed by the parties. See Kaiser Found. Health Plan v. Doe, 903 P.2d 375 (Or. Ct. App. 1995) (enforcing oral mediated settlement where subsequent behavior evidenced agreement).

[109] Sarah R. Cole, Craig A. McEwen, Nancy H. Rogers, James R. Coben & Peter N. Thompson, Mediation: Law, Policy, & Practice § 7:19 (2024) ("In some jurisdictions, privilege rules preclude testimony about oral settlements reached through mediation, but do not preclude oral settlements reached through negotiations without a mediator.").

[110] Helmericks v. Peak Trust Company, 2020 WL 5814200, *5 (Alaska 2020) (stating that an oral mediated settlement can be enforceable even if the parties contemplate that the agreement will be reduced to writing, and it is not reduced to a writing); Ackerman v. Sobol Family Partnership, LLP, 4 A.3d 288, 310 (Conn. 2010) ("The trial court correctly noted that 'the fact that an oral agreement was later to be memorialized in writing does not make it any less enforceable' ").

*(4) Defenses to Enforcement of Mediated Settlements*

Ordinary contract-law defenses—such as misrepresentation, mistake, duress, and undue influence—apply to negotiated settlements (§ 1.40(c)) and apply similarly to mediated settlements. While many parties have asserted such defenses to avoid enforcement of mediated settlements, few prevail.[111] For example, one federal court rejected a litigant's argument that his settlement argument was formed under duress because his lawyer recommended settlement and the mediator predicted he would not fare well at trial.[112] However, in a few contexts, mediated settlements must meet a higher standard than negotiated settlements to be enforceable. For example, some statutes say that a mediated settlement agreement is not legally binding unless it contains a provision stating that it is.[113]

Conversely, in a few contexts, courts hold mediated settlements to a lower standard than negotiated settlements to be enforceable. A Texas example is discussed at the end of the following subsection.

*(5) Agreed Judgments and Consent Decrees*

As Section 1.40 explains, courts generally enforce releases and settlement agreements against plaintiffs by dismissing cases asserting claims the plaintiff has released or promised to release in an agreement the defendant has not breached. This is also true of

---

[111] Sarah R. Cole, Craig A. McEwen, Nancy H. Rogers, James R. Coben & Peter N. Thompson, Mediation: Law, Policy, & Practice § 7:20 (2024) ("courts usually enforce mediated settlement agreements, even in the face of a strong challenge"); id. ("When parties go to court to enforce a mediated settlement agreement, judges readily enforce the agreements. Contract defenses are rarely successful"); id. §§ 7:6–7:13 (discussing cases). See, e.g., Pohlman v. Pohlman, No. 344121, 2020 WL 504775, at *5 (Mich. Ct. App. Jan. 30, 2020) ("when a party asserts that her own attorney coerced or unduly influenced her, courts will not overturn a consent judgment absent a showing that the opposing party participated in the coercion or influence.")

[112] Igani v. Summit Physical Therapy, No. 1:18-CV-155, 2019 WL 13299291, at *6 (E.D. Tenn. Dec. 20, 2019) ("Igani cannot abdicate responsibility for his own decision due to the opinions or predictions of his attorney or the mediator.")

[113] See Cal. Evid. Code § 1123 (providing that a written mediated settlement agreement can be admissible only if the "agreement provides that it is admissible," "enforceable," or contains "words to that effect"); Tex. Fam. Code. Ann. § 6.602(b)(1)–(3) (providing that a mediated settlement agreement is enforceable if it contains a "prominently displayed statement that is in boldface type or capital letters or underlined, that the agreement is not subject to revocation; (2) is signed by each party to the agreement; and (3) is signed by the party's attorney, if any, who is present at the time the agreement is signed"). See also Wetherby v. Wetherby, 50 A.D.3d 1226, 854 N.Y.S.2d 813 (3d Dep't 2008) (refusing to enforce a mediated agreement that was a signed and notarized modification to an "opt out" agreement because it did not have a formal acknowledgement as required by N.Y. Dom. Rel. § 236(B)(3)).

releases and settlement agreements formed in mediation.[114] However, while courts enforce settlement agreements against defendants, this process can be slow and expensive because it often takes two steps (§ 1.40). First, the plaintiff from the underlying settled action starts a new suit (presumably last in line on the court's docket) for breach of the settlement agreement, seeking the remedy of specific performance—a court order requiring that the defendant do what defendant promised in the settlement agreement. Then, if the defendant still does not comply, the plaintiff can enforce the specific performance decree through a contempt proceeding. This two-step burden of bringing a breach of contract suit generally applies to mediated, as well as negotiated, settlements.[115]

In contrast, the enforceability of a settlement agreement can—if the dispute is already in litigation—be expedited by having a court retain jurisdiction over the case. Then the agreement can be enforced on motion without need for a new suit, or by having the court enter judgment on a settlement agreement, which effectively converts it from a private contract to a judgment of the court (§ 1.40). This expedited process generally applies similarly to mediated and negotiated settlements.[116] Such an "agreed judgment" or "consent decree" may be enforced in a single step because it already includes the court's order requiring each party to do what it promised in the settlement agreement. By removing the need for a separate breach of contract suit, an agreed judgment or consent decree enables the party

---

[114] Howard v. Louisiana Citizens Prop. Ins. Corp., 65 So. 3d 697, 698–99 (La. App. 2011) (affirming summary proceeding granting insurer's motion to enforce settlement reached in mediation with homeowner).

[115] Sarah R. Cole, Craig A. McEwen, Nancy H. Rogers, James R. Coben & Peter N. Thompson, Mediation: Law, Policy, & Practice § 7:19 (2024) ("While enforcement procedures vary from state to state, as a general rule, mediated settlement agreements are treated as contracts, which can be enforced in a court of general jurisdiction by beginning a lawsuit.")

[116] See, e.g., id. ("Of course, if the [mediated settlement] agreement is included in a court order, or the court retains jurisdiction over the matter, the court may enforce its order through contempt powers or other procedures for enforcing court orders."); Thomas H. Oehmke, Commercial Arbitration § 26:48 ("The best practice is to reduce any mediation settlement agreement (MSA) to a stipulated or consent judgment and have it entered as an order of the court."); Rachel Elliott, The Eviction Crisis is Rampaging, 2025 J. Disp. Resol. 77 (in eviction mediation, "If a settlement is reached, a mediator will create a stipulated judgment, and the judge will sign it."); U.S. Sec. & Exch. Comm'n v. Silea, No. 4:20-CV-737-SDJ, 2022 WL 2346384, at *1 (E.D. Tex. June 28, 2022) ("parties mediated" "and entered into a partial settlement agreement" the terms of "which were incorporated into consent judgments" "entered by the Court"); M & C Assocs. v. State, Dep't of Transp., 682 So. 2d 640, 640 (Fla. Dist. Ct. App. 1996) ("A stipulated final judgment was entered that incorporated the [mediated] settlement agreement."); Batton v. Batton, No. 09-22-00312-CV, 2024 WL 1914401, at *1 (Tex. App. May 2, 2024) ("Linda and Lawrence reached an Agreed Final Decree of Divorce ('the Decree'), which included a mediated settlement agreement"); id. at *7 ("Once a trial court approves and adopts the parties' agreement into its enforcement order, the agreement becomes the judgment of the court and subject to enforcement").

seeking enforcement to avoid the court's docket queue and obtain sanctions more quickly than if a new lawsuit had to be filed.

While the previous paragraph notes that courts are generally as willing to enter judgment on mediated settlements as they are on negotiated settlements, in a few contexts courts are more willing to enter judgment on mediated settlements. For example, a Texas statute narrows the circumstances in which a family court "may decline to enter a judgment on a mediated settlement agreement," but not on a negotiated settlement agreement.[117] Because "using mediation and engaging a mediator represent the keys to earning this extreme judicial deference," Texas family lawyers created "drive-by mediation," in which they *negotiate* a settlement and then have their clients sign it in a *mediator*'s presence to make it an ostensibly mediated settlement and thus increase its enforceability.[118]

### *(c) Enforceability of Mediated Settlements Beyond the U.S.*

#### *(1) Other Nations*

In the United States, general contract law largely governs negotiated settlement agreements (§ 1.40), and law governing negotiated settlements also generally applies to mediated settlements (§ 2.16). So, general contract law largely governs mediated settlement agreements.

That description of law in the U.S. generally applies as well in other nations with similar legal systems. For example, it is telling that when an English lawyer was asked, "In what circumstances can the mediation settlement agreement be challenged in court?" the lawyer responded about settlement agreements generally because it does not matter whether a settlement was made in mediation or negotiation:

> As a settlement agreement is a contract, it can be challenged as any other contract. Thus, it could be found to be void on grounds of concepts such as mistake, frustration,

---

117 Tex. Fam. Code Ann. § 153.0071. See also Nancy A. Welsh, Drive-By Mediation and Other Opportunistic Distortions of Process, 67 Ariz. L. Rev. 773, 793 (2025) ("in Texas, judges' authority to refuse entry of judgment on parents' mediated settlement agreements remains incredibly narrow. And importantly, using mediation and engaging a mediator represent the keys to earning this extreme judicial deference.")

118 Nancy A. Welsh, Drive-By Mediation and Other Opportunistic Distortions of Process, 67 Ariz. L. Rev. 773, 789–96 (2025).

> fraud and illegality. It could also be set aside on grounds of misrepresentation, duress and undue influence.[119]

Similarly, English procedures for converting a negotiated settlement into a court order also apply to converting a mediated settlement into a court order.[120] And much or all of what this paragraph says about England applies to other major nations based on the English common law, such as Canada and Australia.

By contrast, in many civil law (as distinct from common law) jurisdictions, the law on mediated settlements differs more from the law on negotiated settlements. In particular, the procedures and criteria for making a mediated settlement a court order (roughly, an "enforceable title") tend to differ from the procedures and criteria for making a negotiated settlement a court order.[121]

Special law for enforcement of mediated, but not negotiated, settlements has also been repeatedly promulgated by the United Nations Commission on International Trade Law (UNCITRAL). The 2018 UNCITRAL Model Law on International Commercial Mediation and International Settlement Agreements Resulting from Mediation, adopted by 33 nations plus several U.S. states and Canadian provinces,[122] says that "If the parties conclude an agreement settling a dispute, that settlement agreement is binding and enforceable."[123] However, this Model Law only "applies to international commercial mediation,"[124] not to negotiated settlements. The Model Law defines mediation as

> a process, whether referred to by the expression mediation, conciliation or an expression of similar import, whereby parties request a third person or persons ("the mediator") to

[119] Donald Lambert, Mediation in United Kingdom, Lexology (Sept. 9, 2019), https://www.lexology.com/library/detail.aspx?g=02ee5416-79ba-484b-bd62-eb26318d330b.

[120] General Council of the Bar of England and Wales, Bar Council response to the "Consultation on the United Nations Convention on International Settlement Agreements Resulting from Mediation (New York, 2018) (the "Singapore Convention on Mediation")" consultation paper, 31 March 2022, at 4 ("it is the norm for concluded mediated settlement agreements to be recorded in a Tomlin Order or other form of court order if proceedings have commenced"); Giuseppe De Palo & Mary B. Trevor, Is Mediation Becoming A Core Component of Justice in England and Wales?, 43 Alternatives to High Cost Litig. 35, 46 (2025) ("Agreements reached through mediation can be formalized as legally binding contracts or integrated into Tomlin Orders, which grant them the same enforceability as court orders.")

[121] Stephen J. Ware & Piotr Slawicki, Enforcement of Negotiated and Mediated Settlements in the EU and in the Anglosphere: A Comparative Approach, Studia Iuridica (forthcoming 2026).

[122] https://uncitral.un.org/en/texts/arbitration/modellaw/commercial_conciliation/status.

[123] Art. 15.

[124] Art. 1(1).

> assist them in their attempt to reach an amicable settlement of their dispute arising out of or relating to a contractual or other legal relationship. The mediator does not have the authority to impose upon the parties a solution to the dispute.[125]

This passage uses the phrase "amicable settlement," which seems far more common in civil law systems than in the United States. Perhaps this is because in the U.S. and other English-based systems, "settlement" alone conveys "by agreement, rather than adjudication," but in other places and languages "dispute settlement" includes adjudication, so the phrase "amicable settlement" is needed to clarify settlement by agreement.

The Model Law also contains further sections on *international* settlement agreements resulting from mediation.[126] These sections are designed to coordinate with the treaty discussed next.

*(2) Cross-Border Enforcement and the Singapore Convention*

Section 1.40(d) explains that cross-border enforcement of settlements is challenging, even if the settlement has been converted into a court order, because the orders or judgments of one nation's courts are not reliably enforced by the courts of other nations. Cross-border enforcement of judgments may improve as more nations adopt the 2019 Convention on the Recognition and Enforcement of Foreign Judgments in Civil or Commercial Matters, which obliges contracting states to recognize and enforce civil and commercial judgments rendered in another contracting state.[127] But at present, only 32 countries are parties to this Judgments Convention.[128]

In contrast, 172 nations are parties to the United Nations Convention on the Recognition and Enforcement of Foreign Arbitral Awards (New York Convention).[129] For decades, the New York Convention has made cross-border enforcement of arbitration awards simpler and more assured than cross-border enforcement of court judgments.[130] Under the New York Convention, when a party wins

---

[125] Art. 1(3).

[126] Art. 19.

[127] HCCH (Hague Conference on Private International Law), Convention of 2 July 2019 on the Recognition and Enforcement of Foreign Judgments in Civil or Commercial Matters, https://www.hcch.net/en/instruments/conventions/full-text/?cid=137.

[128] https://www.hcch.net/en/instruments/conventions/status-table/?cid=137.

[129] New York Convention, Contracting States, https://www.newyorkconvention.org/contracting-states.

[130] Yuliya Zeynalova, *The Law on Recognition and Enforcement of Foreign Judgments: Is It Broken and How Do We Fix It?*, 31 Berkeley J. Int'l L. 150, 151 (2013) ("Unlike foreign arbitral awards, which are governed by the New York Convention, no treaty outlines the circumstances under which U.S. courts may recognize foreign

an international commercial arbitration award, that party does not need to get confirmation or approval of its award from a court in the nation where the arbitration was seated. Instead, the party seeking to enforce its award can go straight to a court in the nation where the respondent's (defendant's) assets are, as that court shall enforce the award except upon narrow grounds for denying enforcement.[131] In other words, the basic idea of cross-border enforcement of arbitral awards is to make the award portable, so it is readily enforced by courts wherever assets might be found, without having to attend to differences among various nations' laws.[132] All the courts of the world nearly rubber-stamping the results of a private, contractual alternative dispute resolution process (arbitration) exaggerates the idea only slightly.

Bringing this reliable cross-border enforcement to another private, contractual alternative dispute resolution process (mediation) is the basic goal of the 2018 Convention on International Settlement Agreements Resulting from Mediation ("the Singapore Convention").[133] To encourage mediation of international commercial disputes,[134] the Singapore Convention tries to make resulting

awards and vice versa. Transnational litigants are therefore more likely to encounter difficulties enforcing their foreign court awards than parties seeking to enforce their foreign arbitral awards."); Theodore J. Folkman, Recognition and Enforcement of Foreign Arbitral Awards, Massachusetts Continuing Legal Education, Inc. (2d ed. 2016) ("[T]he absence of an international convention on the recognition and enforcement of foreign judgments makes recognition and enforcement somewhat complex. [In contrast, t]he New York Convention, the convention governing recognition and enforcement of foreign arbitral awards, greatly simplifies matters when the foreign decision is an award rather than a judgment.").

131 Stephen J. Ware & Ariana R Levinson, Principles of Arbitration Law, § 59 (2d ed. 2023) ("For example, if an arbitration tribunal seated outside the United States awards the claimant money damages from the respondent and the respondent has property in the United States then the claimant does not need to involve a court at the seat of the arbitration. The claimant can get a federal court in the U.S. to confirm the award, which converts the award into a judgment of the court."); id. § 60 (discussing narrow grounds for vacatur and non-enforcement of international arbitration awards).

132 Richard Happ, 40 Years New York Convention: Past, Present and Future, 2 Vindobona J. 55 (1998) ("The New York Convention is one of the greatest achievements of modern international economic law. It has been the decisive factor for the development and acceptance of international commercial arbitration around the globe. By requiring states to recognise and enforce arbitral awards rendered in foreign countries if they fulfil certain requirements, and limiting the reasons for which recognition and enforcement can be refused, it has made awards portable and mitigated the complexities of cross-border disputes.")

133 U.N. Convention on International Settlement Agreements Resulting from Mediation, Dec. 20, 2018 (adopted), Aug. 7, 2019 (signed), Sept. 12, 2020 (effective), 3369 U.N.T.S. 154, 2019 [hereinafter Singapore Convention] https://uncitral.un.org/sites/uncitral.un.org/files/media-documents/EN/Texts/UNCITRAL/Arbitration/mediation_convention_v1900316_eng.pdf.

134 The Singapore Convention governs only international commercial settlement agreements resulting from mediation. Rather than define "commercial," Article 1(2) excludes settlements arising from personal, family, or household consumer transactions, as well as those related to family, inheritance, or employment law.

settlement agreements readily enforceable in courts around the world by treating mediated settlements like arbitration awards.[135] The Singapore Convention does not apply to mediated settlements in which the judge with "authority to impose a solution upon the parties" was the mediator,[136] or to mediated settlements "that have been approved by a court or concluded in the course of proceedings before a court" and "are enforceable as a judgment in the State of that court."[137]

To use the Singapore Convention, a party relying on a mediated settlement agreement submits to "the competent authority," (typically a court,[138]) "the settlement agreement signed by the parties" and "evidence that the settlement agreement resulted from mediation," such as "[t]he mediator's signature on the settlement agreement."[139] This Singapore Convention process can be used to enforce a mediated settlement defensively or offensively. Defensively, if Plaintiff sues Defendant on a claim already resolved by a mediated settlement agreement, Defendant can invoke the Convention to use the settlement as a shield against that claim.[140] Conversely, if a settlement obligates Defendant to pay a sum of money to Plaintiff, Plaintiff can invoke the Convention offensively to have the settlement agreement enforced directly by the competent authority against Defendant's property (assets).[141]

---

135 See Timothy Schnabel, The Singapore Convention on Mediation: A Framework for the Cross-Border Recognition and Enforcement of Mediated Settlements, 19 Pepp. Disp. Resol. L.J. 1 (2019) (Singapore Convention provides a framework for enforcing mediated settlement agreements "akin to the framework that the 1958 New York Convention provides for arbitral awards.").

136 Art. 2(3) (defining mediation as "a process. . .whereby parties attempt to reach an amicable settlement of their dispute with the assistance of a third person or persons ('the mediator') lacking the authority to impose a solution upon the parties to the dispute.")

137 Art. 1(3)(a).

138 The person who proposed and negotiated the Singapore Convention on behalf of the United States says "The 'competent authority' before which these issues may arise can be a court or any other authority empowered by the relevant state to address these issues, including an arbitral tribunal." Timothy Schnabel, The Singapore Convention on Mediation: A Framework for the Cross-Border Recognition and Enforcement of Mediated Settlements, 19 Pepp. Disp. Resol. L.J. 1, 34 (2019).

139 Singapore Convention, Art. 4(1).

140 Art. 3(2). Timothy Schnabel, The Singapore Convention on Mediation: A Framework for the Cross-Border Recognition and Enforcement of Mediated Settlements, 19 Pepp. Disp. Resol. L.J. 1, 39–40 (2019) ("Article 3(2) applies if the parties have successfully mediated a dispute but then one party attempts to re-litigate part of the underlying dispute that was resolved via mediation.")

141 Id. at 39 ("In Article 3(1), the Convention requires states to enforce mediated settlements, in accordance with their rules of procedure and under the conditions laid down in the Convention . . . This paragraph thus covers the 'sword'—the relief sought by a party who attempts to affirmatively compel compliance with a mediated settlement in the face of another party's breach of its obligations under the settlement").

The Singapore Convention permits courts to deny enforcement to settlements on narrow grounds similar to the New York Convention's narrow grounds for courts to deny enforcement to arbitration awards. The Singapore Convention's grounds to deny enforcement are:

*(a)* A party to the settlement agreement was under some incapacity;

*(b)* The settlement agreement sought to be relied upon:

(i) Is null and void, inoperative or incapable of being performed under the law to which the parties have validly subjected it or, failing any indication thereon, under the law deemed applicable by the competent authority of the Party to the Convention where relief is sought under article 4;

(ii) Is not binding, or is not final, according to its terms;

or

(iii) Has been subsequently modified;

*(c)* The obligations in the settlement agreement:

(i) Have been performed; or

(ii) Are not clear or comprehensible;

*(d)* Granting relief would be contrary to the terms of the settlement agreement;

*(e)* There was a serious breach by the mediator of standards applicable to the mediator or the mediation without which breach that party would not have entered into the settlement agreement; or

*(f)* There was a failure by the mediator to disclose to the parties circumstances that raise justifiable doubts as to the mediator's impartiality or independence and such failure to disclose had a material impact or undue influence on a party without which failure that party would not have entered into the settlement agreement.[142]

Although about sixty States have signed the Singapore Convention, only nineteen have ratified it, including Bahrain, Belarus, Brazil, Costa Rica, Ecuador, Fiji, Georgia, Honduras, Israel,

[142] Singapore Convention, Art. 5.

Japan, Kazakhstan, Nigeria, Paraguay, Qatar, Singapore, Sri Lanka, Türkiye, and Uruguay.[143]

With the United States among those signatories that have not yet ratified it, courts in the U.S. have not been called upon to interpret and apply the Singapore Convention. However, several states (including California, Texas, Ohio, North Carolina, and Oregon) have enacted statutes, based on the UNCITRAL Model Law discussed in Section 2.16(c)(1), that treat mediated settlements of international commercial disputes like final arbitral awards for enforcement purposes.[144] The American Bar Association, Uniform Law Commission, and U.S. Chamber of Commerce have urged U.S. ratification of the Singapore Convention.[145]

The Singapore Convention is not the only attempt to encourage cross-border enforcement of mediated settlements. The 2008 European Union Directive on Mediation, which applies to cross-border commercial disputes within the EU,[146] says:

> 1. Member States shall ensure that it is possible for the parties, or for one of them with the explicit consent of the others, to request that the content of a written agreement resulting from mediation be made enforceable. The content of such an agreement shall be made enforceable unless, in the case in question, either the content of that agreement is contrary to the law of the Member State where the request is made or the law of that Member State does not provide for its enforceability.
>
> 2. The content of the agreement may be made enforceable by a court or other competent authority in a judgment or decision or in an authentic instrument in

---

143 Link to current signatories, parties, and reservations: https://treaties.un.org/Pages/ViewDetails.aspx?src=TREATY&mtdsg_no=XXII-4&chapter=22&clang=_en (last visited July 16, 2024). See Sean D. Murphy, Principles of International Law 86–87 (3d ed. 2018) ("Most treaties have a two-step process, consisting of first signature and then ratification. . . . When the two-step process is used, a state's signature . . . does not obligate the state to ratify a treaty; The principal reason for this second step is that many states have internal constitutional requirements mandating legislative or parliamentary approval of a signed treaty before it becomes binding on the state. For example, in the United States, the president or his representative signs the treaty and it is then sent to the U.S. Senate for advice and consent. Only after receiving such consent, which may require the passage of implementing legislation, may the president proceed to the next step of ratifying the treaty").

144 Ana Sambold, The Singapore Convention on Mediation: Why It Matters and Where the U.S. Stands, Just Resolutions, Nov. 3, 2025.

145 Id.

146 https://eur-lex.europa.eu/eli/dir/2008/52/oj/eng.

accordance with the law of the Member State where the request is made.[147]

# D. MEDIATION CONTEXTS

## § 2.17 Family

The category of cases long generating the most mediation in the U.S. is family law, especially divorce and child custody disputes. Family mediation sometimes does not involve lawyers. Many family mediators—especially those provided by the court—are non-lawyers, such as marriage counselors, psychologists, and social workers.[148] Moreover, many parties in family mediation represent themselves,[149] usually because they cannot afford a lawyer. Along the same lines, when parties do have lawyers, those lawyers sometimes do not attend mediation sessions, in part to save clients on legal fees. Family case mediators in some states even have authority to exclude lawyers.[150] The relative absence of lawyers from family mediation makes it a mediation context especially likely to raise concerns about the unauthorized practice of law by non-lawyer mediators (§ 2.27(c)(3)), and about issues of professional responsibility for lawyer-mediators (§ 2.27(c)(2)).

If divorce mediation results in an agreement the court approves, the court often incorporates the agreement into the judgment of divorce. A contract is not enough to end the legal relationship of marriage, so a court order is required. If divorce or other family

---

[147] Art. 6.

[148] Debra Berman & James Alfini, Lawyer Colonization of Family Mediation: Consequences and Implications, 95 Marq. L. Rev. 887, 894 (2012) ("many mediators in court-connected settings are still mental health professionals, including social workers and psychologists. In fact, numerous court-connected programs have very few mediators with legal backgrounds on their staffs. The main reason that mental health professionals continue to dominate is that, indeed, many court-based mediation programs tend to focus on custody issues rather than property division. Some court-connected mediation services are limited to parenting plans only.")

[149] Kelly Browe Olson, Post-Grillo: New Family Mediation Protections and Revised Dangers in Discussions in Dispute Resolution 172 (2021) ("family courts have seen an exponential increase in their caseloads and in the number of self-represented parties."); Ellen Waldman, How Mediation Contributes to the "Justice Gap" and Possible Technological Fixes, 88 Fordham L. Rev. 2425, 2426 (2020) ("California tallies indicate that 67 percent of disputants in family court . . . are self-represented").

[150] Cal. Fam. Code § 3182(a) ("The mediator has authority to exclude counsel from participation in the mediation proceedings pursuant to this chapter if, in the mediator's discretion, exclusion of counsel is appropriate or necessary."); S.D. Codified Laws § 25–4–59 ("The mediator shall conduct the mediation proceedings in private. The mediator may exclude counsel from participation in the mediation proceedings."); Mont. Code Ann. § 40–4–302 ("except in cases involving domestic violence, the mediator may exclude attorneys from the mediation sessions").

In some other jurisdictions lawyers developed the practice of non-attendance on their own. See Craig A. McEwen, Lynn Mather & Richard J. Maiman, Mediation, Lawyers, and the Management of Divorce Practice, 28 L. & Soc'y Rev. 149, 180 (1994).

mediation results in agreements on child custody and support, then these agreements must be approved by the court to be binding (§ 1.40(c)(4)). This contrasts with most settlement agreements, which do not require court approval to be binding as simple contracts (§ 1.40(b)).

Divorcing spouses are often encouraged by their lawyers to mediate any contested issues. If the parties do not mediate voluntarily, statutes and courts in many jurisdictions have a presumption and sometimes a requirement for mediation of disputes regarding child custody or visitation.[151] Child custody mediation, whether arising out of a divorce or not, receives especially strong support from many states through government funding, legally mandated participation requirements, and broad evidentiary privileges.[152] In fact, "Court sponsored family [mediation] programs often mediate only issues of [child] custody or visitation and refuse to encourage negotiations regarding economic issues."[153] The case for mediating, rather than litigating, child custody is especially strong because "the parties typically seek different remedies than the courts can provide," and such cases "if prolonged, adversely affect nonparties,"[154] especially children. For example, mediation may result in an agreed schedule of when a child will be with each parent that is more complex and detailed than could be expected of a court's ruling.

Family mediation's advocates say its less-adversarial setting typically minimizes the emotional and financial trauma of separation, divorce, or other family changes—benefiting both parents and any children. Unlike litigation, family mediation can help separating parents appreciate each other's interests and priorities

---

[151] See, e.g., Cal. Fam. Code § 3170(a) ("If it appears on the face of a petition, application, or other pleading to obtain or modify a temporary or permanent custody or visitation order that custody, visitation, or both are contested, the court shall set the contested issues for mediation"); Or. Rev. Stat. § 107.765(1) (permitting mediation in disputes regarding child custody or visitation); Maine Rev. Stat. Ann., Tit. 19-A, § 251(2); La. Rev. Stat. Ann. § 9:332(A) (allowing court-ordered mediation in custody disputes); Kan. Stat. Ann. § 23–3502 (2025) ("The court or hearing officer may order mediation of any contested issue of child custody, residency, visitation, parenting time, division of property or other issues, at any time, upon motion of a party or on the court's own motion").

[152] Sarah R. Cole, Craig A. McEwen, Nancy H. Rogers, James R. Coben & Peter N. Thompson, Mediation: Law, Policy, & Practice § 2:6 (2024) (citing statutes in support of "A substantial number of states support use of mediation more strongly for child custody than for general civil cases, encouraging custody mediation through such provisions as mandated participation, public funding, and broad privileges. The commentary and statutes suggest the advantages of settlement for the parties' children and the superiority of settlement over court rulings in meeting the parties' complex needs").

[153] Id. § 15:2.

[154] Id. § 1:4.

and help them to work together in the future as, for example, children grow older and new parenting issues arise.[155] By facilitating the parents' own decision-making and self-determination, mediation "should enhance continuing family ties and reassert the dignity and importance of the family as a self-governing unit."[156] As noted above with respect to a child's schedule of time with each parent, while the remedies in litigation are limited, mediation can provide personalized, tailor-made arrangements for the particular parties involved. Consequently, "parties 'own' the final result and, therefore, will be more likely to abide by it."[157]

On the other hand, divorce and other family mediation also have strong critics. "Many of these critics are leaders of the women's movement who contend that women will achieve worse results in mediation than in court."[158] This might occur in divorce for a variety of reasons, most based on the premise that wives tend to be less powerful—financially and otherwise—than their husbands. First, some evidence suggests that men are more likely than women to use the *adversarial/competitive* approach to negotiation, while women are more likely than men to use the *cooperative* and *problem-solving* approaches (§ 1.27). There is a significant risk that the adversarial/competitive negotiator will exploit the cooperative or problem-solving one (§§ 1.21, 1.26). This risk is heightened in mediation if the parties do not have, or are unaccompanied by, their own lawyers,[159] which as noted above, is common in family mediation.

---

[155] In this respect, divorce mediation may be an opportunity for the relevant moral growth of the parties. See § 2.8.

[156] H. Jay Folberg, Divorce Mediation: A Workable Alternative, from American Bar Association, Alternative Means of Family Dispute Resolution 11, 17 (1982).

[157] Sarah R. Cole, Craig A. McEwen, Nancy H. Rogers, James R. Coben & Peter N. Thompson, Mediation: Law, Policy, & Practice § 15:2 (2024).

[158] Edward Brunet & Charles B. Craver, Alternative Dispute Resolution: The Advocate's Perspective 277 (2d ed. 2001).

[159] Craig A. McEwen, Nancy H. Rogers & Richard J. Maiman, Bring in the Lawyers: Challenging the Dominant Approaches to Ensuring Fairness In Divorce Mediation, 79 Minn. L. Rev. 1317 (1995) ("Mandatory divorce mediation is under attack. According to some critical commentators, divorce mediation reinforces bargaining imbalances between parties and places women at a disadvantage. Professor Penelope Bryan, for example, concludes that there is an 'insidious nature of mediation' for divorcing women and that 'those who structure court affiliated programs, as well as mediators, now should recognize their complicity in the continued oppression of women and their dependent children.' She and other critics charge that mandatory mediation programs represent an unnecessary step that leaves divorcing parents unprotected by lawyers and makes the divorce process less fair. Bryan claims that mediation 'exploits wives by denigrating their legal entitlements, stripping them of authority, encouraging unwarranted compromise, isolating them from needed support, and placing them across the table from their more powerful husbands and demanding that they fend for themselves.' ")(internal citations omitted).

In addition, mediation lacks compelled discovery. So, if the husband has more property than the wife, or more knowledge about jointly owned property, then litigation enables the wife and her lawyer to acquire that knowledge through court-ordered discovery. In contrast, if mediation occurs prior to discovery, the husband may be able to conceal property, or information about it, from the wife.[160]

Finally, divorce and other family mediation may follow domestic or other intimate partner violence. "A view that victims of intimate partner or other domestic violence are not well served in mediation has led most states to enact exceptions to or other restrictions of mandated mediation in these cases."[161] These exceptions are typically implemented by court-employed screeners and by mediators who increasingly are trained to "identify problematic behavior and coercive acts," and to implement ameliorative measures like "shuttle mediation, video conferencing, asynchronous meetings, and other uses of technology."[162]

## § 2.18 Labor & Employment

Mediation of work-related disputes is common and is often called "conciliation."[163] In the U.S., law governing employment is often divided into two categories: "employment law" which applies to all employees, and "labor law," which governs employees' collective activities, such as forming a labor union. Labor law has its own specialized terminology. Contracts between employers and unions are called "collective bargaining agreements," and claims alleging breach of these contracts are called "grievances."[164]

Mediation (or "conciliation") has been used to resolve labor disputes for at least a century.[165] The Federal Mediation and Conciliation Service ("FMCS") is part of the Department of Labor, and it mediates disputes between labor unions and employers. Its statutory charge is "to assist parties to labor disputes in industries

---

[160] See Laurie Woods, Mediation: A Backlash to Women's Progress on Family Law Issues, 19 Clearinghouse Rev. 431, 435 (1985).

[161] Sarah R. Cole, Craig A. McEwen, Nancy H. Rogers, James R. Coben & Peter N. Thompson, Mediation: Law, Policy, & Practice § 15:2 (2024). See also Anne M. Sidwell, Mandatory Child Custody Mediation: A Call on California to Protect Domestic Violence Survivors, 57 U.S.F. L. Rev. 135, 137 (2022) (arguing that "California should adopt legislation allowing domestic violence survivors to opt out of court mandated mediation.")

[162] Kelly Browe Olson, Post-Grillo: New Family Mediation Protections and Revised Dangers in Discussions in Dispute Resolution 170–71 (2021).

[163] Sarah R. Cole, Craig A. McEwen, Nancy H. Rogers, James R. Coben & Peter N. Thompson, Mediation: Law, Policy, & Practice § 15:8 n.3 (2024).

[164] See Stephen J. Ware & Ariana Levinson, Principles of Arbitration § 43 (2d ed. 2023).

[165] Sarah R. Cole, Craig A. McEwen, Nancy H. Rogers, James R. Coben & Peter N. Thompson, Mediation: Law, Policy, & Practice § 4:1 (2024).

affecting commerce to settle such disputes through conciliation and mediation."[166] Its involvement is usually in *transactional* mediation, specifically the formation of a new collective bargaining agreement.[167] The National Mediation Board plays a similar role in the airline and railroad industries.[168] At the state level, under California's Agricultural Labor Relations Act,

> In certain cases in which an employer and a labor union have failed to reach a first contract, either party may invoke MMC [mandatory mediation and conciliation], which involves a mediation process before a neutral mediator. If the parties do not reach an agreement on all terms through mediation, the mediator resolves the disputed terms and submits a proposed contract to the [California Agricultural Labor Relations] Board, which can then impose that contract on the parties.[169]

The FMCS is also sometimes involved in *dispute* mediation, that is, the resolution of grievances under an existing collective bargaining agreement.[170] Grievances are also mediated by private-sector mediators, and some collective-bargaining agreements provide for disputes to be mediated.[171]

Disputes between employers and employees not represented by a labor union are also mediated.[172] While much employment mediation is conducted by private mediators, the U.S. Equal Employment Opportunity Commission mediates about 10,000 cases

---

166 29 U.S.C. § 173(a).

167 Federal Mediation and Conciliation Services Frequently Asked Questions https://www.fmcs.gov/resources/faqs/#cbm-faqs (last visited June 9, 2025) ("Under the Labor-Management Relations Act of 1947, FMCS provides free mediation services in contract negotiation disputes between employers and their unionized employees").

168 National Mediation Board, Mediation Overview & FAQ, https://nmb.gov/NMB_Application/index.php/meditation-overview-faq/.

169 Gerawan Farming, Inc. v. Agric. Lab. Rels. Bd., 3 Cal. 5th 1118, 1130, 405 P.3d 1087, 1089 (2017).

170 The FMCS may also provide its services for grievance disputes, but "only as a last resort and in exceptional cases." 29 U.S.C. § 173(d). Parties are obligated to "participate fully and promptly" in the sessions called by the FMCS. Id. § 174(a)(3).

171 Maldonado v. SecTek, Inc., No. CV 19-693, 2019 WL 3759451, at *2 (E.D. Pa. Aug. 8, 2019) ("Article 12 of the CBA, entitled 'Grievance Mediation and Arbitration Procedure,' sets forth a multi-step grievance procedure, the last step of which is binding arbitration").

172 See generally Laura J. Cooper, Dennis R. Nolan & Richard A. Bales, ADR in the Workplace, 705–59 (2d ed. 2005).

per year.[173] State departments of labor may have mediators assigned to workers compensation claims.[174]

## § 2.19 Community, Civil Rights, and Housing

Before the 1960s, mediation in the U.S. "was a process used almost exclusively in the labor-management sector."[175] But during the 1960s and 1970s, the U.S. Department of Justice's Community Relations Service (CRS) "initiated a mediation program for civil rights disputes. In the ensuing years, Congress funded a CRS staff that mediated hundreds of prison, school, police-community, and other civil rights conflicts."[176] In recent years, "high numbers of police-related conflicts continue to consume CRS's resources."[177] These can be beyond the typical. For instance, after 9/11, CRS worked with "the nation's Arab, Muslim, and Sikh communities"[178] and law enforcement on complaints about law enforcement profiling and harassing individuals or failing to follow up on alleged hate crime incidents.[179]

Much as CRS began in the 1960s and 1970s, during the same era, government and private money began funding "community mediation centers" or "neighborhood justice centers" around the country. Disputes came to these centers largely through referrals by prosecutors, police, and the courts.[180] These centers—in which parties are rarely accompanied by lawyers—originally mediated the

---

173 U.S. Equal Employment Opportunity Commission, EEOC Mediation Statistics FY 1999 through FY 2020, https://www.eeoc.gov/eeoc-mediation-statistics-fy-1999-through-fy-2020.

174 For example, the Kansas Department of Labor Division of Workers Compensation "promotes and encourages mediation by offering professional services at no cost to the parties." https://www.dol.ks.gov/workers-compensation/mediation-and-judicial-services.

175 Robert A. Baruch Bush, Staying in Orbit, or Breaking Free: The Relationship of Mediation to the Courts over Four Decades, 84 N.D. L. Rev. 705, 709 (2008).

176 Sarah R. Cole, Craig A. McEwen, Nancy H. Rogers, James R. Coben & Peter N. Thompson, Mediation: Law, Policy, & Practice § 4:1 (2024). See also Bertram Levine & Grande Lum, America's Peacemakers: The Community Relations Service and Civil Rights (2020).

177 Demarquin Johnson, Conscious Neutrality for the U.S. Department of Justice Community Relations Service, 21 Berkeley J. Afr.-Am. L. & Pol'y 42, 43 (2020). See also Russel K. Osgood, Prevention and Remediation of Police Excessive Force and Similar Complaints, 66 Wash. U. J.L. & Policy 107, 119 (2021) ("The Community Relations Service of the U.S. Department of Justice has issued a 'Conciliation Handbook' to help communities experiencing conflict over claims of excessive force.").

178 See Grande Lum, The Community Relations Service's Work in Preventing and Responding to Unfounded Racially and Religiously Motivated Violence After 9/11, 5 Tex. A&M J. Prop. L. 139, 141–45 (2019).

179 Id.

180 Leonard L. Riskin, Mediation and Lawyers, 43 Ohio St .L.J. 29, 31–32 (1982).

sorts of disputes commonly found among neighbors, such as landlord-tenant, nuisance, small claims, and misdemeanors.

However, community mediation often extends beyond two-party disputes to disputes involving much of an entire community, such as school segregation,[181] or relationships with the police. "A Rochester, New York community mediation program, for example, has worked with police, other local officials, and leaders within the broader community to plan ahead of civil unrest."[182] Community mediation centers also serve "in the aftermath of a divisive incident. For example, mediation and restorative circles seem to help in some instances to help families and neighbors deal with issues that remain in the aftermath of police shootings."[183] The U.S. Department of Justice included in consent decrees with Baltimore, Maryland, and Ferguson, Missouri, a requirement of community mediation center involvement to mediate citizen complaints against the police.[184]

Some community mediation centers "concentrate special attention on parent-child or school-student conflicts, or the problems of the elderly."[185] These centers may offer peer mediation training in schools and restorative justice programs for juveniles diverted from the court system.

Some states fund community mediation. For instance, Nebraska funded

> six independent nonprofit community mediation centers that undergo an annual review to maintain their approval status through the [State's] Office of Dispute Resolution. . . . Nebraska law mandates access to mediation for everyone in the state, regardless of their ability to pay. The fees for most mediation clients are determined on a

---

181 Tracy Tully, Facing Entrenched School Segregation, New Jersey Tries Something New, N.Y. Times (Sept. 6, 2024), https://www.nytimes.com/2024/09/06/nyregion/new-jersey-schools-segregation.html?te=1&nl=today%27s-headlines&emc=edit_th_20240907 (2018 lawsuit alleging public schools in New Jersey were segregated in violation of the state Constitution led to mediation over many months between the state and the plaintiffs. "The mediator leading the talks, Barry T. Albin, a retired New Jersey Supreme Court justice, has ordered lawyers, plaintiffs and representatives from the attorney general's office and the State Department of Education to keep the details of the negotiations secret.")

182 Id.

183 Id.

184 Brittain McClurg, Reducing the Impact of Racial Discrimination in Policing, 2019 J. Disp. Resol. 201, 212 (2019).

185 Sarah R. Cole, Craig A. McEwen, Nancy H. Rogers, James R. Coben, Peter N. Thompson, 1 Mediation: Law, Policy and Practice § 15:9 (2024) ("these centers mediate disputes involving such issues as assaults, threats, and insults by people in continuing relationships such as neighbors, lovers, relatives, or friends; small claims cases; landlord-tenant conflicts; stalking; and neighborhood noise, pet, boundary, or yard appearance disputes.")

> sliding fee scale for those willing to provide proof of income. . . . Nearly all of the clients of Nebraska's community mediation centers are eligible for reduced fee services due to their income.[186]

The history is somewhat similar in Australia, where by 2001 "government-sponsored mediation centres located throughout Australia" "offer[ed] mediation services either free of charge or for a very low cost," typically for "family, neighbourhood, small business or consumer disputes."[187]

Housing mediation can come in a variety of forms depending on the nature of the housing. Foreclosing on the "family farm" was frequent enough in the 1980s that some people referred to it as a farm crisis, and "states were determined to take action to assist their farmers. In 1985 and 1986, North Dakota, Minnesota, and Iowa were early trailblazers in using mediation as a tool to assist farmers and lenders to find solutions to the crisis."[188] Some of these states require creditors to mediate before pursuing foreclosure.[189] This approach expanded to home foreclosure more generally during the Great Recession of 2008–09, when nearly half the states tried some form of foreclosure mediation or settlement conference program.[190]

> The design and outcomes of foreclosure mediation programs were shaped by the federal government's involvement in the mortgage foreclosure crisis, which rewarded mortgage servicers for reducing or mitigating foreclosure sales. . . . In many jurisdictions mediation, often buttressed by services provided by housing counselors, legal services providers, or both, served as the site for "loan modification conferences" in which loan servicers and

---

186 Kristen M. Blankley & Kelly Riley, Providing Access to Mediation for Rural Participants, 29 Dis. Res. Mag. 24, 25 (September 2023).

187 Nadja Alexander, What's Law Got To Do With It? Mapping Modern Mediation Movements in Civil and Common Law Jurisdictions, 13 Bond. L. Rev. 1, 8 (2001).

188 John Schmitz, Don't Bet the Farm in Litigation Before Considering Mediation: The Case for Agriculture Mediation Program Implementation, 23 Cardozo J. Conflict Resol. 687, 694 (2022).

189 Id. at 708 (2022) ("In states where mediation is mandated for specific disputes, one of the parties may be significantly less committed to finding a workable solution. In those cases, the creditor is likely participating out of fear of sanction or coercion rather than any genuine interest in putting forth a good faith effort to resolving the dispute. In those situations, creditors may view mediation as a simple delay in the foreclosure process rather than a potential alternative.")

190 Alan M. White, Foreclosure Diversion and Mediation in the States, 33 Ga. St. U. L. Rev. 411, 416 (2017).

mortgagors spoke directly and committed to possible alternatives to foreclosure.[191]

Mandatory foreclosure mediation is designed to reduce or delay foreclosures by "impos[ing] burdens on the ability of a mortgagee to enforce their contractual right," which results in "delays in the commencement of an action."[192] Mandatory mediation of foreclosure cases in Maine's state courts led creditor plaintiffs to shift such cases from state courts to federal courts located in Maine. A federal court in Maine presented with such a case detected "the strong scent of forum-shopping," and granted the defendant's motion refer the case to Maine's foreclosure mediation program.[193]

During the Covid pandemic of 2020–21, an expansion of eviction mediation occurred. Jurisdictions from Philadelphia to Hawaii began requiring lessors to mediate before pursuing eviction.[194] While mandating eviction mediation, like mandating foreclosure mediation, aims to keep people from losing their homes, these mandates may often just delay the inevitable because "most tenants facing eviction need rent money, not lawyers."[195]

## § 2.20 Business & Commercial

Mediation of disputes among businesses has grown over the last several decades. The variety of business contexts generating these disputes is endless: sales of goods and services, sales and leases of real estate,[196] real estate development and construction,[197] licenses

---

[191] Deanna Pantín Parrish, Just Diversion: Designing Eviction Mediation to Address Incentives and Inequities, 68 Wash. U. J.L. & Pol'y 63, 67–68 (2022).

[192] MLF3 Jagger v. Kempton, 50 N.Y.S. 3d 247, 249–250 (N.Y. Sup. Ct. 2017). (referring to NY statute requiring courts to "hold a mandatory conference . . . for the purpose of holding settlement discussions").

[193] HSBC Bank USA, Nat'l Ass'n as Tr. for Registered Holders of Ace Sec. Corp. Home Equity Loan Tr., Series 2006-NC3, Asset Backed Pass-Through Certificates v. Lombardo, No. 2:19-CV-00291-NT, 2020 WL 6136213, at *10–11 (D. Me. Oct. 19, 2020).

[194] Deanna Pantín Parrish, Just Diversion: Designing Eviction Mediation to Address Incentives and Inequities, 68 Wash. U. J.L. & Pol'y 63, 79–81 (2022).

[195] Juliet M. Brodie & Larisa G. Bowman, Lawyers Aren't Rent, 75 Stan. L. Rev. 132, 134 (2023).

[196] Jerry M. Slusky, Mediating the Commercial Lease Dispute (with Form) Mediation Gives the Parties What They Really Want-Control over the Dispute Resolution Process, Prac. Real Est. Law., July 2008, at 9, 12 ("Mediation has been successful in commercial real estate disputes for several reasons. Due to the nature of the real estate market, land or rental space may not have the same value at the end of litigation as it did when the dispute arose. The value of the parties' interest may be damaged by injunctions, restraining orders, or other restrictions imposed by the courts. Depending on the characteristics of the deal, the nature of the real estate, and the uses of the property, a variety of disputes can arise from a commercial property lease transaction").

[197] Dean Thomson, Julia Douglass, Comparing Theory and Practice: Survey Results of What Attorneys and Arbitrators Want in Construction Mediation and Arbitration, Constr. Law., 2023, at 27 ("All standard construction industry contract

of technology and intellectual property,[198] franchising,[199] financing, default, and even corporate reorganization bankruptcies.[200]

Mediation is used in business disputes from small family businesses[201] to large, complex matters involving multinational corporations. A leader regarding large companies is CPR, the International Institute for Conflict Prevention & Resolution. Prominent companies like Mastercard, Microsoft, Pepsi, and Pfizer have signed its pledge:

> Our company pledges to commit its resources to manage and resolve disputes through negotiation, mediation and other ADR processes when appropriate, with a view to establishing and practicing global, sustainable dispute management and resolution processes.[202]

Corporate general counsels' charge to reduce legal expenses contributed bigly to the growth of mediation in the U.S., and liability insurers play a role as well.[203] Mediation of cross-border commercial disputes implicates law discussed in Section 2.16(c).

---

forms require mediation of disputes as a condition precedent to proceeding toward binding dispute resolution"); Steven C. Bennett, Construction Mediation: Best Practices for Success, Prac. Real Est. Law., May 2018, at 3, 17 ("Mediation may be especially appropriate in the kind of multi-party, complex disputes that often arise out of construction projects, where no other mechanism can so readily bring constituents into a single forum").

198 Theodore K. Cheng, Considering Arbitration or Mediation for Licensing Disputes, Fed. Law., May/June 2019, at 16, 17 ("Licensing disputes have long been resolved competently, cost-effectively, and expeditiously by arbitrators and mediators"). The Silicon Valley Arbitration & Mediation Center provides a "List of the World's Leading Technology Neutrals" of "exceptionally qualified arbitrators and mediators known globally for their experience and skill in crafting business-practical legal solutions in the technology sector." https://svamc.org/tech-list/.

199 Timothy J. Bryant, Matthew E. Lane, Companion Dispute Resolution: Three-Dimensional Thinking and the Effective Use of Mediation with Traditional Litigation of Franchise Disputes, 33 Franchise L.J. 261 (2013).

200 Laura N. Coordes, 41 Emory Bankr. Dev. J. 153, 163 (2025) (contrasting "the traditional use of bankruptcy mediation" for "discrete, two-party disputes" "such as those involving claims, avoidance actions, or adversary proceedings," with newer and more controversial use of bankruptcy mediation as "a multiparty undertaking involving claimants from all levels of a debtor's capital structure, with the ambitious goal of resolving the entire case through a consensual plan of reorganization."); Edward L. Schnitzer, Bankruptcy Mediation, 28 No. 3 J. Bankr. L. & Prac. Art. 6 (2019) ("Mediation has become a mainstay in bankruptcies, particularly in New York and Delaware, and particularly for plan disputes, mass tort claim objections and adversary proceedings.")

201 See, e.g., Barry Y. Weiner, Mediation and the Business Divorce Resolving Disputes When the Business Relationship Ends, Bus. L. Today, January/February 2008, at 45 (detailing three cases); Lawrence I. Drath, Business Mediation: All in the Family, Disp. Resol. J., Oct. 1996, at 51 (a fourth case).

202 CPR, 21st Century Pledge, https://www.cpradr.org/21st-century-pledge.

203 Jeff Trueman, Mediation in the World of Commercial Dispute Litigation: An Inside Look at the Challenges for Counsel, Mediators, and Insurance Claims

Some business and commercial contracts include "two-step" ADR clauses, providing that the parties shall mediate any dispute that may arise and, if mediation fails to result in a settlement, the parties shall arbitrate the dispute. For example, the dispute resolution clause in a sale of ferric sulfate included the following:

> In the event that a dispute cannot be settled between the parties, the matter shall be mediated within fifteen (15) days after receipt of notice by either party that the other party requests the mediation of a dispute pursuant to this paragraph. If the parties are unable to select a mediator, the Florida Mediation Group shall select a mediator. The parties agree to use their best efforts to mediate a dispute.
>
> In the event that the dispute cannot be settled through mediation, the parties shall submit the matter to arbitration within ten (10) days after receipt of notice by either party. The arbitration shall be conducted in accordance with the Commercial Arbitration Rules of the American Arbitration Association then in effect. The parties shall each select an arbitrator and the two arbitrators thus selected shall select a third arbitrator. These three arbitrators shall constitute the arbitration panel. It is understood that a judgment or award rendered, which may include an award of damages, may be entered in any court having jurisdiction thereof.[204]

## § 2.21 Public Law

### *(a) Generally*

Much law is made, not by legislatures or courts, but by administrative agencies such as the Environmental Protection Agency and the Consumer Financial Protection Bureau. Negotiated rulemaking ("reg-neg") is a form of *transactional mediation*[205] among

---

Professionals, 63 Wash. U. J.L. & Pol'y 207 (2020) ("Insurance claims professionals and other representatives who manage litigation risk for large institutions are concerned with their insureds' exposure to liability").

[204] Kemiron Atl., Inc. v. Aguakem Int'l, Inc., 290 F.3d 1287, 1289 (11th Cir. 2002). See, also Molton, Allen & Williams, LLC v. Cont'l Cas. Ins. Co., No. 09-V-6924, 2010 WL 780353, at *1 (N.D. Ill. Mar. 3, 2010) ("The Agreement contains a mandatory arbitration clause which states: 'In the event of any dispute arising out of or relating to this agreement which cannot be resolved by negotiation, the parties shall endeavor to settle the dispute by non-binding mediation. . . . Any dispute which has not been resolved by mediation within 60 days of the demand for such procedure shall be resolved by final and binding arbitration under the Commercial Arbitration Rules of the American Arbitration Association.") International examples are cited in Anna Howard, EU Cross-Border Commercial Mediation § 6.03[B] (2021).

[205] See § 2.3.

the parties likely to be affected by a regulation. Instead of transactional mediation to form a private contract, the deal formed by the parties in reg-neg is a government regulation. Accordingly, the mediation sessions are open to the public. "In a reg-neg setting, the governmental agency invites stakeholders and their representatives to the bargaining table to help draft a rule which might impact the parties. Usually, a third-party facilitator is involved, deploying mediation-style techniques, to produce the rule by consensus."[206] Reg-neg is encouraged by statutes, and many agencies have used it.[207]

Administrative agencies also use mediation to resolve disputes. According to a 2021 report,[208] at least 25 federal agencies use mediation, including:

- the Environmental Protection Agency,
- the Nuclear Regulatory Commission,
- the International Trade Commission,
- the Department of Education,
- three agencies of the Department of Agriculture,
- the Department of the Interior (DOI),
- the Internal Revenue Service (IRS),
- Health and Human Services, the Federal Energy Regulatory Commission (FERC),
- the Department of Justice Community Relations Service,
- the Department of Transportation, the Department of Commerce,
- the Pension Benefit Guaranty Corporation,
- the National Mediation Board (NMB),

---

[206] The Administrative Conference Commissions: A Deep Dive into Executive Branch ADR, 40 Alternatives to High Cost Litig. 31, 32 (2022).

[207] Peter H. Schuck & Steven Kochevar, Reg Neg Redux: The Career of A Procedural Reform, 15 Theoretical Inquiries L. 417, 423 (2014) ("By 1996, the federal government appeared to fully support reg neg, and Congress permanently reauthorized the Negotiated Rulemaking Act (NRA). The Act has been codified within the Administrative Procedure Act (APA), firmly ensconcing reg neg in the super-statute at the heart of American administrative law."); Jeffrey S. Lubbers, Achieving Policymaking Consensus: The (Unfortunate) Waning of Negotiated Rulemaking, 49 S. Tex. L. Rev. 987, 1007 (2008) (listing statutes).

[208] Kristen Blankley, Kathleen Claussen & Judith Starr, Alternative Dispute Resolution in Agency Administrative Programs 19–20 (December 17, 2021).

- the Federal Mediation and Conciliation Service,
- the Federal Maritime Commission,
- the Office of Special Counsel (OSC),
- the National Labor Relations Board,
- the National Archives and Records Administration,
- the National Center, the Federal Labor Relations Authority,
- the Federal Communications Commission,
- the Federal Election Commission, and
- the Equal Employment Opportunity Commission (EEOC).

### *(b) Environmental*

Several states have enacted statutes designed to encourage mediation of environmental disputes.[209] At the federal level, the Environmental Protection Agency uses mediation in its enforcement actions.[210] Such disputes generally involve multiple parties: polluters, adjacent residents, public-interest groups, and federal, state, and local agencies. The mediator may facilitate both multilateral (many parties) and bilateral (two parties) negotiations.[211]

Similarly, local government agencies have long "relied on mediators to manage contentious adjudicative decisions such as the siting of" a housing development, factory, or waste treatment facility.[212] Increasingly, state and federal courts are mandating mediation of environmental insurance coverage disputes.[213]

---

209 Lauran M. Sturm, Elizabeth A. Hurst, Alternative Dispute Resolution in EPA and State Permit Appeals, Nat. Resources & Env't, Summer 2020, at 23, 25.

210 In addition, EPA may partner with other agencies. Sara A. Colangelo, Forging Complete Justice: Equitable Relief in Environmental Enforcement, 46 Harv. Envtl. L. Rev. 315, 359 (2022) ("For example, in Obama-era settlements, EPA and the DOJ coordinated with DOJ's Community Relations Service and local offices, to assist with community outreach regarding violations and potential remedies, including restorative relief like mitigation and SEPs").

211 See, e.g., Lawrence Susskind, Environmental Mediation and the Accountability Problem, 6 Vt. L. Rev. 1 (1981). Several case studies of multi-party environmental disputes are discussed in ABA Env't Energy, & Resources L.: Year In Rev. Ch. 24 (2015).

212 Sean F. Nolon, Second Best Practices?: Addressing Mediation's Definitional Problems in Environmental Siting Disputes, 49 Idaho L. Rev. 69, 70 (2012).

213 Jay E. Grenig, 1 Alt. Disp. Resol. § 19:22 (4th ed. 2022).

### *(c) Education*

Schools at all levels mediate all sorts of disputes among students that do not involve actual or potential legal claims and thus are not *settlement mediation*, defined in Section 2.3 as mediation of disputes likely to involve lawyers because they are in binding adjudication or likely to go to binding adjudication if mediation fails to reach a settlement. Some of this school-related non-settlement mediation is discussed in Section 2.19.

In addition, schools engage in lots of settlement mediation. The Individuals with Disabilities Education Act gives parents the right to request, and school districts the duty to provide, mediation of disputes about whether the school is complying with that law.[214] Department of Education regulations have taken a variety of positions over the years on mediation of sexual assault and harassment allegations within higher education.[215]

## § 2.22 Personal Injury

Many of the disputes discussed above—family (§ 2.17), labor and employment (§ 2.18), community, civil rights and housing (§ 2.19), business and commercial (§ 2.20), environmental and education (§ 2.21)—are widely considered well-suited to mediation, especially the *problem-solving* approach, because they tend to be disputes between *repeat players*—parties who want or expect their relationships to continue after the dispute is resolved. Disputes between repeat players are more likely than disputes between *one-shotters* to involve multiple issues; they are less likely to be simple disputes about the amount of money one party will pay the other. Multiple issues are crucial to creating opportunities for *positive-sum* negotiation (§ 1.10) and thus making the dispute more amenable to the *problem-solving* approach used by so many mediators (§ 2.7).

In contrast, other disputes involve one-shot parties, that is, parties who do not want or expect their relationship to continue after the dispute is resolved. A classic example of these *one-shot* parties is a personal injury claim arising out of an automobile accident.[216] The plaintiff hopes and expects to have no further interaction with the defendant or the defendant's insurance company once the dispute is resolved and that feeling is likely mutual. These one-shot disputes

---

214 20 U.S.C. § 1415(e).

215 Sarah R. Cole, Craig A. McEwen, Nancy H. Rogers, James R. Coben, Peter N. Thompson, 1 Mediation: Law, Policy and Practice § 15:6 (2024).

216 Janis Sue Porter, Mediation of Personal Injury Cases; Mediation Can Settle Most Personal Injury Cases, Or. St. B. Bull., FEB-MAR 1992, at 34 ("Personal injury cases involve a different set of dynamics than other kinds of mediation cases. There is no long-term relationship which needs to be maintained").

are often *zero-sum* (§ 1.9) situations in which the only issue to be resolved is the amount of money one party will pay the other.[217] Consequently, the parties to one-shot, zero-sum disputes are less likely to benefit from a problem-solving mediator than from a *settlement-oriented* mediator, especially an *evaluative* one (§§ 2.11, 2.13). Accordingly, personal injury lawyers tend to discuss mediation with a focus on evaluating the parties' positions:

> Mediation can be a productive and meaningful process when the parties prepare their proofs of claims and defenses and argue those issues at mediation as they would at trial. Positions taken should be supported by admissible evidence. The strengths and weaknesses of each party's proof will be discussed during individual caucuses.[218]

This 1992 description of personal injury mediation remains representative today:

> If the case settles in mediation, which it does 85 percent to 90 percent of the time, mediation can completely resolve the matter. The claimant walks away with a check and the insurance company walks away with a claim release.
>
> Personal injury cases most appropriate for mediation are ones in which the insurance company admits total or partial liability for the accident and the main question is the extent of damages. If the insurance company denies liability for the claim, we generally do not recommend mediation because there is nothing to negotiate. The insurance company won't pay any money and the claimant thinks it should.
>
> The majority of personal injury cases we mediate involve automobile accidents.[219]

---

[217] Anne MacArthur, Effective Advocacy at Mediation of Personal Injury Cases, Wis. Law., June 2025, at 22, 24 ("In mediating a personal injury lawsuit, the predominant interest is financial: the plaintiff wants the most the insurer will pay, while the insurer wants to pay the lowest amount the plaintiff will accept").

[218] Anne MacArthur, Effective Advocacy at Mediation of Personal Injury Cases, Wis. Law., June 2025, at 22, 25.

[219] Janis Sue Porter, Mediation of Personal Injury Cases; Mediation Can Settle Most Personal Injury Cases, Or. St. B. Bull., FEB-MAR 1992, at 34.

Courts' encouragement of mediation has contributed to some increase in mediation of personal injury and other run-of-the-mill civil cases.[220]

## § 2.23 Criminal Cases

Plea-bargaining is to criminal litigation what settlement negotiation is to civil litigation—the way most cases in the U.S. are resolved (§ 1.44). But the involvement of mediators to facilitate plea bargaining has grown more slowly than the involvement of mediators to facilitate civil settlement negotiation. And much of the plea mediation that has developed—although somewhat under the radar—is with the judge as "mediator" in settlement conferences. Such plea "mediation" is discussed in Section 2.30(f)(2).

Leaving aside judges mediating plea agreements, the mediation that occurs in criminal cases generally departs from the plea-bargaining norm of the defendant (typically represented by a lawyer) negotiating with the charging government (represented by the prosecutor). Instead, mediation of criminal cases is the defendant negotiating with the complainant or victim. This is unusual because crimes have long been treated by the law as offenses against the state or society, rather than just offenses against the victim, so prosecutors, not complainants, have the authority to determine whether a prosecution will proceed. Empowering the complainant, as some criminal mediation does, is an exception to the government-dominated approach of most criminal law. "Agreements to stifle prosecution . . . are traditionally void as against public policy. The courts have treated agreements between a victim and the accused with suspicion."[221]

Where this policy has been overcome, courts and prosecutors can refer at least some criminal cases to mediation before trial, and even before the prosecutor files charges. Agreements reached in such mediation typically have the effect of removing the threat of prosecution in exchange for the payment of restitution to the complainant.[222] While restitution can encompass a broad variety of

---

220 See, e.g., Robert B. Moberly, Ethical Standards for Court-Appointed Mediators and Florida's Mandatory Mediation Experiment, 21 Fla. St. U.L. Rev. 701, 701–03 (1994).

221 Sarah R. Cole, Craig A. McEwen, Nancy H. Rogers, James R. Coben & Peter N. Thompson, Mediation: Law, Policy, & Practice § 15:5 (2024).

222 Nancy Hirshman, Mediating Misdemeanors: As Maryland Experience Shows, Pre-trial Mediation Can Mean Big Success in Small Cases, 7 Disp. Resol. Mag. 12, 13 (Fall 2000) ("subject to approval of the prosecutor . . ., the mediation agreement will be entered on the court docket in lieu of the case proceeding to trial. . . . The parties are responsible for verifying . . . that the assistant state's attorney has approved the agreement, disposed of the criminal charge and excused the parties."); Markus Durk

forms, such as performing community service, the most common form usually involves money.[223]

In contrast, other criminal mediation—often outside the U.S.—occurs "next to the court process and does not replace it."[224] In other words, an agreement made in mediation "will be added to the court file, and will contain all the details about how the offender/suspect is going to compensate the victim and/or how the relationship will be after the agreement is signed," but it remains "up to the court what to do with the offense."[225]

Mediation can occur after conviction. "One or more trained facilitators will conduct a facilitation either in joint session or sometimes by caucus involving the victim, the offender, and support persons."[226] Victim-offender mediation often proceeds in the spirit of *restorative justice*.[227]

> Instead of a punitive model that asks (1) what rules or laws were broken, (2) who broke them, and (3) how should they be punished, restorative practices asks (1) what is the harm caused and to whom, (2) what are the needs and obligations that have arisen, and (3) who has the obligation to address the needs, to repair the harm, and to restore relationships. From a restorative perspective, these questions "cannot be adequately answered without the involvement of those who have been most affected."[228]

Restorative justice ideally seeks to achieve the four Rs: "repair, restore, reconcile, and reintegrate the offenders and victims to each

---

Dubber, The Victim in American Penal Law: A Systematic Overview, 3 Buff. Crim. L. Rev. 3, 22 (1999).

[223] See, e.g., Larysa Simms, Criminal Mediation Is the BASF of the Criminal Justice System: Not Replacing Traditional Criminal Adjudication, Just Making It Better, 22 Ohio St. J. on Disp. Resol. 797, 802 (2007) ("The New Castle County criminal mediation program addresses misdemeanors and disputes that arrive in court with criminal charges which optimally should not result in criminal convictions. Mediation quickly addresses the disputes and often results in both offenders avoiding criminal convictions, and claimants receiving restitution according to mediated agreements.")

[224] Pascal Comvalius, Mediation in Criminal Cases 18 (2022).

[225] Id. at 18–19.

[226] Sarah R. Cole, Craig A. McEwen, Nancy H. Rogers, James R. Coben & Peter N. Thompson, Mediation: Law, Policy, & Practice § 15:5 (2024).

[227] Mark S. Umbreit et al., Restorative Justice in the Twenty-First Century: A Social Movement Full of Opportunities and Pitfalls, 89 Marq. L. Rev. 251 (2005). See also Thalia González, The Legalization of Restorative Justice: A Fifty-State Empirical Analysis, 2019 Utah L. Rev. 1027, 1049 (2019) ("presently forty-five states have codified the term 'restorative justice' into state law. Collectively, 'restorative justice' appears in a total of 229 statutes, court rules, and regulations").

[228] Marilyn Armour, Restorative Practices: Righting the Wrongs of Exclusionary School Discipline, 50 U. Rich. L. Rev. 999, 1018 (2016).

other and to their shared community."[229] "Restitution and apology, rather than incarceration, is a common remedy."[230] Many victim-offender programs focus on juvenile offenders.[231]

Agreements reached in victim-offender mediation may become a condition of probation (and thus effectively reduce or eliminate the offender's prison time) in exchange for the payment of restitution to the victim. If a promise to pay restitution is a condition of probation, then that promise can be enforced by the probation officer. Critics argue that "[a]llowing offenders to buy their way out of prison" undermines the public goals of criminal law such as retribution, incapacitation, deterrence, and rehabilitation.[232]

# E. REPRESENTING CLIENTS IN MEDIATION

## § 2.24 Whether to Mediate

You may find yourself representing a client in mediation even though your client never agreed to mediate. That is because some statutes require mediation of certain types of cases and, in many state and federal courts, judges have authority to order most types of civil cases into mediation (§ 2.30).[233] Leaving aside such *mandatory mediation*, the issue of whether to mediate arises in every dispute any of your clients has, as you can always suggest mediation.

For you and your client to decide whether mediation would be worthwhile, you will consider the particularities of the dispute. Mediation is not for a client whose interests can only be served by a court's verdict.[234] Some clients want, at nearly any cost, the public

---

[229] Carrie Menkel-Meadow, Restorative Justice: What Is It and Does It Work?, 3 Ann. Rev. L. & Soc. Sci. 161, 162 (2007). See also Lynn S. Branham, "Stealing Conflicts" No More?: The Gaps and Anti-Restorative Elements in States' Restorative-Justice Laws, 64 St. Louis U. L.J. 145, 146 (2020) ("Proponents of restorative justice have criticized criminal-justice systems, as currently devised, for their failure to afford a person harmed by a crime and the person who inflicted that harm the opportunity to engage in a dialogue, along with others, about how the crime harmed the victim and what the person who caused that harm could do to best remedy or mitigate it. This failure leaves the harm ensuing from a crime unrepaired and the relationships fractured by it never mended. This harm can take many forms, including the shackling of the victim, the person who harmed the victim, and both of their families with hurt, fear, or shame for which conventional processing of a criminal case typically affords no constructive outlet.").

[230] Sarah R. Cole, Craig A. McEwen, Nancy H. Rogers, James R. Coben & Peter N. Thompson, Mediation: Law, Policy, & Practice § 15:5 (2024).

[231] Id.

[232] Jennifer Gerarda Brown, The Use of Mediation to Resolve Criminal Cases: A Procedural Critique, 43 Emory L.J. 1247, 1296–1301 (1994).

[233] See also Sarah R. Cole, Craig A. McEwen, Nancy H. Rogers, James R. Coben & Peter N. Thompson, Mediation: Law, Policy, & Practice § 9:2 (2024).

[234] Sarah R. Cole, Craig A. McEwen, Nancy H. Rogers, James R. Coben & Peter N. Thompson, Mediation: Law, Policy, & Practice § 5:10 (2024) ("mediation is contraindicated" when a party has a "need for precedent," or "public vindication").

vindication that comes from a favorable verdict, to "make law" with a favorable precedent, or to develop reputations for being fierce litigators to intimidate future adversaries (§§ 1.35, 1.39). But most clients who want these things will give them up for a price, in the form of money or something else they want. So, if settlement is truly out of the question for your client, then mediation, like negotiation, is pointless. But it is the rare client who will flatly refuse any settlement offer, no matter how good and no matter when offered. For all but these rare clients, mediation is worth considering simply because a settlement might be in your client's interests.

Once you and your client have decided to consider the possibility of settlement, how do you decide between negotiating with the other side and mediating with them? Mediation has advantages over negotiation in all kinds of disputes, positive-sum and zero-sum. Some cases present opportunities for *positive-sum* negotiation, that is, for finding those settlement terms that are better for both parties than other settlement terms. Such cases tend to involve issues other than, or in addition to, money and to involve *repeat* parties who expect or want to continue their relationship after the case is resolved (§§ 1.09–1.10). Positive-sum opportunities may go unexploited in negotiation because negotiators often have strong incentives not to reveal their interests and priorities (§ 1.26). Mediation, especially with a *problem-solving* mediator, can alter these incentives to facilitate positive-sum negotiation (§ 2.12). In short, mediation can expand a pie that negotiation would only have divided.

In zero-sum cases, such as a case about nothing other than how much money Defendant will pay Plaintiff, dividing the pie is the only issue (§§ 1.09–1.10(a)). In these cases, negotiators often fail to discover whether a *settlement zone* exists and, even if they discover that it does, they still often fail to reach a settlement (§ 1.39). A *settlement-oriented* mediation (§ 2.6) would likely be better than negotiation in quickly identifying whether a settlement zone exists, and narrowing differences between the parties' positions, that is, bringing them closer to agreement (§§ 2.11, 2.13).

So, mediation has advantages over negotiation in all cases, positive-sum and zero-sum. But the benefits of mediation should be weighed against the costs.

Mediation is likely to have costs not present in negotiation. For example, the cost of paying the mediator often must be borne by the parties. Another cost is time, both the lawyer's and the client's, if they will both be participating in mediation. The relevant time includes not just the mediation session(s), but also preparation for mediation, which can be much more elaborate than preparation for negotiation. Preparing for mediation, if done thoroughly, can be quite time-consuming and, if not done thoroughly, can make mediation risky (§ 2.25).

Many lawyers who handle large numbers of small cases—such as auto accidents or slip-and-fall cases—spend little time negotiating settlements. Such so-called "settlement mills" are repeat players on both the plaintiff and (typically insurance company) defendant sides, so settlement values are predictable and lawyers tend to settle cases quickly for formulaic "going rates" (§ 1.39(f)). This "assembly line" vibe is even greater for lawyers pursuing evictions, unpaid credit card bills, and the like against defendants who cannot afford lawyers (§ 1.37(b)). So, any negotiation in these circumstances is likely to be even more perfunctory. Where the assembly-line plaintiff can easily win a default judgment, or when negotiating a settlement takes just an hour or two of the lawyer's time, spending even a few hours and a thousand dollars on mediation may be excessive. Unless the mediator's settlement rate is near 100 percent, she is not cost-effective. Outside of these small cases, however, the money and time for a single mediation session are relatively minor costs.

A bigger cost can be the risk that suggesting mediation, or participating in it, will hurt one's position against the other side.[235] Some lawyers worry that suggesting mediation to the other side is a sign of weakness that an adversarial/competitive counterpart will exploit.[236] Participating in mediation also presents—potentially the biggest cost—a risk that you or your client will reveal sensitive information to the mediator that, for whatever reason, does not remain confidential (§ 2.28).

If you and your client decide to pursue mediation, when would you like it to occur? Thoughtful commentators "identify four distinct opportunities, each with benefits and risks:

- before a legal action is filed,
- after preliminary discovery,
- 'in the shadow' of a significant ruling, and

[235] Id. (the possible costs of mediation "may include strategic damage incurred if the matter is later tried. In many jurisdictions, statements from the mediation will sometimes be admissible against the parties at trial. Even if confidentiality laws preclude trial use, disclosure may harm the case strategically by, for example, helping an adversary to develop a subsequent well-targeted discovery plan").

[236] Id. § 13:2 ("Absent compulsory mediation, a decision by lawyer and client to use the process takes them only halfway; opposing parties must also agree to participate. Reluctant parties might have a variety of reasons for declining participation, including fear of appearing weak"). This is an argument for judges ordering, or at least encouraging, mediation. If the idea comes from the judge, and both sides say they are mediating just to stay in the judge's good graces, then neither side looks weak. See Jeffrey Z. Rubin & Bert R. Brown, The Social Psychology of Bargaining and Negotiation 47, 58 (1975).

- shortly before trial."[237]

Of course, the earlier mediation occurs, the more time, money, and aggravation it will save if it produces a settlement. But one or more of the parties (or, more likely, their lawyers) may believe some discovery and pre-trial rulings from the court are needed to develop the case enough for each side to value it accurately, and thus to assess whether particular settlement terms are in their interest compared to continued litigation (§ 1.35(d)).[238]

## § 2.25 Preparing for Mediation

As a lawyer preparing to represent a client in mediation, you should do everything you would do to prepare for negotiation (§§ 1.29–1.33), and more. The "more" begins with learning about the mediator. You will want to learn about the mediator's background and qualifications, of course. What is her expertise regarding the subject matter of this dispute? Such expertise is very important for an accurate *evaluation* (§ 2.13) and will be helpful even in a non-evaluative mediation.[239] In addition, you will want to learn the mediator's usual approach to mediation.[240] Is she focused just on reaching settlement or does she emphasize positive-sum opportunities or strengthening the parties' dispute-resolution skills (§§ 2.5–2.8)? Does she evaluate (§ 2.13)? Will she keep all communications in the strictest confidence?[241] You can gather information on all this by asking the mediator and by asking parties and lawyers who have previously participated in mediations with this mediator.

You and your client will probably have a role in selecting the mediator. Voluntary mediation will not occur unless you agree (on behalf of your client) to use a particular mediator. And even in mandatory mediation, a common procedure is for you and the other side to agree on a mediator; so only if you cannot reach an agreement will the court appoint one for you (§ 2.27(c)(1)). Before selecting a

---

237 Sarah R. Cole, Craig A. McEwen, Nancy H. Rogers, James R. Coben & Peter N. Thompson, Mediation: Law, Policy, & Practice § 5:11 (2024) (citing Jay Folberg et al., Resolving Disputes: Theory, Practice, and Law 312–14 (2005)).

238 See, e.g., ABA Section on Dispute Resolution, Task Force on Improving Mediation Quality, Final Report 12 (2006–2008) (noting that 81% of users and 77% of mediators believed that the preferred time for mediation is generally after "critical" discovery is completed, but before full completion of discovery).

239 Joseph B. Stulberg, Facilitative Versus Evaluative Mediator Orientations: Piercing the "Grid" Lock, 24 Fla. St. U.L. Rev. 985, 996–97 (1997).

240 See, e.g., Layn R. Phillips, Laying Foundation for Successful Mediation: Questions Neutrals and Parties Need to Ask, 13 Alternatives to the High Cost of Litig. 132 (1995).

241 Answering this question may require research about the law as well as about the mediator. Even a mediator who wants to keep confidences may be compelled by subpoena to reveal them. See § 2.28.

mediator, you will want to learn about the candidates. You would like to learn, with respect to each candidate, all the information discussed in the previous paragraph. On the other hand, you may find that it costs too much time and money to gather so much information.

Preparing for mediation has an added dimension if your client will be participating in the mediation.[242] If you expect an *evaluative* (§ 2.13) mediator, or one who may reveal confidences, then you might prepare your client for mediation as you would prepare your client for his deposition. In this mode, you will caution your client not to depart from his prepared script.[243] If he wants to say anything not on the script, he should call for a break in which he will consult with you, his lawyer, privately. Preparation of your client is especially important if the mediator is likely to ask to meet with the parties without lawyers present. If you think your client would be disadvantaged in such a forum, you can refuse the mediator's request to leave the room.[244]

On the other hand, if you plan to take a *problem-solving* approach, your discussions with your client would focus on his interests and priorities (§§ 1.22–1.26). You will encourage him to speak freely during the mediation so the mediator can identify positive-sum opportunities.

## § 2.26 During Mediation

How you best represent your client during mediation will depend on the specifics of the case and the participants. And no matter how well you prepare for mediation, you will need to adapt in the moment. Mediation is facilitated negotiation and, as with any negotiation, you should think jazz improv. As Section 1.32 noted, because "negotiation involves interacting with others, both *analysis* (conceptualizing the issues being negotiated) and *behavior* are dynamic works-in-progress and must be revised before, during, and after engagements and processing of new information."[245] "[M]ost effective negotiators will moderate their behavior as needed (respond in kind or respond to change the situation, ask questions to get information or ask questions to build rapport, etc.) throughout the course of the

---

[242] See § 2.13(b)(1) for reasons why some mediators seek to increase the participation of clients and reduce the participation of lawyers. For a list of questions the mediator is likely to ask your client, see Tom Arnold, 20 Common Errors in Mediation Advocacy, 13 Alternatives to the High Cost of Litig. 69, 71 (1995).

[243] John W. Cooley, Mediation Advocacy 90 (1996) ("If you decide that your client is to participate verbally at the mediation, discuss the nature and extent of the participation in detail prior to the session.")

[244] In the family law area, however, there are some jurisdictions in which the mediator has the authority to exclude lawyers. See § 2.17.

[245] Carrie Menkel-Meadow, Negotiation: A Very Short Introduction 3 (2022).

negotiation."[246] In this regard, "some have analogized negotiation to jazz. Jazz, like negotiation, relies on some measure of intuition and improvisation."[247]

So, there are no hard-and-fast rules for representing clients in mediation. But there are some generalizations. On one hand, "compared to the lawyer in adjudication, the lawyer contemplating using mediation or advising clients during mediation tends to focus less on determining how to persuade a third party and more on assessing whether and how participation in mediation will result in an acceptable agreement."[248] But on the other hand, "because the parties may not settle, the lawyer representing a client in mediation will need to avoid compromising the client's posture for litigation."[249]

More specifically, in representing your client in mediation, your behavior should be influenced by at least two things about the mediator: the likelihood that the mediator will *evaluate* (§ 2.13), and the likelihood that the mediator will keep confidential any sensitive information you give her. If the mediator is certain not to evaluate at all, and certain never to reveal any of your confidences, then you can be open to the mediator about your side's interests and priorities. In other words, you can take a *problem-solving* approach (§ 1.22). This will best enable the mediator to help identify and exploit *positive-sum* opportunities (§ 2.12). On the other hand, if the mediator evaluates, the evaluation may be worse for your side if you disclose your side's interests and priorities, rather than argue your case to the mediator (§ 2.13(b)(1)). Furthermore, if the mediator, perhaps compelled by subpoena, reveals sensitive information you told her, then you may regret your forthright disclosure (§ 2.28).

Finally, you, the lawyer, may not be present in mediation. For example, some states prohibit lawyers from attending family mediation sessions (§ 2.17). You may advise your client not to agree to anything until he has a chance to consult with you. Where lawyers are not present during mediation, clients often ask their lawyers to review the mediated settlement agreement before the client signs it. "Lawyers, however, express frustration over their limited ability to advise on these agreements, because they do not witness the give-and-take of the negotiations that created them and lack access to the

---

[246] Andrea Kupfer Schneider, Teaching A New Negotiation Skills Paradigm, 39 Wash. U. J.L. & Pol'y 13, 23 (2012).

[247] Michael Moffitt, Settlement Malpractice, 86 U. Chi. L. Rev. 1825, 1848 (2019).

[248] Sarah R. Cole, Craig A. McEwen, Nancy H. Rogers, James R. Coben & Peter N. Thompson, Mediation: Law, Policy, & Practice § 1:2 (2024).

[249] Id.

information needed to evaluate properly alternatives to settlement."[250]

# F. LAW GOVERNING MEDIATION

## § 2.27 Mediators' Professional Duties

### *(a) Overview*

This section discusses three ways to establish and enforce mediators' professional duties. The first is the lawsuit. A private party suing a professional for negligence, breach of contract, or other legal violation is an important way in which various professionals' duties are enforced. It has been substantially disabled, however, as a way of enforcing mediators' professional duties (§ 2.27(b)).

The second way of establishing and enforcing professional duties is administrative regulation, specifically occupational licensing. Lawyers, for example, must meet certain requirements to receive from the state a license to practice law, and that license can be revoked if the lawyer violates certain professional duties, typically those in the Model Rules of Professional Conduct (§ 2.27(c)(2)). No analogous system of general licensing for mediators exists, but something approximating a licensing requirement is part of many mandatory and court-sponsored mediation programs (§ 2.27(c)).

The third way of establishing and enforcing professional duties is with private, rather than governmental, sanctions. This approach is developing with respect to mediation (§ 2.27(d)).

### *(b) Liability Suits Against Mediators*

Doctors, lawyers, psychologists, accountants, engineers, architects, and others are sued for alleged failures in their performance of professional services. In contrast, judges are immune from suit for the performance of their judicial duties,[251] so the remedy for the party who dislikes a judge's ruling is to appeal, not to sue the

---

[250] Craig A. McEwen, Nancy H. Rogers & Richard J. Maiman, Bring in the Lawyers: Challenging the Dominant Approaches to Ensuring Fairness In Divorce Mediation, 79 Minn. L. Rev. 1346 (1995).

[251] Mireles v. Waco, 502 U.S. 9, 9 (1991) ("A long line of this Court's precedents acknowledges that, generally, a judge is immune from a suit for money damages."); id. at 11 ("Like other forms of official immunity, judicial immunity is an immunity from suit, not just from ultimate assessment of damages. Accordingly, judicial immunity is not overcome by allegations of bad faith or malice, the existence of which ordinarily cannot be resolved without engaging in discovery and eventual trial") (citations omitted).

Judicial immunity applies only to acts that are judicial in nature. A judge who fires a probation officer, for example, is acting in an administrative, rather than judicial, capacity and is therefore not immune. Forrester v. White, 484 U.S. 219 (1988).

judge. Immunity has spread from judges to other actors in the court system such as prosecutors, jurors, witnesses, and court reporters.[252]

Some state statutes grant mediators immunity in the same manner and to the same extent as judges, and even in the absence of statute, courts may hold mediators immune as a matter of common law.[253] However, these statutes and case holdings vary on whether they protect all mediators or only court-appointed mediators.[254] In addition, "willful and wanton misconduct" may be an exception to mediator immunity.[255]

Courts denying mediator immunity typically reason that a mediator lacks the "discretionary decision-making authority" that is characteristic of judicial proceedings.[256] Even a statutorily appointed mediator's purpose "is not to conduct a proceeding wherein he or she is the final arbiter of fact or law."[257] Thoughtful scholars have articulated similar arguments against mediator immunity.[258]

---

[252] Caroline Turner English, Mediator Immunity, 63 Geo. Wash. L. Rev. 759, 765 (1995); Barbara E. Bergman, Theresa M. Duncan & Marlo Cadeddu, 1 Wharton's Criminal Procedure § 1:13 (14th ed. 2025) ("Generally, prosecutors are absolutely immune in both federal and state courts from civil lawsuits for malicious prosecution based upon the exercise of their discretion to prosecute."); Rodney A. Smolla, 2 Federal Civil Rights Acts § 14:45 (3d ed. 2025) ("Lower courts have also granted absolute immunity to other witnesses in judicial proceedings, as well as to jurors." (footnotes omitted)); Murrell v. Consiglio, 841 F. App'x 357, 360 (3d Cir. 2021) (holding that court reporter was "protected, not by absolute immunity, but by qualified immunity").

[253] Sarah R. Cole, Craig A. McEwen, Nancy H. Rogers, James R. Coben & Peter N. Thompson, Mediation: Law, Policy, & Practice §§ 11:11–11:12 (2024). See, e.g., Fla. Stat. Ann. § 44.107(1) (extending to mediators "judicial immunity in the same manner and to the same extent as a judge").

[254] See, e.g., Hutchinson v. San Diego Superior Court, 2019 WL 211979, *3 (S.D. Cal. 2019) (mediator acting on behalf of the County Family Court Services ("FCS") was protected by quasi-judicial immunity because the FCS is an entity of the Superior Court and the state); Todd v. Shoopman, 2012 WL 3531563 (E.D. Cal. 2012) (court-appointed mediator entitled to immunity because the family court judge who appointed the mediator ordered the mediator to interview the plaintiff's son so the mediator could make findings and issue recommendations as to custody and visitation).

[255] Colo. Rev. Stat. Ann. § 13–22–305(6).

[256] Ralston v. Garabedian, 2021 WL 6072881, *11 (E.D. Pa. 2021).

[257] M&T Bank v. Carlin, 2024 WL 164802, *2 (Conn. Super. Ct. 2024). See also DiGiuseppe v. Talbot, No. HDCV166069963S, 2017 WL 2324303, at *2 (Conn. Super. Ct. May 4, 2017) (denying immunity to defendant mediator because although "[C]ourts have extended absolute immunity to a variety of judicial and quasi-judicial officers . . . The determining factor . . . is whether the official was performing a function that was integral to the judicial process."); id. ("In the present case, the defendant does not cite, and the court cannot find, any case law determining that a private mediator functions in such a manner as to be intimately involved in or integral to the judicial process. . . . the defendant in the present case is neither a court-appointed mediator nor a judicial branch employee.")

[258] See Sharon Press, Against Quasi-Judicial Immunity for Mediators, 30 Disp. Resol. Mag. 32 (2024) (arguing that quasi-judicial immunity should not be extended to

A thorough search found only one lawsuit in the U.S. in which the mediator had been held liable, and "that circumstance involved a conviction on two dozen criminal charges, suggesting that it cannot accurately be treated as a simple case of mediator malpractice."[259] In sum, "lawsuits against mediators virtually always fail."[260] The same is true across several other common law jurisdictions.[261]

### *(c) Licensing Mediators*

#### *(1) Court Appointments and Rosters*

Law permits anyone to mediate; no license is required. But much mediation is mandated or funded by government, and in these cases, government often mandates or influences the choice of mediator.

In mandatory mediation, the mediator may be a government employee.[262] For example, the Sixth Circuit "employs four mediators,"[263] and the Superior Court of Placer County, California, includes Family Court Services Staff who mediate child custody and visitation disputes.[264] When courts in some jurisdictions order parties to mediate, the court selects the mediator.[265] More commonly,

mediators because mediators do not render substantive decisions); Michael Moffitt, Suing Mediators, 83 B.U. L. Rev. 147, 200–06 (2003).

[259] Michael Moffitt, No News (Read: Successful Lawsuits Against Mediators) Is Good News?, 12 Tex. A&M L. Rev. 709, 731 (2025).

[260] Id. at 733.

[261] Jennifer L. Schulz Mediator Liability 23 Years Later: The "Three C's" of Case Law, Codes, & Custom, 55 Ottawa L. Rev. 151 (2024) ("I have reviewed the case law from Canada, the United States, England, Australia, New Zealand, and South Africa and found that courts are still not holding mediators liable, even where their conduct is negligent.")

[262] Sarah R. Cole, Craig A. McEwen, Nancy H. Rogers, James R. Coben & Peter N. Thompson, Mediation: Law, Policy, & Practice § 14:19 (2024) (citing Wayne Brazil, Comparing Structures for the Delivery of ADR Services by Courts: Critical Values and Concerns, 14 Ohio St. J. on Disp. Resol. 715, 747–48 (1999)) (five models for recruiting mediators to a court's mediation program: "court staff, court contracts with a private mediation provider, court-paid private practitioners (on a limited roster or not), private practitioner volunteers from a roster, and party-paid private practitioners from a roster.")

[263] U.S. Court of Appeals for the Sixth Circuit, Mediation, https://www.ca6.uscourts.gov/mediation.

[264] Superior Court of California, County of Placer, Parenting Plan Mediation and Family Court Services, https://www.placer.courts.ca.gov/divisions/family/child-custody-mediation.

[265] Roger A. Hansona & Richard Becker, Appellate Mediation in New Mexico: An Evaluation, 4 J. App. Prac. & Process 167, 172 (2002) (New Mexico Court of Appeals' mediation program "continues to operate with the resources of a single mediator and a part-time administrative assistant. The mediator, one of this paper's authors, is an attorney trained in modern mediation methods and hired by the Court"); Carrie-Anne Tondoa et al., Mediation Trends: A Survey of the States, 39 Fam. Ct. Rev. 431, 433 (2001) ("mediation of family relations is not used in the precise manner in any two states. . . . In most instances, the court appoints a qualified mediator; however, many states allow the parties to select a mediator subject to court approval.")

the parties are allowed to agree on a mediator but, if they cannot agree, the judge or other court employee will appoint one.[266] Even where the court permits parties to select a mediator, the court may require or encourage the parties to choose someone from a roster of mediators approved by the court or other government agency. If the court requires parties to pick from the roster, then getting on the roster amounts to getting a license to mediate this category of cases.[267]

To get on the roster, a mediator may have to meet certain qualifications, such as:

- letters of recommendation,[268]
- co-mediating with a mediator mentor who provides feedback,[269]
- completing a mediator training course,[270] and continuing education,[271] and
- complying with a mandatory disclosure requirement to reveal to the parties the mediator's qualifications, education, and training.[272]

And to get on the roster for particular sorts of cases, such as family cases, a mediator may need:

---

266 See, e.g., Ala. Civ. Ct. Mediation Rule 3 ("Upon an order for mediation, the court, or such authority as the court may designate, shall appoint a qualified mediator. The mediator appointed shall be agreed upon by the parties concerned, subject to the qualifications provisions of Rule 4, except that if the parties do not agree upon a mediator, then the selection of the mediator shall be in the discretion of the court or its designated authority."); Fla.R.Civ.P. 1.720(j)(2).

267 For instance, a Kansas Supreme Court rule says, "When referring a dispute to mediation, a district court must appoint a person who . . . has received a certificate of approval." Kan. Mediation Rule 907. Earning that certificate requires letters of recommendation, 16 or more hours of training depending on the type cases for which the mediator is approved, and participation "in an approved practicum," id. Rule 911, which includes co-mediating with a mediator mentor who provides feedback. Id. Rule 915.

268 Id.

269 Id. See also La. Stat. Ann. § 9:334 ("a minimum of eight hours of co-mediation training under the direct supervision of a mediator").

270 710 Ill. Comp. Stat. Ann. 20/5(a)(2) (30 hours); Tex. Civ. Prac. & Rem.Code Ann. § 154.052(a) (40 hours); Minn. Gen. Prac. Rule 114.12 ("All Qualified Neutrals providing facilitative or hybrid services, that include a mediation component in civil, non-family matters, must have received a minimum of 30 hours of classroom training, with an emphasis on experiential learning").

271 Nev. Foreclosure Mediation Rule 3 ("all mediators must participate in approved biennial continuing education of at least 4 hours and consisting of education in the area of real property law").

272 Minn. Stat. Ann. § 572.37.

- a master's degree in psychology, social work, counseling, or other discipline,[273] or
- experience as a counselor or psychotherapist,[274] and
- "training on the dynamics of domestic violence and the effects of domestic violence on victims of domestic violence and on children."[275]

In short, government intervenes in the mediation market by requiring certain qualifications to mediate certain cases. Government also intervenes in the mediation market by funding certain mediation programs.[276] Some courts impose filing fee surcharges on all civil litigants and use that money to fund mediation programs.[277]

In contrast, outside the contexts of mandatory and other court-sponsored mediation, law does not restrict who can mediate or impose standards for competence and ethics. So, "as a practical matter, anyone can hold herself out to be a mediator."[278]

*(2) Lawyer-Mediators*

While no license is required to mediate (§ 2.27(c)(1)), a license is required to practice law.[279] A lawyer may lose her license (be disbarred or suspended from practice) if she violates the conditions of her license, such as her state's Rules of Professional Conduct. Nearly every state (except California) has largely adopted a version of the American Bar Association's Model Rules of Professional

---

[273] Id. §§ 1815(a)(1), 3164(b). (a). See also Mo. Prac., Civil Rules Practice R 88.05 (2025 ed.) ("A mediator who performs mediation in domestic relations and paternity cases pursuant to this Rule 88 shall be . . . an attorney or a person who possesses a graduate degree in a field that includes the study of psychiatry, psychology, social work, counseling, or other behavioral science substantially related to marriage and family interpersonal relationships").

[274] Cal. Fam. Code §§ 1815(a)(2), 3164(b).

[275] Wis. Stat. Ann. § 767.405.

[276] Sarah R. Cole, Craig A. McEwen, Nancy H. Rogers, James R. Coben & Peter N. Thompson, Mediation: Law, Policy, & Practice § 4:3 (2024) ("By the early 1990's, . . . judicial systems in California and elsewhere funded mediation and other programs.")

[277] Jessica G. Mayer, Family Court Mediation After the Financial Crisis: A Struggle Worth New York's Attention, 15 Cardozo J. Conflict Resol. 333, 355 (2013) ("States with large mediation programs often enact permanent funding mechanisms to support these programs. For example, California (which mandates mediation for custody and visitation issues) funds their mediation program in part through marriage license and marriage certificate fees.")

[278] Leonard L. Riskin et al., Dispute Resolution and Lawyers 349 (6th ed. 2019).

[279] See ABA, Compendium of Professional Responsibility: Rules and Standards (2025).

Conduct.[280] These are often thought to be *ethical* rules and they are, but they are also *legal* rules because they are enacted and enforced by government. The state bar committees and courts that enforce these rules are government agencies administering occupational licensing regulations to determine who is, and is not, legally permitted to practice law.

The Model Rules speak to lawyers serving as mediators. Model Rule 2.4 provides:

> Rule 2.4 Lawyer Serving as Third-Party Neutral
>
> (a) A lawyer serves as a third-party neutral when the lawyer assists two or more persons who are not clients of the lawyer to reach a resolution of a dispute or other matter that has arisen between them. Service as a third-party neutral may include service as an arbitrator, a mediator or in such other capacity as will enable the lawyer to assist the parties to resolve the matter.
>
> (b) A lawyer serving as a third-party neutral shall inform unrepresented parties that the lawyer is not representing them. When the lawyer knows or reasonably should know that a party does not understand the lawyer's role in the matter, the lawyer shall explain the difference between the lawyer's role as a third-party neutral and a lawyer's role as one who represents a client.[281]

In short, Rule 2.4(b) indicates that a lawyer-mediator does not represent the parties.

Note, however, the special concern for unrepresented parties in Rule 2.4(b). One-lawyer mediation, in which the mediator is the only lawyer, differs importantly from three-lawyer mediation, in which each party has its own lawyer.[282] While three-lawyer mediation is the norm for most settlement mediation, one-lawyer mediation is common in family law matters (§ 2.17). So, it should be no surprise that issues surrounding the application of the Model Rules to lawyer-mediators have arisen most frequently in the family context.

---

[280] ABA, Alphabetical List of Jurisdictions Adopting Model Rules, https://www.americanbar.org/groups/professional_responsibility/publications/model_rules_of_professional_conduct/alpha_list_state_adopting_model_rules/; ABA, Ctr. for Prof'l Resp., Jurisdictional Rules Comparison Charts, https://www.americanbar.org/groups/professional_responsibility/policy/rule_charts/.

[281] Model Rules of Prof'l Conduct R.2.4 (2013).

[282] With multiple parties, more than three lawyers can be involved. Two-lawyer mediation is when the mediator is a lawyer, and one of the two parties is unrepresented or when both parties are represented and the mediator is a non-lawyer.

A lawyer-mediator should explain to both parties that they are not her clients.[283] Although she is a lawyer, she is performing mediation services for them, not legal services.[284] Many agreements to mediate expressly state that no attorney-client relationship is formed between the mediator and any party.[285] Furthermore, the lawyer-mediator should explain to the parties that she cannot, in the future, represent either party in the matter.[286] There is also authority for the proposition that the lawyer-mediator cannot in the future represent either party in a related matter.[287]

In some states, a lawyer-mediator who wants to avoid an attorney-client relationship with the parties must refrain from giving the parties legal advice.[288] For example, parties lacking their own lawyers might ask the lawyer-mediator how their dispute would likely be resolved by a court. Rather than try to answer such a question, the lawyer-mediator in these states should tell the parties that they each have the right to hire a lawyer if they want legal advice.

---

[283] In order to appear impartial, the participants should not have been her clients in the past. See Model Standards for Family and Divorce Mediation, Standard IV (The Symposium on Standards of Practice 2000). See also Model Standards of Conduct for Mediators, Standard III(A) (Am. Arb. Ass'n et al. 2005), available at www.abanet.org/dispute/documents/model_standards_conduct_april2006.pdf ("A mediator shall avoid a conflict of interest or the appearance of a conflict of interest during and after mediation. A conflict of interest can arise . . . from any relationship between a mediator and any mediation participant, whether past or present, personal or professional, that reasonably raises a question of a mediator's impartiality."). However, it is possible that the participants could waive any conflicts of interest with written informed consent as long as the mediator could still remain impartial. Model Standards for Family and Divorce Mediation, Standard IV (The Symposium on Standards of Practice 2000).

[284] See, e.g., State Bar of Michigan, Ethics Op. No. RI-256, 75 Mich. B.J. 364, 365 (1996); Arizona State Bar Committee on Rules of Prof'l Conduct, Op. No. 96–01 (1996).

[285] See, e.g., Jay E. Grenig, 26 West's Legal Forms, Alt. Disp. Res. § 2:34 (4th ed.) (Pre-Suit Mediation Agreement, Para. 3) ("Although the mediator is an attorney, the mediator does not represent any party and does not offer and will not give legal advice or counsel").

[286] See Model Rules of Prof'l Conduct, R.1.12(a) (2020) (allowing subsequent representation only when all parties to the mediation give informed consent in writing).

[287] Sarah R. Cole, Craig A. McEwen, Nancy H. Rogers, James R. Coben & Peter N. Thompson, Mediation: Law, Policy, & Practice § 10:6 (2025) ("Although some exceptions exist, the general view among regulators is that a lawyer-mediator may not represent a party to a previous mediation. This view seems to be an extension of the principle that a lawyer may not represent an individual whose interests are adverse to a previous client"); Poly Software Int'l Inc. v. Su, 880 F. Supp. 1487, 1494 (D. Utah 1995) ("where a mediator has received confidential information in the course of mediation, that mediator should not thereafter represent anyone in connection with the same or a substantially factually related matter unless all parties to the mediation proceeding consent after disclosure.")

[288] Sarah R. Cole, Craig A. McEwen, Nancy H. Rogers, James R. Coben & Peter N. Thompson, Mediation: Law, Policy, & Practice § 10:3 (2025).

In contrast, other states permit lawyer-mediators to give legal advice, generally with the requirement that the advice be given in the presence of all parties.[289] An intermediate position allows lawyer-mediators to give legal information, but not legal advice.[290]

There is a similar variety and doubt about the extent to which the lawyer-mediator may be involved in drafting the settlement agreement while still avoiding an attorney-client relationship with the parties. Certainly, giving legal advice and drafting settlement agreements have long been core activities of lawyers representing clients.[291] But these activities differ when done by a neutral mediator than when done by an advocate seeking to advance only one party's interests. Accordingly, the American Bar Association Section on Dispute Resolution resolved that:

> The preparation of a memorandum of understanding or settlement agreement by a mediator, incorporating the terms of settlement specified by the parties, does not constitute the practice of law. If the mediator drafts an agreement that goes beyond the terms specified by the parties, he or she may be engaged in the practice of law. However, in such a case, a mediator shall not be engaged in the practice of law if (a) all parties are represented by counsel and (b) the mediator discloses that any proposal that he or she makes with respect to the terms of settlement is informational as opposed to the practice of law, and that the parties should not view or rely upon such proposals as advice of counsel, but merely consider them in consultation with their own attorneys.[292]

*(3) Non-Lawyer Mediators*

A license from the state is required to practice law.[293] Only when one acquires this license (becomes a lawyer) is she generally

---

[289] Id. § 10:4.

[290] Virginia State Bar Standing Committee on Legal Ethics, LE Op. No. 511 (1983) & 590 (1985).

[291] See Carrie Menkel-Meadow, Is Mediation the Practice of Law?, 14 Alternatives to the High Cost of Litig. 57, 61 (1996) ("When mediators engage in some prediction or application of legal standards to concrete facts—and especially when they draft settlement agreements, I think they are 'practicing' law.")

[292] ABA Section of Dispute Resolution, Resolution on Mediation and the Unauthorized Practice of Law, Feb. 2, 2002.

[293] ABA, Compendium of Professional Responsibility: Rules and Standards 115–19 (2006). Deborah Rhode, Policing the Professional Monopoly: A Constitutional and Empirical Analysis of Unauthorized Practice Prohibitions, 34 Stan. L. Rev. 1 (1981).

permitted to give legal advice,[294] draft legal documents,[295] and engage in the other activities constituting the practice of law. Non-lawyer mediators, like other non-lawyers, are subject to penalty if they engage in these activities. However, prohibitions on the unauthorized (un-licensed) practice of law (UPL) are enforced more rigorously in some states than others.[296]

Only a few cases discuss what non-lawyer mediators can and cannot do without "practicing law."[297] A Virginia court enjoined a non-lawyer mediator from "giving legal advice to persons relating to the specific questions, problems or desires of such person."[298] The First Circuit dismissed a constitutional challenge to a bar association's warning to a non-lawyer mediator who was, the bar association concluded, practicing law.[299]

Otherwise, the issue has been left to the UPL rules of state supreme courts and bar associations. Arizona's are among the most specific to mediation:

> (A) A person who is not authorized under Rule 31.1(a) to engage in the practice of law in Arizona may prepare a written agreement settling a dispute or file such an agreement with the appropriate court if:
>
> > (i) the person is employed, appointed, or referred by a court or government entity and is serving as a mediator at the direction of the court or a governmental entity; or
> >
> > (ii) the person is participating without compensation in a nonprofit mediation program, a

[294] See, e.g., Ga. Code Ann. § 15–19–51(a)(4) ("It shall be unlawful for any person other than a duly licensed attorney at law: . . . (4) To render or furnish legal services or advice").

[295] See, e.g., La. Rev. Stat. Ann. § 37:212(A)(1) ("The practice of law means and includes . . . In a representative capacity, the appearance as an advocate, or the drawing of papers, pleadings or documents, or the performance of any act in connection with pending or prospective proceedings before any court of record in this state.")

[296] Jacqueline M. Nolan-Haley, Lawyers, Non-Lawyers and Mediation: Rethinking the Professional Monopoly from a Problem Solving Perspective, 7 Harv. Negotiation L. Rev. 235, 264 (2002).

[297] It is still true that "Case law is sparse and thus to a large degree mediation practice by non-lawyers operates more under the shadow or threat of UPL regulations rather than under an active enforcement regime." Jacqueline M. Nolan-Haley, Lawyers, Non-Lawyers and Mediation: Rethinking the Professional Monopoly from a Problem Solving Perspective, 7 Harv. Negotiation L. Rev. 235, 269–70 (2002).

[298] Sarah R. Cole, Craig A. McEwen, Nancy H. Rogers, James R. Coben & Peter N. Thompson, Mediation: Law, Policy, & Practice § 10:10 (2025) (quoting Commonwealth of Virginia v. Steinberg, Va. Cir. Ct., Henrico Co., Case No. CL-96-504.)

[299] Werle v. Rhode Island Bar Ass'n, 755 F.2d 195, 199–200 (1st Cir. 1985).

community-based organization, or a professional association.

(B) Unless specifically authorized in Rule 31.3(e)(5)(A), a mediator who is not authorized under Rule 31.1(a) to engage in the practice of law in Arizona and who prepares or provides legal documents for the parties without attorney supervision must be certified as a legal document preparer in compliance with the Arizona Code of Judicial Administration § 7–708.[300]

Other bar association opinions have disapproved the giving of legal advice by non-lawyer mediators.[301]

On the other hand, leading mediation scholars state that unauthorized practice prohibitions are not violated by a nonlawyer-mediator who "communicates legal advice or drafting suggestions to the parties' lawyers."[302] This fits the important distinction between one-lawyer mediation and three-lawyer mediation. In addition, "Court-employed mediators have also avoided unauthorized practice problems, presumably because courts already regulate their activities."[303] Finally, bar associations and courts seem to apply unauthorized practice restrictions less rigorously to non-profit mediation programs than to for-profit mediators.[304] Thus, three large categories of non-lawyer mediators—those dealing with represented parties and those working for courts or non-profit programs—seem somewhat protected from liability for engaging in the unauthorized practice of law. The more serious liability risk is confined to private, for-profit mediators with one or more parties not represented by a lawyer.

### *(d) Private Certification of Mediators*

Organizations such as the American Arbitration Association, JAMS, and the CPR Institute for Dispute Resolution maintain rosters (or "panels") of mediators. To be on the roster, the mediator may have to possess certain qualifications relating to background, credentials, training, and experience. So, these organizations' roster requirements are the private sector analog to the requirements for

---

300 Ariz. Sup. Ct. R. 31.3(e)(5).

301 Connecticut Bar Ass'n Committee on Professional Ethics Informal Op No. 83–1 (1982), 9 Fam L. Rep. 2013 (1982); Bar Ass'n of Nassau Co. [NY] Committee on Professional Ethics Op No. 84–1 (1984).

302 Sarah R. Cole, Craig A. McEwen, Nancy H. Rogers, James R. Coben & Peter N. Thompson, Mediation: Law, Policy, & Practice § 10:10 (2024).

303 Id.

304 Id. § 10:11.

being a mediator on the roster of a court or other government agency, discussed in Section 2.27(c)(1).

Professional associations of mediators—such as the Association for Conflict Resolution and the International Academy of Mediators—have membership requirements along the same lines.[305] So membership in the organization functions as a sort of "seal of approval" for the mediator.

## § 2.28 Confidentiality

### *(a) Generally*

Settlement mediation, like settlement negotiation, is a means of discovery in litigation. So, lawyers guard against revealing anything in mediation that could come back to haunt them or their clients if mediation fails to reach a settlement and litigation continues. Lawyers are especially careful about what information to share with the other side of a dispute, and lawyers are also often cautious about the information they or their clients give the mediator. Two of the major factors inhibiting disclosure to mediators are worries that disclosure will harm the disclosing party if the mediator evaluates the dispute, or if the mediator fails to keep the disclosed information confidential. Evaluation is discussed in Section 2.13. Confidentiality is discussed in this section.

A mediator can often help the parties more as they disclose more to the mediator, especially when the mediator learns the parties' sensitive information. For example, if the mediator learns each party's *bottom line*, she can quickly identify whether there is a *settlement zone* and, if so, where it is (§ 2.11). And if the parties are open to the mediator about their interests and priorities, the mediator can best help the parties identify and exploit *positive-sum* opportunities (§ 2.12). In short, the more important the information lawyers and parties share with the mediator, the better mediation tends to work. But as the previous paragraph explains, factors inhibiting such sharing include worries that the mediator may not keep the disclosed information confidential.

Consequently, mediators generally claim to be trustworthy—good at keeping secrets. Mediators generally tell parties and lawyers that what they tell the mediator will remain confidential, unless the discloser gives the mediator permission to reveal it.[306] Many mediations achieve better results for both parties than negotiation

---

[305] See, e.g., Ass'n for Conflict Resolution, Criteria for Advanced Levels of ACR Membership, https://acrnet.org/page/AdvancedPractitioner (last visited Oct.3, 2022); Int'l Acad. of Mediators, Membership Policy, https://iamed.org/membership-nomination-process-criteria/ (last visited Oct. 3, 2022).

[306] See § 2.10(f) (sample agreement to mediate, paragraphs 11 and 12).

would have achieved because the mediator receives each side's otherwise confidential information in private caucus and then combines that information (§§ 2.11–2.12). The mediator can only accomplish this if the parties and lawyers believe that what they tell the mediator will remain confidential. So, mediation benefits from tools to increase the certainty that mediators can be trusted not to reveal confidences. Also, in some cases, parties are willing to reveal things to each other that they do not want revealed to others, such as journalists or business competitors. Thus, mediation also benefits from tools to increase the certainty that parties (and their lawyers) can be trusted not to reveal more broadly confidences shared within mediation.

### *(b) Confidentiality Agreements Prior to Mediation*

One way to reduce the risk of information disclosed in mediation being shared more broadly is to make such further sharing a breach of contract. At the outset of mediation, participants may agree that any information revealed during the mediation will remain confidential. These agreements are often signed writings and may include express promises not to subpoena the mediator.[307] An agreement to mediate pursuant to the rules of an organization, such as the American Arbitration Association, may be a confidentiality agreement because the rules incorporated into the contract require confidentiality. For example, the AAA Commercial Rules say "confidential information disclosed to a mediator by the parties or by other participants (witnesses) in the course of the mediation shall not be divulged by the mediator."[308] And "[t]he parties shall maintain the confidentiality of the mediation and shall not rely on, or introduce as evidence in any arbitral, judicial, or other proceeding the following, unless agreed to by the parties or required by applicable law."[309]

Confidentiality agreements in settlement negotiation are discussed in Section 1.43, and that discussion generally applies to settlement mediation. While courts have enforced mediation

---

[307] James D. Yellen et al., Mediator Redux: Now More Than Ever Suggestions for Practitioners 338 (Practicing Law Institute 2006) ("The parties shall not subpoena or otherwise require the mediator to testify or produce documents received, reviewed or prepared by the mediator."); Stephen G. Bullock & Linda Rose, Gallagher, Surveying the State of the Mediative Art: A Guide to Institutionalizing Mediation in Louisiana, 57 La. L. Rev. 885, 995 (1997) ("[T]he parties generally promise not to call the mediator to testify if the case does not settle nor to subpoena records maintained by the mediator").

[308] See, e.g., Am. Arb. Ass'n, Commercial Arbitration Rules and Mediation Procedures, Rules, M–10, M–12 (2020).

[309] Id.

confidentiality agreements in a variety of ways,[310] relatively few courts have enjoined disclosure that would breach the agreement.[311]

### *(c) Rules of Evidence and Discovery*

Suppose mediation fails to achieve a settlement and the parties go to trial. One side may seek to introduce as evidence what the other side said during mediation—either to the mediator in a private caucus or to the other side in a joint session. Either way, such statements are not likely to be admitted into evidence.

Federal Rule of Evidence 408 says, "conduct or statements made in compromise negotiations" are not admissible "to prove liability or invalidity of the claim or its amount."[312] Rule 408 does not expressly state that it applies to statements in *mediation* as well as to statements in *negotiation*. But some states' versions of Rule 408 do.[313] And in other states, most courts sensibly hold that the presence of a mediator does not reduce statements' protection from admission into evidence below Rule 408's protection.[314]

However, Rule 408 does not invariably exclude from evidence all statements made in mediation or negotiation. Rule 408 may not exclude statements relating to a dispute not yet on the verge of litigation (§ 1.43(b)). And even statements related to disputes in litigation are admissible if offered for purposes other than "proving liability for or invalidity of the claim or its amount." Such purposes include proving bias or prejudice, undue delay, or obstruction of justice (§ 1.43(b)). Also, Rule 408, like any evidence rule, only applies to courts. It does not apply to administrative hearings, for example, and may not apply to arbitration (§ 1.43(b)).

---

[310] Sarah R. Cole, Craig A. McEwen, Nancy H. Rogers, James R. Coben & Peter N. Thompson, Mediation: Law, Policy, & Practice § 8:39 (2024).

[311] C.R. & S.R. v. E., 573 So. 2d 1088 (Fla. Dist. Ct. App. 1991) (priest accused of child molestation granted preliminary injunction enjoining child's parents from disclosing information from mediation/arbitration proceeding).

[312] The full text of Rule 408 and further discussion of it, are contained in § 1.43(c).

[313] See also Haw. R. Evid. 408 ("Evidence of conduct or statements made in compromise negotiations or mediation proceedings is likewise not admissible."); Me. R. Evid. 408(b); Mo. Rev. Stat. § 435.014(2) ("Arbitration, conciliation and mediation proceedings shall be regarded as settlement negotiations."); Vt. R. Evid. 408.

[314] See, e.g., Cribari v. Allstate Fire & Casualty Insurance Company, 2021 WL 2255008, *12–13 (10th Cir. 2021) (affirming exclusion of claim log entries related to mediation, and a check drafted by defendant but never delivered to the plaintiff, as well as a letter from the defendant's accounting department asking why plaintiff had not cashed the check, reasoning that the entries, check and letter were sufficiently "so causally connected" to the mediation to warrant protection under Rule 408); Berg v. Berg, 170 N.E.3d 224 (Ind. 2021) (holding that a balance sheet containing information about marital assets and debts exchanged specifically to assist in mediation but disclosed prior to the mediation falls under Rule 408 protection); Rogers v. Dupree, 799 S.E.2d 1, 21–22 (Ga. App. 2017) (deeming inadmissible a prelitigation demand letter and demand made during private mediation).

Moreover, Rule 408 and similar state statutes do not explicitly protect statements made in negotiation from pre-trial discovery. Of course, the party to whom information is revealed in mediation will not need to discover it. But that party may receive discovery requests from other parties to that litigation or from parties to other cases. Such discovery requests are likely to be granted by courts applying civil procedure rules allowing discovery of, not just admissible evidence, but anything reasonably calculated to lead to the discovery of admissible evidence.[315]

However, "several courts have held that the same public policy concerns that support [Federal Rule of Evidence] 408 also support protection from discovery into confidential settlement negotiations."[316] For instance, recognizing that "[c]onfidentiality is an important feature of [ ] mediation," the Second Circuit ruled that "[a] party seeking disclosure of confidential mediation communications must demonstrate (1) a special need for the confidential material, (2) resulting unfairness from a lack of discovery, and (3) that the need for the evidence outweighs the interest in maintaining confidentiality."[317]

### *(d) Mediation Privilege*

Sections 2.28(b) and (c) discuss the limitations of confidentiality agreements and rules of evidence and discovery as tools to ensure the confidentiality of mediation. These limitations have led to the development of a mediation privilege. Much as communications

---

[315] Fed. R. Civ. P. 26(b) ("Unless otherwise limited by court order, the scope of discovery is as follows: Parties may obtain discovery regarding any nonprivileged matter that is relevant to any party's claim or defense and proportional to the needs of the case, considering the importance of the issues at stake in the action, the amount in controversy, the parties' relative access to relevant information, the parties' resources, the importance of the discovery in resolving the issues, and whether the burden or expense of the proposed discovery outweighs its likely benefit. Information within this scope of discovery need not be admissible in evidence to be discoverable.")

[316] In re RDM Sports Group, Inc., 277 B.R. 415, 433 (Bankr. N.D. Ga. 2002) (citing cases). But see Leading Mfg. Sols., LP v. Hitco, Ltd., No. 15CV1852-LAB (PCS), 2017 WL 1336939, at *3 (S.D. Cal. Mar. 24, 2017)) ("communications during settlement negotiations are discoverable").

[317] In re Teligent, Inc., 640 F.3d 53, 57–58 (2d Cir. 2011). See also Accent Delight Int'l Ltd. v. Sotheby's, 505 F. Supp. 3d 281, 287 (S.D.N.Y. 2020) (extending Second Circuit's holding from court-ordered mediations to private mediations); id. ("providing weaker protections to communications during a confidential private mediation than to communications during a court-sponsored mediation would discourage parties from agreeing to engage in private mediation. But in many cases, particularly more complex cases, private mediation (which is often conducted with a paid, highly experienced mediator who can devote more time to the matter) may be preferable to, and more likely to succeed than, court-ordered or -sponsored mediation. Incentivizing private mediations (or, to be more precise, not disincentivizing them) benefits not only the parties in such cases, but also the court system generally, both because it alleviates the burdens on court-sponsored mediation programs (which are often thinly staffed by unpaid volunteers) and because, when successful, it lightens the court's docket").

between attorney and client or between spouses are privileged, so in many states are communications between a party or its lawyer and the mediator privileged. Mediation privileges generally protect mediators and other participants in mediation from being compelled to testify about what was said at the mediation, even if the evidence is offered for a purpose permitted by Federal Rule of Evidence 408 or similar state rules. Mediation privileges also generally protect statements made in mediation from the pre-trial discovery process and from disclosure outside of court, such as at administrative hearings,[318] or to journalists or business competitors. Some mediation privileges go beyond protecting statements made in mediation to protect the records of the mediator or mediation program, agreements to mediate, settlement agreements formed at mediation, and so forth.[319]

Most states have created mediation privileges, either by statute or caselaw,[320] and some federal courts have followed.[321] However, some state privilege statutes apply "only to particular mediation programs, such as court-supervised child custody mediation. If not tied to a program, the statute often protects only those sessions conducted by mediators who meet training or other requirements."[322] In contrast, other privileges (including that found in the Uniform Mediation Act,[323] which has been adopted in over 12 states,[324]) are more broadly written to cover all mediators or mediation programs

---

318 Sarah R. Cole, Craig A. McEwen, Nancy H. Rogers, James R. Coben & Peter N. Thompson, Mediation: Law, Policy, & Practice § 8:20 (2024) ("Most mediation privileges preclude disclosure or use of the protected information in any forum in the jurisdiction—whether at trial, during pretrial proceedings, discovery, or in administrative proceedings. Courts seem disinclined to narrowly interpret this aspect of confidentiality coverage").

319 Id. § 8:24.

320 See id. § 8:12 at 311 & App. B.

321 See, e.g., Folb v. Motion Picture Industry Pension & Health Plans, 16 F. Supp. 2d 1164 (C.D. Cal. 1998); Sheldone v. Pennsylvania Turnpike Commn., 104 F. Supp. 2d 511 (W.D. Pa. 2000); In re RDM Sports Group, Inc., 277 B.R. 415 (Bankr. N.D. Ga. 2002). But see In re Grand Jury Subpoena Dated Dec. 17, 1996, 148 F.3d 487, 493 (5th Cir. 1998) ("Because privileges are not lightly created, United States v. Nixon, 418 U.S. 683, 710 (1974), we will not infer one where Congress has not clearly manifested an intent to create one. Thus, we hold that [7 U.S.C.] § 5101(c)(3)(D) does not protect documents relating to mediation proceedings involving the Moczygembas from disclosure to the grand jury").

322 Sarah R. Cole, Craig A. McEwen, Nancy H. Rogers, James R. Coben & Peter N. Thompson, Mediation: Law, Policy, & Practice § 8:12 (2024).

323 Unif. Mediation Act § 4. See Ellen E. Deason, Procedural Rules for Complementary Systems of Litigation and Mediation—Worldwide, 80 Notre Dame L. Rev. 553 (2005).

324 Uniform Law Commission, Mediation Act, https://www.uniformlaws.org/committees/community-home?communitykey=45565a5f-0c57-4bba-bbab-fc7de9a59110.

meeting certain requirements.[325] In some states, the privilege extends to mediations in which the parties "agree in writing to submit their dispute to" mediation.[326]

A privilege can be waived by the person holding the privilege. States vary on whether the mediation privilege is held only by the party making the pertinent communication,[327] all the parties,[328] or also the mediator.[329] The holders of the privilege under the Uniform Mediation Act include the parties, the mediator, and non-party participants.[330] Many mediation privilege statutes fail to identify the holder.[331]

The downside of any privilege, of course, is that it suppresses information that, if revealed, might have changed the outcome of a trial or other legal proceeding. The mediation privilege's suppression of information may even shield criminal or other wrongful activity. Suppose a parent admits to the child-custody mediator that the parent has physically abused his children and is not sure whether he will do it again. A broad mediation privilege would prevent the mediator from revealing that information to the court, and a court deprived of this information may award primary residential custody to the abusive parent. A broad mediation privilege would also prevent the mediator from revealing this information to a state social services agency which, if it had the information, would monitor and counsel the parent. Consequently, statutes creating a mediation privilege typically make an exception allowing for disclosure of such information.[332] More broadly, many privilege statutes make an exception for when allegations of crime are involved or limit the assertion of privilege to civil proceedings.[333] Still other privileges are defeated when the court finds that the need for evidence in a particular case outweighs the benefit created by the privilege.[334]

---

[325] Id. § 8:24.

[326] Mo. Ann. Stat. § 435.014.

[327] See, e.g., Conn. Gen. Stat. Ann. § 31–96 (labor mediation).

[328] See, e.g., Colo. Rev. Stat. § 13–22–307.

[329] Olam v. Congress Mortg. Co., 68 F. Supp. 2d 1110, 1130 (N.D. Cal. 1999) ("California law confers on mediators a privilege that is independent of the privilege conferred on parties to a mediation."); Fenton v. Howard, 575 P.2d 318, 319 (Ariz. 1978).

[330] Unif. Mediation Act § 4(b).

[331] Sarah R. Cole, Craig A. McEwen, Nancy H. Rogers, James R. Coben & Peter N. Thompson, Mediation: Law, Policy, & Practice § 8:21 (2024).

[332] Unif. Mediation Act, § 6(a)(7).

[333] Sarah R. Cole, Craig A. McEwen, Nancy H. Rogers, James R. Coben & Peter N. Thompson, Mediation: Law, Policy, & Practice § 8:20 (2024).

[334] See, e.g., 5 U.S.C. § 574(b)(5). Such privileges are "qualified," rather than "absolute."

Another exception to some privilege statutes is when testimony goes to the question of whether a settlement agreement was formed in mediation.[335] Suppose that Plaintiff and Defendant sign a written settlement agreement at the end of mediation. If Defendant, for example, breaches the agreement, Plaintiff may seek to enforce it in court. But Defendant may argue that no settlement agreement was formed, and that the mediation privilege precludes admission of any evidence to the contrary. The privilege, Defendant argues, prevents Plaintiff or the mediator from testifying that an agreement was formed or from introducing the signed document into evidence. These arguments are a real obstacle to the enforceability of mediated settlements. If such settlements are to be enforceable, then surely the written settlement agreement signed at the end of mediation must be admissible.[336] How can a court enforce it if the court cannot see it?

On the other hand, as discussed in Section 2.16(b)(3), some courts have invoked the mediation privilege to exclude evidence that an *oral* settlement agreement was formed at mediation.[337] Such case law makes a mediation privilege, in effect, a Statute of Frauds for mediated settlement agreements; such agreements are enforceable only if written or otherwise recorded.[338]

### *(e) Confidentiality Clauses in Settlement Agreements*

Once a settlement agreement is reached in mediation, the parties may agree to keep the settlement's terms confidential. However, parties sometimes breach such non-disclosure agreements.[339] The law on the enforceability of confidentiality provisions in *negotiated* settlements is discussed in Section 1.43, and that discussion generally applies to mediated settlements as well. In

---

[335] Sarah R. Cole, Craig A. McEwen, Nancy H. Rogers, James R. Coben & Peter N. Thompson, Mediation: Law, Policy, & Practice § 8:25 (2024).

[336] Unif. Mediation Act § 6(a)(1) (2002) (privilege exception for "agreement evidenced by a record signed by all parties to the agreement"); Stewart v. Preston Pipeline Inc., 36 Cal. Rptr. 3d 901 (Ct. App. 2005).

[337] See § 2.16(b)(3). See also Unif. Mediation Act, § 6(c) (2002).

[338] See § 2.16(b) (discussing enforceability of mediated settlement agreements). See also Ellen E. Deason, Procedural Rules for Complementary Systems of Litigation and Mediation—Worldwide, 80 Notre Dame L. Rev. 553, 102 (2005) ("predictable confidentiality is a value that justifies requiring that mediated settlements be evidenced by a record—either a signed writing or a modern substitute—to preclude the need for testimony on the course of the mediation.")

[339] Rivera v. Sharp, No. 21-2254, 2022 WL 2712869, at *1 (3d Cir. July 13, 2022) ("Fourteen years ago, Rivera sued the Defendants for employment discrimination. Mediation produced an agreement releasing Rivera's claims in exchange for a monetary sum, and requiring both parties to keep the terms confidential."); id. ("None of that happened. Instead, Rivera filed an unsealed 'motion to enforce settlement' revealing the existence of the deal and many material terms, including the settlement amount.")

addition, the confidentiality of mediated settlements may be further enhanced by any applicable mediation privilege (§ 2.28(d)).

## § 2.29 Agreements to Mediate

Parties with a dispute can agree to mediate that dispute. Such *post-dispute* mediation agreements can be formed before or after litigation starts. Much mediation is the result of such agreements, which are usually but not always written. A sample post-dispute mediation agreement appears in Section 2.10(f).

More interesting, perhaps, are *pre-dispute* mediation agreements. Any sort of contract can include a clause obligating the parties to mediate any dispute that may arise between them.[340] An example of such a clause is in Section 2.20 and another example is:

> 1. In the event any controversy arising under this agreement is not resolved by informal negotiations within (30) days (or any mutually agreed extension of time) after either party requests such negotiations, the case shall be referred to the nearest office of [appointing agency] for mediation, that is, an informal, nonbinding conference or conferences between the parties in which a mediator will seek to guide the parties to a resolution of the case.
>
> 2. The parties are free to select any mutually acceptable panel member from the list of mediators at [appointing agency]. If the parties cannot agree or have no particular choice of mediator and simply request that the [appointing agency] assign one to the case, then a list and resumes of available mediators, numbering one more than there are parties, will be sent to the parties, each of whom may strike one name leaving the remaining name as the mediator. If more than one name remains, the designated mediator shall be selected by the Administrator of the [appointing agency] from the remaining names.
>
> 3. The mediation process shall continue until the case is resolved or the mediator makes a finding that there is no possibility of settlement through mediation or either party chooses not to continue further.[341]

Organizations selling mediation services encourage contracting parties to specify their organization. For instance, the American Arbitration Association says:

---

[340] See generally, Sarah R. Cole, Craig A. McEwen, Nancy H. Rogers, James R. Coben & Peter N. Thompson, Mediation: Law, Policy, & Practice §§ 6:1–6:8 (2024).

[341] Jay E. Grenig, Alternative Dispute Resolution App. R Form 1 (4th ed. 2022).

Parties can copy and paste this clause into their contracts.

> *If a dispute arises out of or relates to this contract, or the breach thereof, and if the dispute cannot be settled through negotiation, the parties agree first to try in good faith to settle the dispute by mediation administered by the American Arbitration Association under its Commercial Mediation Procedures before resorting to arbitration, litigation, or some other dispute resolution procedure.*[342]

If a party who has formed such a pre-dispute mediation agreement refuses to participate in mediation, what will a court do to enforce the agreement? While courts' usual method of contract-enforcement is money damages, how would these damages be calculated when the breach is the refusal to mediate? To put the non-breaching party in the position it would have been in had the contract been performed,[343] the court would have to predict the results of both mediation and litigation, then award as damages the difference (in terms of value to the non-breaching party) between the two. The speculativeness of such an approach is daunting,[344] and at least one court has refused to award money damages on that ground.[345] Little judicial authority supports the award of money damages for breach of agreements to mediate.[346]

In contrast, more authority supports granting specific performance for breach of agreements to mediate. Courts routinely enforce agreements to *arbitrate* with the remedy of specific

---

[342] AAA-ICDR Clause Drafting, https://www.adr.org/Clauses.

[343] This is the way to calculate the "expectation damages" normally awarded for breach of contract. See Restatement (Second) of Contracts §§ 344, 347 (1981).

[344] See Marland v. Safeway, Inc., 65 Fed. Appx. 442 (4th Cir. 2003).

> The contract does contain a clause which compels the parties to resolve any dispute through mediation. While Marland may at one time have had an action for specific performance to compel mediation, it sought only damages resulting from failure to mediate. We do not find any evidence in the record supporting such a damage claim.
>
> Further, even if such evidence had been submitted, Marland would be required to prove that such damages were foreseeable to Safeway at the time the contract was entered into. Because no such evidence was submitted, we hold that the district court appropriately granted summary judgment for Safeway on this count.

Id. at 448–49.

[345] DKH Homes, LP v. Kilgo, 2011 WL 1811435 (Tex. App. 2011) (DKH's claim that it should receive attorney's fees for prosecuting suit following Kilgos' failure to mediate presupposes that the parties would have reached an agreement had they mediated the case; such a claim is too speculative to constitute relevant evidence).

[346] Sarah R. Cole, Craig A. McEwen, Nancy H. Rogers, James R. Coben & Peter N. Thompson, Mediation: Law, Policy, & Practice § 6:1 (2024).

performance, that is, ordering the breaching party to arbitrate.[347] Similarly, "courts consistently dismiss litigation when one party fails to comply with mediation or other nonbinding dispute resolution clauses," in various sorts of contracts.[348] Such decisions can be found in a variety of courts enforcing mediation clauses in a variety of contracts.[349]

A party may waive its right to enforce an agreement to mediate.[350] And, like other contracts, an agreement to mediate may be unenforceable under contract defenses such as misrepresentation, mistake, and duress. However, "[t]hese challenges may themselves be subject to mediation under a mediation clause."[351]

Pre-dispute agreements to mediate are rarely held unconscionable. However, an unconscionability holding may occur when the agreement to mediate is part of a broader "ADR agreement" that includes an adhesive arbitration agreement and unusually harsh terms on the adhering party. For instance, the Hooters Restaurants' take-it-or-leave-it ADR agreement for its employees required the employee to travel a great distance for the mediation session "from which lawyers are excluded from participating."[352] Another court refused to enforce against the employee an Early

---

[347] See Stephen J. Ware & Ariana R. Levinson, Principles of Arbitration Law §§ 3, 11 (2d ed. 2023).

[348] Sarah R. Cole, Craig A. McEwen, Nancy H. Rogers, James R. Coben & Peter N. Thompson, Mediation: Law, Policy, & Practice § 6.1 (2024).

[349] DeValk Lincoln Mercury, Inc. v. Ford Motor Co., 811 F.2d 326, 335–37 (7th Cir. 1987) (affirming summary judgment for defendant because plaintiff failed to mediate; mediation was a condition precedent to plaintiff's right to pursue any other remedy); Begley v. Fullana-Morales, 2021 WL 2580601, *3–4 (D.P.R. 2021) (dismissing a case without prejudice because plaintiff failed to participate in mediation which was a contractual condition to other legal remedies); Sohmer v. Hwang, 2021 WL 2582804, *2 (W.D. N.C. 2021) (dismissing a case without prejudice when the plaintiff failed to attempt mediation in accordance with the dispute resolution clause of the agreement); KPH Healthcare Services, Inc. v. Mylan N.V., 2020 WL 3288057 (D. Kan. 2020) (enforcing pre-suit mediation requirement as condition precedent to litigation for antitrust claims); Primov v. Serco, Inc., 817 S.E.2d 811 (Va. 2018) ("employee's failure to comply with employment agreement's condition precedent requiring that written request to mediate be made prior to bringing suit warranted dismissal of action rather than staying action"); Smith v. Smith, 112 N.Y.S.3d 580, 581 (App. Div. 2019) (enforcing mediation clause in marital settlement agreement); US Magnesium, LLC v. ATI Titanium, LLC, 2017 WL 913596 (D. Utah 2017) (finding dismissal necessary where party failed to engage in mediation prior to filing suit as contract required); Cullenen v. Town of Rockingham, 2016 WL 6496225 (D. Vt. 2016) (granting motion to compel mediation in accordance with parties' agreement); Santana v. Olguin, 208 P.3d 328 (Kan. App. 2009) (dismissing case because plaintiff failed to comply with mediation condition in contract).

[350] Sarah R. Cole, Craig A. McEwen, Nancy H. Rogers, James R. Coben & Peter N. Thompson, Mediation: Law, Policy, & Practice § 6:6 (2024) ("Courts have found that delay in seeking mediation or refusal to mediate will result in waiver of the mediation clause").

[351] Id. § 6:7 (citing cases).

[352] Garrett v. Hooters-Toledo, 295 F. Supp. 2d 774, 781–82 (N.D. Ohio 2003).

Resolution Conference provision requiring the employee to give the employer 14 days written notice before violating or challenging other contract provisions and obligating the employee to "participate in a mediation or in-person conference if requested to do so by" the employer.[353] The court objected that this provision "contains no parallel requirement that [Employer] submit to mediation at [Employee]'s request, or a commitment on [Employer]'s part to mandatory mediation. Because this provision does not bind [Employer], it lacks consideration."[354]

## § 2.30 Mandatory Mediation

### *(a) Common in the U.S. and Some Other Places*

Courts and other government agencies in the U.S. often encourage, and even require, disputing parties to mediate before proceeding to trial or other decision by the court. Some statutes expressly require mediation of certain types of cases.[355] Examples include mandatory mediation of cases involving child custody (§ 2.17), labor (§ 2.18), and foreclosure (§ 2.19). Other statutes require certain types of agreements to include clauses requiring mediation of any disputes arising out of the agreement,[356] and such agreements are generally enforceable (§ 2.29).

More broadly, courts interpret statutes generally authorizing them to make "necessary or proper" orders as statutes authorizing them to order mediation.[357] As a result, throughout many state and

[353] Aerotek, Inc. v. Obercian, 377 F. Supp. 3d 539, 544 (D. Md. 2019).

[354] Id. at 554. Compare CJ Consultants Inc. v. Window World Inc, 2022 WL 4354265 (W.D. Mich. 2022) (enforcing pre-dispute mediation agreement after rejecting franchisee's argument that it is unconscionable because it applies only to claims against franchisor and because of the mediation's location).

[355] See, e.g., Iowa Code Ann. § 654A.6 (requiring mediation before farm foreclosure); Ocasio v. Froedtert Mem'l Lutheran Hosp., 646 N.W.2d 381, 382 (Wisc. 2002) (remanding to determine remedy for suit in violation of statute providing that "no court action may be commenced unless a request for mediation has been filed" for bodily injury or death because of a tort or breach of contract based on professional services rendered or that should have been rendered by a health care provider") (discussing Wis. Stat. Ann. § 655.44(1), (5)).

[356] Sarah Cole et al., Mediation: Law, Policy and Practice § 6:1 (2024) ("Under a Washington statute, dispute resolution clauses are a mandatory part of any agreement between divorcing parents settling custody and visitation disputes."); id. ("States have imposed mandatory mediation clauses in various other contexts including: Kansas for disability provider contracts; New Jersey for housing liens; Indiana for environmental work plans; Minnesota for agricultural commodity agreements; Tennessee for parenting plans; New Jersey for local government contracts; and California for environmental agreements between Native American tribes and regulatory agencies.")

[357] See, e.g., Breslin v. Breslin, 276 Cal. Rptr. 3d 913, 918 (Ct. App. 2021) ("The probate court has the power to order the parties into mediation.") (citing Cal. Prob. Code § 17206, which says "The court in its discretion may make any orders and take any other action necessary or proper to dispose of the matters presented by the petition, including appointment of a temporary trustee to administer the trust in

federal courts, statutes or rules give judges authority to order most types of civil cases into mediation.[358] However, Section 2.17 notes that states mandating mediation of family disputes often make exceptions for cases in which domestic violence is alleged. Going further, Oregon allows a party to any civil action to escape mandatory mediation simply by filing a written objection to it.[359] So while mandatory mediation is prevalent throughout the U.S., exceptions can in some jurisdictions come from parties as well as from judicial discretion.

While mandatory mediation may be especially prevalent in the U.S., other jurisdictions have it too. Perhaps closest to the U.S. is Ontario, Canada, which has long had "an extensive system of . . . mandatory mediation in civil and family matters."[360] England's "reluctance to embrace mandatory mediation began to wane in the 2010s, as economic pressures and caseload burdens on courts underscored the need for alternative mechanisms."[361] England in 2024 instituted mandatory mediation for small claims.[362] More broadly, England's rules of civil procedure permit a court to stay litigation ("proceedings") for "the parties try to settle the case by alternative dispute resolution or other means."[363] While appellate decisions in England have held that trial courts in some circumstances have the power to stay litigation for mediation,[364] no

whole or in part.")); Fraternal Ord. of Police v. District of Columbia, 139 A.3d 853, 870 (D.C. 2016) (ordering mediation based on D.C. Code § 17–306 (2013 Repl.), which authorizes the court, "in the disposition of an appeal, to 'direct the entry of such appropriate order, judgment, or decision, or require such further proceedings to be had, as is just in the circumstances' "); Ky. Farm Bureau Mut. Ins. Co. v. Wright, 136 S.W.3d 455, 458–59 (Ky. 2004) (upholding the trial court's mediation order based on the court's inherent power and Ky. R. Civ. P. 16(1)(f), which granted the court "jurisdiction to do what it deemed reasonably necessary to 'aid in the disposition of the action' ").

358 Sarah Cole et al., Mediation: Law, Policy and Practice § 9:2 (2024) (referring to and citing examples of "the growing number of statutes and court rules that authorize a court to order parties to mediation"); id. ("Courts uphold this power to compel mediation and treat it as an accepted part of litigation practice. Successful challenges to judicially compelled mediation are rare. Court orders requiring parties to mediate are not readily appealable in many jurisdictions because they are interlocutory orders.")

359 Or. Rev. Stat. § 36.185.

360 Julie Macfarlane & John Manwaring, Reconciling Professional Legal Education with the Evolving (Trial-Less) Reality of Legal Practice, 2006 J. Disp. Resol. 253, 257 (2006) (citing Ont. R. Civ. P. 24.1 (mandatory mediation).

361 Giuseppe De Palo, Mary B. Trevor, Is Mediation Becoming A Core Component of Justice in England and Wales?, 43 Alternatives to High Cost Litig. 35, 46 (2025).

362 Akshatha Achar, Integrating Mandatory Mediation: Transforming the U.K.'s Small Claims Process, 42 Alternatives to High Cost Litig. 130 (2024).

363 Civil Procedure Rule Part 26.5(1), (3).

364 In Churchill v. Merthyr Tydfil County Borough Council [2023] EWCA Civ 1416, the trial court refused to stay proceedings for mediation, holding it lacked power to compel it. However, the appellate court, at [22], said "the court can lawfully stay

example of a trial court doing so has, at this writing, been affirmed on appeal. And at least one English appellate court found that on the facts in that case mandating mediation would be an "unacceptable constraint on the right of access to the court and therefore a violation of article 6"[365] of the European Human Rights Convention, which says

> In the determination of his civil rights and obligations or of any criminal charge against him, everyone is entitled to a fair and public hearing within a reasonable time by an independent and impartial tribunal established by law.[366]

In contrast, the highest court of the European Union, the European Court of Justice (ECJ), held that Article 6 was not violated by Italy's mandatory mediation.[367] In doing so, the ECJ conditioned its endorsement of mandatory mediation on the following provisos:

a) the mandatory mediation procedures cannot result in a binding decision;

b) cannot cause substantial delay in bringing proceedings;

c) mediation time suspends any time-bar period; and

d) cannot give rise to more than minimal costs.[368]

---

existing proceedings for, or order, the parties to engage in a non-court-based dispute resolution process." See also id. at [65] ("the court should only stay proceedings for, or order, the parties to engage in a non-court-based dispute resolution process provided that the order made does not impair the very essence of the claimant's right to proceed to a judicial hearing, and is proportionate to achieving the legitimate aim of settling the dispute fairly, quickly and at reasonable cost.")

365 Halsey v. Milton Keynes NHS Trust [2004] EWCA Civ 576.

366 European Convention on Human Rights, https://www.echr.coe.int/documents/d/echr/convention_ENG. In Romania, mandatory mediation, been held unconstitutional. Anna Howard, EU Cross-Border Commercial Mediation § 2.04[A] & n.126 (2021).

367 Alassini v. Telecom Italia SpA, 2010 E.C.R. 134; Rosalba Alassini v. Telecom Italia SpA Legge 31 luglio 1997, n. 249 (It.).

368 Joined Cases C-317/08, C-318/08, C-319/08 & C-320/08, Rosalba Alassini v. Telecom Italia SpA, 2010 E.C.R. I-02213.

French law mandates mediation or conciliation for some cases involving employment,[369] small debts,[370] and if the court mandates, divorce.[371]

People may disagree about whether mediation is "mandatory" when law does not require it but nevertheless penalizes parties who do not mediate. For example, a Florida statute provides that in certain cases, "[i]f a party requests mediation and the opposing party refuses to agree to mediate upon proper request, the party refusing to mediate shall not be entitled to attorney's fees in any action relating to [the] dispute."[372] Sometimes mediation is encouraged by a judge who suggests to the opposing lawyers and parties that their case "looks appropriate for mediation," and asks the lawyers if they and their clients would be willing to try mediation. Although the judge has been subtle about it, the judge's message is received by the lawyers loud and clear: any party who refuses to mediate will have displeased the judge. So, each lawyer will likely advise her client to mediate, if only to stay in the good graces of the judge who will be presiding over the case if no settlement occurs.[373]

---

369 Code du Travail [Labor Code], Art. L1411-1 (Fr.) ("Le conseil de prud'hommes règle par voie de conciliation les différends qui peuvent s'élever à l'occasion de tout contrat de travail soumis aux dispositions du présent code entre les employeurs, ou leurs représentants, et les salariés qu'ils emploient.") ("The labor court settles by way of conciliation the disputes which may arise in connection with any employment contract subject to the provisions of this code between employers, or their representatives, and the employees they employ.")

370 Code de procédure civile [Civil Procedure Code], Art. 750 1 (Fr.) (" . . . demande en justice est précédée, au choix des parties, d'une tentative de conciliation menée par un conciliateur de justice, d'une tentative de médiation ou d'une tentative de procédure participative, lorsqu'elle tend au paiement d'une somme n'excédant pas 5000 euros . . . .") (" . . . the legal claim must be preceded, at the parties' choice, by an attempt at conciliation conducted by a court-appointed conciliator, an attempt at mediation or an attempt at participatory procedure, when it seeks payment of a sum not exceeding 5000 euros . . . .").

371 Code civil [Civil Code], Art. 255 (Fr.) ("Le juge peut . . . [e]njoindre aux époux, sauf si des violences sont alléguées par l'un des époux sur l'autre époux ou sur l'enfant, ou sauf emprise manifeste de l'un des époux sur son conjoint, de rencontrer un médiateur familial qui les informera sur l'objet et le déroulement de la mediation . . . .") ("The judge may . . . order the spouses, unless violence is alleged by one of the spouses against the other spouse or against the child, or unless there is manifest control of one of the spouses over their partner, to meet with a family mediator who will inform them about the purpose and process of mediation . . . .").

372 Fla. Stat. Ann. § 723.037(6).

373 Dorcas Quek, Mandatory Mediation: An Oxymoron? Examining the Feasibility of Implementing A Court-Mandated Mediation Program, 11 Cardozo J. Conflict Resol. 479, 487 (2010) ("In one study of New York state mediation centers, mediation program staff revealed that disputants often agreed to participate in mediation because they wished to impress the judge and they thought that their case would not be damaged if they told the judge that they made an effort to mediate").

### *(b) Policy Arguments for and Against*

Many courts and other government agencies encourage and even require disputing parties to mediate in the hope of increasing the percentage of cases that settle (§ 2.6). The more cases that settle, the fewer that go to trial. Increasing the number of cases that settle allows judges to devote more attention to those cases that remain.

That is attractive to judges and others who believe that the court system is overwhelmed with more cases than it can handle.[374] Bar associations have been sounding the alarms about "dangerously crowded dockets" and "overburdened judges" each decade since at least the 1950s.[375] The endorsement of mediation to reduce court congestion, delay, and expense is even found in legislation. For example, a North Carolina statute says,

> The General Assembly finds that a system of court-ordered mediated settlement conferences should be established to facilitate the settlement of superior court civil actions and to make civil litigation more economical, efficient, and satisfactory to litigants and the State.[376]

There is reason to believe that mediation does facilitate settlement. *Evaluation* by the mediator is likely to cause a convergence in the parties' expectations about the results of litigation (§ 2.13(a)). The closer the parties' expectations are to each other, the larger any settlement zone is likely to be. Also, mediation is more likely than negotiation to foster settlements because of mediation's tendency to facilitate communication and exploit *positive-sum* opportunities, which can also expand the settlement zone (§ 2.12).

On the other hand, some studies indicate that mediation does little to encourage settlement. These studies indicate that settlement rates with mediation are only slightly higher than, or even the same as, settlement rates without mediation.[377] In other words, mediated

---

[374] Simmons v. Ghaderi, 187 P.3d 934, 939 (Cal. 2008) ("California's Legislature has a strong policy favoring mediation as an alternative to litigation. Because mediation provides a simple, quick, and economical means of resolving disputes, and because it may also help reduce the court system's backlog of cases, it is in the public interest to encourage its use.")

[375] Stephen J. Ware, Is Adjudication A Public Good? "Overcrowded Courts" and the Private Sector Alternative of Arbitration, 14 Cardozo J. Conflict Resol. 899, 901–03 (2013) (quoting bar associations).

[376] N.C. Gen. Stat. § 7A–38.1. See also Ark. Code Ann. § 9–31–405 ("The Arkansas Youth Mediation Program's goals are to: (1) Reduce economic, psychological, and social costs to individuals and public and private institutions arising from disputes involving youth; (2) Reduce court dockets and delays; . . .[and] reducing unnecessary adversarial behavior and expense in litigation throughout Arkansas.")

[377] Michael D. Campbell & Sharon L. Pizzuti, Case Evaluation and Mediation in Michigan Circuit Courts: A Follow Up Study, Courtland Consulting 51 (2018), https://www.courts.michigan.gov/4a9f38/siteassets/reports/odr/2018-mediation-and-case-

settlements largely replace negotiated settlements, not trials. The cases that settle in mediation may be the cases that would have settled without mediation. So, if the goal is to clear congested trial dockets or save money in the court system, then encouraging or requiring mediation may do little to achieve the goal.

Another rationale for encouraging or requiring mediation is to achieve not *more* settlements, but *better* settlements.[378] And some empirical data suggests that mediation tends to make settlements come earlier in litigation, rather than on the eve of trial.[379] Earlier settlements are, all else equal, better settlements because they tend to save the parties time, money, and aggravation. In addition, mediated settlements are better settlements to the extent they tend to be more positive sum than negotiated settlements (§ 2.12). So, plausible reasons exist for courts to encourage, or even require, mediation. Doing so may produce a slightly higher settlement rate and seems to produce settlements that tend overall to be faster and better than they would be without mediation.

On the other hand, the arguments against encouraging, and especially requiring, mediation reflect concerns about costs, party autonomy, and disempowered groups.[380] Mandating mediation may do nothing but require the parties to spend time and money on a mediation that will not increase the chance of settlement. The parties presumably know better than a judge or other court employee whether mediation is worthwhile for their particular dispute, so if they do not voluntarily choose it, they should not be forced into it.[381]

---

evaluation-study.pdf (In a study of 221 tort case records, "[t]he tort cases that did not use ADR had a 71% rate of settlement/consent. While the rates of settlement were higher for cases that used case evaluation (82%) and mediation (92%), these were not statistically significant increases. The lack of significance was likely due to the fact that the high rate of settlement for non-ADR cases left relatively little room for improvement when ADR was used."), https://www.courts.michigan.gov/498849/siteassets/reports/odr/2018-mediation-and-case-evaluation-study.pdf; Roselle L. Wissler, The Effectiveness of Court-Connected Dispute Resolution in Civil Cases, 22 Conflict Resol. Q. 55, 65 (2004) (of "eight studies that included a comparison group of non-mediation cases, half found that cases referred to mediation tended to have a somewhat higher rate of settlement . . ., but half found no differences.")

378 See S.D. Ala., ADR Plan ("The purposes of mediation are to increase the chances of settlement, help the litigants devise better settlements, and improve relationships among the litigants.")

379 Roselle L. Wissler, The Effectiveness of Court-Connected Dispute Resolution in Civil Cases, 22 Conflict Resol. Q. 55, 67 (2004) ("Five studies reported that mediation cases terminated faster than nonmediation cases . . . . However, four studies found no differences in disposition time.")

380 See generally Society of Professionals in Dispute Resolution, Mandated Participation and Settlement Coercion: Dispute Resolution as It Relates to the Courts (1991).

381 Nancy A. Welsh, The Place of Court-Connected Mediation in A Democratic Justice System, 5 Cardozo J. Conflict Resol. 117, 142 (2004) ("Courts should end their reliance on mandatory mediation. . . .If mediation is truly a valuable process that

This opposition to mediation may be a mutual view of both opposing parties, or the defendant may see mandating mediation as helpful precisely because it adds another hurdle of time and money the plaintiff must pay before it can get a court's ruling on the merits. For example, Section 2.19 notes that mandating foreclosure and eviction mediation is designed to make foreclosing and evicting slower and more expensive for creditors.

Those untroubled by mandating that creditors mediate may be more troubled by mandates' applications to disempowered groups. Some contend that mediation, when compared to litigation, "increase[s] the risk of unfair treatment for minority disputants, women and the poor,"[382] so law should not require these parties to mediate. These party-autonomy arguments, combined with concern for domestic violence victims, have influenced the law. As Section 2.17 explains, some statutes exempt from the mandatory mediation of family disputes cases involving domestic violence,[383] with one rationale being that it is wrong to force a victim of abuse to mediate with the abuser.[384] More broadly, the party-autonomy principle also appears in Oregon legislation allowing a party to escape mandatory mediation simply by filing a written objection to it.[385]

---

responds to citizens' desires for an alternative means to resolve disputes, the process should be able to stand on its own, freely selected by parties as their disputes arise."); Trina Grillo, The Mediation Alternative: Process Dangers for Women, 100 Yale L.J. 1545, 1582 (1991) ("It is presumptuous to assume that the state has a better idea than the parties themselves about whether mediation will work in their particular case.")

[382] Richard Delgado et al., Fairness and Formality: Minimizing the Risk of Prejudice in Alternative Dispute Resolution, 1985 Wis. L. Rev. 1359, 1400. And there is one study suggesting "that minority participants generally fare worse than whites in both mediation and adjudication, and that these effects are most severe in mediation." Michele Hermann et al., Metrocourt Project Final Report: A Study of the Effects of Ethnicity and Gender in Mediated and Adjudicated Cases at the Metropolitan Court Mediation Center viii–xii (1993).

[383] Sarah R. Cole, Craig A. McEwen, Nancy H. Rogers, James R. Coben & Peter N. Thompson, Mediation: Law, Policy, & Practice § 15:2 (2024) ("A view that victims of intimate partner or other domestic violence are not well served in mediation has led most states to enact exceptions to or other restrictions of mandated mediation in these cases. These exceptions may exclude about a quarter or more of cases eligible for mediation—some studies suggest that the figure is half or more—and have generated controversy about whether empirical evidence supports arguments for exclusion"). Some statutes distinguish between mediation with and without lawyers present. See, e.g., Minn. Stat. Ann. § 518.619 ("If the court determines that there is probable cause that one of the parties, or a child of a party, has been physically or sexually abused by the other party, the court shall not require or refer the parties to mediation or any other process that requires parties to meet and confer without counsel, if any, present.").

[384] See Sarah R. Cole, Craig A. McEwen, Nancy H. Rogers, James R. Coben & Peter N. Thompson, Mediation: Law, Policy, & Practice § 15:5 (2024). But as noted in § 2.17, some jurisdictions implement ameliorative measures like "shuttle mediation, video conferencing, asynchronous meetings, and other uses of technology."

[385] Or. Rev. Stat. § 36.185.

These seem to be exceptions to a general long-term trend of increased mandatory mediation.[386] Lawmakers, including courts, in the U.S., generally seem to believe that merely participating in mediation is a small burden and that the coercion of requiring it is a price worth paying to achieve the hoped-for benefits of mediation. Notice, however, that the parties' burden from mandatory mediation may include some or all of the following costs:

- the parties' time,
- paying for the lawyers' time,
- paying for the mediator,[387]
- travel costs to the mediation, and
- the delay of another hurdle before trial.

### *(c) Who Must Participate?*

One of the costs mandatory mediation imposes on the parties is the consumption of their time. If a party can avoid participating in mediation by sending a lawyer, then the burden of mandatory mediation on the party's time is quite low. And many parties choose to have their lawyers participate in mediation on their behalf, just as they choose to have their lawyers participate in negotiation on their behalf. Some court orders mandating mediation, however, require participation of the client as well as the lawyer.[388] And some family

---

[386] Sarah R. Cole, Craig A. McEwen, Nancy H. Rogers, James R. Coben & Peter N. Thompson, Mediation: Law, Policy, & Practice § 3:3 (2024) ("Mandatory mediation has become increasingly common in the last two decades—either on a case-by-case basis or for a whole category of cases.")

[387] Id. § 9:11 ("Many jurisdictions require that the parties pay for court-ordered mediation. The expenses of mediation may, in some jurisdictions, be taxed as costs and recovered by the prevailing party. Thus, a part of compliance with the mediation obligations may include payment of the mediator's fee to the court or to a private provider. Failure to pay the mediator when required by a court order or rule may result in sanctions"). For examples of mandatory mediation requiring parties to pay for the mediator, see, e.g., N.M. Stat. Ann. §§ 40–12–5 ("Parents shall pay the cost of the domestic relations mediation program pursuant to a sliding fee scale approved by the supreme court. The sliding fee scale shall be based on ability to pay for the specific service rendered by the counselor. The fees shall be paid to the district court to be credited to the fund."); Ala. Code § 6–6–20(b)(2) ("The party asking for mediation shall pay the costs of mediation, except attorney fees, unless otherwise agreed.").

[388] Doorstep Beverages of Longwood, Inc. v. Collier, 928 So. 2d 482, 483 (Fla. Ct. App. 2006) (imposing sanctions on counsel for the failure of the client to appear at the appellate mediation where counsel admitted to the court that he failed to advise his client that this attendance was required); Long v. Am. Family Mut. Ins. Co., S.I., 2019 WL 5819968, *3 (D. Kan. 2019) (granting sanctions when counsel of record, but no insurance company representative, attended the mediation); Roanoke Country Club, Inc. v. Town of Williamston, 759 S.E.2d 711 (N.C. Ct. App. 2014) (granting sanctions when parties' wives, who were also parties, did not attend the mediation arguing that they had authorized their husbands to represent them).

mediation statutes allow the mediator to require the participation of the client unaccompanied by a lawyer (§ 2.17).

Some clients cannot participate in mediation except through lawyers or other agents. For example, corporations cannot participate except through the humans who represent them. When a corporation is required to participate in mediation, can it send a low-level employee, or must it send the Chief Executive Officer or even a quorum of the entire Board of Directors? The time of high-level executives and directors is quite precious to the corporation so any mediation rule that consumes a significant amount of their time imposes a severe burden.[389] On the other hand, sending an agent who lacks full settlement authority is an old trick to prevent settlement at anything but one-sided terms (§ 1.17(e)).

### *(d) Good Faith*

Suppose a party and his lawyer arrive for mandatory mediation at the appointed time, but they refuse to speak, and each insists on wearing noise-cancelling headphones to avoid hearing anything the mediator or other party says. Has that party satisfied his duty to mediate? If so, mandatory mediation is pointless. The presence at mediation of a party who refuses to speak or listen is not going to promote settlement, let alone a fast or good settlement. For this reason, some mandatory mediation requirements impose a duty to mediate in "good faith."[390] If the court finds that a party failed to make a good faith effort to mediate, the court may punish that party financially or even render a default judgment against that party.[391]

---

[389] Compare G. Heileman Brewing Co. v. Joseph Oat Corp., 871 F.2d 648, 655 (7th Cir. 1989) (enforcing order that corporate party send to pretrial conference an agent with "full authority to settle the case or to make decisions and grant authority to counsel with respect to all matters that may be reasonably anticipated to come before the conference"), with id. at 663–65 (Easterbrook, J. dissenting) (sending agent with full settlement authority might require sending a quorum of the entire Board of Directors). See also Physicians Protective Trust Fund v. Overman, 636 So.2d 827 (Fla. Dist. Ct. App. 1994) (ordering attendance of entire Board of Directors).

[390] Sarah R. Cole, Craig A. McEwen, Nancy H. Rogers, James R. Coben & Peter N. Thompson, Mediation: Law, Policy, & Practice § 9:3 (2024) (in some laws duties to participate in mediation "are defined in specific terms, such as a duty to prepare documents for mediation, to appear at the mediation, or to appear at the mediation with a person who has settlement authority. It is common, however, to define the duty in general terms, usually requiring the parties to mediate in good faith. Typically, the court or court rule does not define 'good faith,' leaving it to the litigation process to flesh out the details of precisely what bargaining behavior is required.") See, e.g., Kan. Stat. Ann. § 72–2235(c)(4); Me. Rev. Stat. Ann. tit. 19-A, § 251(4). Federal Rule of Civil Procedure 16(f), which is often used as authority for ordering pretrial conferences or mediation, goes further to sanction a party who is "substantially unprepared to participate." Fed. R. Civ. P. 16(f). Compare § 1.16(e) (discussing usual lack of duty to negotiate in good faith).

[391] Me. R. Civ. P. 16B(e); Nick v. Morgan's Foods, Inc. 270 F.3d 590 (8th Cir. 2001) (financial sanctions); Wahle v. Medical Center of Delaware, Inc., 559 A.2d 1228 (Del.

One practical problem with a "good faith" standard, of course, is that it is so indeterminate. Good faith is in the eye of the beholder; what may look like bad faith to you, may not look like bad faith to me. Case law may or may not provide some guidance.[392] For instance, one Fifth Circuit case holds that good faith does not require making a settlement offer.[393] But another Fifth Circuit case, only a year later, sanctioned a defendant that offered to pay only $100,000 (in a case resulting in a $6 million jury verdict) because the defendant "concealed its true position that it never intended to settle the case."[394]

Another practical problem with a "good faith" standard is that, to determine whether a party's participation was in good faith, a court may have to learn things about the mediation that break the confidentiality of mediation discussed in Section 2.28.[395] Some jurisdictions with mandatory mediation avoid these problems by refusing to impose any good-faith requirement.[396] How those jurisdictions would deal with the party who insists on wearing headphones to mediation remains to be seen.

A variation on the requirement to mediate in good faith is the requirement to keep mediating after a party has given it a good faith try. If a case drags on for many months or even years after a court-mandated mediation session, the court may be tempted to mandate another round of mediation. This repeated mandatory mediation may

1989) (failure to attend court-sponsored arbitration and to comply with other pretrial orders resulted in dismissal); Triad Mack Sales & Serv. v. Clement Bros. Co., 438 S.E.2d 485 (N.C. Ct. App. 1994) (failure to attend mediation without good cause resulted in default judgment).

392 Generally, courts have "limited their interpretation of good faith to attendance, submission of pre-mediation memoranda, and, in some cases, attendance of organizational representatives with settlement authority." John Lande, Using Dispute System Design Methods to Promote Good-Faith Participation in Court-Connected Mediation Programs, 50 UCLA L. Rev. 69, 86 (2002).

393 Dawson v. United States, 68 F.3d 886 (5th Cir. 1995). See also Hess v. New Jersey Transit Rail Operations, Inc., 846 F.2d 114 (2d Cir. 1988).

394 Guillory v. Domtar Industries Inc., 95 F.3d 1320, 1335 (5th Cir. 1996).

395 See In re A.T. Reynolds & Sons, Inc., 452 B.R. 374, 383–84 (S.D.N.Y. 2011) ("Inquiring into the parties' level of participation also imperils the confidentiality of mediation."); id. ("Accordingly, this Court holds the confidentiality considerations preclude a court from inquiring into the level of a party's participation in mandatory court-ordered mediation, i.e., the extent to which a party discusses the issues, listens to opposing viewpoints and analyzes its liability. This holding provides a clear and objective standard with minimal intrusion into confidentiality and a party's right to refuse to settle. This holding is also consistent with the general pattern of interpretation by the courts, which have interpreted good faith narrowly to require compliance with orders to attend mediation, provide pre-mediation memoranda, and, in some cases, produce organizational representatives with sufficient settlement authority."); Foxgate Homeowner's Assoc. v. Bramalea, 25 P.3d 1117 (Cal. 2001) (mediation privilege bars testimony about whether party had bargained in good faith).

396 Decker v. Lindsay, 824 S.W.2d 247 (Tex. Ct. App. 1992); Graham v. Baker, 447 N.W.2d 397 (Iowa 1989).

achieve a settlement on the second or third try, but at some point, access to justice requires the judge to move from mandating mediation to scheduling the case for trial.[397] As one family lawyer put it,

> To add to the delays, the court may order the parties to engage in multiple mediations to: (1) develop their Temporary Parenting Plan, (2) address other immediate but piecemeal relief, (3) develop their Permanent Parenting Plan and (4) reach global resolution. If any mediations fail, the judge may order the parties to attend mediation again.
>
> . . . requiring parties to reach consensus may be inappropriate where there is a pre-existing or current power differential between them. One party's repeated request for mediation after it has already failed can be used as a tactic to reduce the other party's wherewithal, emotional stamina and access to justice. If they are unable to reach consensus, parties lose time and money and gain no resolution.
>
> Multiple mediations increase the overall expenses and attorney's fees to litigate family law issues. Each time they attend mediation, family law litigants must pay their own attorney's fees and the mediator's fees. In complex, high-conflict cases involving custody, the parties may also be required to pay fees for other attorneys who are court-appointed to assist the court. Guardians ad litem and attorneys ad litem are examples of other attorneys that are court-appointed in family law cases. Though they perform a function for the court, litigants are required to pay these attorneys' hourly rates throughout the case.[398]

### *(e) Additional Pressures to Settle: Mediator's Evaluation and Report to the Court*

As noted in § 2.30(b), requiring mediation may somewhat increase the likelihood of settlement. To further increase the likelihood of settlement, mandatory mediation can include *evaluation* by the mediator. A mediator's evaluation tends to narrow the divergence between the parties' expectations about the result of

---

[397] Bankruptcy judges may be particularly tempted to rely for too long on mandating mediation due to their "docket pressure or concern about the complexity of the case." Laura N. Coordes, Chapter 11 Mediation, 41 Emory Bankr. Dev. J. 153, 189 (2025).

[398] K.O. Herston, Everything You Need to Know about the Tennessee Domestic Relations Arbitration Act, March 13, 2023, https://herstontennesseefamilylaw.com/2023/03/13/everything-you-need-to-know-about-the-tennessee-domestic-relations-arbitration-act/.

litigation, and this convergence makes settlement more likely (§ 2.13). Evaluative mediation inches closer to the processes of *neutral evaluation* (§ 2.32) and *non-binding arbitration* (§ 2.33).

The versions of mandatory mediation with the strongest pressures to settle send the mediator's evaluation to the judge.[399] This makes the evaluation not merely a prediction of how the case will be decided but also an influence on how the case is decided and thus arguably converts mediation into adjudication (§ 2.2). When parties expect the so-called mediator's evaluation will go to the court, the parties should argue their cases to the "mediator" much as they would argue to the judge, thus converting the "mediator" into an adjudicator. This loses the benefits of mediation as a process encouraging parties to disclose their interests and priorities (§ 2.12) and their bottom lines and weaknesses (§ 2.13).

These benefits of mediation are protected by confidentiality, (§ 2.28(a)), so at least one appellate court has reversed a trial court whose ruling was based on the report of a mediator who violated mediation's confidentiality by issuing a report expressing the mediator's opinion about which party was standing in the way of settlement.

> The mediator here went beyond his permitted authority in disclosing more than just whether the mediation had occurred or was terminated; whether a settlement was reached; and the attendance of the parties. Rather, the mediator provided a factual background of the matter as well as injected his opinion and reasoning as to which party was not at fault. Furthermore, the trial court, in its judgment entry, concluded that the plaintiff failed to "negotiate in good faith," a conclusion based on improper reliance upon a "mediation communication" that exceeded the boundaries of [the statute permitting only the above mediator disclosures].
>
> Accordingly, we conclude the court erred in considering and basing its ruling on mediation communication and an improper mediation report.[400]

---

399 See Cal, Fam Code § 3183(a) (2025) ("the mediator may, consistent with local court rules, submit a recommendation to the court as to the custody of or visitation with the child"); Sarah R. Cole, Craig A. McEwen, Nancy H. Rogers, James R. Coben & Peter N. Thompson, Mediation: Law, Policy, & Practice § 8:40 (2024) ("to increase settlement rates, some statutory schemes permit the mediator to issue a more substantive report or recommendation if no settlement is reached.").

400 BAC Home Loans Servicing v. Testa, No. 2011-P-0045, 2012 WL 5844892 (Ohio Ct. App. Nov. 19, 2012).

### *(f) Settlement Conferences as Mandatory Mediation*

#### *(1) Civil*

Settlement conferences in court vary. Sometimes the "settlement conference" is as simple and ineffective as the judge merely asking the lawyers at a pre-trial conference whether they have tried to settle the case.[401] If the lawyers say they tried unsuccessfully, many judges will let the subject drop.

In contrast, other settlement conferences—while not often called "mandatory mediation"—become just that, with the judge as the mediator.[402] The judge's mere presence can facilitate negotiation by encouraging the lawyers to be constructive and positive. The judge may require that the parties, as well as their lawyers, be present at the settlement conference.[403] The judge may become involved in the discussion, perhaps helping to focus issues, or even evaluating the merits of the case.[404] The most evaluative judges even propose terms of settlement, although this sometimes leads to the settlement being overturned on appeal.[405] Occasionally a judge goes so far as to

---

[401] Fed. R. Civ. P. 16(a)(5) ("the court may order the attorneys and any unrepresented parties to appear for one or more pretrial conferences for such purposes as . . . facilitating settlement.").

[402] Ellen E. Deason, Beyond "Managerial Judges": Appropriate Roles in Settlement, 78 Ohio St. L.J. 73, 99 (2017) ("The labels 'mediation' and 'settlement conference' are not very helpful for informing parties what to expect in a settlement process. As a starting point, although local court rules frequently authorize the two processes separately, creating an implication that they are distinct processes with separate identities, there is no precise understanding of the differences between them. The labels encompass widely varying and overlapping practices, making their use problematic."); id. at 102 ("If it is difficult to separate judges' behaviors in court settlement conferences from those of private mediators, it is even more difficult to distinguish between behaviors in 'settlement conferences' and 'mediation' when both are court processes conducted by judicial officers.")

[403] See 28 U.S.C. § 473(b)(5) ("a requirement that, upon notice by the court, representatives of the parties with authority to bind them in settlement discussions be present or available by telephone during any settlement conference"); G. Heileman Brewing Co. v. Joseph Oat Corp., 871 F.2d 648 (7th Cir. 1989).

[404] Ellen E. Deason, Beyond "Managerial Judges": Appropriate Roles in Settlement, 78 Ohio St. L.J. 73, 113 (2017) (referring to "a traditional settlement conference that involves an evaluative approach").

[405] See, e.g., Carvalhos Masonry, LLC v. S & L Variety Contractors, LLC, 183 A.3d 697, 699–700 (Conn. App. Ct. 2018) (after bench trial, but before trial court rendered judgment, trial court suggested the parties stipulate to a judgment for a specific dollar amount; defendant refused and trial court entered judgment for the exact amount that it had suggested; appellate court held that trial court should have disqualified itself from deciding the issues of liability and damages following its failed attempt to convince the parties to stipulate to judgment); McKenna v. Ass'n of Apt. Owners of Elima Lani, 470 P.3d 1110, 1114, 1120 (Haw. 2020) (vacating order enforcing settlement agreement when plaintiff alleged, among other things, that trial judge "improperly introduced [the] confidential Mediation amount as a starting point for settlement negotiations" (alteration in original) (quoting plaintiff's brief)); Deikan v. Blackwelder, 2011 Mass. App. Div. 66, 71 (2011) (vacating enforcement of a judge-proposed $9,000 settlement agreement); Kothe v. Smith, 771 F.2d 667 (2d Cir. 1985)

perform "shuttle diplomacy." Each side is in its own room and the judge travels back and forth.[406] The judge may tell Plaintiff how weak her case is and then, minutes later, tell Defendant that the judge expects a high dollar verdict.[407]

These tactics tend to increase the likelihood of settlement. A neutral's evaluation tends to narrow the divergence between the parties' expectations about the results of litigation, and this convergence makes settlement more likely (§ 2.13(a)). This is especially true if the neutral is the judge who will be presiding over the case. The judge's evaluation is an excellent predictor of how the case will be decided because the judge can influence the case to be decided that way.

Judges can "be forceful arm twisters," and "the authority of the office accompanies a judge even in an informal process such as a settlement conference or mediation," which can "turn the judge into a coercive authority figure in the parties' eyes."[408] "The potential for coercion is elevated many fold when the arm twisting," "comes from a judge who will have decisional power over the case if it does not settle" because parties know that judges are under pressure to clear

(reversing award of sanctions against party who refused to settle in range suggested by judge); Dodds v. Commission on Judicial Performance, 906 P.2d 1260 (Cal. 1995); Peskin v. Peskin, 638 A.2d 849 (N.J. Super. Ct. App. Div. 1994) (reversing settlement coerced by trial judge); Stanley Ryan & John Wickham, Pre-trial Practice in Wisconsin Courts, 1954 Wisc. L. Rev. 5, 16 ("I offer suggestions, intimate to the attorneys and clients the possibility and extent of liability, suggest the range of what I believe to be a fair settlement, and then also attempt to persuade the parties and their attorneys to accept a settlement within that range."). Other judicial tactics to encourage settlement also meet with criticism from lawyers. See, e.g., Daisy Hurst Floyd, Can the Judge Do That? The Need for a Clearer Judicial Role in Settlement, 26 Ariz. St. L.J. 45, 55–56 (1994).

[406] Sharon Press, Mediator Ethical Breaches: Implications for Public Policy, 6 Y.B. On Arb. & Mediation 107, 140 (2014) ("The [judge] then went back and forth between the two rooms during the course of the negotiations . . . described as 'Kissinger-style shuttle diplomacy.' "); Peter H. Schuck, The Role of Judges in Settling Complex Cases: The Agent Orange Example, 53 U. Chi. L. Rev. 337 (1986).

> [T]he special masters undertook a grueling two-day course of shuttle diplomacy, holding separate meetings with each side interspersed with private conferences with Judge Weinstein. On several occasions, the judge met privately with each side.
>
> Several features of the discussion were particularly salient in generating the settlement agreement. First, the court did not permit the two sides to meet face-to-face until the very end, after the terms of the deal had been defined. This strategy preserved the court's control over the negotiations and prevented them from fragmenting.

Id. at 345.

[407] See Sharon Press, Mediator Ethical Breaches: Implications for Public Policy, 6 Y.B. On Arb. & Mediation 107, 167 (2014) ("If one compares what happens during judicial settlement conferences versus mediations, it is not uncommon for a judge to 'beat-up' on the lawyers in an effort to settle the case.").

[408] Ellen E. Deason, Beyond "Managerial Judges": Appropriate Roles in Settlement, 78 Ohio St. L.J. 73, 109–10 (2017).

their dockets,[409] so parties worry that the judge's later rulings will not favor a party who rejected a settlement proposal backed by the judge.

> [T]here are too many troubling accounts of behavior that, even if only isolated instances, could be coercive. Consider the judge who reportedly instructed plaintiff's counsel to "tell his client he'd better settle or there would be 'reverse interest' if the damage award was lower." Or the judge who threatened contempt and warned that he would take defendant's refusal to settle into account in considering any fee application. Then there was the judge who allegedly threatened to report a party to the ethics committee if the mediation did not succeed. Even less explicit threats, such as an admonition to settle "because I can guarantee you much pain," or a judge's antagonistic reaction to counsel's statement that mediation would not "work out right now," can be interpreted as coercive.[410]

We lack practical ways "to remedy coercive judicial settlement behavior,"[411] so instead of mediation by the judge who will be presiding over the case, the mediator is often another judge in the same or neighboring district.[412] Similarly, in federal courts "it has become common for presiding judges to select other judges to 'mediate' in their cases."[413] "Magistrate judges regularly serve as mediating judges at the request of district judges and each other," while "82% of bankruptcy judges reported that their courts had used non-presiding judges for settlement or mediation."[414] And ongoing litigation over school desegregation, prison reform, and the like can involve ongoing mediation by a special master.[415]

---

409 Id.

410 Id. at 110–12.

411 Id.

412 Id. at 134–35 (citing federal court local rules under which "Neutral roles are typically kept separate by a rule specifying that the judicial officer who is assigned to try the case may not serve as the mediator"); id. at 136 (for settlement conferences, "a substantial number of districts have adopted" similar rules "that explicitly exclude the assigned judge from serving as the presiding neutral at a settlement conference").

413 Melissa B. Jacoby, Other Judges' Cases, 78 N.Y.U. Ann. Surv. Am. L. 39, 45 (2022).

414 Id. at 45–46.

415 See James S. Degraw, Note: Rule 53, Inherent Powers, And Institutional Reform: The Lack Of Limits On Special Masters., 66 N.Y.U. L. Rev. 800, 801 (1991) ("Special masters can play essential roles in modern litigation [such as] conducting settlement conferences"); id. at 802 ("when drafting the terms of [ ] a [remedial] decree and overseeing an institution's compliance with it, judges are relying upon special masters for assistance . . . during judicial efforts to transform prisons, integrate schools, draft community housing plans, oversee institutions for the mentally retarded, and supervise affirmative action programs.").

### (2) *Criminal (Plea Bargaining)*

According to a leading scholar writing in the 1970s, "[t]he general consensus, seems to be that trial judges should not participate in the pretrial negotiations that currently lead the overwhelming majority of American criminal defendants to plead guilty."[416] Back then, judicial participation in plea bargaining tended to be "with a wink and a nod, or in secret;" in contrast, it "is now institutionalized and embedded in the very structure of many court systems in ways never dreamed of in the 1970s."[417] In some jurisdictions, routine conferences of the judge, prosecutor, and defendant's lawyer "are incorporated into normal case processing."[418]

> At the meeting, if the parties have not yet agreed on a possible resolution, they usually present a short summary to the judge of important evidence, the defendant's criminal history, and the likely scoring under sentencing guidelines, if any, for the charges. After listening to these summaries, the judge responds with language along the lines of, "Based on the information I have now, this is what I would give him if he decides to plead guilty." When the parties float a proposed sentence deal, the judge indicates whether it is acceptable.[419]

These conferences can be off the record in the judge's chambers, or "on the record, whether it be in a courtroom, at the bench, or recorded in chambers."[420]

Much as judicial mediation of civil cases is often conducted by a judge other than the judge presiding over the case, some states have used a similar approach with judicial involvement in facilitating plea negotiations.[421]

---

416 Albert W. Alschuler, The Trial Judge's Role in Plea Bargaining, Part I, 76 Colum. L. Rev. 1059 (1976).

417 Nancy J. King & Ronald F. Wright, The Invisible Revolution in Plea Bargaining: Managerial Judging and Judicial Participation in Negotiations, 95 Tex. L. Rev. 325, 326 (2016).

418 Id. at 338.

419 Id. at 340.

420 Id. at 341.

421 Id. at 352 (Oregon "mediators in these [ ] cases are a subset of the county's judges . . . Each judge devotes at least one afternoon a week to these conferences, which are held off the record, in the courtroom, 'about forty-five days out' from first appearance. At the conference, the judge might meet with the prosecution separately from meeting with defense counsel and the defendant. Those separate meetings make it easier for the mediator to 'unstick' the parties from their initial negotiating"); id. at 354 ("In Kansas, . . . a small number of counties have quietly started, without any rule or statutory change, to conduct mediation in criminal cases similar to the process described in Oregon. . . . The judge assigned to try the case selects a mediator for the case, often another sitting or retired judge who has volunteered to take mediations.")

# G. OTHER PROCESSES IN AID OF NEGOTIATION

## § 2.31 Introduction to Other Processes in Aid of Negotiation

The previous sections of this chapter discuss mediation, the most important process in aid of negotiation. This section discusses two other processes in aid of negotiation: neutral evaluation (§ 2.32), and non-binding arbitration (§ 2.33). Like mediation, these processes involve a third-party neutral but do not by themselves resolve disputes as litigation and arbitration do. Rather, neutral evaluation and non-binding arbitration, like mediation, help the parties negotiate a resolution to the dispute (§ 2.2). Accordingly, they can be called "processes in aid of negotiation."[422]

> These processes promote settlement through adversarial presentations of evidence (or summaries of evidence) and arguments, which result in advisory findings by a neutral. . . . These findings, together with the experience of the hearing process itself, may provide parties with a clearer recognition of the strengths and weaknesses of their case and a more realistic assessment of likely litigated outcomes.[423]

In short, neutral evaluation and non-binding arbitration aim to facilitate settlement by showing parties what will happen if they don't settle.

## § 2.32 Neutral Evaluation

As Sections 2.2 and 2.13 explain, evaluation is less precise than adjudication. *Evaluation* is an assessment of the merits of a case that does not go so far as to decree a specific, concrete result. For example, an adjudicator (judge, jury, or arbitrator) tells the parties that "Defendant is liable to Plaintiff in the amount of $250,000." In contrast, an evaluator might say "Plaintiff has a very strong argument that Defendant breached the contract, and damages

---

See also State v. Niblack, 220 Conn. 270, 280, 596 A.2d 407, 412 (1991) ("The judge was responsible for conducting plea negotiations and, if an agreement was reached, for holding a plea and sentencing hearing. If negotiations were not successful, however, a judge who was not involved in the plea negotiations would have presided at trial and pronounced sentence if the defendant were found guilty. We approve of the procedure followed in reaching the plea agreement.")

422 Sarah R. Cole, Craig A. McEwen, Nancy H. Rogers, James R. Coben & Peter N. Thompson, Mediation: Law, Policy, & Practice § 3:4 (2024) ("nonbinding arbitration, mini-trials, and summary jury trials, aid the settlement process but differ procedurally from mediation").

423 Sarah R. Cole, Craig A. McEwen, Nancy H. Rogers, James R. Coben & Peter N. Thompson, Mediation: Law, Policy, & Practice § 5:4 (2024).

appear to be in the low six figures," or "I've seen verdicts in similar cases range around two or three hundred thousand dollars." Other examples of evaluation include "Defendant's contributory negligence argument is unlikely to persuade a jury," or "Plaintiff seems to have shown strong evidence of price-fixing."

As Section 2.13(a) (discussing evaluative mediation) explains, parties' over-optimism about their success at litigation can prevent settlement zones. So, advocates of settlement seek to reduce party over-optimism and thus make the parties' expectations about litigation results converge. Neutral evaluation tends to do that. It reduces the gap between the parties' expectations by giving them information (the neutral's evaluation of the case) that causes the parties' expectations about the results of litigation to converge around the neutral's evaluation. The neutral, because her judgment is respected by the parties, persuades the parties to change their expectations.

While that neutral evaluation discussed in Section 2.13(a) was neutral evaluation by a mediator, neutral evaluation can also be provided by someone who does not mediate but only evaluates. Such a person may be called a neutral evaluator, and the process may be called neutral evaluation. When it occurs soon after a case is filed, it may be called Early Neutral Evaluation ("ENE").

For example, the rules of the United States District Court for the District of Vermont say,

> ENE is meant to reduce costs and litigation by providing litigants the opportunity:
>
> (1) to articulate respective positions;
>
> (2) to hear, first-hand, opponent's views on disputed matters;
>
> (3) to hear a neutral assessment of the strengths and weaknesses of each party's case;
>
> (4) for realistic settlement negotiations; and
>
> (5) in the absence of settlement, to narrow issues and structure discovery and trial preparation.[424]

Neutral evaluation can be agreed to by the parties or, and this seems to occur more often, required by the court. For example, the local rules of the United States District Court for the Southern District of California require:

---

[424] VT R US DCT LR 16.1.

> Within forty-five (45) days of the filing of an answer, counsel and the parties must appear before the assigned judge for an early neutral evaluation conference; this appearance must be made with complete authority to discuss and enter into settlement.[425]

In courts that use ENE, a lawyer selected by the court usually serves as the evaluator, and some courts have at least one full-time evaluator. The evaluator meets with the parties and their lawyers for a few hours. This meeting generally occurs early in the case, typically before discovery. The meeting typically begins with the evaluator asking the clients to describe the case. Then the evaluator "asks questions of both sides to clarify issues, arguments, and evidence, to fill in evidentiary gaps, and to probe for strengths and weaknesses."[426] "The evaluator tries to help the parties to identify common ground, and to convert this to stipulations or informal agreements," as well as "to isolate the areas of disagreement most central to the case."[427]

The evaluator writes an evaluation of the merits of the case. This evaluation can be quite detailed, predicting how the court will likely rule on each disputed issue and suggesting a range of damages. Before communicating the evaluation to the parties, the evaluator encourages the parties to discuss settlement. If the parties do not settle, the evaluator communicates the evaluation to the parties and encourages further settlement negotiation. If the parties still have not settled, the evaluator "outlines a case development plan, identifying key areas of disagreement and suggesting ways to posture the case and to conduct discovery as efficiently as possible."[428] ENE is designed, not only to promote settlement, but to streamline the litigation of cases that do not settle. ENE can be seen as the most evaluative form of mediation, taking evaluation by the mediator (§ 2.13) to the next level of dropping the mediation and leaving just the evaluation.

ENE can raise many of the same legal issues as mandatory mediation. In one federal case, for instance, a neutral evaluator "preside[d] over the settlement discussions" "with the parties and their attorneys," and then "provided the district court with a report

---

[425] Rule 16.1.

[426] Joshua D. Rosenberg & H. Jay Folberg, Alternative Dispute Resolution: An Empirical Analysis, 46 Stan. L. Rev. 1487, 1490 (1994).

[427] Lawyers Get Tips on Using Early Neutral Evaluation From ENE Originator and Experience Trial Lawyer in Alternative Dispute Resolution: Practice and Perspectives 83 (Martha A. Matthew ed., 1990).

[428] Id. at 84.

indicating that the parties had agreed to settle the case."[429] Defendants' lawyer purportedly reduced the oral settlement agreement to writing, but the plaintiff refused to sign it, "believing [its] terms were unfair and inconsistent with the[ ] oral agreement."[430] The district court determined that a binding oral agreement had been reached and granted the defendants' motion to enforce it—a ruling the Sixth Circuit affirmed.[431] Section 2.16(b)(3) discusses similar issues regarding settlements allegedly formed in mediation.

In another noteworthy case, *Wagshal v. Foster*,[432] the D.C. Circuit held that court-appointed evaluators enjoy quasi-judicial immunity. Section 2.27(b) discusses somewhat similar mediator immunity.

## § 2.33 Non-Binding Arbitration

*Adjudication* is a process by which somebody (the adjudicator) decides the result of a dispute (§ 1.2(a)). Rather than the disputing parties agreeing on the result of the dispute, as in *negotiation* or *mediation* or neutral evaluation (§§ 2.2, 2.32), adjudication is the adjudicator telling the parties the result. Judges and jurors are the adjudicators in *litigation*, which is adjudication in a government forum, such as a court. *Arbitration* is adjudication in a private (non-government) forum (§ 1.2(a)).[433]

What makes litigation and arbitration *binding* adjudication is that the adjudicator's decision is backed with the force of government. The adjudicators' decisions in litigation and arbitration are enforced, ultimately, by sheriffs and marshals with guns and badges. Parties who fail to comply with these adjudicators' decisions may find their property forcibly taken from them or even find themselves jailed.

In contrast, *non-binding* adjudication lacks such enforcement. The parties to non-binding adjudication get a decision from the adjudicator but a party's failure to comply with that decision does not subject that party to enforcement by the sheriff or similar government agent. Instead, a party is free to disregard the non-binding adjudicator's decision and to pursue binding adjudication to

429 Stewart v. Carter Mach. Co., 82 F. App'x 433, 434 (6th Cir. 2003).

430 Id.

431 Id.

432 Wagshal v. Foster, 28 F.3d 1249 (D.C.Cir. 1994).

433 See Stephen J. Ware & Ariana R. Levinson, Principles of Arbitration Law (2d ed. 2023).

its conclusion. The most common form of non-binding adjudication is non-binding arbitration.[434]

Parties can agree to non-binding arbitration, and courts have generally enforced such agreements by requiring parties to try non-binding arbitration before litigating the dispute.[435] In contrast, other non-binding arbitration arises not from an agreement but from a court order. Such court-connected arbitration is "relatively rare,"[436] compared to contractual arbitration. But courts in "eighteen states and three federal districts are believed to have compulsory court-connected arbitration in their general jurisdiction trial courts."[437] Delaware, Hawaii, Nevada, and Washington are four states that have compulsory court-connected arbitration in their general jurisdiction trial courts, typically for low-dollar claims.[438] Arizona's statute mandating arbitration of low-dollar claims says, "The court may waive the arbitration requirement on a showing of good cause if

---

[434] Others are the mini trial and the summary jury trial, neither of which seems much used in recent decades.

[435] See, e.g., Endurance Am. Specialty Ins. Co. v. Shelter Corp., No. 5:21-CV-45-DAE, 2021 WL 7707815, at *5 (W.D. Tex. July 7, 2021) ("the Court finds it proper to compel Endurance to participate in arbitration pursuant to the 'Non-binding Arbitration Endorsement' of the Policy"); United States v. Bankers Ins. Co., 245 F.3d 315, 322 (4th Cir. 2001) (enforcing agreement to use non-binding arbitration before commencing litigation); Wolsey, Ltd. v. Foodmaker, Inc., 144 F.3d 1205, 1209 (9th Cir. 1998) (same); Russell County Sch. Board v. Conseco Life Ins. Co., 2001 WL 1593233, at *1–5 (W.D. Va. Dec. 12, 2001); Hartford Acc. & Indem. Co. v. Ace Am. Reins. Co., 2003 WL 22245421, at * 6 (Conn. Super. Ct. 2003) (same); Pettus v. Olga Coal Co., 72 S.E.2d 881, 885–86 (W.Va. 1952) (same).

Some contracts are not clear on whether they require binding or non-binding arbitration. See, e.g., Rainwater v. Nat'l Home Ins. Co., 944 F.2d 190, 194 (4th Cir. 1991) (contract stating that arbitration is a "condition precedent" to the commencement of litigation held to require binding arbitration; "we read 'condition precedent' to some extent as an artifact left over from the days of [judicial] hostility toward arbitration. To the extent that the phrase has meaning, we find that it does not undermine the binding nature of arbitration, but instead applies to the confirmation process permitted by 9 U.S.C. § 9, or to other litigation in which the arbitration award would be final but just a sub-text in some larger litigation context.")

[436] Leonard L. Riskin et al., Dispute Resolution and Lawyers 663 (6th ed. 2019)

[437] Id.

[438] Del. Super. Ct. R. Civ. P. 16.1(a) ("all civil actions . . . in which (1) trial is available; (2) monetary damages are sought; (3) any nonmonetary claims are nominal; and (4) counsel for claimant has made an election on the Civil Case Information Sheet for mandatory non-binding arbitration . . . are subject to mandatory non-binding arbitration"); Haw. Cir. Ct. Arb. R. 6(A), 8(A) ("All tort cases having a probable jury award value . . . not in excess of One Hundred Fifty Thousand Dollars ($150,000.00) . . . [are automatically accepted] into the [Court Annexed Arbitration Program]"); Nev. Rev. Stat. Ann. § 38.250(1)(a) ("All civil actions filed in district court for damages, if the cause of action arises in the State of Nevada and the amount in issue does not exceed $50,000 per plaintiff . . . must be submitted to nonbinding arbitration . . . ."); Wash. Rev. Code. Ann. § 7.06.020 ("All civil actions . . . which are at issue in the superior court in counties which have authorized arbitration, where the sole relief sought is a money judgment, and where no party asserts a claim in excess of fifteen thousand dollars. . . are subject to civil arbitration.") (authorized by over half of Wash. counties).

all parties file a written stipulation waiving the arbitration requirement."[439] Similarly, while the United States District Court for the Eastern District of New York compels arbitration for almost all civil claims not exceeding $150,000, However, the court shall exempt any case from arbitration for good cause, such as complexity, novelty, or predominance of legal issues.[440]

Court-connected arbitration is non-binding because the party that loses in arbitration may pursue the case in litigation and the court will hear the case *de novo*, giving no deference to the arbitrator's decision. However, most court-connected arbitration rules impose something to deter the losing party from pursuing litigation. For example, that party often "must deposit with the court a sum equal to the fees of the arbitrators. The deposit is returned only if the result at the trial de novo is more favorable to the appellant than the award of the arbitrators."[441]

Some state statutes require non-binding arbitration of medical malpractice claims, in particular.[442] While the arbitrator's decision is non-binding, in some states that decision is admissible in any later

---

[439] Ariz. Rev. Stat. Ann. § 12–133.

[440] E.D.N.Y. Local Rule 83.7(e)(2) (Oct. 29, 2018).

[441] Ian R. Macneil, Richard E. Speidel & Thomas J. Stipanowich, Federal Arbitration Law § 2.4.2.2, at 2:34 (1995). See, e.g., Ariz. R. of Civ. P., Rule 77(g) ("The clerk must refund the deposit on appeal to the appellant if: (1) the judgment on the trial de novo is at least 23 percent more favorable than the monetary relief or other type of relief granted by the arbitration award; or (2) there is no order from the court for the disposition of the deposit on appeal upon the action's final disposition."); Haw. Arbitration Rules 25 (defining "Prevailing Party" in a trial de novo as "the party who (1) appealed and improved upon the arbitration award by 30% or more, or (2) did not appeal and the appealing party failed to improve upon the arbitration award by 30% or more."); id. Rule 26 (sanctions for failure to prevail in trial de novo include reasonable costs and fees incurred (such as expert witness fees, travel, and deposition costs, costs of jurors, attorneys' fees not to exceed $15,000)); Or. Rev. Stat. § 36.425(4)–(5). Italy does something similar with what it calls a "mediator's proposal". "The parties are free to accept or decline [the proposal], however declining may produce fee shifting at the later trial. Under Art. 13, if the proposal is declined and later corresponds with the subsequent judgement at trial, the judge will exclude costs incurred at trial from the award if the winning party declined the proposal (this can also occur in certain circumstances even if they are not equivalent." EuroNetMediation—Legal Frame of Mediation in Italy, EuroNetMediation (Med.-Net), https://mediation-net.eu/index.php/en/law/19-italy/61-legal-frame-of-mediation-in-italy. See also Federal Rule of Civil Procedure 68, which provides that a plaintiff who rejects the defendant's settlement offer and then receives a judgment "not more favorable than the offer" must pay the defendant's court costs and fees incurred after the offer.

[442] Md. Code Cts. & Judic. Proc. §§ 3–2A–01–10. Id. § 3–2A–02 ("All claims, suits, and actions, . . . by a person against a health care provider for medical injury allegedly suffered by the person in which damages of more than the limit of the concurrent jurisdiction of the District Court are sought are subject to and shall be governed by the provisions of this subtitle")

trial.[443] Making the arbitrator's decision admissible increases the pressure to settle because admission makes the arbitrator's decision not merely a prediction of how the case will be decided but also an influence on how the case is decided. See Section 2.30(e), which makes a similar point about mediator reports going to the court.

## § 2.34 Policy Arguments for and Against Mandatory Evaluation and Non-Binding Arbitration

### *(a) Arguments for Mandating Evaluation or Non-Binding Adjudication*

Courts sometimes require parties to use neutral evaluation or non-binding arbitration. The rationale for requiring one of these non-binding processes is to promote settlement,[444] and there is reason to believe that they do.

*Evaluation* by the mediator is likely to cause a convergence in the parties' expectations about the results of litigation. A case cannot settle unless there is a *settlement zone* (§ 1.39(b)). With few exceptions, the only cases lacking a settlement zone are those in which Plaintiff expects a more pro-Plaintiff result from litigation than Defendant expects (§ 1.39(c)). If, for example, Plaintiff expects a $250,000 verdict, while Defendant expects a $200,000 verdict, there may be no settlement zone. These cases in which Plaintiff expects a more pro-Plaintiff result than Defendant expects, can be called cases of over-optimism. If Plaintiff expects a verdict of $250,000 and Defendant expects a verdict of $200,000, then at least one of the parties is overly optimistic about its likely success at litigation. Cases lacking a settlement zone are those in which at least one of the parties is in for a disappointment when the court rules.

Because parties' over-optimism about their success at litigation can prevent settlement zones, advocates of settlement seek to reduce over-optimism and thus make the parties' expectations about the results of litigation converge. Non-binding arbitration and evaluation tend to do that. They reduce the gap between the parties' expectations by giving them information (the neutral's decision or evaluation of the case) that causes the parties' expectations about the results of litigation to converge around the neutral's decision or

---

443 Md. Code Cts. & Jud. Proc. § 3–2A–06(d) ("Unless vacated by the court pursuant to subsection (c) of this section, the unmodified arbitration award is admissible as evidence in the judicial proceeding. The award shall be presumed to be correct, and the burden is on the party rejecting it to prove that it is not correct.")

444 See, e.g., Leonard L. Riskin & James E. Westbrook, Dispute Resolution and Lawyers 3 (2d ed. 1997) ("a right to a trial de novo means that the process is fundamentally an effort to promote settlement.")

evaluation. The neutral, because her judgment is respected by the parties, persuades the parties to change their expectations.[445]

Suppose, for example, Plaintiff expected a verdict of $800,000, and Defendant expected a verdict of $100,000, before the non-binding arbitrator declared a verdict of $300,000 or the neutral evaluator predicted a verdict "somewhere in the $200,000 to $400,000 range." The non-binding arbitration or evaluation succeeded if it caused Plaintiff to now expect a verdict below $800,000 and Defendant to expect a verdict above $100,000. The evaluation succeeded marvelously if it caused each party now to expect a verdict of $300,000. The more the evaluation reduced the $700,000 gap between the parties' expectations, the more the evaluation succeeded.

Consequently, successful non-binding arbitrations and evaluations come from a neutral whose judgment is respected by the parties as a good predictor of litigation. For instance, in a personal injury case arising out of an auto accident, if the neutral is a local judge who has presided over the trial of hundreds of similar cases, the parties and lawyers may have great confidence that this neutral can predict quite well the results of litigating this case. The better a predictor of litigation the parties believe non-binding arbitration or evaluation to be, the more non-binding arbitration or evaluation is likely to reduce the gap in the parties' expectations.

### *(b) Arguments Against Mandating Evaluation or Non-Binding Arbitration or Evaluation*

Much like studies of mandatory mediation, studies of courts mandating evaluation[446] and non-binding arbitration[447] do not, on

---

[445] Sarah R. Cole, Craig A. McEwen, Nancy H. Rogers, James R. Coben & Peter N. Thompson, Mediation: Law, Policy, & Practice § 3:4 (2024) (non-binding adjudication "involve[s] adversarial presentation of evidence (or summaries of evidence) and arguments, resulting in a nonbinding finding or decision.")

> Presumably, the experience of hearing the presentation of the case by both sides, the clearer recognition of the strengths and weaknesses on each side, and the tentative finding of a neutral third party all provide more information that the parties may use to assess settlement. In theory, the advisory finding of arbitrator, judge, or jury particularly influences the settlement equation by predicting more closely than either party could what the outcome in court might be. As a consequence of the anticipated expense and time for preparation, the very scheduling of such a procedure may by itself induce negotiation and settlement.

Id.

[446] Joshua D. Rosenberg & H. Jay Folberg, Alternative Dispute Resolution: An Empirical Analysis, 46 Stan. L. Rev. 1487 (1994).

[447] See, e.g., Jane W. Adler, Deborah R. Hensler & Charles Nelson, Simple Justice: How Litigants Fare in the Pittsburgh Court Arbitration Program (1983); Lisa Bernstein, Understanding the Limits of Court-Connected ADR: A Critique of Federal Court-Annexed Arbitration Programs, 141 U.Pa.L.Rev. 2169 (1993); Deborah R.

the whole, show significantly higher settlement rates. Cases settling after using any of these procedures may be the cases that would have settled without them. On the other hand, mandating these procedures may tend to make settlements come earlier, which tends to save the parties time, money, and aggravation.

Even assuming that evaluation and non-binding arbitration promote settlement, one may still argue against making these processes mandatory for the same reasons people argue against mandating mediation (§ 2.30(b)). Perhaps the parties know better than a judge or other court employee whether one of these processes is appropriate for their particular dispute, so if they do not voluntarily choose it, they should not be forced into it. Moreover, mandating these processes may be especially harmful to poor plaintiffs because these processes increase the time and money plaintiffs must spend before trial.[448] However, courts have rejected arguments that this increased burden violates constitutional rights, including the right to a jury trial.[449]

## § 2.35 Court System Resources

Ultimately the competing arguments about mandating mediation (§ 2.30(b)), evaluation (§ 2.32), or non-binding arbitration (§ 2.33) must consider court system resources. What would happen if every case went to trial? Would there be enough judges, jurors, and courtrooms to handle the work? Most courts around the country

Hensler, Does ADR Really Save Money? The Jury's Still Out, Nat. L.J., at C2 (Apr.11, 1994); Keilitz, Court-Annexed Arbitration, in Nat'l Symposium on Court-Connected Dispute Resolution Research 43 (Nat'l Center for State Cts. and State Jus. Instit. 1994); Levine, Court-Annexed Arbitration, 16 J. Law Reform 537, 542–43 (1983); Voluntary Arbitration in Eight Federal District Courts: An Evaluation 6 (Federal Judicial Center 1994).

448 Lisa Bernstein, Understanding the Limits of Court-Connected ADR: A Critique of Federal Court-Annexed Arbitration Programs, 141 U. Pa. L. Rev. 2169 (1993); G. Thomas Eisle, The Case Against Mandatory Court-Annexed ADR Programs, 75 Judicature 34, 40 (June 1991).

449 See, e.g., Jersey Cent. Power & Light Co. v. Melcar Util. Co., 59 A.3d 561, 573–74 (N.J. 2013) ("The judicial process in New Jersey uses mandatory, nonbinding arbitration in certain limited circumstances. . . . Importantly, however, arbitration does not cut off the right to a jury trial."); Zamora v. Price, 213 P.3d 490, 492, 496 (Nev. 2009) (rejecting litigant's argument that Nevada's mandated nonbinding arbitration program's "requirement that the arbitration award be admitted at a new trial violated his constitutional right to a jury trial"); Fisher v. Edgerton, 336 P.3d 167, 177 (Ariz. Ct. App. 2014) (rejecting litigant's argument that "the prospect of having to pay an opposing party's attorneys' fees [because of a mandatory arbitration program] would chill her fundamental right to a jury trial because she would fear being held liable for such fees" because "[a]lthough the right to a jury trial is constitutionally protected, it is also subject to reasonable regulation. Under Arizona law, the state has the power to set reasonable prerequisites to exercise the right to a jury trial, provided the right is not eliminated").

routinely say they are operating at or near capacity.[450] Many judges routinely say they are overworked and cannot give each case the attention it deserves. Surely, the judicial system would be overwhelmed if cases never settled. Settlement and its criminal-law analog, the plea bargain, are practical necessities.

But this conclusion assumes that courts continue to receive the same level of resources. In fact, we could build more courthouses, elect and appoint more judges, and call jurors more frequently. We could, in short, devote more resources to the courts. This would—all else equal—enable the courts to try more cases.[451] Perhaps it would be possible to devote enough resources to courts to try all cases without delay.

However, this would consume resources that are now devoted elsewhere. And one might argue that the court system is already consuming too many resources. Some money now going to the courts might be better spent on, for example, schools, roads, or healthcare. Perhaps time people now spend on jury duty would be better spent at their jobs or with their families. The court system's current level of resources is not the only possible level. Is the current level too high, too low, or about right? If lawyers tend to think it is too low, lawyers might recall that they, like most people, tend to think that what they do is important and deserves more resources.

Courts receive some of their revenue from fees paid by litigants, but most comes from the taxpayer. In short, litigation, and especially trials, are subsidized by government.[452] As with other subsidized goods and services, demand exceeds supply. So, litigants must wait for a trial, sometimes for years. Trial time is allocated according to willingness to wait. In contrast, many other goods and services are, in a market economy, allocated according to willingness to pay. If parties had to pay more to use the court system, fewer parties would use it so those who did would not have to wait as long.[453]

---

[450] Stephen J. Ware, Is Adjudication A Public Good? "Overcrowded Courts" and the Private Sector Alternative of Arbitration, 14 Cardozo J. Conflict Resol. 899, 901 (2013) (providing quotes showing that "cries of alarm about underfunded courts, crowded dockets and justice delayed, which we all know is justice denied, have been sounded by lawyers and courts for over a half a century").

[451] See, e.g., Albert Alschuler, Mediation with a Mugger: The Shortage of Adjudicative Services and the Need for a Two-Tier Trial System in Civil Cases, 99 Harv. L. Rev. 1808, 1818 (1986) ("[t]he crisis in our courts that observers decry may be the product of an inadequate supply of adjudication rather than of the excessive litigiousness of our society.")

[452] See, e.g., Richard A. Posner, The Federal Courts: Crisis and Reform 132 (1985).

[453] Arbitration generally has these features of a party-funded "court" system. Stephen J. Ware, Is Adjudication A Public Good? "Overcrowded Courts" and the Private Sector Alternative of Arbitration, 14 Cardozo J. Conflict Resol. 899 (2013).

## § 2.36 Dispute Resolution vs. Public Justice

If the court system's only purpose is to resolve disputes, then settlement should be encouraged. Settlements and court adjudications (at trial or otherwise) both resolve disputes, but settlements generally do so at a lower cost of time, money, and aggravation. So, court adjudications should be discouraged unless they accomplish something other than resolving disputes. Many people argue that court adjudications promote justice in ways settlements do not. This argument, Sections 1.40 and 1.43 explain, has persuaded courts and legislatures to withhold enforcement from settlements in some circumstances. But it has not persuaded courts and legislatures to displace settlement as they usual way parties represented by lawyers resolve disputes in the United States.

# Appendix

# UNITED NATIONS CONVENTION ON INTERNATIONAL SETTLEMENT AGREEMENT RESULTING FROM MEDIATION (SINGAPORE CONVENTION)

Resolution adopted by the General Assembly on 20 December 2018 *[on the report of the Sixth Committee (A/73/496)]*

73/198. United Nations Convention on International Settlement Agreements Resulting from Mediation

*The General Assembly,*

*Recalling* its resolution 2205 (XXI) of 17 December 1966, by which it established the United Nations Commission on International Trade Law with a mandate to further the progressive harmonization and unification of the law of international trade and in that respect to bear in mind the interests of all peoples, in particular those of developing countries, in the extensive development of international trade,

*Recalling also* its resolution 57/18 of 19 November 2002, in which it noted the adoption by the Commission of the Model Law on International Commercial Conciliation and expressed the conviction that the Model Law, together with the Conciliation Rules of the Commission recommended in its resolution 35/52 of 4 December 1980, contributes significantly to the establishment of a harmonized legal framework for the fair and efficient settlement of disputes arising in international commercial relations,

*Recognizing* the value of mediation as a method of amicably settling disputes arising in the context of international commercial relations,

*Convinced* that the adoption of a convention on international settlement agreements resulting from mediation that is acceptable to States with different legal, social and economic systems would complement the existing legal framework on international mediation and contribute to the development of harmonious international economic relations,

*Noting* that the decision of the Commission to concurrently prepare a convention on international settlement agreements resulting from mediation and an amendment to the Model Law on International Commercial Conciliation was intended to accommodate the different levels of experience with mediation in different jurisdictions and to provide States with consistent standards on the cross-border enforcement of international settlement agreements resulting from mediation, without creating any expectation that interested States may adopt either instrument,

*Noting with satisfaction* that the preparation of the draft convention was the subject of due deliberation and that the draft convention benefited from consultations with Governments as well as intergovernmental and non-governmental organizations,

*Taking note* of the decision of the Commission at its fifty-first session to submit the draft convention to the General Assembly for its consideration,

*Taking note with satisfaction* of the draft convention approved by the Commission,

*Expressing its appreciation* to the Government of Singapore for its offer to host a signing ceremony for the Convention in Singapore,

*Commends* the United Nations Commission on International Trade Law for preparing the draft convention on international settlement agreements resulting from mediation;

*Adopts* the United Nations Convention on International Settlement Agreements Resulting from Mediation, contained in the annex to the present resolution;

*Authorizes* a ceremony for the opening for signature of the Convention to be held in Singapore on 7 August 2019, and recommends that the Convention be known as the "Singapore Convention on Mediation";

*Calls upon* those Governments and regional economic integration organizations that wish to strengthen the legal framework on international dispute settlement to consider becoming a party to the Convention.

*62nd plenary meeting 20 December 2018*

**United Nations Convention on International Settlement Agreements Resulting from Mediation**

***Preamble***

*The Parties to this Convention,*

*Recognizing* the value for international trade of mediation as a method for settling commercial disputes in which the parties in dispute request a third person or persons to assist them in their attempt to settle the dispute amicably,

*Noting* that mediation is increasingly used in international and domestic commercial practice as an alternative to litigation,

*Considering* that the use of mediation results in significant benefits, such as reducing the instances where a dispute leads to the termination of a commercial relationship, facilitating the administration of international transactions by commercial parties and producing savings in the administration of justice by States,

*Convinced* that the establishment of a framework for international settlement agreements resulting from mediation that is acceptable to States with different legal, social and economic systems would contribute to the development of harmonious international economic relations,

*Have agreed* as follows:

***Article 1. Scope of application***

1. This Convention applies to an agreement resulting from mediation and concluded in writing by parties to resolve a commercial dispute ("settlement agreement") which, at the time of its conclusion, is international in that:

(a) At least two parties to the settlement agreement have their places of business in different States; or

(b) The State in which the parties to the settlement agreement have their places of business is different from either:

(i) The State in which a substantial part of the obligations under the settlement agreement is performed; or

(ii) The State with which the subject matter of the settlement agreement is most closely connected.

2. This Convention does not apply to settlement agreements:

(a) Concluded to resolve a dispute arising from transactions engaged in by one of the parties (a consumer) for personal, family or household purposes;

(b) Relating to family, inheritance or employment law.

3. This Convention does not apply to:

(a) Settlement agreements:

(i) That have been approved by a court or concluded in the course of proceedings before a court; and

(ii) That are enforceable as a judgment in the State of that court;

(b) Settlement agreements that have been recorded and are enforceable as an arbitral award.

***Article 2. Definitions***

1. For the purposes of article 1, paragraph 1:

(a) If a party has more than one place of business, the relevant place of business is that which has the closest relationship to the dispute resolved by the settlement agreement, having regard to the circumstances known to, or contemplated by, the parties at the time of the conclusion of the settlement agreement;

(b) If a party does not have a place of business, reference is to be made to the party's habitual residence.

2. A settlement agreement is "in writing" if its content is recorded in any form. The requirement that a settlement agreement be in writing is met by an electronic communication if the information contained therein is accessible so as to be useable for subsequent reference.

3. "Mediation" means a process, irrespective of the expression used or the basis upon which the process is carried out, whereby parties attempt to reach an amicable settlement of their dispute with the assistance of a third person or persons ("the mediator") lacking the authority to impose a solution upon the parties to the dispute.

***Article 3. General principles***

1. Each Party to the Convention shall enforce a settlement agreement in accordance with its rules of procedure and under the conditions laid down in this Convention.

2. If a dispute arises concerning a matter that a party claims was already resolved by a settlement agreement, a Party to the Convention shall allow the party to invoke the settlement agreement in accordance with its rules of procedure and under the conditions laid down in this Convention, in order to prove that the matter has already been resolved.

### *Article 4. Requirements for reliance on settlement agreements*

1. A party relying on a settlement agreement under this Convention shall supply to the competent authority of the Party to the Convention where relief is sought:

(a) The settlement agreement signed by the parties;

(b) Evidence that the settlement agreement resulted from mediation, such as:

(i) The mediator's signature on the settlement agreement;

(ii) A document signed by the mediator indicating that the mediation was carried out;

(iii) An attestation by the institution that administered the mediation; or

(iv) In the absence of (i), (ii) or (iii), any other evidence acceptable to the competent authority.

2. The requirement that a settlement agreement shall be signed by the parties or, where applicable, the mediator is met in relation to an electronic communication if:

(a) A method is used to identify the parties or the mediator and to indicate the parties' or mediator's intention in respect of the information contained in the electronic communication; and

(b) The method used is either:

(i) As reliable as appropriate for the purpose for which the electronic communication was generated or communicated, in the light of all the circumstances, including any relevant agreement; or

(ii) Proven in fact to have fulfilled the functions described in subparagraph *(a)* above, by itself or together with further evidence.

3. If the settlement agreement is not in an official language of the Party to the Convention where relief is sought, the competent authority may request a translation thereof into such language.

4. The competent authority may require any necessary document in order to verify that the requirements of the Convention have been complied with.

5. When considering the request for relief, the competent authority shall act expeditiously.

### *Article 5. Grounds for refusing to grant relief*

1. The competent authority of the Party to the Convention where relief is sought under article 4 may refuse to grant relief at the request of the party against whom the relief is sought only if that party furnishes to the competent authority proof that:

(a) A party to the settlement agreement was under some incapacity;

(b) The settlement agreement sought to be relied upon:

(i) Is null and void, inoperative or incapable of being performed under the law to which the parties have validly subjected it or, failing any indication thereon, under the law deemed applicable by the competent authority of the Party to the Convention where relief is sought under article 4;

(ii) Is not binding, or is not final, according to its terms; or

(iii) Has been subsequently modified;

(c) The obligations in the settlement agreement:

(i) Have been performed; or

(ii) Are not clear or comprehensible;

(d) Granting relief would be contrary to the terms of the settlement agreement;

(e) There was a serious breach by the mediator of standards applicable to the mediator or the mediation without which breach that party would not have entered into the settlement agreement; or

(f) There was a failure by the mediator to disclose to the parties circumstances that raise justifiable doubts as to the mediator's impartiality or independence and such failure to disclose had a material impact or undue influence on a party without which failure that party would not have entered into the settlement agreement.

2. The competent authority of the Party to the Convention where relief is sought under article 4 may also refuse to grant relief if it finds that:

(a) Granting relief would be contrary to the public policy of that Party; or

(b) The subject matter of the dispute is not capable of settlement by mediation under the law of that Party.

### *Article 6. Parallel applications or claims*

If an application or a claim relating to a settlement agreement has been made to a court, an arbitral tribunal or any other competent authority which may affect the relief being sought under article 4, the competent authority of the Party to the Convention where such relief is sought may, if it considers it proper, adjourn the decision and may also, on the request of a party, order the other party to give suitable security.

### *Article 7. Other laws or treaties*

This Convention shall not deprive any interested party of any right it may have to avail itself of a settlement agreement in the manner and to the extent allowed by the law or the treaties of the Party to the Convention where such settlement agreement is sought to be relied upon.

### *Article 8. Reservations*

1. A Party to the Convention may declare that:

    (a) It shall not apply this Convention to settlement agreements to which it is a party, or to which any governmental agencies or any person acting on behalf of a governmental agency is a party, to the extent specified in the declaration;

    (b) It shall apply this Convention only to the extent that the parties to the settlement agreement have agreed to the application of the Convention.

2. No reservations are permitted except those expressly authorized in this article.

3. Reservations may be made by a Party to the Convention at any time. Reservations made at the time of signature shall be subject to confirmation upon ratification, acceptance or approval. Such reservations shall take effect simultaneously with the entry into force of this Convention in respect of the Party to the Convention concerned. Reservations made at the time of ratification, acceptance or approval of this Convention or accession thereto, or at the time of making a declaration under article 13 shall take effect simultaneously with the entry into force of this Convention in respect of the Party to the Convention concerned. Reservations deposited after the entry into force of the Convention for that Party to the Convention shall take effect six months after the date of the deposit.

4. Reservations and their confirmations shall be deposited with the depositary.

5. Any Party to the Convention that makes a reservation under this Convention may withdraw it at any time. Such withdrawals are

to be deposited with the depositary, and shall take effect six months after deposit.

***Article 9. Effect on settlement agreements***

The Convention and any reservation or withdrawal thereof shall apply only to settlement agreements concluded after the date when the Convention, reservation or withdrawal thereof enters into force for the Party to the Convention concerned.

***Article 10. Depositary***

The Secretary-General of the United Nations is hereby designated as the depositary of this Convention.

***Article 11. Signature, ratification, acceptance, approval, accession***

1. This Convention is open for signature by all States in Singapore, on 7 August 2019, and thereafter at United Nations Headquarters in New York.

2. This Convention is subject to ratification, acceptance or approval by the signatories.

3. This Convention is open for accession by all States that are not signatories as from the date it is open for signature.

4. Instruments of ratification, acceptance, approval or accession are to be deposited with the depositary.

***Article 12. Participation by regional economic integration organizations***

1. A regional economic integration organization that is constituted by sovereign States and has competence over certain matters governed by this Convention may similarly sign, ratify, accept, approve or accede to this Convention. The regional economic integration organization shall in that case have the rights and obligations of a Party to the Convention, to the extent that that organization has competence over matters governed by this Convention. Where the number of Parties to the Convention is relevant in this Convention, the regional economic integration organization shall not count as a Party to the Convention in addition to its member States that are Parties to the Convention.

2. The regional economic integration organization shall, at the time of signature, ratification, acceptance, approval or accession, make a declaration to the depositary specifying the matters governed by this Convention in respect of which competence has been transferred to that organization by its member States. The regional

economic integration organization shall promptly notify the depositary of any changes to the distribution of competence, including new transfers of competence, specified in the declaration under this paragraph.

3. Any reference to a "Party to the Convention", "Parties to the Convention", a "State" or "States" in this Convention applies equally to a regional economic integration organization where the context so requires.

4. This Convention shall not prevail over conflicting rules of a regional economic integration organization, whether such rules were adopted or entered into force before or after this Convention: *(a)* if, under article 4, relief is sought in a State that is member of such an organization and all the States relevant under article 1, paragraph 1, are members of such an organization; or *(b)* as concerns the recognition or enforcement of judgments between member States of such an organization.

***Article 13. Non-unified legal systems***

1. If a Party to the Convention has two or more territorial units in which different systems of law are applicable in relation to the matters dealt with in this Convention, it may, at the time of signature, ratification, acceptance, approval or accession, declare that this Convention is to extend to all its territorial units or only to one or more of them, and may amend its declaration by submitting another declaration at any time.

2. These declarations are to be notified to the depositary and are to state expressly the territorial units to which the Convention extends.

3. If a Party to the Convention has two or more territorial units in which different systems of law are applicable in relation to the matters dealt with in this Convention:

(a) Any reference to the law or rule of procedure of a State shall be construed as referring, where appropriate, to the law or rule of procedure in force in the relevant territorial unit;

(b) Any reference to the place of business in a State shall be construed as referring, where appropriate, to the place of business in the relevant territorial unit;

(c) Any reference to the competent authority of the State shall be construed as referring, where appropriate, to the competent authority in the relevant territorial unit.

4. If a Party to the Convention makes no declaration under paragraph 1 of this article, the Convention is to extend to all territorial units of that State.

### *Article 14. Entry into force*

1. This Convention shall enter into force six months after deposit of the third instrument of ratification, acceptance, approval or accession.

2. When a State ratifies, accepts, approves or accedes to this Convention after the deposit of the third instrument of ratification, acceptance, approval or accession, this Convention shall enter into force in respect of that State six months after the date of the deposit of its instrument of ratification, acceptance, approval or accession. The Convention shall enter into force for a territorial unit to which this Convention has been extended in accordance with article 13 six months after the notification of the declaration referred to in that article.

### *Article 15. Amendment*

1. Any Party to the Convention may propose an amendment to the present Convention by submitting it to the Secretary-General of the United Nations. The Secretary-General shall thereupon communicate the proposed amendment to the Parties to the Convention with a request that they indicate whether they favour a conference of Parties to the Convention for the purpose of considering and voting upon the proposal. In the event that within four months from the date of such communication at least one third of the Parties to the Convention favour such a conference, the Secretary-General shall convene the conference under the auspices of the United Nations.

2. The conference of Parties to the Convention shall make every effort to achieve consensus on each amendment. If all efforts at consensus are exhausted and no consensus is reached, the amendment shall, as a last resort, require for its adoption a two-thirds majority vote of the Parties to the Convention present and voting at the conference.

3. An adopted amendment shall be submitted by the depositary to all the Parties to the Convention for ratification, acceptance or approval.

4. An adopted amendment shall enter into force six months after the date of deposit of the third instrument of ratification, acceptance or approval. When an amendment enters into force, it shall be binding on those Parties to the Convention that have expressed consent to be bound by it.

5. When a Party to the Convention ratifies, accepts or approves an amendment following the deposit of the third instrument of ratification, acceptance or approval, the amendment shall enter into

force in respect of that Party to the Convention six months after the date of the deposit of its instrument of ratification, acceptance or approval.

***Article 16. Denunciations***

1. A Party to the Convention may denounce this Convention by a formal notification in writing addressed to the depositary. The denunciation may be limited to certain territorial units of a non-unified legal system to which this Convention applies.

2. The denunciation shall take effect 12 months after the notification is received by the depositary. Where a longer period for the denunciation to take effect is specified in the notification, the denunciation shall take effect upon the expiration of such longer period after the notification is received by the depositary. The Convention shall continue to apply to settlement agreements concluded before the denunciation takes effect.

DONE in a single original, of which the Arabic, Chinese, English, French, Russian and Spanish texts are equally authentic.

# Table of Cases

# Index

References are to Sections